Accounting in Networks

Routledge Studies in Accounting

Accounting in Networks

Edited by Håkan Håkansson,
Kalle Kraus, and Johnny Lind

Routledge
Taylor & Francis Group
NEW YORK AND LONDON

First published 2010
by Routledge
711 Third Avenue, New York, NY 10017

Simultaneously published in the UK
by Routledge
2 Park Square, Milton Park, Abingdon, Oxfordshire OX14 4RN

First issued in paperback 2014

Routledge is an imprint of the Taylor and Francis Group, an informa company

© 2010 Taylor & Francis

Typeset in Sabon by IBT Global.

Library of Congress Cataloging-in-Publication Data
Håkansson, Håkan, 1947–
    Accounting in networks / by Hakan Hakansson, Kalle Kraus, and Johnny Lind. — 1st ed.
        p. cm. — (Routledge studies in accounting)
    Includes bibliographical references and index.
    1. Accounting. 2. Business communication. 3. Business networks. I. Kraus, Kalle.
II. Lind, Johnny. III. Title.
    HF5636.H35 2010
    657—dc22
    2009041824

ISBN13: 978-0-415-80647-3 (hbk)
ISBN13: 978-0-415-75445-3 (pbk)

Contents

PART II
Accounting Techniques

PART III
Theoretical Perspectives on Accounting in Networks

Figures

Figures

Tables

Abbreviations

ABC	Activity-based costing
ANT	Actor-network theory
BCG	Boston Consulting Group
BPI	Business process indicators
CA	Customer accounting
CAPM	Capital Asset Pricing Model
CCM	Concurrent cost management
CLV	Customer life-time value
CMG	Cost management group
CP	Customer profitability
CRM	Customer relationship management
DCF	Discounted cash flow
DTI	Department of Trade and Industry
FPQ	Functionality-price-quality
GLT	Groningen Long Term
HSRA	Huissaannemer Shell Research Amsterdam
ICS	Industrial control system
IFA	Inter-firm accounting
IMP	Industrial Marketing and Purchasing

IOCM	Inter-organisational cost management
IJV	International joint venture
JIT	Just-in-time
JV	Joint venture
KAM	Key account management
NAM	Nederlandse Aardolie Maatschappij
NIE	New institutional economics
NIS	New institutional sociology
NPM	New public management
OBA	Open-book accounting
OIE	Old institutional economics
PA	Product area
PFI	Private financing initiatives
PPP	Public-Private Partnerships
RBV	Resource-based view
SCDG	Supply Chain Development Group
SCM	Supply chain management
SRTCA	Shell Research and Technology Centre Amsterdam
TBM	Time-based management
TCC	Total cost control
TCE	Transaction cost economics
TCO	Total cost of ownership
TQM	Total quality management
VCA	Value chain analysis
VMI	Vendor management inventory

Acknowledgments

We are grateful to Suzanne Lidström for help with editing the book and, for financial assistance, to Svenska Handelsbanken Foundation for Social Science Research and Stockholm School of Economics. We are also grateful to the following for permission to reproduce copyright material: Chapter 3, Table 3.3, Reprinted from *Management Accounting Research,* vol. 19, Van der Meer-Kooistra, J., and Scapens, R. W., The governance of lateral relations *between* and *within* organizations, 365–384, 2009, with permission from Elsevier; Chapter 5, Tables 5.1 and 5.2, reprinted from *Accounting, Organizations and Society,* vol. 32, Kamminga, P. E., and Van der Meer-Kooistra, J., Management control patterns in joint venture relationships: A model and an exploratory study, 131–154, 2009, with permission from Elsevier; Chapter 9, Figure 9.1, reprinted from *Journal of Purchasing and Supply Management,* vol. 10, Kulmala, H. I., Developing cost management in customer-supplier relationships: Three case studies, 65–77, 2009, with permission from Elsevier; Chapter 9, Tables 9.2, 9.3, and 9.4, reprinted from *Management Accounting Research,* vol. 16, Kajüter, P., and Kulmala, H. I., Open-book accounting in networks: Potential achievements and reasons for failures, 179–204, 2009, with permission from Elsevier.

1 Accounting in Networks as a New Research Field

Håkan Håkansson, Kalle Kraus, and Johnny Lind

1 A NEW ISSUE FOR ACCOUNTING SCHOLARS

In the mid-1990s, several accounting scholars emphasised the importance of extending the domain of accounting across the traditional boundary taken—that of the firm. Two important contributions were those of Hopwood (1996) and Otley et al. (1995). Hopwood (1996) stressed that, historically, accounting has been concerned with the management of vertical relationships within firms and that its key functions have been to constitute the boundary of the firm and reinforce the organisational hierarchy. Further, he stated that even the accounting innovations that were developed in the 1980s and early 1990s share this concern with the hierarchy. This historical picture of the vertical focus of accounting is in contrast with the contemporary and often conflicting changes in the organisational arrangements between companies, such as outsourcing, which emphasises the horizontal relations between legally independent firms rather than the vertical activities within firms.

Otley et al. (1995) examined the development of management control up to the mid-1990s and gave an overview of this, from which the authors concluded that it was still dominated by a closed and functionalistic view of management control. In this way, the development described by Otley and his coauthors corresponds well with the picture painted by Hopwood (1996). At this time, management control was largely comprised of 'financial numbers'; it was developed within large, hierarchically structured organisations and the firm and its subunits were the natural focus of the research. Hence, management control had a clear vertical orientation and took place within the boundary of the firm. Just as Hopwood would come to note in the following year, Otley and his co-workers discussed how the existing 'orientation' of management control did not correspond with an environment of contemporary organisations facing challenges such as business process re-engineering and the outsourcing of noncore activities, i.e., a world in which the importance of horizontal relations across legal boundaries was increasing.

Both of the preceding contributions point out that the development of production processes that are integrated across firm boundaries, thereby becoming embedded in several companies, put new demands on the management processes that also need to transcend the legal organisational boundaries. A particular problem encountered in this situation is that of the interdependence of the organisational tasks within the companies involved and how to manage tasks of this type. Integration, collaboration, and joint actions are some central aspects that need to be considered if one is to understand a firm's success in this environment. However, accounting, with its focus on hierarchical coordination within a single company, is in conflict with changes in the business landscape of this kind, which increase the importance of horizontal coordination between independent companies. Hopwood (1996) and Otley et al. (1995) concluded that, in the mid-1990s, little knowledge existed about accounting and its role within networks of embedded companies. Hence, in their view, accounting in networks was an important and promising field for further investigation.

Shields and Scapens and Bromwich drew similar conclusions in their literature reviews, which considered published articles by North Americans (Shields 1997) and the first decade of publications in Management Accounting Research (Scapens and Bromwich 2001). One of the key suggestions for future research put forward by Shields was horizontal accounting, whereas Scapens and Bromwich called for management accounting in new organizational forms that would be able to go beyond existing organisational boundaries.

Many scholars have responded to these calls for research on accounting in inter-organisational settings and, since the mid-1990s, a growing body of literature has appeared. One relatively early and influential contribution is that of Tomkins (2001). In his analytical paper on interdependences, trust, and information in dyadic relationships and networks, he analysed the interaction between trust and information in personal relationships. He used his findings to distinguish the information needed to support trust from that needed for the mastery of events. In the same paper, he also touched upon the consequences on the design and use of accounting of viewing a relationship as an element in a network of embedded relationships. One clear illustration of this paper's influence is that the majority of chapters in this book refer to it.

Accounting in inter-organisational relationships has been viewed as an emerging field within accounting research, and it promises to become one of the most interesting areas for future research. This has been manifested in numerous publications in leading accounting journals, such as *Accounting, Organizations and Society, Journal of Accounting Research, Management Accounting Research,* and *The Accounting Review,* as well as in recent reviews on the topic (Håkansson and Lind 2007; Kraus and Lind 2007; Caglio and Ditillo 2008). However, this emerging issue has yet to be adequately dealt with in mainstream textbooks, and there is no comprehensive publication covering the whole field. The intention, therefore, of this book is to fill this gap by providing a comprehensive account of accounting in inter-organisational relationships and networks.

In a literature review of the field, Håkansson and Lind (2007) concluded that most of the articles that had been published at that time gave extensive empirical descriptions, while the theoretical base was still limited. However, during the last five years, some papers have applied theoretical frameworks derived from different theoretical approaches. The theoretical articles have been dominated by transaction cost economics and agency theory, but there are also an increasing number of publications using other theoretical approaches. In our view, the subject area has now reached the state—both with regard to empirical observations and theoretical considerations—when it is appropriate to assemble all these different threads into a comprehensive summary of what has been achieved so far, and to examine what the interesting developments for the coming ten years are likely to be.

This introductory chapter is organised as follows. In the next section, some indicators and development processes are identified that can illustrate and explain the increased importance of inter-organisational relationships. Thereafter, the obstacles contemporary accounting presents when firms want to increase their engagement in long-term horizontal relationships are discussed. Section 4 comments on the various conceptualisations of accounting in networks and provides a short summary of the different chapters of the book.

2 INTER-ORGANISATIONAL RELATIONSHIPS AND NETWORKS

The increase in the importance of horizontal processes in the business landscape during the past few decades is manifested by a large number of different forms of inter-organisational relationships that take place under names like joint ventures, strategic alliances, technology licensing, research consortia, strategic partnerships, business relationships, supply chain relationships, and outsourcing relationships.

The very diversity of names is itself an indicator of the increased importance of horizontal relationships in the contemporary business landscape. Two other more substantial ones were identified by Håkansson and Lind, 2007. The first of these is a large number of empirical studies that show that the business relationships between companies are more organised than they were previously. These studies have covered diverse industries and all major geographical regions of the economic world and include both broad survey studies and a large number of detailed case studies of single dyadic relationships and even of relationships embedded in networks. The second type of indicator is the popularity and increased use of management tools such as just-in-time (JIT) management, time-based management (TBM), and total quality management (TQM). The justification for the implementation of these general management tools is based on the existence of closer relationships with customer and suppliers. Several other management tools have also been developed, such as customer relationship management (CRM), supply chain management (SCM), and the appointment of key account managers (KAM), which are dedicated to the handling of specific customer or supplier relationships. These two indicators together suggest the existence and importance of inter-organisational relationships in today's business landscape.

It is also possible to identify two types of development process that support the appearance and increased importance of inter-organisational relationships in network structures (Håkansson and Lind 2007; Kraus and Lind 2007). One such process is the nurturing of more extensive and long-term business relationships between companies that buy and sell products or services to each other. These types of relationships have probably existed for a long time. However, they have been accentuated in recent decades as companies have successively become more specialised, and have been forced to prioritise their counterparts and collaborate more intensively with some of them. The extensiveness of the relationships is shown by the high level of involvement of a large number of individuals from different functional specialities within each of the collaborating firms. The firms that prioritise one another adapt their products, production processes, and administrative and logistical activities. Furthermore, they seek combined involvement early in the product development processes and, thereby, embark on joint product development projects.

The second type of development process is related to the outsourcing of units, functions, and activities from companies. Outsourcing is of increased importance within large firms because of the need to reduce costs, to increase specialisation, and to improve the development capabilities through closer collaboration with a chosen supplier. The outsourcing takes various forms, such as the breaking up of large hierarchically controlled companies into independent units, as well as the more commonly understood interpretation, that of outsourcing operations that were previously viewed as core operations. Hence, one difference in the outsourcing activities during the last decade is that firms outsource both production and product development processes to a greater extent than before.

3   ACCOUNTING AND ITS REINFORCEMENT OF THE HIERARCHY

In the first section, we described how Hopwood (1996) and Otley et al. (1995) stated that, historically, accounting has been focused on the vertical relations within the firm and, as such, has supported the hierarchical coordination. Some authors even claim that the development of accounting methods was a prerequisite for the formation of large multinational companies (Chandler and Daems 1979; Johnson 1983). Hence, accounting methods such as responsibility accounting, transfer prices, and budgeting have been developed in symbiosis with the growth of companies solving internal hierarchical problems.

However, at the beginning of the 1990s, some researchers argued that this close connection to the vertical dimension has negative effects on handling the horizontal dimension with counterparts. They claimed that the design and use of the contemporary accounting that was focused on the hierarchically structured organisations was an obstacle for the establishment of long-term cooperative horizontal relationships (Shank and Govindarajan 1993; Gietzmann 1996). Shank and Govindarajan (1993) emphasised the importance of the change in focus when firms apply cost analysis, from a value-added perspective to a value chain perspective. According to them, the shortcomings of contemporary cost analysis were that it started too late for the firm's suppliers and ended too soon for the customers, as it started and finished at the firm's boundary. In their view, one consequence of the strong focus on the firm was that the decision makers within the firm did not consider the effects that the decisions made would have on the firm's customers and suppliers. Thus, the contemporary accounting methods within the firm supported the individual firm's attempts to improve its bargaining position with respect to its customers and suppliers, but did not take into account the fact that this was in conflict with the possibility of exploiting the relationships with suppliers and customers. An attempt to address the latter was identified as being of key potential for the implementation of cost reductions. Thus, the aim was to consider the competitiveness of the overall value chain in which a firm was situated (Shank and Govindarajan 1993).

Gietzmann (1996) analysed the classical make-or-buy decision and concluded that traditional management accounting does not motivate suppliers to invest specific resources in a relationship. The classical make-or-buy decision is presented in traditional management accounting texts as a competition between a company's internal operations and an arm's-length supplier. In such classical literature, however, it is argued that the most efficient form of governance is identified by competitive short-term bidding over price between a large numbers of suppliers. The lowest purchasing price, which is the outcome of this bidding process, is then compared with the company's internal production costs to identify the cheapest form of governance. Short-term price bidding is an efficient solution for standardised components that the suppliers can supply off the shelf. However, it gives little incentive to the supplier to invest in cooperative design and development work with the buyer. According to Gietzmann (1996, p. 624), it was necessary that "the focus on accounting moves from how to apply competitive bidding to minimize supplier bargaining strength, to issues such as which subcontractors should be promoted to become design approved subcontractors."

The preceding examples illustrate a central point in this book, namely, that the use of accounting methods is always based on some very specific assumptions about how individual companies are—and even how they should be—related to counterparts such as customers and suppliers and other third parties. From this, one can deduce that the theoretical dimension is closely connected to the empirical application of accounting methods and, as a consequence, a certain accounting method ought to be able to support or hinder the development of a specific type of business relationship.

4   ACCOUNTING IN NETWORKS, INTER-ORGANISATIONAL ACCOUNTING, AND MANAGEMENT CONTROL OF INTER-ORGANISATIONAL RELATIONSHIPS

The previous section shows that contemporary accounting, with its reinforcement of the hierarchy and its preference for short-term competitive bidding in external relations, is not just ignorant of, but even an obstacle to, the development of extensive long-term cooperative horizontal relationships. The critique of the contemporary accounting and the urge for research on accounting in horizontal relations have resulted in an increasing number of published papers on the issue.

However, accounting in horizontal relations has been taken up in discussions coming under a large variety of headings. Some examples are inter-organisational accounting, accounting in networks, inter-organisational cost management, open-book accounting, network accounting, supply chain accounting, target costing, horizontal information systems, management control of hierarchical networks, value chain accounting, management control of joint ventures, horizontal accounting, interfirm accounting, and management control of inter-organisational relationships. This variation is interesting as it indicates that there are a large number of subjects touched upon when focusing on relationships with external counterparts. However, all these issues are related to the conceptualisations of accounting and horizontal relations across legal boundaries. A number of authors have defined and studied accounting and the inter-organisational setting in accordance with the aim of their research, which has been varied, sometimes having an empirical focus and on other occasions being aimed at the ongoing construction of the theoretical base. This variation is at the core of this book, and the intention is not to compare or choose between these different ways to define and classify the issues and concepts. Instead, we want to create a map to describe and with which to clarify this variation and its consequences. Different conceptualisations, as well as empirical methods with their specific focus, definition, and theoretical bases, will appear in the chapters that follow.

By way of giving an indication of what is to come, we elaborate on three key conceptualisations that have been used in the existing accounting literature: inter-organisational accounting, management control of inter-organisational relationships, and accounting in networks.

Inter-organisational accounting is closely linked to certain accounting techniques, like open-book accounting, target costing, and value chain accounting. The research that has studied inter-organisational accounting has focused on accounting design encompassing at least two firms. Accounting of this kind can take form of open-book accounting, where one or both firms have access to the counterpart's internal financial and nonfinancial data. Another example can be one firm measuring and influencing its suppliers' or customers' operations. In almost all empirical studies this means that the focus is on a dyadic relationship. Typical inter-organisational accounting studies are Carr and Ng (1995), Nicolini et al. (2000), and Dekker (2003).

Management control of inter-organisational relationships has many similarities with inter-organisational accounting and in, several studies, the conceptualisations seem to be interchangeable. Research designed to study the management control of inter-organisational relationships is characterised by a focus on control patterns in dyadic relationships. The point of departure in most of these studies is a buyer-supplier relationship (or a joint-venture relationship), where the buyer needs to choose an appropriate control pattern with which to control its supplier. Studies on management control of inter-organisational relationships show a greater emphasis on other types of controls, such as behaviour controls and social controls, than on outcome controls. However, independent of the mixture of types of control, they all cross the focal firm's legal boundary. Management control of inter-organisational relationships is illustrated in studies by Van der Meer-Kooistra and Vosselman (2000), Baiman and Rajan (2002) and Dekker (2004). A specific form of these types of studies is the management control of joint ventures (Kamminga and Van der Meer-Kooistra 2007).

A characteristic of research on accounting in networks is the concern about the effects on and the impact of third parties on the firm or firms under investigation. The focus on these indirect effects means that research on accounting in networks extends the perspective to include parties other than the pair involved in the dyadic relationship. However, it should be noted that it is the indirect effects of accounting on or of third parties that are characteristic of accounting in networks, and not necessarily the design of the accounting. Hence, intra-organisational accounting, inter-organisational accounting in a dyad, and inter-organisational accounting in a formalized network can all be studied under the heading of accounting in networks. In this way, accounting in networks is a more general topic than the previously discussed ones. It is more general in the sense that it is possible to include studies of how firms use inter-organisational accounting and other controls in dyadic relationships to influence their counterparts within the network approach. Papers that illustrate accounting in networks are Tomkins (2001), Håkansson and Lind (2004), and Mouritsen and Thrane (2006).

The title of this book—*Accounting in Networks*—has been chosen because it includes intra- and inter-organisational accounting and management control. The title is intended to convey the variety of empirical and theoretical approaches and discussions included within this book. Each chapter focuses on a specific aspect of accounting in networks, assessing theoretical and empirical evidence, summarising the current debate, and discussing promising avenues for future research. The book starts with a general chapter on inter-organisational relationships and networks and the role of accounting in these relationships. Thereafter, it is divided into three main parts. First, a variety of inter-organisational settings are discussed, including dyads, networks, joint ventures, and the public sector, and the roles of accounting in each of these settings are considered. The second part of the book deals with specific accounting techniques that companies use to manage their business in a world of inter-organisational relationships and networks, namely, customer accounting, target costing, and open-book accounting. The third part of the book covers different theoretical perspectives on accounting in networks, and examines transaction cost economics, the industrial-network approach, actor-network theory, and institutional theory. The book ends with a summary in the chapter entitled "Accounting in Networks—the Next Step".

In Chapter 2, David Ford and Håkan Håkansson provide us with an overview of accounting in networks. They develop a 2×2 matrix with the degree of change in the business landscape on one axis and the degree of change in the theoretical approaches to accounting on the other. The analysis of the four boxes in the matrix illustrates the dynamic interplay between the theoretical and empirical aspects of accounting in inter-organisational relationships and explains and describes the large variety of accounting issues and methods. Thus, the chapter does not just give a picture of the complexities and difficulties in the development of accounting in networks, but clarifies why a distinction is made between chapters addressing accounting techniques and chapters describing different theoretical perspectives.

John Cullen and Juliana Meira, in Chapter 3, commence Part I of the book by presenting an in-depth analysis of inter-organisational accounting in dyadic settings, that is, they restrict their discussion to studies that have conceptualised and analysed inter-organisational relationships as independent dyadic pairs. They conclude that the vast majority of the published studies on accounting in networks fall into this group. The authors focus on using the supply chain maturity model to analyse the published research available. They find that most of the inter-organisational relationships carried out in dyadic settings that have been analysed can be considered to represent serial dependence (dominant customer). Management controls and accounting tools and techniques are mainly used to control suppliers or outsourced parties. A smaller number of the studies present cases demonstrating reciprocal dependence (where there is a certain degree of collaboration between customer and suppliers) or mutual dependence (where partnership takes the form of collaboration, arising out of mutual interests), and here inter-organisational accounting information is more openly exchanged.

Chapter 4 has been written by Johnny Lind and Sof Thrane. They introduce a framework presenting the various types of situations that a firm needs to handle in relation to counterparts within a network setting. The situations, therefore, range from how to handle one relationship in isolation to networks consisting of suppliers, customers, and third parties such as competitors, regulators, and suppliers' suppliers. The authors have sought to investigate how managerial issues and the roles of accounting are related to inter-organisational relationships. The framework shows that different conceptualisations of these inter-organisational relationships raise different managerial issues and indicate the potential suitability of specific types of control mechanisms. Furthermore, conceptualisations of different types of situations tend to use different theories, ranging from economic theories at one extreme, and institutional theory, actor-network theory, the industrial-network approach, and complexity theory at the other.

In Chapter 5, Jeltje van der Meer-Kooistra and Pieter E. Kamminga analyse the role management control can play in establishing and maintaining joint venture relationships. They stress that joint ventures are open to influences from the environment, as well as from within the relationship. These influences could threaten or strengthen the joint-venture relationship and could lead to changes in joint-venture management control. The authors discuss the issues of coordination, opportunistic behaviour, and relational atmosphere that the parent companies of a joint venture are confronted with and examine how they use management control to deal with these issues. Van der Meer-Kooistra and Kamminga also stress the dynamic character of joint-venture relationships and show how joint-venture management control develops over the life of a joint venture.

Kalle Kraus and Cecilia Lindholm's chapter, Chapter 6, deals with accounting in inter-organisational relationships within the public sector. The work reviewed is from a significant set of accounting journals from 1990 to 2008, and the authors conclude that the overall themes in the articles were related to different ways of organising the public sector and of delivering public sector services, and to the role of accounting and management control in these new organisational structures. Little discussion was found on ongoing day-to-day cooperation between interdependent public sector units/organisations and the role of accounting therein. Further, the studies did not conduct a theoretical evaluation of the distinctive characteristics of public sector organisations, such as the existence and role of strong professions. With this in mind, Kraus and Lindholm have elaborated on the construction of three different forms of accountability—professional accountability, managerial accountability, and inter-organisational accountability—within domestic health and social care for the elderly.

Mikael Cäker and Torkel Strömsten open the discussion in Part II with a chapter on customer accounting. Customer accounting is viewed as an internal tool that firms use to measure and manage their customer relationships. Two lines of research were identified, with the focus either on customer profitability, measured on an accrual basis over a specific period of time, or on customer lifetime value, where cash flows are emphasised, and where the time horizon is extended to capture value creation over several years. The authors conclude that customer profitability research was mainly undertaken by accounting researchers, while research on customer lifetime value was conducted primarily by marketing researchers and that there was little interaction between the two sets of literature. Cäker and Strömsten state that the field of customer accounting would benefit if the borders between the different streams of research were to be reduced. They also stress the need to account for embeddedness when evaluating customers. In addition, formal customer accounting techniques and models need to be adapted to an inter-organisational context, where indirect effects should be taken into consideration.

In Chapter 8, Martin Carlsson-Wall and Kalle Kraus review the literature on target costing in inter-organisational relationships and networks. They conclude that, even though target costing is seen as a central accounting practice that is vital for product development, a vast majority of existing studies have paid little attention to discussing the underlying theoretical assumptions of product development. The authors have assessed target costing in networks by examining the relationship between target costing and how companies conduct their product development. Through an empirical case study, the authors showed that target costing had "combinatory roles" during a product development project. Sometimes target costing was used to manage time and quality on a dyadic level to attain preset goals, but on other occasions it was used to arrive at pragmatic compromises where preliminary target costs were set and then interactively revised when new interdependencies, often on a network level, were discovered.

In Chapter 9, Peter Kajüter and Harri I. Kulmala discuss the practice of disclosing and sharing cost information between firms in inter-organisational relationships through open-book accounting, and illustrate the achievements and problems in both dyadic and network settings. The authors conclude that research on open-book accounting, especially in the network context, is still at an exploratory stage and the empirical evidence is largely based on case studies and on interventionist research. Kajüter and Kulmala find that most of the case study research analyses the practice and the problems associated with the implementation of open-book accounting in dyadic buyer-supplier relationships. The authors acknowledge that there is no coherent theory of open-book accounting, but state that given the nature of open-book accounting practice, two theories seem to be particularly useful to gain a deeper understanding of open-book accounting, namely, contingency theory and agency theory.

Shannon Anderson and Henri Dekker's chapter, Chapter 10, on transaction cost economics is the first chapter in Part III. Transaction cost economics (TCE) is, as the authors state in the introduction, the dominant theory used to analyse accounting in inter-organisational relationships. Anderson and Dekker assess how TCE has been used as a theoretical lens to analyse accounting in relation to the stages of alliance decision and choice of governance mode, partner search and selection, management control design, and dynamic evolution and change. From the studies reviewed, the authors conclude that TCE appears most useful for identifying when changes and adaptation of control design in inter-organisational relationships can be expected, and less useful for providing researchers with the tools required to study how and through which processes change takes place. They also find that, in recent years, TCE-based research has often been complemented by other theoretical perspectives, such as strategic behaviour and organisational theory.

Chapter 11, written by Håkan Håkansson, Kalle Kraus, Johnny Lind, and Torkel Strömsten, examines the industrial network approach and discusses its implications for the understanding of accounting in networks. The industrial-network approach is centred on two basic assumptions, those of resource heterogeneity and interdependence. As heterogeneity and interdependence are not isolated to dyads, there will always be third parties that are affected by any changes in inter-organisational relationships through indirect effects that may even be larger than the direct ones. Accounting design needs to take this into account, as does its use. Another conclusion in this chapter is that accounting and management control should shift its prioritisations from the optimisation and follow-up of pre-set goals to facilitation of the collective process of finding temporarily valid "solutions". The primary role of accounting may be to help create interaction between different companies, leading to temporarily valid pragmatic compromises, rather than to help identify a perfect solution to coordination problems.

In Chapter 12, Jan Mouritsen, Habib Mahama, and Wai Fong Chua apply actor-network theory to accounting, with the starting point being given by the device "follow accounting in action". One basic standpoint is that accounting can be seen as an interdependent actor influencing, in a very direct way, how knowledge is structured and thereby also determining what qualifies as useful knowledge. The authors show how accounting, as an actor in its own right, mediates and constructs inter-organisational relationships through self-regulation and orchestration mechanisms. These conclusions are important as they describe accounting much more actively, and as an evolving entity, than is the case in most other literature on accounting in networks. The authors state that accounting calculations should not be seen as passive tools, but more as an active knowledge-influencing factor. Thus, the design of the accounting system is vital for how the whole company will function within its environment.

The final chapter of Part III has been written by Robert W. Scapens and Evangelia Varoutsa, who explore how institutional theory could be used to study accounting in inter-organisational relationships. They conclude that the existing research is sparse and identify a need for studies that emphasise the complexity of the institutional context of the inter-organisational relationships. The authors state that more research is needed to explore the way in which accounting and cost-management techniques can become embedded in the broader institutional context, and to determine how such embedded techniques can form and influence the nature of inter-organisational relationships as they develop. Another conclusion is the need for research that explores why some accounting practices become institutionalised in inter-organisational relationships, while others do not. This is based on the contradictory findings in the studies by Coad and Cullen (2006), where inter-organisational cost management was replicated across the supply chain, and Free (2008), where the attempts to introduce category management as a catalyst for new supplier-retailer relationships damaged the existing trust and the new accounting techniques did not become embedded in the relationships.

Thus, the reader has an extensive piece of work in front of her/him, which looks back over the developments of the past, examines the situation at present, and highlights the many areas in which further research on accounting in networks is required. It will be exciting to see what the next decade will bring.

BIBLIOGRAPHY

Baiman, S., and Rajan, M. V. 2002. The Role of Information and Opportunism in the Choice of Buyer-Supplier Relationships. *Journal of Accounting Research* 40: 247–278.

Caglio, A., and Ditillo, A. 2008. A review and discussion of management control in inter-firm relationships: Achievements and future directions. *Accounting, Organizations and Society* 33: 865–898.

Carr, C., and Ng, J. 1995. Total cost control: Nissan and its U.K. supplier partnerships. *Management Accounting Research* 6: 347–365.

Chandler, A. D. Jr., and Daems, H. 1979. Administrative coordination, allocation and monitoring: A comparative analysis of the emergence of accounting and organization in USA and Europe. *Accounting, Organizations and Society* 4: 3–20.

Coad, A. F., and Cullen, J. 2006. Inter-organisational cost management: Towards an evolutionary perspective. *Management Accounting Research* 17: 342–369.

Dekker, H. C. 2003. Value chain analysis in interfirm relationships: A field study. *Management Accounting Research* 14: 1–23.

Dekker, H. C. 2004. Control of inter-organizational relationships: Evidences on appropriation concerns and coordination requirements. *Accounting, Organizations and Society* 29: 27–49.

Free, C. 2008. Walking the talk? Supply chain accounting and trust among UK supermarkets and suppliers. *Accounting, Organizations and Society* 33: 629–662.

Gietzmann, M. B. 1996. Incomplete contracts and the make or buy decisions: Governance design and attainable flexibility. *Accounting, Organizations and Society* 21: 611–626.

Håkansson, H., and Lind, J. 2004. Accounting and network coordination. *Accounting, Organizations and Society* 29: 51–72.

Håkansson, H., and Lind, J. 2007. Accounting in an interorganisational setting. In *Handbook of Management Accounting Research*, ed. Chapman, C. S., Hopwood, A. G., and Shields, M. D. 885–902. Oxford: Elsevier.

Hopwood, A. G. 1996. Looking across rather than up and down: On the need to explore the lateral processing of information. *Accounting, Organizations and Society* 21: 589–590.

Johnson, H. T. 1983. The search for gain in markets and firms: A review of the historical emergence of management accounting systems. *Accounting, Organizations and Society* 8: 139–146.

Kamminga, P. E., and Van der Meer-Kooistra, J. 2007. Management control patterns in joint venture relationships: A model and an exploratory study. *Accounting, Organizations and Society* 32: 131–154.

Kraus, K., and Lind, J. 2007. Management control in inter-organisational relationships. In *Issues in Management Accounting*, ed. Hopper, T., Scapens, R. W. and Northcott, D. 269–296. Harlow, UK: Financial Times Prentice Hall.

Mouritsen, J., and Thrane, S. 2006. Accounting, network complementarities and the development of inter-organizational relations. *Accounting, Organizations and Society* 31: 241–275.

Nicolini, D., Tomkins, C., Holti, R., Oldman, A., and Smalley, M. 2000. Can target costing and whole life costing be applied in the construction industry?: Evidence from two case studies. *British Journal of Management* 11: 303–324.

Otley, D., Broadbent, J., and Berry, A. 1995. Research in management control: An overview of its development. *British Journal of Management* 6: 31–44.

Scapens, R. W., and Bromwich, M. 2001. Editorial report–management accounting research: The first decade. *Management Accounting Research* 12: 245–254.

Shank, J. K., and Govindarajan, V. 1993. *Strategic Cost Management—The New Tool for Competitive Advantage*. New York: The Free Press.

Shields, M. D. 1997. Research in management accounting by North Americans in the 1990s. *Journal of Management Accounting Research* 9: 3–61.

Tomkins, C. 2001. Interdependencies, trust and information in relationships, alliances and networks. *Accounting, Organizations and Society* 26: 161–191.

Van der Meer-Kooistra, J., and Vosselman, E. 2000. Management control of inter-firm transactional relationships: The case of industrial renovation and maintenance. *Accounting, Organizations and Society* 25: 51–77.

2 Accounting and Inter-Organisational Issues

David Ford and Håkan Håkansson

1 INTRODUCTION

This book is an example of the growing interest during the past decade in the implications that a range of inter-organisational issues have on accounting. This increased interest can be interpreted in two different ways:

Firstly, it can be explained as an attempt to provide a fresh insight into the theoretical analysis of management practice and, thereby, also of accounting. According to this explanation, the inter-organisational issues that have been raised recently have already been addressed in practice, but they have not been covered by the conceptual approaches on which accounting is based. Thus, the interest in the new issues has arisen from the development of new theoretical perspectives on the continuing practice of business. In later chapters, we will see how transaction cost economics (Chapter 10), the industrial-network approach (Chapter 11), actor-network theory (Chapter 12), and institutional theory (Chapter 13) have been used to identify issues that are complementary or alternative to the classical issues in accounting theory. According to this explanation, the trend in accounting is based on a recognition of existing problems that have now been identified as the outcome of new theories about the functioning of firms. Within this explanation, it can be claimed that the newly identified issues have a largely theoretical origin: There is no major change in the business world.

However, the argument can be reversed: The current interest in inter-organisational issues can be seen as a reaction by companies and a change in accounting practice that have arisen from changes in the business landscape and in the ways that companies function in relation to their environment. In this explanation, an important change is occurring in the business landscape and this has been recognised and adapted to by companies. This view may be seen as an explanation of why open-book accounting, target costing, and other new accounting methods have been developed.

The two alternative explanations are important because they indicate that the issues identified in the contemporary inter-organisational accounting literature might have two very different origins. They have developed in a context where there is an interesting mix of practical and theoretical developments. This context has been characterised in recent decades by changes in the theories applied to accounting and/or by changes in the reality facing businesses. The result is a mix of issues, some of which have a very practical and hands-on character, while others are much more theoretical in both their characteristics and origins.

We will start this chapter by looking in some detail into this mixture of theory and reality and consider how it affects the issues addressed in the extended inter-organisational literature on accounting problems. We will do this in order to create a map for the reader on which the discussions in later chapters can be placed.

2   THEORY AND PRACTICE IN THE INTER-ORGANISATIONAL BUSINESS LANDSCAPE

We will start this mapping exercise using a simple 2×2 matrix (see Figure 2.1). On one axis of the matrix, we have two different theories, labelled M and N; on the other, two types of business landscapes are labelled A and B. In this way, four situations are identified, each of which has some particular features, and each of which has its own set of problems.

Contemporary accounting has developed over quite a long time period on the basis of a particular theory and in a particular landscape; this is referred to as Situation 1 (Figure 2.1). During this development process, the theory and the way that the business landscape is viewed have become embedded into each other. The theory has become taken for granted and has become more or less black-boxed, as actor-network theory would argue. One important consequence is that the theory and its concepts are used to describe the landscape.

BUSINESS LANDSCAPES

THEORIES	Landscape A	Landscape B
Theory M	SITUATION 1	SITUATION 2
Theory N	SITUATION 3	SITUATION 4

Figure 2.1   Theory and practice in the inter-organisational business landscape.

In the introduction, we identified two possible changes in relation to this situation:

The first possible change is a move in the direction of Situation 2 in the matrix. In Situation 2 a major change in the business landscape has occurred towards Landscape B. But despite this change, accounting theory is more or less the same, so it can be anticipated that the new landscape will create problems that cannot be readily handled by the existing theory, M. In addition, the use of Theory M is likely to create problems because the landscape no longer works in the way assumed by the theory.

An alternative change is towards Situation 3, in which a new theory, N, has been developed in response to the identification of previously unrecognised aspects of the business landscape, but the landscape itself has remained unchanged. Thus, the new theory (N) incorporates new dimensions or addresses issues that have always existed, but which have not been considered to be significant within the previous theory (M).

Finally, Situation 4 exists when a new theory has been developed based on the characteristics of Landscape B. Thus in this case, Theory N is the outcome of that landscape and is different from M.

We will now look at each of these four situations in turn and use an empirical example to illustrate the interplay between theory and change in the business landscape. The intention is not to make a final judgment about which of the four possible situations best describes the reality facing accounting today, but rather to clarify why there are so many ways of structuring current issues and determining what these mean for the practice and theory of accounting.

Situation 1   Accounting in the World of the Market

Accounting is a very practice-dominated area of study that has evolved in an interaction between the companies that apply it and the stakeholders that use the outcomes from it. However, modern accounting has been built on some basic theoretical assumptions about the nature of companies and the business world that must be accepted by companies and most of their stakeholders as users of accounting. These assumptions have been quite simple: The market model of the business landscape and of the operation of the business firm dominates both theoretical analysis and practice. The theory has been so systematically applied in a normative sense that it can be traced in all aspects of accounting, as well as in the way that the landscape is described: Concepts such as demand, supply, market, competition, and so on are used to characterise the business landscape. Perhaps because of its ubiquity, it is easy to forget that the idea of the market is a theoretical concept that is based on a particular set of assumptions that have profound implications for both the practice of management and for accounting. Later we will see how the centrality of the theory of the market has affected key issues in accounting principles and practices for measuring, controlling, predicting, and auditing company practice.

Accounting is important for both internal and external stakeholders. The management of a company needs accounting to analyse and control current operations and to provide comprehensive and logical information about the choices related to its future development. These activities relate both to the subunits of a business and to the business as a whole. In contrast, external actors require information to be provided to them about how well the company is functioning. There are two different aspects of accounting that are of interest both to the internal and external users: The first is concerned with the continuing characteristics or *flow* of a company's · operations over time, expressed in such terms as its expenditure, receipts, and overall cash flow; the second concerns the company's overall *position* at a particular point in time, expressed in a variety of ways, such as its inventories, debts, and capitalisation and discussed in terms of the company's solidity or liquidity. A company's management needs to be able to make comparisons between flows at different periods of time and against previously set goals and targets and to obtain an assessment of its overall position at any point in time. Thus, accounting provides the basis for the assessment and control of the business as a whole, as well as for specific aspects of the firm's operations. In this way, accounting can function as an alarm bell announcing when something has to be done. However, even more importantly, accounting must not be restricted to warning that something has to be done, but must also be able to indicate what could be done. This is one reason why it is important to separate the continuing flow in a company's operations from its overall position. There is a significant difference between the situations facing a company with a problem in its daily operations, represented by the flow, compared to a positional problem. The accounting system has developed to take care of these aspects. Let us have a look at some important elements in the contemporary accounting system and examine how they are influenced by the market model.

One central factor in the existing accounting system is how the boundary of an individual company is defined. The market model assumes the existence of a clear borderline between the company and its environment. This distinct economic interface makes it possible to decide which assets are held by and within the company and which are outside it. Similarly, the flow of activities within the company and the costs incurred by it can be separated from the activities and costs of other entities outside the firm. Further, the clear economic interface between the company and its surroundings provides a fixed boundary across which transactions take place and to which costs and revenues can be ascribed. The boundary between the company and the environment means that transactions can be interpreted as taking place between autonomous and independent companies. Taken together, this clear borderline means that it is possible to measure and account for each transaction and for the total assets of the company, and to see how those assets are financed, whether the company is generating a surplus and if its overall balance sheet position is improving or not. Let us look a little closer at these issues:

Transactions form an important element in the analysis of the flow of a company's business. There are three types of transaction that are important for the classical manufacturing company relating to labour, other inputs, and to revenues. The costs of labour are particular and relate to both the internal organisation of the firm and its relationship with unions and we will not deal with them in this paper. The two other types of transactions take place with counterparts such as suppliers and customers within markets, and this makes them particularly useful from an accounting perspective. Within the market context, the prices received and paid provide a relevant estimate of revenues and of the costs of direct inputs.

The three types of transactions mentioned earlier are central in accounting because many calculations are built up around direct labour costs, costs of inputs, and prices charged to customers. Direct labour costs and direct input materials are two central cost items in most product or project calculations, and other costs are often considered in relation to them. For the purposes of calculation, these other costs are often considered as a percentage of the direct costs of labour or input materials. Consequently, product-related calculations are based on the price received from the output market and the volume of transactions. These together provide a figure for the revenue, which is then considered with the direct costs of labour, plus some indirect labour-related costs, the cost of purchased materials, and some indirect material-related costs, to arrive at a figure related to the profit. The efficiency of a company is determined by how well it combines labour and materials in the production process. A large proportion of accounting activity is directed at analysing how this takes place and at examining how different changes affect this mix. Over the years, a number of measurements have evolved that enable comparisons to be made between different companies and different situations. In constructing these measures, "rules" have been developed within companies and industries to determine what are considered acceptable or reasonable profit margins, what are reasonable direct costs, what are reasonable indirect costs, and so on. The revenue side of a company mainly shows up over time through repeated transactions with customers that may be influenced by some sales-cost-related activities. These could then be optimised, within the production structure and the demands of individual customers over time.

Transactions with suppliers and customers produce a vital part of the informational input for the accounting system. One important assumption made is that these measurements can be used directly to describe important costs. Given the existence of markets, then the prices received and paid provide the required information, and there is no need for further calculations to be made in order to obtain good estimates of the flow of business. Thus, there is an assumption that markets have led to "standardisation" and therefore eliminated differences: A company is assumed to buy standardised inputs and to sell products and services in competition with others, so that the price alone provides all relevant information.

The analysis of a company's position involves estimating the value of its assets and relating this estimate to the sources of funding. The valuation of assets is problematic and a large number of accounting rules specify how different types of investments should be valued. This valuation involves consideration of capital investments and holdings in equipment and systems, as well as financial investments and holdings in shares and financial instruments. One main rule that is used is that these assets should be valued in "market" terms, that is, at the value that the company would receive if they were to sell the asset in the market. Similarly, a number of types of measurement have evolved as standards for different types of companies for the balance between assets and the use of financial sources.

There is also an important connection between the flow of a company's business and its overall position. A large proportion of the indirect costs of a company's operation are related to its investments in capital goods, which may be made with the specific intention of reducing its direct costs. One consequence of this is that the more a company invests in modern equipment, the greater its indirect costs. This has been one of the key issues that accounting has had to address; how will new investments affect its direct and indirect costs?

Situation 1 represents a very well-developed accounting theory which is in more or less perfect harmony with the business landscape, as perceived by the companies involved in the market. The theory has helped companies to develop measurements and tools that are directly related to this accounting system.

But the second situation is one in which companies start to work systematically in a way that is at odds with the market model.

Situation 2   A Changed Business Landscape

What happens to the accounting system if there is a change in the business landscape? Situation 2 in the matrix occurs if major changes give rise to a landscape that is significantly novel for it to be considered to be totally different. These changes could be external to the individual firm, involving new technologies, political regimes, governmental policies, or customer or supplier structures. Alternatively, the changes could be internal to the firm, relating to the development of different forms of organisational design or the application of new strategies or policies, which, in turn, lead to modified patterns of internal or external behaviour. In both cases, the result is that the business landscape is no longer the same: It does not have the features of a market and this creates at least two new groups of problems for companies. The first appears in the form of new issues faced by practitioners that are unacknowledged by the existing theory, or to which it offers no answers. The second type of problem is that it becomes problematic to apply the existing issues, principles, and measurements within Theory M. We will now consider both of these problems by using a case study based on a turnaround by the Italian motorbike producer Ducati.

Ducati's Turnaround

Ducati encountered major problems at the end of last century (Bocconcelli and Håkansson 2008). In order to survive, it had to achieve a major turnaround. As a first step, the company made an analysis of its internal productivity and found that this could be increased by 20 per cent. However, this analysis also revealed that such an increase in internal productivity would only reduce its product costs by 4 per cent because purchased components accounted for 80 per cent of its product costs. In other words, it would be extremely difficult, if not impossible, for the company to make the turnaround by itself.

Thus, the company found itself in a position far removed from that described in Situation 1, in which the company is assumed to buy standardised raw materials from the market and then carry out a number of manufacturing operations on them, resulting in a final product. In that case, the key efficiency issue for the company would have been to streamline its production activities. In turn, this would mean that its management needed information about how costs were distributed over operational activities and different end products and, if possible, how these costs varied from those of other producers in the same market. But in Ducati's case, the situation was quite different: Ducati's suppliers deliver a number of purpose-designed subsystems, produced according to a schedule that matches that of Ducati, which then assembles them into a motorbike. Thus, "its" production is spread over many highly specialised production sites, each owned by other companies.

The consequence of this situation for Ducati was obvious: It would have to mobilise its suppliers if it was to achieve a turnaround. The next question was how to do this. Ducati could apply the market model and try to pressure its suppliers into reducing their prices by threatening to change suppliers. Alternatively, it could take the opposite approach by developing a more intimate cooperation with some of its suppliers to combine forces to reduce costs and to increase the efficiency of their combined production and product flows. Ducati opted to enter into close cooperation with just a few suppliers. In this way, the company chose to reduce the total number of suppliers by 50 per cent, and the nine suppliers that accounted for 40 per cent of its total volume of purchases became its key suppliers.

In order to achieve positive results in these relationships, Ducati had to introduce two types of changes. Firstly, it had to develop its own ability to work with the suppliers. This required a number of internal changes. One of these was to reorganise its purchasing function and the ways in which it was related both to the company's internal production and even more to the way it worked with the suppliers. It had to develop a number of tools to describe and analyse all the activities and flows between Ducati and its suppliers, and to include their related costs and revenues. It also had to convince its suppliers that this was a change that could be positive for them, because the suppliers would have to make their own internal changes in order to work more effectively with Ducati.

This case is an example of where the accounting methods developed for Situation 1 are of little help, making it necessary for Ducati to develop new tools. The case provides an illustration of a situation where a company recognised that the landscape in which it operated had changed, and was now radically different from that associated with the market purchase of standardised components. The key aspects of the company's costs in this situation were not those of its own internal operations or the overall prices paid for its purchases. Instead, the key costs for the company were those involved in the interplay between its own operations and those of its counterparts. Each of these relationships with a particular supplier will be unique, will have its own dynamics and involve specific costs and benefits for the companies concerned. This specificity means that the costs and benefits in one relationship cannot readily be compared with the costs of identical purchases from other suppliers, as was the case in Situation 1. In other words, the critical issue in Situation 2, and in the case of Ducati, is not how the company's internal operations function, but how they are integrated with preceding and subsequent operations. Furthermore, in this situation of operational and financial interdependence between the company and its suppliers (and distributors), the price of a single transaction is no longer able to indicate the relevant costs and revenues. Instead, the company's concerns must shift to the ways in which a range of less readily quantifiable costs and benefits arise over a series of transactions with a particular counterpart over a period of time. These issues will be further discussed in later chapters under headings such as target costing and open-book accounting.

It is obvious that there are a number of aspects in the new situation that are not covered by the accounting developed for Situation 1. However, it is also interesting to note that there will be issues that come to be seen as problematic because of the established theory; one such example could be the issue of control. Control is important, given the theory and the landscape in Situation 1, in which it is quite straightforward: In Situation 1, the company is assumed to have control over, or is at least responsible for, all the costs that arise within its boundary and to have no control at all over what happens outside it. In this situation, these external activities are subject to the operation of the market and are thus beyond the control of any one company. But if we look at the Ducati case, characterising Situation 2 from a market point of view, the company's interdependencies with 'specific others' indicates some major problems for control. On the one hand, these interdependencies mean that the company is subject to the control of others over significant aspects of its own operations and their costs. On the other hand, those same interdependencies may provide it with some measure of control over certain aspects of the operations of its counterparts. This might not be perceived to be a problem at all by the company itself, but it will certainly be experienced as a major one by someone attempting to apply the market model to this new situation! The problem of control, so often discussed in inter-organisational studies, may be more of a theoretical consequence than a practical issue in need of a solution.

Situation 3   New Theory Identifying New Issues in the Existing Landscape

Cell 3 represents the situation in which the business landscape remains unchanged, but the development of new theories provides a different perspective or fresh insights into the nature of business activity. These insights may lead to the identification of new problems and issues that need to be addressed by both analysts and management alike. But the battle in this situation is likely to be more concerned with theory and centre on consideration of the questions or problems on which the analysis should focus. This debate has interesting parallels in physics and psychology, where major theoretical battles have been conducted about how nature or man works, but it is equally relevant in other scientific areas. The main elements in the debate are the extent to which the old theory can be kept, and how the new theories can be seen as complements or alternatives to the existing one.

The Ducati case presented earlier was used as an example of a situation where a company is faced with a new business landscape. However, this particular case could also be seen as an example of a company having developed a new way to see the pre-existing business landscape. The argument would then be that each individual company has always had important counterparts with which it is interdependent and that the only change is that the theories that have come to be used recognise this aspect. Thus, from this point of view, there has basically been no change in the business landscape, only a change in the way in which we see it.

In this instance, we can concentrate on a discussion of what is the most appropriate way to conceptualise and portray the business world. The Ducati case can also be used as an example of this reconceptualisation. The company adopted a different view of how it relates to its surroundings: not as a totality or as a market, but as a set of unique relationships. This redefinition leads to different accounting requirements involving changed cost and benefit structures, time frames, and units of analysis.

In this book we exemplify this kind of development with a number of theories. In later chapters we will use transaction cost economics, the industrial-network approach, actor-network theory, and institutional theory to discuss different accounting issues. Each of these theories will create its own set of issues which are related to the logic of the theory. All of these can be seen as examples of Situation 3 because none of them requires that the assumption be made that the business landscape has changed: They can all be applied to the business landscape depicted in Situation A, but they make the assumption that there are some specific aspects of the situation that the earlier theory, M, did not cover in a reasonable way.

However, there is a major difference between these theories, namely, the ease with which they can be combined with the existing theory, M. This is a key issue in this situation because it influences how well the new theories can be integrated with the previous one. If it is still the same business landscape, then one would imagine that the old theory would still be useful: It would be strange if the earlier model became completely wrong when there is no change in the landscape. Theories that are easy to integrate can live side by side with the established theory, M, for a considerable time. This continuity is likely to be reinforced in a field such as accounting that is so dominated by practice, and in which there are also important legal interfaces that are difficult to change.

An interesting example of this continuity is given by transaction cost economics. This is probably the theory that has been used by most researchers challenging Situation 1; it can be seen as a complement to the market model, extending it to include some situations depicted as "market failures", meaning those situations when Theory M does not work. Transaction cost economics can be used to explain why there is a need for companies to use all three of the governance forms: hierarchy (corresponding to the use of authority), bilateral governance (where relationships are built on trust), and markets (where price is the decisive factor). It does this by identifying some specific situation-dependent characteristics that require different governance modes from an efficiency point of view (to obtain the lowest transaction costs). The theory can be combined easily with the earlier theory: It is identical in many respects, but at the same time, it includes a couple of previously unexplained and unidentified empirical phenomena (the efficiency of hierarchies and business relationships). In later chapters we will see how this theory affects the approach to accounting.

One consequence of applying new theories is that their use might also change the business landscape. This has already been discussed in Situation 1, where it was mentioned that Theory M has become embedded into the business landscape, A. In the long run, the use of new theories will affect the business landscape.

The use of new theories also has practical consequences. For example, in the case of accounting, a newly identified but important issue is the long-term interdependence of a company with its important counterparts. This interdependency is likely to challenge how existing theory accounts for novel costs and benefits within conventional accounting periods and the issue of accounting over time periods that extend beyond the conventional ones. An example of these challenges is frequently faced by companies when attempting to account for R&D spent on specific projects with potential long-term payoffs, especially when the R&D is embedded in specific relationships.

Situation 4   A New Theory for a New Business Landscape

Finally, cell 4 in the matrix represents the situation where there has been a change in both the business landscape and in the theory developed for its analysis. This situation is likely to occur when a novel theory has been developed that is oriented towards some of the particular features that characterise the new business landscape. We may also expect that the newly developed theory may be concerned with normative claims about operation in the changed landscape.

Many years are likely to be required to develop a general theory for a new type of business landscape. As yet, there is no such theory. Of those mentioned for Situation 3, actor-network theory and the industrial-network approach are the two that take the majority of their starting assumptions from empirical findings and, for this reason, can be seen to have the greatest potential for such eventual development. As there is no general theory, we need to concentrate here on the question of whether there is a need for such a theory. We will use the Ducati case to discuss whether some major changes have occurred in the business landscape. We will argue that the Ducati case is not an isolated instance. Instead, we will suggest that it is an example of widespread phenomena in which the business landscape is so different from that assumed in the market model that it requires the development of a new theory. Such a theory could, possibly, be used to make normative statements applicable to Ducati and others.

A hundred years ago many companies were integrated organisations carrying out most of the operations that were needed to transform basic raw materials into offerings suitable for their customers. The most striking examples of this integration could be seen in railway and automotive companies. Since that time, the characteristics of individual companies and the business landscape as a whole have evolved to the situation in which the modern enterprise (exemplified by Ducati) is generally a much more specialised company that limits itself to just a few operations that contribute only a minor part of the eventual offering that is required by ultimate customers. In Håkansson et al. (2009), the research about this development has been described and discussed in terms of relatedness, variety, and motion. The same three aspects can be identified in the Ducati case.

Relatedness can be seen in the way that the requirements of customers have grown more complex and changed so that they can rarely be satisfied by buying conventional or generic products. These requirements now involve complex combinations of service and product that address their particular problems and enable them to simplify, reduce, and specialise their own operations. Companies have become, by choice or by necessity, highly dependent on specific suppliers and customers.

The Ducati case is a good example of the development of the increased importance of counterparts in the operations of companies. In the Ducati case, we concentrated on the role of a small number of suppliers that produced major elements of the company's products, with significant developmental input and costs being borne by both supplier and customer. But the case could also be used to describe the increased importance of Ducati and similar customers for producers of components, subsystems, and equipment. We could have equally well presented other cases that highlight the enhanced importance of distributors and other customers that receive dedicated supplies from a chosen company and together make similar relationship-specific investments alongside one another. In all of these cases, other companies are responsible for a significant proportion of the costs and revenues of a particular focal company. They are also responsible for a significant proportion of the total activities involved in the business of a company.

Relatedness is closely connected to variety and motion. The Ducati case illustrates an important possibility for both suppliers and customers that, through investing in a business relationship, are able to contribute to and take advantage of existing variety and of successive changes over time. The production structure of a company may develop in this way: It can become more embedded into the production structure of other companies and, together, the companies involved may find ways to co-evolve. This development goes against the generalised factors associated with a market. Nor is this process likely to be uniform across different companies in the same "industry" or those that produce nominally similar products. Instead, the nature and extent of a company's interdependence with its customers, suppliers, and others will depend on what happens within particular relationships with specific counterparts. The processes within specific relationships will lead over time to an increase in the variety of the business landscape. Sometimes specific and company-wide evolution will be the result of the interplay between the conscious outsourcing of one and the marketing strategy of the other in a particular relationship.[1] Sometimes this evolution may be unconscious; on other occasions the evolution of a relationship may be heavily influenced by developments that have occurred in one of the company's relationships with other customers or suppliers. On yet more occasions, evolution can be attributed to changes occurring elsewhere in the network of interconnected relationships and interdependencies. But in all cases, the multiplicity of factors that affect the interdependencies and relationships between a company and its counterparts means that those relationships will not be within the direct or sole control of the company, or of anyone else. One outcome of these processes between companies is that they contribute to the relatedness, variety, and motion of the business landscape. Thus, we can expect that the business landscape moves further and further away from that which is characterised by the market model. In other words, there are some important reasons for arguing for the need to develop new theories that are based on other assumptions than the market model and that can be used for the development of accounting practice.

3   SOME CRUCIAL AND URGENT INTER-ORGANISATIONAL ISSUES

The four cells exemplified and discussed earlier make it possible to distinguish between different types of changes and their effects. But the background to theoretical discussion is always mixed in real-life situations. For this reason, we now concentrate on some specific features of the inter-organisational landscape that need to be addressed independently of currently employed theory and for which contemporary companies need advice. How they are addressed will depend on which of the situations in the matrix to which they correspond. We will now examine four significant features and their implications for accounting. In doing this, we will be particularly concerned with how these features affect the key accounting concepts of "transactions" and "assets".

The Importance of Having Few Counterparts

A contemporary specialised company usually produces only a minor part of the offering that it supplies to others and it uses suppliers in a quite different way from the classical company. These suppliers are generally responsible for a large part of the total value creation of a company's ultimate offering, as in the Ducati case. Similarly, contemporary companies are also often highly dependent on just a few customers as in the case of the suppliers to Ducati.

The importance of particular counterparts in contemporary business places a considerable emphasis on the choice of counterparts. This importance is compounded because of the processes that take place between these counterparts and the implications of these processes for the companies and individuals involved in them. The development of interdependence in this situation is likely to involve significant investment by companies in their relationships. These relationships frequently involve adaptations to the products, services, overall offerings, operations, capital investments, and administrative procedures of either or both of the companies to meet the requirements of their counterpart and to develop the relationship between them. The nature of this development process means that a company's interface will be different with each of its relatively few major counterparts and characterised by significant variation in how the activities and the resources of the company are related to and integrated with the activities and resources of these few others.

As well as incurring costs, the development of business relationships takes time and business relationships are often long-lasting. They are frequently complex, involving contacts between large numbers of individuals in each company. Many of the preoccupations of managers and the activities of individuals in a company will centre on particular relationships, or even on particular *episodes* within them. The complexity of these relationships and the interdependence between the resources, activities, and people involved in them mean that no clear boundary can be seen to exist between the operations of the two companies.

Thus, a contemporary specialised company faces a major challenge in the analysis, establishment, development, and management of its business relationships. But a business relationship is not managed by either of the counterparts alone. Suppliers cannot manage their relationships with "their" customers nor can customers manage "their" suppliers. The evolution of a business relationship is in part the outcome of what happens around it and in part the outcome of the aims and actions of the counterparts and their view of that relationship and their others. Hence, the management of business relationships requires skills in analysing the progression and potential of particular relationships and skills in interaction with counterparts; working with, through, and at times against them. These management tasks represent a challenge to accounting in terms of recording and controlling expenditure, costs, charges, margins, and profit in these relationships.

The time taken and investments made by a particular company in a counterpart will be intended to reduce the costs of transactions between the companies concerned and to produce benefits directly arising from the more or less dedicated or adapted abilities of the two companies. Some of these benefits may be realised in relationships with other counterparts, through enhanced offerings made to them. The benefits may also be manifested in cost reduction in other aspects of the company's operations that are away from the direct costs or physical presence of the products in a particular relationship. This complexity of interconnections and the length of "relationship time" make it difficult for companies to cope with the intricacies of relationship accounting. For example, companies are likely to have to make cost and revenue comparisons and choices between the investment of time and resources in alternative, currently existing relationships or between established relationships and potential new counterparts. These choices need to involve consideration of any new investments required, benefits of previous investments foregone, direct and indirect costs, and benefits over extended periods of time. However, in contrast, it is common for customer analysis to be limited to the comparison of short-term sales volumes, price achieved, and immediate direct and allocated costs.

A further complexity for accounting arises because the important relationships of a company are not isolated in themselves. Each relationship will have important connections with others that together create a network-like structure across the business landscape. The structure of this business network also has implications for the ideas of managerial discretion, decision, and control. The interconnections and interdependencies that enmesh a company in the network link it specifically and uniquely to individually significant others and, more generally, to myriad other companies with entirely different operations and technologies. These economic interconnections mean that it is unrealistic to consider that a network can have a single centre, or that any one company can be its "hub", or that a realistic view of the operation of a network can be obtained from the perspective of a single company. For example, a company's view that others are part of "its" supply chain or "its" distribution channel will neglect the impact on its relationships with these companies of their wider position in the network and their relationships with others. In the networked business landscape, business management and the development of strategy cannot realistically be regarded as activities of individual companies. Thus, the decision making of any one company with respect to its counterparts is unlikely to be generalised, but will have to relate explicitly or implicitly to the positions in the network and the past and possible future actions, reactions, and re-reactions of specific others. Similarly, what happens to and within a company and its operations, finances, and performance cannot be regarded as the result of that company's own actions and the behaviour of a generalised market, but as subject to the intentions and actions of specific counterparts. The interdependencies between companies mean that operations, investments, cash flows, costs, and revenues are intimately connected between specific companies across the network. The elements of a business are effectively *multi-located* and each element has numerous discrete and measurable effects on particular companies. These companies are doing more than just assembling products or transacting services for money. The interfaces between counterparts have become more specialised and unique, which means that each interface has to be handled differently and they have to be systematically combined with each other.

The Impact of Limited Abilities

Companies face the pressures of the increasing costs of technological intensity and technology acquisition. In other words, the number of different technologies required to design and fulfil an offering to meet a customer's requirements has increased and the costs of developing those technologies increase with each subsequent generation of those technologies. Increased specialisation allows companies to focus on a limited number of skills or technologies and to apply these in some specific applications. This has obvious cost advantages for specialising companies and marks an important contrast between the contemporary situation and that characterised as a market in Situation 1. Situation 1 was characterised by companies that held most or all of the technologies needed to provide offerings to their customers in-house. A major feature of the contemporary business landscape is that these technologies are distributed in different companies across the network. So, for example, it is now common for some companies to concentrate solely on the design of offerings, whilst others manufacture according to the designs developed by counterparts and use dedicated intermediaries to provide supporting services and logistics specialists for deliveries. The resultant dependence on a limited number of suppliers or customers would be a cause for concern in a market because it would leave the dependent customer or supplier vulnerable to price pressure from its counterpart for the supply or purchase of products. But dependence is frequently chosen by counterparts in the contemporary situation. This is because choosing to be dependent on a particular counterpart and on its abilities and technologies (whether general or relationship specific) frees up a company to invest its scarce resources in other more productive areas either in that relationship or in others. However, specialisation places great emphasis on the need for the decisions on technological investment (and relationship choice) to be appropriate. These decisions are always long-term and cover a time span greater than the life of single products. They are likely to be major investments and, in some cases, involve funding greater than the net worth of companies making them. The time and costs involved in developing specialisation mean that many decisions related to specialisation effectively oblige companies to forfeit all other avenues that could have been followed. Thus, decisions on technological and operational specialisation are, in some cases, effectively irreversible.

The particular characteristics of technological and operational specialisation in contemporary business involve challenges for accounting. Accounts reporting commonly takes place at the level of individual products or operating units and is based on costs and revenues either measured in terms of transactions or over fixed time periods. But accounting for technological specialisation involves consideration of the return on technological investments that transcend individual products or operating units and which involve time periods relating to the life of the technology itself. It is common for accounting to accommodate individual development projects or particular products. But it is rare to find accounting that takes an appropriately broad perspective on the returns to technological investment. This would involve assessment of the long-term returns that may be achieved by a technological investment incorporated in multiple products, used in multiple applications or over multiple time periods, or the overall returns on combinations of technologies.

The Impact of Time

The implications for accounting of limited counterparts and limited abilities are complicated by the issue of time. We have already noted that business relationships are likely to take time to develop and involve considerable investment by the counterparts. However, business relationships do not all develop at the same rate, nor do they necessarily proceed towards a situation of ever-closer ties. "Relationship time", referring to the duration of a relationship, varies depending on the commitment and investment of the counterparts. Some relationships become inert after only a short period, whilst others continue to develop over decades. A business relationship may be built round a single transaction, as in the case of a major capital purchase and sale, or it may involve frequent and regular transactions; others may continue to involve infrequent and irregular purchases. In many cases, the cost and revenues associated with a single transaction will give an erroneous idea of the actual profitability of that transaction, or of the offering involved or of the customer relationship. The development of a business relationship is likely to involve negative cash flows, particularly in its early stages as contacts are made, time is spent, and adaptations and investments occur. However, even long-established and well-developed relationships will still incur costs of operation, maintenance, and adaptation. As a relationship develops, a vendor is likely to receive positive cash flow from the customer, and the customer is likely to gain financial benefits from the relationship in terms of cost reductions or through benefits in its other relationships. However, even though individual transactions may be profitable at any time in the relationship, the relationship itself will only become profitable for the counterparts when its *cumulative* cash flow or cost savings or wider benefits becomes positive. The time for this to be achieved is frequently measured in years. The importance of small numbers of individually important relationships to companies and their impact over time involves a reorientation in accounting theory towards performance over the duration of a relationship rather than over calendar time or for individual transactions or products.

The Impact of Redefined Assets

The development of company specialisation and interdependence in important business relationships also has implications for the concept, evaluation, and use of business assets. In the contemporary business landscape, the relationship is a central asset, without which the modern business enterprise cannot trade. The valuation of relationships is often subsumed in company accounts under the generalised concept of "goodwill". But we have suggested that, for a modern company, a relatively small number of relationships are of major importance, and that each is unique. This means that companies are faced with the need to evaluate and to re-evaluate each of these assets over time. Business relationship assets are also important in relation to other assets. It is generally considered important for companies to apply a realistic value to their assets in market terms. However, in the current business landscape, many assets represent investments made as part of the development of specific relationships, so that some of these assets will have little or no value in other relationships or in a generalised or hypothetical market. Further, if many business assets have only a relationship-specific value, then that value is tied to the other assets involved in a particular relationship, many of which may be held on the books of the counterparts. Thus, the value of these company-held assets is tied to the continuing relationship investment of both counterparts, making their asset value more a property of a relationship, rather than of a single company. This commonality of asset value between companies raises important issues for accounting. But more importantly, it reinforces the importance of interdependence in business and suggests that the unit for strategic analysis extends beyond the boundaries of an individual firm.

4 CONCLUSIONS: ACCOUNTING THEORY IN A DIFFERENT SITUATION

We have suggested in this chapter that accounting theory faces the challenge of developing new approaches to a changed empirical situation. Many of the changes that we have suggested have evolved slowly over many years and have been captured to a greater or lesser extent within accounting practice. Other aspects of the current business situation, such as the importance of business relationships, have been of significance since business began. Nevertheless, the driving forces of technological cost and the ability to communicate effectively at a distance have intensified corporate specialisation and the interdependence of companies. These forces and their effects reinforce the need for the development of accounting theory to cope with the reality of business in complex networks.

In simple terms, the development of theory will be built on changes in the units of analysis used by accounting in addressing the flow within companies and the positions of those companies. Interdependence between companies means that the flows within companies cannot be separated from the flows between them. Indeed, a major conclusion from the empirical observation of business in networks is that a company's identity is less about what it does or has itself and more about its position in the flow of others companies' activities across the network and its ability to access the resources of these other companies.

Thus, the units of analysis for developing accounting theory for the flow of business are likely to move from transactions themselves to the relationships within which those transactions take place. Accounting for relationships is less about individual or collective sales and costs within each relationship and more about investment and returns. Similarly, the units of analysis for assets are less about their notional value in the market and more about their value in specific relationships. It is important to develop an approach in accounting theory that is able to deal with the transactions, sales, purchases, and assets in a single company in the contemporary business world. But it is more important to develop a theory to relate flows, assets, and corporate positions across the wider network as the location and arena for interdependent flows, assets, strategies, and the single company.

NOTES

1. It is worth noting, as an example of interconnections within business networks, that outsourcing by one company involves insourcing by another. This insourcing may result in the company concerned concentrating on the insourced activity for several counterparts, and outsourcing some of its own activities to others, and so on.

BIBLIOGRAPHY

Bocconcelli, R., and Håkansson, H. 2008. External interaction as a means of making changes in a company: The role of purchasing in a major turnaround for Ducati. *IMP Journal* 2: 25–37.
Håkansson, H., Ford, D., Gadde, L.-E., Snehota, I., and Waluszewski, A. 2009. *Business in Networks*. London and New York: Wiley.

Part I

Accounting in Different Settings

3 Inter-Organisational Accounting in Dyadic Settings

John Cullen and Juliana Meira

1 INTRODUCTION

Inter-organisational accounting is a growing field of research. Since Otley's (1994) and Hopwood's (1996) call for deeper investigations regarding the accounting and management controls used in new forms of organisations, there have been an increasing number of studies addressing the theme. A recent review of the published literature was presented by Caglio and Ditillo (2008), who analysed the literature according to the different management control solutions used in each case. Whereas Caglio and Ditillo (2008) covered both dyadic and network settings, this chapter presents a more in-depth analysis of inter-organisational accounting in dyadic settings. It is important to recognise, however, that, in some cases, the distinction between dyads and networks might be problematic.[1] The issue of the development of accounting in network settings is the subject of the next chapter, Chapter 4, in which a framework is developed.

Kraus and Lind (2007) identify dyadic relationships as relationships between collaborating companies. They suggest that these relationships may take the form of either vertical or horizontal collaboration:

- Vertical collaboration is collaboration between a company and its suppliers or customers in the supply chain.
- Horizontal collaboration is collaboration between companies targeting the same customers.

Such collaboration can take the form of, for example, technology licensing, research consortia, joint ventures, and strategic alliances (Kraus and Lind 2007). Vertical dyadic relationships tend to be the most common, although any of the forms identified can be evident in horizontal collaboration (e.g., Volvo and Mitsubishi in forming NedCar, the Dutch car manufacturing company, Kraus and Lind 2007).

According to the *Oxford University Press Dictionary* (2008), dyad refers to "something that consists of two parts". In the inter-organisational accounting literature, this term has been used when relationships are examined as a pair of companies. In fact, a great deal of the literature in this field of research refers to dyadic relationships. In addition to the vertical and horizontal distinction, dyads can differ in relation to whether there are formal or informal agreements between inter-organisational links; the length of time the relationship has endured; and whether the relationship is a close cooperation or not.

This chapter shows how accounting differs from one type of inter-organisational dyadic setting to another. Although Caglio and Ditillo (2008) classify the literature according to the role of cost and accounting controls in vertical and horizontal relationships, no attempt has been made to relate the maturity of the relationship and the inter-organisational accounting tools and techniques used.

Whilst Kraus and Lind (2007) suggest that, in the main, vertical dyadic relationships are usually long-term, this particular chapter will analyse such relationships at different stages of maturity. It will also identify the different management accounting techniques that have been used during different stages of supply chain maturity.

2 THE RISE OF INTER-ORGANISATIONAL ACCOUNTING

Accounting and management controls were primarily developed for internal use in organisations. They considered only the companies' internal operations because they took into account the market-hierarchy dichotomy. However, as a result of competitive pressures and the need to improve results, managers have started to pay more attention to relationships with external links. In this context, it has been recognised that traditional management accounting practices may not provide managers with appropriate information. Indeed, it has been argued that the traditional make-or-buy calculus may act as a potential major obstacle to the development of partnerships and alliances (Gietzmann 1996). Management accounting systems, therefore, must be adapted to handle the management of new organisational forms (e.g., strategic alliances, partnerships, networks, and virtual organisations), the growth of which has been a significant factor in creating competitive advantage in a dynamic market.

One of the major problems with traditional models is the emphasis on the calculation of the alternative between market and hierarchy that minimises costs, rather than on the development of long-term relationships with suppliers. From this perspective, when outsourcing operations, the price mechanism is used predominantly. If the supplier can meet quality specifications and delivery requirements, then a price discount can be negotiated. The problem is that, with the focus on price, there is no incentive for the supplier to work in cooperation with the assembler (Gietzmann 1996). In addition, the make-or-buy accounting calculus does not take into account the risk of the supplier acting opportunistically or performing poorly. The need to revise this calculus has been acknowledged in the accounting literature (Gietzmann 1996; Van der Meer-Kooistra and Vosselman 2000).

Moreover, as already mentioned, the need for change has been emphasised by Otley (1994) and Hopwood (1996). Challenging accounting and management controls that have traditionally been used by hierarchical organisations has been considered to be essential as the new organisational forms have started to emerge. Since the call for further investigation of the "wider functionings of accounting and the implications which these have for the form of organized activity" (Hopwood 1996, p. 590), a considerable number of studies have been published (e.g., Berry et al. 1997; Cullen et al. 1999; Seal et al. 1999; Mouritsen et al. 2001; Tomkins 2001; Dekker 2003; Cooper and Slagmulder 2004; Dekker 2004; Håkansson and Lind 2004; Seal et al. 2004; Kajüter and Kulmala 2005; Coad and Cullen 2006; Mouritsen and Thrane 2006; Chua and Mahama 2007).

Today, it can be said that accounting "is the result of a mixture of companies' experiences and normative advice and models originating from scientific studies" (Håkansson and Lind 2007, p. 885). Closer relationships developed in the inter-organisational environment and the idea of managing operations beyond legal barriers has brought the need for change in both the accountants' role and in the accounting tools and techniques that they use. As a result, inter-organisational accounting techniques are now used by organisations at the inter-organisational level.

In the *inter-organisational accounting* literature, a variety of terms have been used. Indeed, it might be said that the literature is messy and there is a need for order and clarification. Some examples of the diversity that exists are the following: *supply chain accounting* (e.g., Free 2008); *inter-firm accounting—IFA* (e.g., Seal et al. 2004); *inter-organisational cost management—IOCM* (e.g., Cooper and Slagmulder 2004; Coad and Cullen 2006); and *accounting and network coordination* (e.g., Håkansson and Lind 2004). Although the reasons for the appearance of several different terms are not always clear, it might be said that one justification is that this field of research is still a new one. Another important point is that they may vary according to the inter-organisational setting under analysis in each case. For example, while the study by Free (2008) focuses on the role of accounting in the UK supermarket supply chain, the analysis of Håkansson and Lind (2004) concentrates on accounting and management controls used by organisational units embedded in the Ericsson and Telia Mobile network. Exploring all the different terminologies used goes beyond the scope of this chapter. The most important ones will be considered later in this book, notably in Chapters 7, 8, and 9. The important issue here is that inter-organisational accounting can be used as an umbrella to cover all these possibilities.

3   SUPPLY CHAIN MATURITY

A model of supply chain maturity was illustrated by Berry et al. (2000) in their investigation of management accounting control practices in the UK in relation to the development of supply chain management. They identified relationships starting off with the autonomous firm and then moving through different stages of cooperation, identified as serial dependence (dominant customer), reciprocal dependence (some forms of collaboration between customer and suppliers), and mutual dependence (partnership models of collaboration arising out of mutual interests).

Previously, Lamming (1993) also constructed a model of customer-supplier relationships that recognised four different phases of development. The four phases were the traditional approach, stress, resolved, and partnership. In the traditional model, the supplier with the lowest bid would be awarded a contract. In the stress phase, favoured suppliers were encouraged to invest, and gain benefits from the competitive advantage associated with new practices and plants. In this phase, the involvement of suppliers was driven by attempts to reduce costs. In the resolved phase, there was an increased recognition of the importance of relationships and this resulted in more collaboration. In the partnership phase, it was recognised that the resolved model was not sufficiently progressive for best practice relationships. Best practice was identified by Lamming as being a partnership between two firms, showing respect for and valuing each other's contribution, engaged in the relationship.

The important messages coming out from Berry et al. (2000) and Lamming (1993)[2] are that management accounting systems must facilitate supply chain relationships at different levels of maturity. Where arm's-length relationships exist, inter-organisational accounting techniques tend to focus on the lowest cost option that meets required quality standards. The use of tendering and on-off supply agreements may be the norm here, and traditional techniques of management accounting will be required. As relationships move through the maturity, or development, cycle, inter-organisational accounting techniques will be used differently. At the mutual dependence/partnership stage, techniques such as open-book accounting become more acceptable since the parties engaged in the relationship can gain mutual benefit from improvements made to both cost and quality. These benefits can be shared between the collaborating partners. It is also feasible that two organisations can engage in relationships at different stages of development, depending on the specific

Table 3.1 Stages of Supply Chain Maturity

	Berry et al. (2000)	*Lamming (1993)*
Arm's-length relationship	Autonomous firm	Traditional
Management of suppliers	Serial dependence	Stress
Collaboration with suppliers	Reciprocal dependence	Resolved
Systemic management	Mutual dependence	Partnership

circumstances of a particular business transaction. One company could, for example, be in a partnership arrangement with another in a certain product area, whilst maintaining an arm's-length relationship in another product area. For example, large retail organisations may collaborate with competitors and suppliers in certain activities whilst acting purely at arm's length in others. Any inter-organisational accounting techniques used should reflect the nature of the business relationship being enacted.

Tomkins (2001) also provides an interesting insight into the role of information at different stages of relationship building. Here, there is a particular emphasis on the interaction between trust and information. Tomkins identifies two information types:

- Type 1 is information that relates to the willingness to trust; that is, what is needed to create trust and to check on the state of the relationship. This is concerned with planning for a collaborative future.
- Type 2 is information needed for mastery of events by that relationship as an entity in its own right. As implied, this focuses on the use of information to master events collaboratively.

These two different types of information then need to be related to the relationship life cycle and the way in which the impact of interdependence changes with the evolution of the relationship. Caglio and Ditillo (2008, p. 875) summarise this relationship as follows:

> When interdependence is very low, at the beginning of the relationship, Type 1 information is used to control the partner's attributes, values, integrity and ethics, while Type 2 information is adopted to assess the costs and benefits of the relationship. When interdependence is medium, at the exploratory/screening stage, more detailed (internal) Type 1 information on a specific partner's attributes and aspirations is exchanged, and more articulated Type 2 (external) information on scenario development, strategic options and alternative relationships is collected. With the growth of interdependence at higher levels, in the commitment development stage, Type 1 information is used to control the achievement of milestones and processes, whereas Type 2 information is collected to assess joint competitive positions, investments and profit/risk-sharing schemes. Finally, when interdependence is high, at the commitment development stage, while information exchanged for cooperation purposes regards open-book accounting and transparency of activities available for inspection, information used for mastery of events concerns the results and the future returns from the relationship, together with the exploration of possibilities for extending the relationship and an assessment of the portfolio of investments and endowments.

Tomkins (2001) talks about relating aggregate information needs to trust intensity and the maturity of the relationship and argues that, while requests for excessive information may reduce trust, the provision of more information is needed to create more trust in the upswing of the relationship. The suggestion is that "information influences trust, which influences information need, which influences trust, and so on" (Tomkins 2001, p. 171). In the following section, we will analyse the way in which inter-organisational accounting has been used at different stages of supply chain maturity.

4   INTER-ORGANISATIONAL ACCOUNTING AND SUPPLY CHAIN MATURITY

This section focuses on using the supply chain maturity model to analyse the studies in the literature on inter-organisational accounting in dyadic settings. Table 3.2 identifies different studies at different stages of supply chain maturity.

Table 3.2   Inter-Organisational Accounting and Supply Chain Maturity

Maturity	Inter-organisational accounting	Papers
Serial dependence	Open-book accounting	Mouritsen et al. (2001) Free (2008)
	Target costing	Nicolini et al. (2000) Mouritsen et al. (2001)
	Total cost control	Carr and Ng (1995)
	Value chain analysis	Dekker (2003)
	Inter-organisational cost management	Cooper and Slagmulder (2004)
	Cost for inter-organisational control	Cäker (2008)
	Other forms of IOA (e.g., pricing, suppliers' assessment, contracting)	Frances and Garnsey (1996) Seal et al. (2004)
Reciprocal dependence	Open-book accounting possibilities	Seal et al. (2004)
	Inter-organisational cost management	Coad and Cullen (2006)
	Management control and Governance	Van der Meer-Kooistra and Vosselman (2000)
Mutual dependence	Open-book accounting	Seal et al. (1999) Langfield-Smith and Smith (2003) Dekker (2004)
	Governance practices	Van der Meer-Kooistra and Scapens (2008)

Serial Dependence

Open-book Accounting

Although this technique was initially associated with Japanese companies, it has gradually spread all over the world. This appears to be the most complete and, though logically simple (Kraus and Lind 2007), the most complex technique to apply in inter-organisational settings. The logic of open-book accounting (OBA) is that one or both companies in a relationship 'open their books' to their counterpart(s) and disclose internal information. The development of reliable relationships between the companies is necessary for this to occur. The idea is to facilitate cooperation in relation to the identification of critical areas and the subsequent cost reduction throughout the supply chain (Ellram 1996; Berry et al. 1997; Mouritsen et al. 2001; Kulmala et al. 2002; Kajüter and Kulmala 2005).

An example of the use of OBA would be the supplier allowing the customer to have access to its cost information. This was the most common situation observed in previous studies (Håkansson and Lind 2007; Kraus and Lind 2007) and happens as a result of power asymmetry in the supply chain. As a consequence, the supplier might also want to gain access to cost information from the customer and might not find reciprocity. In a different situation, the supplier might gain access to the customer's cost information and find that the profits are being shared unfairly throughout the supply chain. This issue is related to the reflexivity between actors in the inter-organisational context (Seal et al. 2004).

In fact, in practice, most of the empirical evidence regarding the adoption of OBA is one-sided (Kraus and Lind 2007) or unidirectional (Håkansson and Lind 2007). Usually, there is "a strong customer requiring its supplier to give it access to financial and non-financial information, thereby enabling it to become actively involved in improving its supplier's operations" (Kraus and Lind 2007, p. 277). From the perspective of the supply chain maturity model, this is what takes place at the serial dependence level, in which one part (the supplier) 'opens its books'. At the reciprocal and mutual dependence levels, as will be discussed further in this section, two-way information exchange takes place.

As shown in Table 3.2, at the serial dependence level, empirical evidence related to OBA is presented by Mouritsen et al. (2001) and Free (2008). However, it should be noted that the cases in which the OBA terminology was not used predominantly were not included under the OBA heading. For example, in the study by Carr and Ng (1995), the suppliers share cost information with the automotive manufacturer Nissan and the terminology of OBA was mentioned in the paper. However, in Table 3.2, it was included under the "target-costing" heading because this is the specific inter-organisational accounting tool adopted. In fact, the other types of inter-organisational accounting tools and techniques presented in Table 3.2 will to some extent incorporate open-book accounting because of the need to share some sort of accounting information between the organisations. Nevertheless, as there are more specific types of inter-organisational accounting mechanisms, such as target costing and value chain analysis, they are discussed separately.

The study by Mouritsen et al. (2001) appears twice in Table 3.2, as it presents two case studies in the electronics industry in Denmark: one related to the implementation of OBA and the other to target costing. The former is discussed here, and the latter appears later in this section under the heading of target costing. The inter-organisational accounting tools were implemented to improve the information exchange between interorganisational links. Both companies had recently outsourced important processes. The high-tech company that chose to implement OBA operated in the communication equipment market and was designated in the paper as LeanTech. The tool was a way of controlling operations at a distance and enhancing production flexibility. Time and cost information about production processes was available to the logistics manager. Bar-coding systems were used to monitor the flows from materials delivery to the final shipment of the product to the customer (Mouritsen et al. 2001). In this way, OBA was a way of covering the black hole in management activities created when operations were initially outsourced.

Free (2008) presented a case demonstrating the use of OBA in the UK supermarket sector. Empirical data were collected in two phases. The first phase aimed to identify key issues in the sector. Interviews were conducted with staff in eight major retailers and eleven suppliers. Category management was identified as the most important recent development in the sector. "The term 'category management' has many definitions and is somewhat ambiguous, denoting an array of buyer-supplier relationships ranging from computer-aided space planning to full-blown partnerships. The concept is built on two basic premises: (i) the supply base is a source of competitive advantage that requires strategic investment; and (ii) dealing with fewer, larger and more sophisticated suppliers reduces risk and transaction costs. It suggests a number of roles for management accounting aimed at enabling collaborative relations, which include open-book costing, joint costing, joint performance measurement, joint forecasting and risk management approaches, pricing guidance, consumer profitability analysis, cost analysis and formal profit sharing arrangements" (Free 2008, pp. 637–638).

The second phase of the study was a field study of the relationship between one of the UK's largest retail chains (ConCo) and one of the world's leading paper products producers (PulpCo). The relationship had endured almost twenty years and both organisations had grown considerably over this period; despite the initial intentions, however, the relationship between trust (or the 'trust talk') and accounting was seen as problematic. As Free (2008) put it, despite the initial emphasis on the trust talk, during the process of implementation of the project, accounting was used by the organisations to preserve their original organisational boundaries. Indeed, the author argues that the divergence between the initial idea and the ensuing developments might be the result of unrealistic expectations about trust-based benefits. This holds true especially in organisations where, historically, power relations are based on hierarchical, autocratic, and adversarial relationships between customers and suppliers.

Target Costing

Target costing was first used in the Japanese context to improve the management of just-in-time (JIT) production systems (Kato 1993). Japanese companies had been motivated by the demand to find new ways of reducing costs, following previous cost reductions at the production stage obtained with JIT production systems. Target costing is not a costing system; rather, it is a concept focused on minimising costs throughout a new product's life cycle (Kato 1993). As such, it seeks to reduce costs with the support of all internal departments and also the suppliers (Kraus and Lind 2007). Nevertheless, it is important to ensure that quality, reliability, and other requirements are not affected if all the cost reductions intended are to be achieved.

Target costing and the functional analysis closely related to it are first used in the planning stage of a product, before its production. The key idea is to analyse possible cost reductions in all stages of a product's lifetime, like planning, research and development, and creating a prototype. As Berry et al. (1997, p. 75) explain: "Target Cost (allowable cost) equals Target Sales Price minus Target Profit. The target sales price is determined primarily from market analysis. The target profit is derived from a view of the total profit requirements of the organisation which is then decomposed into a target profit for each product. For a particular product, any gap between the as-if cost and the target cost will then be the focus of attention using techniques such as value engineering."

Mouritsen et al. (2001) presented a case of target-costing implementation in the electronic sector in Denmark. The company, designated New-Tech, produced burglar and fire alarm systems for industry incorporating cutting edge technology in their highly complex systems. As a consequence of the need for innovation, the adoption of tight controls was considered inappropriate. Thus, the target-costing approach was not adopted in a formalised way to avoid the inhibition of innovation. The key aspect of the target-costing approach was the functional analysis, which provided the data for the discussions between NewTech and its suppliers. The company was a market leader in technology, so presenting innovative concepts for their products was far more important than concerns related to achieving a certain market price.

Nicolini et al. (2000) also found it hard to apply target costing thoroughly in the construction industry in the UK. Their study was carried out in relation to two pilot projects. The projects were initiatives of the

Ministry of Defence (MoD) and concerned the construction of two training and recreational facilities for the army. The Tavistock Institute and
two major contractors in the UK were also engaged in the projects. The
main intention was to try out new modes of purchasing in the construction
sector. The MoD was interested in exploring new ways of procurement to
avoid high costs, poor quality, and a high level of adversarialism, which
had been encountered before in this industry (Nicolini et al. 2000). A key
issue was to improve the integration of the parties: the MoD client, the
designers, the main contractors, and main subcontractors.

Although a fully fledged version of the target-costing approach was not
adopted, the cost model was used to assess costs and to monitor the impact
of modifications in the processes. An iterative process enabled cost reductions to be made even though, in reality, this was still achieved through a
more traditional approach, whereby initial bids were submitted by cluster
leaders.[3] These bids included a single gross figure, but there were no detailed
analyses provided, nor were enquiries made regarding functionality or the
detailed costs of components. One of the difficulties in implementing the
new approach was related to the absence of reliable costing systems. However, as the authors emphasised, industry issues were a "determinant bar-
rier". Indeed, the results corroborate with prior research, which points out
"the existence of some deep-seated limitations and defence mechanisms at
the industry level which prevent the introduction of change" (Nicolini et
al. 2000, p. 321).

Total Cost Control or Total Cost of Ownership

The paper by Carr and Ng (1995) presents a case of serial dependence
or stress in which the dominant party, Nissan Motor Company UK, uses
the total cost control inter-organisational accounting technique to manage
and control its first-tier suppliers. Total cost control (TCC) or total cost of
ownership (TCO) represents an extension of target costing. The idea has
spread following their work related to the development of this approach
at Nissan Group, both in Japanese and in British companies. The Nissan
Group's approach to cost control is a strategic one and uses some principles
of target costing (Carr and Ng 1995). Nissan had to take into account
suppliers' costs as they accounted for more than 80 per cent of the entire
production costs. With the aim of addressing the challenge of developing a
way to control costs throughout the supply chain, the company developed
an approach to TCC that includes strategic elements and focuses on monitoring costs along the supply chain (Carr and Ng 1995).

Indeed, this tool adopts a structured approach to understanding the
costs in the supply chain as a whole. By using slightly different terminology, total cost modelling, Ellram (1996) explains: "while other techniques
focus on the supplier's cost structure, total cost modelling looks at the *cost
of doing business* with a particular supplier for a particular item over the

life of that item" (p. 16, original emphasis). Not only are the purchasing costs of the item analysed, but also the cost of activities associated with the purchase that do not add value, such as service costs, inspection, losses, administration, maintenance, and so on. The idea is to identify these costs and to reduce or even eliminate them (Carr and Ng 1995; Ellram 1996; Berry et al. 1997).

In addition, it is important to emphasise that this approach at Nissan was related to the buyer and the supplier philosophy, as the development of TCC "requires a commitment by the customer and supplier to a long-term relationship based on clear, mutually agreed objectives to strive for world-class capability and competitiveness" (Berry et al. 1997, p. 75). Indeed, the idea of TCC can be considered to be closely linked to the open-book accounting perspective, as there is a need to share relevant and strategic information between different links in the supply chain (Berry et al. 1997). Classification into different stages of supply chain maturity, as signalled here, can be problematic since the language of reciprocal dependence and mutuality are being used in a situation that we include under the heading of serial dependence. It can be argued that our classifications are questionable, but such analysis does allow us to open up the debate about inter-organisational accounting tools and concepts of supply chain maturity.

Value Chain Analysis

Value chain analysis (VCA) is related to Porter's (1985) concept of a value chain, and to further developments by Shank and Govindarajan (1993). Such analysis presupposes that the value chain be divided into strategically relevant parts in order to improve the understanding of cost behaviour and sources of differentiation (Porter 1985). It can be used "to analyse, coordinate and optimise linkages between interdependent activities in the value chain" (Kraus and Lind 2007, p. 278). Thus, value chain analysis represents an important innovation in the accounting field, as traditional management accounting is not capable of recognising the potential of exploring inter-organisational links (Berry et al. 1997).

Dekker (2003) provides an example of an entity—a supermarket chain (Sainsbury)—using VCA. The case analyses the adoption of the VCA model in the relationship between Sainsbury and a group of its suppliers. The focus was on identifying supply chain cost-reduction opportunities based on assumptions related to the VCA approach. According to Dekker (2003), at Sainsbury, the VCA not only encompassed the idea of analysing the activities from an external perspective, but also the management of costs in cooperation with suppliers through the integration of cost data in the supply chain. The model was used with three specific aims in mind: to assess the performance of supply chain activities, to analyse modifications to supply chain operations, and to evaluate the development of supply chain costs over time.

This study adds to the empirical evidence of the application of value chain analysis and is a good example of a successful application of the technique. The maturity of the inter-organisational relationship can be classified as serial dependence because of the evident power of the customer in relation to the suppliers. Even though Dekker (2003) emphasises that implementing inter-organisational accounting mechanisms is a result of the confidence between the parties, Sainsbury's control over its suppliers is evident in his case study. In addition, the use of value chain analysis or value chain accounting has brought some additional problems. Håkansson and Lind (2007) suggest that this model has largely been used to reduce value chain costs rather than focusing on adding value.

Inter-Organisational Cost Management

Further developments in the exchange of cost and accounting information have resulted in so-called inter-organisational cost management (IOCM). While some believe (e.g., Kraus and Lind 2007) that the focus of IOCM is to work together with suppliers to identify potential opportunities for cost reduction, others (e.g., Coad and Cullen 2006) go beyond this and regard not only the cost reduction as an important characteristic of the IOCM, but also the creation of value. IOCM relies upon cooperation between the links in the supply chain to achieve both cost reductions and value creation (Coad and Cullen 2006).

In relation to the use of IOCM practices, Cooper and Slagmulder note that managing costs along the supply chain is even more important for lean organisations with high levels of outsourcing of the manufacture and design of the total added value of their products. Levels of outsourcing may be as high as 70 per cent. In their studies, Cooper and Slagmulder (2004, 2006) have emphasised the relevance of target costing for IOCM and have identified three main techniques: functionality-price-quality (FPQ) trade-offs, inter-organisational cost investigations, and concurrent cost management.

The FPQ trade-off is helpful when the supplier's cost of production is expected to be higher than its target costing, and the only way to bring its costs back to the target level is by relaxing the functionality and/or quality specifications of the product (Cooper and Slagmulder 2004, 2006). After potential sources of relaxation are identified, the buyer's and supplier's design teams meet to discuss the changes that would be required. Generally, the relaxations are proposed by the supplier team and must be approved by the buyer. Thus, to be successful, the supplier should ensure that the resultant product will generate adequate returns. Cooper and Slagmulder (2004) emphasise that an effective value-engineering program is the key for the success of this IOCM technique. They add that, usually, an FPQ trade-off is an outcome of an initial stage value-engineering project. Despite this, it can take place at any stage from the design to the release of the product into mass production.

Inter-organisational cost investigations will be used when the FPQ trade-offs identified bring about insufficiently large savings to reduce the manufacturing cost to the target level. The main difference between the two is that in the case of inter-organisational cost investigations, design engineers from more than two firms in the supply chain are involved in solving the problem. Normally, there are two solutions: either the product is redesigned to avoid or minimise the need for certain activities identified, or the activities might be outsourced to a different company or performed by a different unit within the firm in order to reduce costs. "However, just as with FPQ tradeoffs, the fundamental design of the end product still remains essentially fixed" (Cooper and Slagmulder 2004, p. 7).

Concurrent cost management "aggressively reduces costs by increasing the scope of design changes that the supplier can undertake" (Cooper and Slagmulder 2004, p. 8). It is suitable when fundamental changes in both the buyer's product and the supplier's component are needed (Kraus and Lind 2007). Moreover, concurrent cost management is often initiated by the buyer once it has been recognised that only sustained and coordinated cost-reduction actions by both the supplier's and the buyer's design teams can achieve the desired cost reduction. Although this technique is used in a situation when the most substantial cost reductions are necessary, typically it is introduced at a much earlier stage than the cost-saving measures associated with the other two IOCM techniques (Cooper and Slagmulder 2006).

At the serial dependence level, the study by Cooper and Slagmulder (2004) presents the case of implementation of IOCM in the manufacturing and automotive Japanese industries. Three supply chains were analysed. In two of them, the focus was on the relationship between the manufacturer and a first-tier supplier, and in the other, there were the manufacturer and a first-tier and a second-tier supplier. Data were collected in all seven of the companies in the sample. In addition, IOCM practices were observed in one of the dyadic pairs to enrich the analysis. The authors observed that IOCM techniques were developed to overcome information asymmetry between buyers and suppliers, and to enhance coordination and cooperation in their design teams as they seek to identify ways of changing the specifications and lowering costs.

Cost For Inter-Organisational Control

Cäker (2008) analysed the interrelation between bureaucratic mechanisms and social mechanisms in the management of inter-organisational processes where the customer has a dominant position in the market. His case study was carried out in three companies: The Customer, Supplier 1, and Supplier 2. The Customer is a large multinational corporation which supplies assembling units with technically advanced and complex products, most of the time within the corporation. The two suppliers are small companies, each providing 20–30 critical, customised products to The Customer which are used by it on a daily basis. However, both suppliers are regarded as being replaceable because, in the long term, their skills are not considered to be exclusive (Cäker 2008). In addition, the suppliers fear losing The Customer and the paper views the relationship from the perspective of the dominated supplier.

As a consequence of the power dominance of The Customer, suppliers are continuously assessed and ranked, especially in relation to quality and delivery precision. Cäker (2008) analysed the implementation of the vendor management inventory (VMI) in a pilot study with the two selected suppliers just mentioned. He identifies the costs of bureaucratic, inter-organisational control from the suppliers' perspectives. One of them is the cost of lost flexibility and is related to the consequences of The Customer directly managing delivery schedules from the suppliers. As the suppliers are forced to meet The Customer's requirements, they lose much of their previous flexibility and incur additional costs. The costs are not only related to delivery, but also to the loss of flexibility in production. For example, Supplier 1 used to hold higher inventories to meet The Customer's deliveries on time. The other cost of inter-organisational control is the cost of inefficient deployment of resources. The VMI project itself was seen to create this type of cost. There was a lack of balance in the amount of resources employed by The Customer and the suppliers for carrying out the project. As Supplier 1 and Supplier 2 were both small companies, hiring additional staff to deal with the new activities was not considered appropriate.

Despite these problems, suppliers were devoted to the execution of the VMI project and the adoption of the inter-organisational controls. Their main motivation for collaborating was the relationship itself. Trust, which is usually regarded as central to this process, was not a major issue. "The suppliers do trust The Customer to honour agreements. However, the prevalence of negative expectations suggesting that The Customer will use their power to claim financial gains and to expect obedience, dominate expectations of whether the suppliers will make any gains in the coming negotiations" (Cäker 2008, pp. 242–243). In addition, market pressures were on the agenda. The Customer was considering the possibility of replacing the suppliers with Eastern European suppliers who could provide cheaper products.

On the other hand, at the operational level, social control mechanisms, such as trust, had played an essential role. In several circumstances, the rigidity of bureaucratic inter-organisational controls was compensated by informal information exchange resulting from the trust between the parties. For example, information regarding the 'real need' or demands of The Customer was obtained as a result of personal relationships developed between employees of the companies. The formal demand plan was thereby updated through the contacts, and the necessary adjustments in deliveries took place without affecting The Customer's production plans. Based on these contrasts, Cäker (2008) argues that his findings question the usually positive view that bureaucratic mechanisms are when managing interorganisational relationships.

Other Tools and Techniques

Frances and Garnsey (1996) presented an example in the UK supermarket supply chain. In addition to the focus on accounting, these authors analysed the role of information technology in replacing marketing relations. Pricing, stock control and monitoring, and the assessment of suppliers are examples of accounting methods introduced by supermarkets, such as Sainsbury and Tesco. Dominating customers are likely to manage relationships in order to enforce cost pressures.

Finally, Seal et al. (2004) has provided an interesting illustration of the changing phases of supply chain relationships and the associated change in the accounting techniques used in the UK electronics sector. The case study organisation, Dextron, designed, assembled, and built computers. It was in an interesting situation since it had both powerful suppliers (microchip and software giants) and less powerful suppliers (local metal-bashers and cable makers). The relationships with the latter can be classified as serial dependence, and Dextron used cost-management techniques associated with value engineering and teardown analysis in its dealings with these companies However, it was not in a position to use open-book accounting with, for example, the microchip producers, who were considered to be world-class manufacturers in their own right.

Reciprocal Dependence

Open-Book Accounting Possibilities

The study by Seal et al. (2004) has already been covered under serial dependence, but it is interesting to note that, in the third phase of development described in the paper, Dextron moved away from more adversarial forms of relationship towards more collaborative relationships. This involved more information sharing across organisational boundaries and opened up the possibility of sharing accounting information. This opening up of accounting information was a consequence of moving through the supply chain maturity model from serial dependence to reciprocal dependence. Accountants within Dextron, specifically in the Cost Management Group, took on additional production, commercial, organisational, and change management roles in addition to their substantive accounting contribution. Accountants within the Cost Management Group were searching for a revised cost model that could more accurately reflect the actual operation of the supply chain. The case does not identify any specific examples of open-book accounting, but it does open up the dialogue of possibilities of open-book arrangements at the more collaborative phase of relationships.

Inter-Organisational Cost Management

Coad and Cullen (2006) reported on an action research project at School Trends Ltd, where they observed cost management of an evolutionary nature, and process mapping and activities management were used to innovate across organisational boundaries. The value chain analysis (VCA) project involved visits to an external supplier of decorative embroidery, a supplier of garments, a logistics supplier and schools within both the primary and secondary sectors. Examples of reciprocal benefits are provided through boundary-spanning activities involving benchmarking, outsourcing, sharing information, and the redesign of packaging. In the context of this chapter, whilst a number of supply chain relationships were examined, the relationships were essentially considered to be dyadic, although interestingly, Caglio and Ditillo (2008) actually place this work under the network category, with one-to-one relationships. This highlights some of the problems of categorising individual pieces of work into specific categories, and the same limitation can be made about our attempts in this chapter to categorise studies in terms of supply chain maturity.

One interesting aspect of Coad and Cullen's (2006) approach to IOCM is the importance of the cooperation between partners to improve costs and create value, even in those situations in which the involvement of management accounting and/or accountants is not completely clear. For them, "IOCM may or may not involve methods recognisable as management accounting, and may or may not involve management accountants. But, whilst its practices are varied, its central concern is with cooperative efforts by members of separate organisational units to modify cost structures and create value for its participants" (p. 343).

Three main findings from their study are highlighted. First, they found it important to describe cost-management practices in the intra- and inter-organisational contexts, but they also emphasise that the boundaries between the two are still not clear. They argue that the processes of institutionalisation, capabilities in resource utilisation, and learning and change will be mutually interchanged between intra- and inter-organisational domains. Second, they concluded that decisions related to how boundaries are established between companies are closely related to social relations affected by historical aspects of current institutions (Coad and Cullen 2006).

This emphasises the relevance of social aspects (as opposed to just economic aspects) in influencing the way managers make decisions related to outsourcing and partnering. Finally, Coad and Cullen regarded power and politics as important in the evolutionary perspective, as proposed by Burns (2000). Power may be used at three levels. At one level, it can be used to introduce new organisational rules. At a second level, power may be used in a subtler manner to introduce organisational routines (including management accounting) to favour particular groups. At a third level, power can be closely linked to institutionalised routines, which influences the way people act and think, in this way bringing stability and building up organisational knowledge (Burns and Scapens 2000).

As a consequence, depending on the situation, power may make changes more difficult or may be an important factor facilitating accounting change and bringing stability back (Burns 2000). In relation to the latter, Coad and Cullen (2006) highlight their belief that notions of power asymmetries in the organisational context give support to the idea that institutionalised routines allow the establishment of a *truce* in contradictory situations. Consequently, they start to question the existence of trust in inter-organisational relationships, as noted by previous studies (Van der Meer-Kooistra and Vosselman 2000; Tomkins 2001; Langfield-Smith and Smith 2003; Cooper and Slagmulder 2004; Dekker 2004). They believe the issue of truce instead of trust is one that warrants further research.

Management Control Structure and Governance

Van der Meer-Kooistra and Vosselman (2000) compared two cases of using accounting and management controls in outsourcing operations in Dutch organisations. In one case, a joint venture between the two oil companies Shell and Esso, called NAM (Nederlandse Aardolie Maatschappij), the way that renovation and maintenance activities were contracted was changed. NAM is the biggest gas producing company in the Netherlands. As part of the Groningen Long Term Project (GLT project), which had a planned duration of twenty-five years, NAM established renovation and maintenance contracts with a consortium of contractors. This consortium became responsible for subcontracting all maintenance activities, from painting to the maintenance of installations. As a result, NAM started to deal with only one party, instead of a number of them.

On the one hand, NAM could benefit from the consortium's specific knowledge, making it easier to coordinate activities. On the other hand, "this may pose a threat, because NAM will become more dependent on the contractor, and may also lose knowledge about planning and coordinating the outsourced activities due to which it will be more difficult to measure and evaluate the quality of the contractor's activities and output" (Van der Meer-Kooistra and Vosselman 2000, p. 65). In order to deal with these potential drawbacks, NAM required very detailed contracts from the competing consortiums at the tendering stage of the project. These contracts should include plans and bids based on the total cost of ownership concept. NAM also influenced the relationships between the companies involved in the consortium by requiring them to draw up a legal partnership.

In addition to the total cost of ownership, the contract between NAM and the selected consortium included several details regarding controlling and performance evaluation. "NAM has the right to audit the activities and their registration. Audits will take place on an ad hoc basis and NAM is to have access to all information (open-book principle). NAM will also carry out regular 'quantity surveys' by means of which NAM measures the physical progress" (Van der Meer-Kooistra and Vosselman 2000, pp. 67–68). As identified by these authors, the controls used by NAM at the initial stages of the development of the inter-organisational relationship are the result of the bureaucratic-based control pattern.

In their paper, Van der Meer-Kooistra and Vosselman (2000) identified three management control patterns in interfirm (or inter-organisational) relationships: the market-based pattern, bureaucracy-based pattern, and trust-based pattern. The control mechanism applied varies according to the pattern; for example, in the market-based pattern, the dominant mechanism is based on the prices found in the market; in the bureaucracy-based pattern, norms, standards, and rules are the essential mechanisms; in the trust-based pattern, control is a result of the trust between the contracting parties. The predominance of bureaucratic control mechanisms in NAM shows the use of accounting and management controls in the inter-organisational relationship by the dominant partner to reduce the risk of having to rely on an external partner, the consortium. However, it is important to stress that the use of these types of controls is seen to be a consequence of NAM's vertical and formal internal structures and of the European regulations with which it has to comply.

In a different way, in the second case presented by Van der Meer-Kooistra and Vosselman (2000), a trust-based pattern for the development of the inter-organisational relationship was presented. The case was carried out at the Shell Research and Technology Centre Amsterdam (SRTCA). SRTCA contracted a consortium to perform the maintenance activities and to deal with the management, coordination, and engineering associated with these activities. The consortium operates under the name Huissaannemer Shell Research Amsterdam (HSRA). Although there was internal resistance to change, the emphasis on the development of the relationship and on enhancing trust was clear from the beginning.

As a consequence of the trust-based pattern, contracts were less detailed than in more adversarial situations. For example, the results of productivity improvements were not established in the initial contract. However, after two years, this subject was discussed and, in conjunction with the development of a system with which to measure the results, SRTCA and HSRA agreed on a bonus system for sharing the benefits from improvements. Therefore, in this case, inter-organisational accounting information only started to become important during the development of the inter-organisational relationship, perhaps as a result of the level of trust between the organisations involved. In terms of supply chain maturity, we classify the work of Van der Meer-Kooistra and Vosselman (2000) as illustrating aspects of reciprocal dependence. However, in the later work of Van der Meer-Kooistra and Scapens (2008), we classify the developments in the relationships in the NAM case study as an example of mutual dependence. The reason for this will be examined in the next section.

Mutual Dependence

Open-Book Accounting

Seal et al. (1999) found that accounting can contribute to the establishment of trusting and collaborative business relationships. They carried out a piece of action research focused on the establishment of a strategic supply partnership. The two companies involved were subsidiaries of major multinational organisations and they had been doing business together for around twenty-five years. However, during this time, business had been done under traditional arm's-length relationship transactions. The procurement director at the assembler organisation (the customer) was keen to engage in a strategic alliance with the supplier and the researchers were engaged as "honest brokers" in the process. The initial draft alliance agreement stressed the importance of open and trusting relationships that enabled tangible and measurable benefits to be gained by both sides over a long period of time and emphasised the desire to share ideas and information. Discussions showed a willingness to look across organisational boundaries and to allow open-book analysis within pre-agreed limits. Target costing was identified as a tool that allowed members of both organisations to "think outside the box" and collaborate on an inter-organisational basis. The sharing of information was intended to deliver mutually beneficial innovative solutions to both parties involved in the alliance. However, in terms of utilising open-book accounting, difficulties arose because of evident weaknesses in both firms' internal cost systems. The intent to use open-book accounting was there, and management accounting notions of cost, cost reduction, and performance measurement were fully embedded in the discussions around product and process improvements. In Tomkins's (2001) terminology, Type 2 information was being used to master events collaboratively.

Langfield-Smith and Smith (2003) reported on a case study of the role of control mechanisms and trust in developing relationships between an electricity company and its outsourced IT operations. In this particular instance, control was achieved through outcome controls and social controls developed over time. The particular focus was on the role of goodwill trust as the relationship developed, and this fits neatly into the mutual dependence phase of supply chain maturity models. Initially, relationships between the organisations involved were difficult, and new management systems were implemented in Central (the electricity company) to achieve cost control and management of IT developments (outsourced to Global). Eighteen months into the contract, a new risk-reward scheme was devised to monitor Global's performance. Two years after the commencement of the new contract, a strategic alliance was formed with a cable manufacturer that was characterised by an open-book approach to the sharing of information. Performance under the new strategic alliance was tied up to risk return, and a joint steering committee (comprised of representatives from both firms) was set up to develop performance indicators to support areas such as growth, delivery time, and costs. Mutual benefits were at the centre of this agreement, and accounting mechanisms were used to support the relationship. In summary, Langfield-Smith and Smith argued that the development of trust may, in fact, be compatible with the development of tighter accounting controls and contracts provided that trust is well established and the controls are used, by both parties, in a supportive and cooperative manner. Again, therefore, in Tomkins's terminology, Type 2 information is being used in this mutual stage of supply chain relationships (Tomkins 2001).

Dekker (2004) provides another example of the role of accounting in a strategic alliance arrangement, this time between NMA (a supplier of railway safety systems) and Nedelandse Spoorwegen (Dutch Railways). Cost control, linked to innovations, featured as the main goal of the alliance, and the cost data that were used to assess performance in this area were calculated on the basis of open-book accounting. Dekker (2004) also analyses the formal and informal control mechanisms used in the alliance under the headings of outcome controls, behaviour controls, and social controls. It is interesting to note that, despite the choice of a good partner and a high level of trust between the two organisations, the partners developed this relatively detailed governance structure. The argument for this, which fits in with Tomkins's Type 2 thinking (Tomkins 2001), is that the strong governance structures facilitated mutual transparency of behaviours and results. In this context, therefore, management accounting plays an essential role in governance through the use of formal controls to facilitate and promote mutual benefits for both organisations involved in a dyadic relationship.

Governance

Recent research (Van der Meer-Kooistra and Scapens 2008) was also carried out taking into account the implementation of the GLT project by NAM. Interestingly, the new empirics collected reveal the progress in the nature of the inter-organisational relationship and the exchange of information between NAM and the outsourced partner. This is in line with both the supply chain maturity model presented in this chapter and a shift from Type 1 to 2 of Tomkins's categories for information (2001) as the level of interdependence in the relationship increases. In the initial stage, the relationship can be classified as reciprocal dependence, as some sort of collaboration between the parties takes place. As the relationship matures, dependence becomes mutual and information sharing becomes more intense. This can be observed in terms of governance practices.

Van der Meer-Kooistra and Scapens (2008) propose directions towards the development of a framework of governance for lateral relations. The lateral relations are regarded as being relatively equal (in a hierarchical sense), and there is a high level of interdependence between the parties. Governance is used instead of control because the former is seen as a wider concept than the latter as it appears in the traditional management accounting literature. The model divides the governance aspects into hierarchical practices, relationship practices, and market prices. Examples of the governance practices observed in the NAM case are presented in Table 3.3.

These governance practices enhanced both collaboration and competition between NAM and the consortium. "The GLT project indicates that a variety of governance practices can be needed, some of which may appear contradictory, with hierarchical practices being used alongside relationship practices, and even market practices" (Van der Meer-Kooistra and Scapens 2008, p. 377). However, the authors emphasise that these contradictions are related to the nature of lateral relations that makes the

Table 3.3 Overview of the GLT-Project Governance Practices

Hierarchical practices	Relationship practices	Market practices
Work orders	Design competition	Search of suitable parties
Monthly information on progress, costs, technical developments and problems, hours worked, deliveries, stocks of materials, etc.	Structure of NAM-consortium relationship	Possibility of terminating the relationship after the renovation of the first eleven sites
Quantity surveys	Structure of the consortium	
Ad hoc audits	Framework contract	
Incentives	In-depth evaluation of the first renovation contract	
	Face-to-face meetings and workshops	
	Information about competencies and approval of changes in key personnel	
	Shared office	
	Dispute and conflict resolution procedures	

(Source: Van der Meer-Kooistra and Scapens 2008, p. 377)

combination of cooperation and competition and flexibility and standardisation necessary.

4   CONCLUDING COMMENTS

The chapter focuses on using the supply chain maturity model to analyse
the studies in the literature on inter-organisational accounting in dyadic
settings. Indeed, in addition to differences in the stage of the relationship,
other characteristics of the dyads were also taken into account. As predicted in the supply chain maturity model, with time, relationships become
closer and the exchange of accounting information is intensified. Whilst
open-book accounting appears at all three stages identified by Berry et al.
(2000), the difference in their use relates to the change from a dominant
customer in serial dependence towards more collaborative approaches at
the reciprocal and mutual dependence stages.

Table 3.2 shows that most of the inter-organisational relationships
analysed in research carried out in dyadic settings can be classified as
serial dependence. In most of the cases, the power of the dominant party
is evident. A smaller number of the studies present reciprocal or mutual
dependence cases. It might be said that, at the serial dependence stage,
Type 1 information (Tomkins 2001) is predominant. Management controls and accounting tools and techniques are mainly used to control suppliers or outsourced parties. They seem to vary according to the needs of
each specific relationship. Total cost control, target costing, value chain
analysis, and inter-organisational cost management are examples found
at this stage.

As relationships progress, at the reciprocal and mutual dependence stages,
inter-organisational accounting information is more openly exchanged.
Open-book accounting agreements are predominant. However, it is important to stress that the implementation of the tool does not take place in all
cases. Indeed, accounting may play a more symbolic role, ". . . although
we found no applications of suggested techniques for inter-firm accounting such as open-book costing and sanction budgets, the limited nature of
the inter-firm accounting was not a result of the technical inadequacy but
rather a reflection of the lack of shared destiny type relations in the electronics industry" (Seal et al. 2004).

Outcome controls, behaviour controls, and social controls are evident at
the various stages of supply chain maturity. Their use depends on related
concepts, such as trust and power, although it is clear to see that outcome
controls are used at all stages of developing supply chain relationships.
Concepts such as goodwill trust are more evident at reciprocal and mutual
stages of dependence. Whilst debates about governance structures impact at
all three levels of dependence, our analysis in Table 3.2 particularly focuses
on governance structures at reciprocal and mutual stages of dependence.

Finally, this chapter has focused on dyadic relationships. Such a focus can be criticised because a dyadic relationship can be viewed as being an isolated island (Kraus and Lind 2007). An alternative is to view inter-organisational relationships as an element within a network of relationships. It might be suggested that networks, value networks, or supply networks would fit better with the current global and competitive business environment. The role of inter-organisational accounting in networks is covered in later chapters in the book.

NOTES

1. In this chapter, papers which refer to supply chains and supply networks were also included when the relationships were analysed as dyadic pairs. For example, the Carr and Ng (1995) study encompasses the case of an automotive supply chain and the research by Coad and Cullen (2006) looks at the relationships of a customised school-wear manufacturer and some of its network relationships, such as suppliers and logistic partners. However, in both cases, the relationships were studied in dyadic pairs.
2. The terminology suggested by Berry et al. (2000) is used predominantly hereafter.
3. Nicolini et al. (2000, p. 311): "A cluster is, in many respects, a design and construct mini project that takes place within the larger framework of the project. It is a place where a limited number of designers, suppliers of materials or components engage in intensive collaboration to design and deliver a significant, recognizable element of the overall building, working to reduce costs, improve value and minimise waste. Clusters operate as semi-independent parts of the project under the overall coordination of the contractor or project manager, replicating the logic of single point responsibility down the supply chain.

BIBLIOGRAPHY

Berry, T., Ahmed, A., Cullen, J., Dunlop, A., and Seal, W. 1997. The consequences of inter-firm supply chains for management accounting. *Management Accounting* 75: 74–75.

Berry, A. J., Ahmed, A., Cullen, J., Dunlop, A., and Seal, W. 2000. *The consequences of inter-firm supply chains for management accounting.* London: CIMA.

Burns, J. 2000. The dynamics of accounting change: Interplay between new practices, routines, institutions, power and politics. *Accounting Auditing and Accountability Journal* 13: 566–596.

Burns, J., and Scapens, R. W. 2000. Conceptualizing management accounting change: An institutional framework. *Management Accounting Research* 11: 3–25.

Caglio, A., and Ditillo, A. 2008. A review and discussion of management control in inter-firm relationships: Achievements and future directions. *Accounting, Organizations and Society* 33: 865–898.

Cäker, M. 2008. Intertwined coordination mechanisms in interorganizational relationships with dominated suppliers. *Management Accounting Research* 19: 231–251.

Carr, C., and Ng, J. 1995. Total cost control: Nissan and its U.K. supplier partnerships. *Management Accounting Research* 6: 347–365.

Chua, W. F., and Mahama, H. 2007. The effect of network ties on accounting controls in a supply alliance: Field study evidence. *Contemporary Accounting Research* 24: 1–44.

Coad, A. F., and Cullen, J. 2006. Inter-organisational cost management: Towards an evolutionary perspective. *Management Accounting Research* 17: 342–369.

Cooper, R., and Slagmulder, R. 2004. Interorganizational cost management and relational context. *Accounting, Organizations and Society* 29: 1–26.

Cooper, R., and Slagmulder, R. 2006. Integrated cost management. In *Contemporary issues in management accounting*, ed. Bhimani, A. 117–145. Oxford: Oxford University Press.

Cullen, J., Berry, A. J., Seal, W., Dunlop, A., Ahmed, M., and Marson, J. 1999. Interfirm supply chains—The contribution of management accounting. *Management Accounting* 77: 30–32.

Dekker, H. C. 2003. Value chain analysis in interfirm relationships: A field study. *Management Accounting Research* 14: 1–23.

Dekker, H. C. 2004. Control of inter-organizational relationships: Evidence on appropriation concerns and coordination requirements. *Accounting, Organizations and Society* 29: 27–49.

Ellram, L. M. 1996. A structured method for applying purchasing cost management tools. *International Journal of Purchasing and Materials Management* 32: 11–19.

Frances, J., and Garnsey, E. 1996. Supermarkets and suppliers in the United Kingdom: System integration, information and control. *Accounting, Organizations and Society* 21: 591–610.

Free, C. 2008. Walking the talk? Supply chain accounting and trust among UK supermarkets and suppliers. *Accounting, Organizations and Society* 33: 629–662.

Gietzmann, M. B. 1996. Incomplete contracts and the make or buy decision: Governance design and attainable flexibility. *Accounting, Organizations and Society* 21: 611–626.

Håkansson, H., and Lind, J. 2004. Accounting and network coordination. *Accounting, Organizations and Society* 29: 51–72.

Håkansson, H., and Lind, J. 2007. Accounting in an interorganizational setting. In *Handbook of management accounting research*, ed. Chapman, C S., Hopwood, A G., and Shields, M D. 885–902. Oxford: Elsevier.

Hopwood, A. G. 1996. Looking across rather than up and down: On the need to explore the lateral processing of information. *Accounting, Organizations and Society* 21: 589–590.

Kajüter, P., and Kulmala, H. I. 2005. Open-book accounting in networks: Potential achievement and reasons for failures. *Management Accounting Research* 16: 179–204.

Kato, Y. 1993. Target costing support systems: Lessons from leading Japanese companies. *Management Accounting Research* 4: 33–47.

Kraus, K., and Lind, J. 2007. Management control in inter-organisational relationships. In *Issues in management accounting*, ed. Hopper, T., Scapens, R. W., and Northcott, D. 269–296. Harlow, UK: Financial Times Prentice Hall.

Kulmala, H. I., Paranko, J., and Uusi-Rauva, E. 2002. The role of cost management in network relationships. *International Journal of Production Economics* 79: 33–43.

Lamming, R. 1993. *Beyond partnership, strategies for innovation and lean supply*. New York: Prentice-Hall.

Langfield-Smith, K., and Smith, D. 2003. Management control systems and trust in outsourcing relationships. *Management Accounting Research* 14: 281–307.

Mouritsen, J., Hansen, A., and Hansen, C. O. 2001. Inter-organizational controls and organizational competencies: Episodes around target cost management/functional analysis and open book accounting. *Management Accounting Research* 12: 221–244.

Mouritsen, J., and Thrane, S. 2006. Accounting, network complementarities and the development of inter-organisational relations. *Accounting, Organizations and Society* 31: 241–275.

Nicolini, D., Tomkins, C., Holti, R., Oldman, A., and Smalley, M. 2000. Can target costing and whole life costing be applied in the construction industry?: Evidence from two case studies. *British Journal of Management* 11: 303–324.

Otley, D. 1994. Management control in contemporary organizations: Towards a wider framework. *Management Accounting Research* 5: 289–299.

Porter, M. E. 1985. *Competitive advantage, creating and sustaining superior performance.* New York: Free Press.

Seal, W., Berry, A., and Cullen, J. 2004. Disembedding the supply chain: Institutionalized reflexivity and inter-firm accounting. *Accounting, Organizations and Society* 29: 73–92.

Seal, W., Cullen, J., Dunlop, A., Berry, T., and Ahmed, M. 1999. Enacting a European supply chain: A case study on the role of management accounting. *Management Accounting Research* 10: 303–322.

Shank, J. K., and Govindarajan, V. 1993. *Strategic cost management: The new tool for competitive advantage.* New York: Free Press.

Tomkins, C. 2001. Interdependencies, trust and information in relationships, alliances and networks. *Accounting, Organizations and Society* 26: 161–191.

Van der Meer-Kooistra, J., and Scapens, R. W. 2008. The governance of lateral relations between and within organisations. *Management Accounting Research* 19: 365–384.

Van der Meer-Kooistra, J., and Vosselman, E. G. J. 2000. Management control of interfirm transactional relationships: The case of industrial renovation and maintenance. *Accounting, Organizations and Society* 25: 51–77.

4 Towards Accounting in Network Settings

Johnny Lind and Sof Thrane

1 INTRODUCTION

The literature on accounting in an inter-organisational setting has been steadily increasing over the past fifteen years (Frances and Garnsey 1996; Gietzmann 1996; Hopwood 1996) and studies have covered several types of inter-organisational relationships, such as outsourcing relationships, customer relationships, supplier relationships, partnerships, and strategic alliances (Carr and Ng 1995; Seal et al. 1999; Van der Meer-Kooistra and Vosselman 2000; Dekker 2004). However, independently of the label given to the inter-organisational relationship considered, they generally focus on collaborations between two legally independent organisations.

A large majority of the papers are studies of buyer-supplier relationships, and most of the authors have theorised their findings through transaction cost economics or agency theory (Håkansson and Lind 2007). These studies have been successful in developing knowledge about key managerial issues, such as make-or-buy decisions and the alignment of the pattern of control with the characteristics of the relationship. However, there has been little discussion of managerial issues and the role of accounting in more complex situations, where, for example, multiple buyers compete for resources, thereby driving the consumption of overheads, or considering how issues of customer relationship management are associated with supplier relationship management through production planning and scheduling. If a relationship is viewed as an element within a network of relationships (Anderson et al. 1994), it is possible to identify at least five significantly different situations a firm needs to handle in relation to counterparts such as customers, suppliers, and competitors.

This chapter introduces a framework of five types of situations that a firm needs to handle in relation to counterparts within a network setting. The situations, therefore, range from how to handle one relationship in isolation to networks consisting of suppliers, customers, and third parties such as competitors, regulators, and suppliers' suppliers. In this chapter the key managerial issues and the related types and roles of accounting are considered for each type of situations identified in the framework. The literature on accounting in an inter-organisational setting has been used to generate these contingencies.

The five types of situations that a firm is likely to find itself in are illustrated in each of the relevant sections. The first type of situation is that of managing just one relationship. This often means that the inter-organisational relationship is conceptualised as a dyadic one. Dyadic settings were the topic of the last chapter; however, we will give dyadic settings the same degree of consideration as the others. Although there is a certain degree of overlap, the topics covered in this chapter are complementary to those in the last one. The type of situation focuses on the coordination and management of serial relationships in a chain. This is manifested by how calculations are performed for relationships with customers and suppliers without differentiating between one relationship and another in a string of relationships, known as a value chain as just calculation on undifferentiated relations to both customers and suppliers in a value chain. The third type of situation has to do with managing several counterparts all active in a certain 'direction' with respect to a focal company, an example of this being that of a firm needing to handle heterogeneous supplier relationships simultaneously. The fourth type deals with the management and coordination of multiple counterparts in two directions. In this instance, the focus is on the management and coordination of multiple supply chains between heterogeneous sets of suppliers and customers relationships. The fifth type of situation focuses on the management of complex systems/networks including third parties such as competitors and regulators. This case deals with the management of multiple relations between buyers, sellers, partners, and linked competitors in a network of interconnected relationships (Lind and Thrane 2005).

This chapter seeks to investigate how managerial issues and the roles of accounting are related to the type of situation that the conceptualisation of the inter-organisational relationships focuses on. The key contribution of this chapter is the development of the framework used to conceptualise the various types of situations in a network setting and their linkages to key managerial issues and to the types and role of accounting.[1] The framework helps to understand the variety of findings in terms of the roles and types of accounting used in inter-organisational relationships. The framework shows that different conceptualisations of the inter-organisational relationships raise different managerial issues and point towards specific types of control mechanisms. Furthermore, conceptualisations of different types of situations tend to use different theories, ranging from economic theories at Situation 1 to institutional, actor network, industrial networks, and complexity theories at Situation 5.

2   ONE RELATIONSHIP

The first and, generally, the most straightforward type of situation for a company within a network of interconnected relationships is that of management within a single, dyadic relationship. The large majority of published studies on accounting in inter-organisational relationships have been on this setting (Håkansson and Lind 2007). The inter-organisational accounting literature has focused on different forms of dyadic relationships, such as collaboration in the supply chain between a company and its customers or suppliers or collaboration between two firms that potentially target the same customers.

However, independently of the form of collaboration, the first type of situation is limited to the relation between two legally independent organisations. This type of research studies and identifies issues and problems within the two collaborating parties. The studies are focused on the transactions that take place between the two organisations.

Further, differences in the types of control are understood and explained within the dyadic relationship. The relationship is viewed as an isolated island in a competitive market. Figure 4.1 shows the first type of situation, that of how to handle one relationship.

Key managerial issues when inter-organisational relationships are conceptualised as a dyadic relationship are as follows: the decision of when and whether to make or buy, the allocation and balance of control and responsibility in the dyadic relationship, information exchange and issues concerning incentives (Anderson et al. 2000; Van der Meer-Kooistra and Vosselman 2000; Baiman and Rajan 2002; Dekker 2004).

Make-or-buy decisions in a transaction cost economics (TCE) perspective have to do with firms' choices between different forms of governance for their transactions, given the characteristics of the context of the transactions, such as asset specificity and uncertainty. The key question is to decide when a company should produce a product/service by itself or when it should buy it from its suppliers. Traditional management accounting has, according to Gietzmann (1996), viewed this issue as a short-term sourcing decision. Managers need detailed cost information

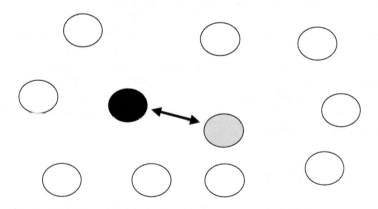

Figure 4.1   One relationship.

about their own operations, which makes it possible to compare possible purchasing prices from potential suppliers with the internal production cost for a component/service. The comparison makes it possible for the managers to choose the most efficient form of governance for the transaction.

Anderson et al. (2000) have contributed to the dialogue on make-or-buy decisions by conducting a study in the U.S. auto industry. They showed that the company outsourced the production of more complex components and components belonging to more complex interdependent subassemblies. This change in the type of components outsourced was introduced at the same time as the number of suppliers of outsourced components was reduced. The findings were not as expected, however, and according to the authors (p. 746), "Our research indicates that it is less appropriate than ever for accountants charged with developing data for sourcing decisions to focus narrowly on production costs. The value chain perspective of strategic cost management with its focus on 'costs of ownership' rather than supplier price is essential, and we can not assume that 'costs of ownership' are minimised with internal production."

In a dyadic relationship, managers need to choose between the most suitable combination of outcome, behaviour, and social controls. Van der Meer-Kooistra and Vosselman (2000), in their research on industrial renovation and maintenance, and Dekker (2004), in his study of a Dutch strategic alliance in the railway sector, show that different dyadic relationships are associated with different control patterns. This research shows that, depending of the characteristics of the dyadic relationship, managers should rely on different combinations of control methods such as budgets, responsibility accounting, performance measurements, rules, quality plans, task groups, board monitoring, values, norms, and cultures.

According to Van der Meer-Kooistra and Vosselman (2000) and Dekker (2004), outcome and behaviour control are needed when the relationship is characterised by a low to medium frequency of transactions, medium to high asset specificity, and medium to high market risks. Outcome and social control are emphasised when the relationship is characterised by a low frequency of transactions, high levels of investment in specific assets, and a high degree of market risk. In situations when transactions are frequently repeated, low asset specificity and the environment are characterised by low uncertainty, firms use outcome control based on standardised activities or output and characterised by competitive bidding. Van der Meer-Kooistra and Vosselman (2000) identified three different control patterns: market-based, bureaucracy-based, and trust-based. Other studies have also shown that managers align different control patterns to different dyadic relationships (Speklé 2001; Langfield-Smith and Smith 2003).

Information exchange and incentive-related issues are closely related to each other (Baiman and Rajan 2002). Increasing the exchange of information between two companies makes it easier for the companies to identify improvements and cost reductions in the relationship. For example, Kulp (2002) studied information sharing between retailers and manufacturers through a vendor-managed inventory system where the retailer delegated inventory decisions to the manufacturer. She demonstrated that increased information sharing with more precise and reliable information was more likely lead to profits in the relationship.

However, making more information available also increases the potential for opportunistic behaviour (Baiman and Rajan 2002). A company can use the information received to increase its bargaining power in the relationship. A critical issue, then, for the company is to develop safeguarding mechanisms in the relationship through which it can protect itself against this eventuality. The control system is a central ingredient in this development and it is important to design an inter-organisational control system that can mitigate the risk of opportunistic behaviour.

In summary, this strand of inter-organisational accounting research focuses on dyadic relationships, and the described management issues and associated type and role of accounting have mainly theorised their work by using TCE and agency theory. There are two types of key managerial issues at this level: Firstly, there is the make-or-buy decision based on transactions characteristics such as asset specificity; and secondly, the motivation and incentives of self-interested firms and individuals in dyadic relations are key issues. Finally, it should be noted that the literature focuses on how the control pattern is aligned with characteristics of the dyadic relationship.

3   SERIAL RELATIONSHIPS IN A CHAIN

The second type of situation for a company in a network setting is related to the management of serial relationships in a chain. This level adds a focal actor, which is located between a buyer and a supplier in the value chain. In contrast to the first type of situation, this situation focuses on both upstream and downstream relations. In this instance, there is a need for coordination and the distribution of revenues and costs between a firm and its customers as well as its suppliers. The second type of situation is associated with the linkages between firms in a chain. In contrast to the dyadic case discussed earlier that focuses on direct dyadic relations between two firms, this type of situation focuses on relations amongst, as a minimum, a supplier, a focal firm, and a customer. The relationships to customers and suppliers are, however, conceptualised as an undifferentiated mass. The second type of situation emphasises the importance of extending the decision horizon and its consequences within a company beyond the most immediate customer and supplier relationships.

The company is often viewed as an actor in a value chain with homogenous relationships to customers and suppliers. Figure 4.2 exemplifies this situation, one of how to handle serial relationships in a chain.

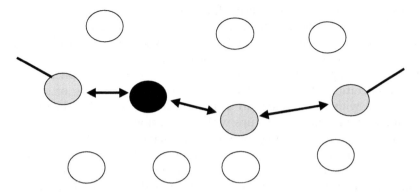

Figure 4.2   Serial relationships to both customers and suppliers in a chain.

The key contribution within this part of the inter-organisational accounting literature is the value chain analysis, introduced in the late 1980s by Herget and Morris (1989) and Shank and Govindarajan (1989, 1993). These writers combined management accounting and value chain analysis to enable them to estimate profitability on each level in the chain. Later, Herget and Morris (1989) and Shank and Govindarjan (1989, 1993) emphasised the necessity of extending the horizons for decision making and argued that the decisions should be analysed in terms of their implications in a wider context than that of just the company's most immediate customers or suppliers.

According to Shank and Govindarajan (1993), it is important to extend the horizon for decisions to include their effects on the entire value chain. In the view of these authors, it is not enough for a company to reduce its costs by passing them up to its suppliers. The competitive position for the value chain as a whole will not be enhanced by such behaviour. The authors state that, instead of passing costs up, a company should focus on actions that reduce costs for the value chain by eliminating nonvalue-adding activities. In their view, companies should analyse and improve the linkages between the companies in the value chain as well as the linkages between different units within a specific company.

Moving on from the early analytical research by Shank and Govindarajan (1989) to consider empirical research on serial relationships in a chain, Dekker and Van Goor (2000) examined how an activity-based costing (ABC) model could be used to estimate the effects of the implementation of the VMI (vendor managed inventory) in a supply chain. Dekker and Van Goor (2000) illustrated that the relocation of activities—especially stock keeping—was contingent on information supplied in the ABC and the model, and that profit sharing was a precondition for the implementation of VMI.

Another empirical illustration of accounting design and use in this type of situation is given by Mouritsen et al. (2001). They showed how target costing and open-book accounting facilitated the relocation of activities in the value chain and how management accounting aided companies to retain some control over the outsourced activities. Another lesson to be drawn from their paper is that target costing generated information from customers that was important in the management and control of suppliers.

Consideration of a value chain shifted the previous type of situation associated with counterparts to a discussion that needed to incorporate the undifferentiated relationships with both customers and suppliers. This opened up a whole new range of issues. The make-or-buy decision is still a key managerial issue, however, as it is more extensive than the traditional make-or-buy decision within a dyad, because companies in a value chain must base their decisions on the profitability within different parts of the value chain. The 'extensive' make-or-buy decision emphasises the importance of understanding the overall effects of a sourcing decision along the chain. This is critical, according to the writers engaged in research on value chain accounting, because different value chains compete against each other (Herget and Morris 1989). Thus, Shank and Govindarajan (1993) found that a value chain analysis generated different solutions to strategic decision making than, for example, the Boston Consulting Group (BCG) matrix as the firm had a higher relative return in the commodity segment/ value chain than in the differentiated segment/value chain. According to these writers, is it important that companies make decisions that reduce the total value chain costs and not only reallocate the costs in the value chain. This should be done through managing structural and executional cost drivers.

A company can use the information from value chain accounting analysis to compare the attractiveness of different value chains as well as to estimate the attractiveness of different parts within a value chain. This information gives the company the opportunity to make more informative choices when it has the opportunity to choose which value chain it should be involved in. It is important for a company to optimise the value chain, but it is perhaps even more important to be an actor within the most successful value chain. However, a company can also use information in its possession to improve its position within the value chain. The company can focus its effort on the attractive parts of the value chain and de-integrate those operations which are located in unattractive parts of the value chain.

The published papers that can be associated with the second type of problem are mainly analytical. The most significant contributors are Shank and Govindarajan (1989, 1993), who have given empirical examples to illustrate the strength of the value chain concept. Writers on undifferentiated relations within the value chain have theorised their work by applying Porter (1985) and focus primarily on two types of problems. Firstly, the choice of position and type of value chain that the firm should compete in and secondly cost cutting in the value chain through the relocation of activities in the chain.

4   SEVERAL COUNTERPARTS IN ONE DIRECTION

The third type of situation considered for a company in a network setting is associated with the management of several counterparts in one direction. This type of context differs from the previous ones through its focus on multiple buyers or suppliers, as well as because it only focuses on one direction (either upstream or downstream). Thus, the issue can be one of how a firm handles multiple supplier relationships simultaneously. This type of situation is limited to directly linked relationships to the firm in one direction. The third type of situation means that a company has several supplier relationships which are seen as heterogeneous and where there are interactions between the supplier relationships. The company will manage the suppliers differently. Some of them will be closer to the focal company than others.

Often the third type of situation has to do with different forms of supplier management or customer relationship management and the control thereof. Figure 4.3 shows the third level of situation: how to handle several counterparts in one direction.

The conceptualisation of inter-organisational relationships as multiple heterogeneous dyadic relationships brings new key managerial issues and the related types and role of accounting to the fore. An early contribution at the third level of problem is Gietzmann (1996), who used a framework based on agency theory. He studied make-or-buy decisions and extended the dyadic relationship view by including the company's treatment of several different supplier relationships in his study. He thoroughly discussed the general view of Japanese subcontracting practices and explicitly studied the subcontracting practices of a Japanese assembler's European operations through a questionnaire.

A key managerial issue that comes to the fore in his study is the importance of segmentation of supplier relationships. According to Gietzmann

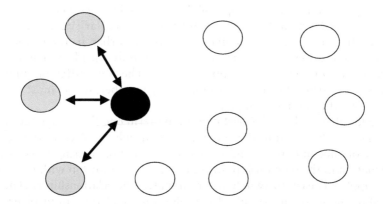

Figure 4.3   Several counterparts in one direction.

(1996), Japanese assemblers organised their suppliers into different and distinguishable groups. One group of subcontractors, comprised of the preferred suppliers, was described as being excellent and consisting of companies with which the focal company wanted to build a long-term relationship. This group of suppliers was subject to frequent appraisal and had a good potential for cooperation. Another group of suppliers was that consisting of important suppliers, and the assemblers found this group to have the potential required for the companies concerned to become most preferred suppliers. A third group of subcontractors was viewed as containing marginal suppliers and these companies were used as reserve suppliers. A fourth group was made up of suppliers that were identified as offering little benefit and had been earmarked as companies with which trading would probably be terminated. This segment did not fulfil the assemblers' demands for cost and performance. Incentives, from this perspective, are generated through segmentation of suppliers. The suppliers were rewarded by adapting the business volume in accordance with their ranking. A supplier that improved its position from the marginal supplier segment to the important supplier segment received increased business volume.

Several other writers have emphasised that the segmentation of customers or suppliers is a key managerial issue (Kaplan and Cooper 1998; Dekker 2003; Cooper and Slagmulder 2004; Kajüter and Kulmala 2005). Dekker (2003), to provide one example, studied supply chain management at Sainsbury, which also organised its supplier relationships into different segments of suppliers; it based the segmentation on the delivered volume and the strategic importance of the products supplied. The most important group consisted of twenty-four key suppliers, which together formed a group called the Supply Chain Development Group (SCDG), and which initiated activities for improving the supply chain. The members of the SCDG exchanged information through web-EDI, joint promotion planning, performance measurement systems, and they developed a collaborative planning system. Kajüter and Kulmala (2005) illustrated various links between suppliers and described how suppliers were assigned responsibility for monitoring other suppliers.

Cooper and Slagmulder (2004) illustrated a similar segmentation of the suppliers to that of Gietzmann discussed earlier in their study of seven Japanese manufacturing companies: family member, major supplier, subcontractor, and common supplier. The four different supplier groups range from the closest group, family member, to the most arm's-length one, the common supplier.

The family member relationship is a long-term one that is characterised by being closely linked to the company, and deeply involved in the development of subcomponents and intensive information sharing of strategic information in the relationship. In contrast, the relationship with the common supplier is easy to switch and terminate. The relationship is characterised by the search for standardised solutions, an absence of involvement in the development of subcomponents, and strategic information sharing was absent. Here, the 'relationship depth' defines the level of disclosure of information about costs and level of cooperation in cost-cutting.

Another key managerial issue closely linked to supplier segmentation that is put forward by Cooper and Slagmulder (2004) is that of inter-organisational cost management (IOCM). They argue that a company needs to introduce IOCM and thereby reduce information asymmetry between the buyer and supplier to make the relationship more efficient. Concurrent cost-management technique was the predominant inter-or-ganisational cost-management technique utilised in the closest supplier group, namely, family members. This technique helps the involved firms to achieve cost savings in the range of 10 to 15 per cent, mainly through additional design changes. In their view (p. 24), "A single outsourcing deci-sion will rarely result in savings sufficient to justify the adoption of a new IOCM technique and its associated relational context. Instead, the analy-sis must be applied to the savings associated with all of the suppliers likely to be affected by the adoption of the new IOCM technique discounted over the time period that they occur." Hence, Cooper and Slagmulder argued that a new IOCM technique that is developed within a supplier relationship should be applied in other similar supplier relationships.

Most studies on the third level are focused on suppliers. However, Lind and Strömsten (2006) developed a framework for customer segmen-tation. The framework shows that a company will apply different cus-tomer accounting techniques depending on the company's interface to a particular customer. The framework identified four types of customer relationships and associated customer accounting techniques. These are as follows: transactional customer relationships and customer segment profitability analysis, facilitative customer relationships and customer profitability analysis, integrative customer relationships and lifetime prof-itability analysis, and connective customer relationships and customer val-uation. Transactional customer relationships, with their low technical and organisational interface, result in little adaptation and, according to the framework, it is not necessary to evaluate each customer individually.

Another study that already illustrated the importance of customer seg-mentation at the beginning of the 1990s is that of Shank and Govindarajan (1993), in which they adapted adopted value chain analysis in the Baldwin Bicycle Company case. They showed that an offer to deliver a large number of private-label bikes to the supermarket Hi-Value, which seemed to be very profitable from a contribution margin analysis, turned out to be uninteresting after an application of value chain analysis. This is because the value chain analysis revealed that the new customer, Hi-Value, would compete directly with Baldwin's current dealers. Thus, if Baldwin accepted the offer from Hi-Value, it would have a negative impact on its ongoing business, in addition to which, some of its current dealers might even decide to terminate their rela-tionship with Baldwin. This illustration by Shank and Govindarjan indicates the importance of simultaneous consideration of multiple customers.

Contributions to the existing state of knowledge relevant to this third group have tended to synthesise different frameworks. For example, Dekker (2004) used Gulati and Singh's (1998) synthesis of organisation theory (coordination cost) and transaction cost economics (appropriation concerns) when he studied Sainsbury's management of suppliers. Cooper and Slagmulder (2004) developed a synthesis incorporating different approaches to prospective inclusive transaction cost economics to examine Japanese supplier cost-management practices.

Contributions to research at this level have concentrated on two foci: firstly, segmentation of relationships, the measurement and management of the segmented relationships, and the generation of incentives for different types of relationships. Secondly, the literature argues that the level of inter-organisational control implemented is dependent on the type of dyadic relationship between the focal firm and each of the suppliers or customers.

5   MULTIPLE COUNTERPARTS IN TWO DIRECTIONS

The fourth situation in a network setting being considered in this chapter is related to the management and effects of multiple counterparts active in two directions. In this instance, the focus is on the simultaneous handling of individualised customer and individualised supplier relationships. It differs from the previous situation by focusing on both directions of relationships: upstream and downstream. The firm needs to link and coordinate the demand and supply between firms upstream and downstream from the firm. This type of situation is limited to the firm's immediate relationships. However, the relationships are viewed as heterogeneous and they impose different demands on the firm. Figure 4.4 shows the fourth type of situation, that of how to handle multiple counterparts in two directions.

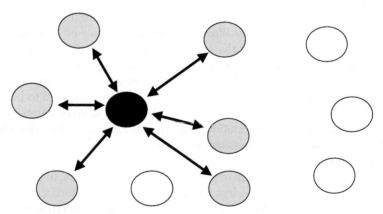

Figure 4.4   Multiple counterparts active in two directions.

Thrane and Hald (2006) examined how, in relation to the introduction of products-specific flows from supplier, to production, to customer interrupted the flows of other products in the supply chain. Some customers were able to make the manufacturing and delivery of their purchased goods more important than those of other customers, which had consequences for the focal firm's relations with its customers. However, the prioritisation of customers also influenced the focal firm's relationships with its suppliers, because they need to change their production plans to accommodate the prioritised customers.

In general, Thrane and Hald (2006) illustrated how relations to suppliers and customers were integrated through the intermediation of control and how that fragmented the focal firm, that is, interactions at both ends of the value chain were connected through the impact that they had on the focal firm. Furthermore, they demonstrated that there was competition between different product supply chains within the firm.

In their recent study of distributed product development, Carlsson-Wall et al. (2009) illustrated how target costing has numerous roles, notably that of facilitating the simultaneous handling of heterogeneous customer and supplier relationships. In their study, they showed how two key customers, A and B, demanded specific adaptations be made to and functionality changed in a robot system that was under development, in combination with a request for large cost reductions. During the product development, several new and, at that time, unsolved technical problems associated with the demands of customers A and B were discovered. The studied firm interacted intensively with its suppliers to solve these problems; however, a solution to one technical problem often created new ones in another supplier relationship.

Target costing impacted on the process of identifying viable solutions. It formed the basis for the rejection of technically well-functioning solutions when they exceeded the target cost. Furthermore, through functional analysis, target costing created boundaries for the different functions that the firm and its suppliers tried to avoid crossing. The parties attempted to find plausible solutions within the given boundaries of a function before they crossed the function's boundary and involved other suppliers. In this way, target costing shapes the search pattern when a firm and its suppliers attempt to identify plausible solutions.

Research involving several counterparts active in two directions illustrates two further issues related to control. Firstly, the competition between different product supply chains within a firm requires that certain chains be prioritised over others. Secondly, effects from relational dynamics at one end of the chain are related to relations and dynamics at the other end of chain, for example, how interaction with different customers affects relations with suppliers.

6   COMPLEX SYSTEMS/NETWORKS INCLUDING THIRD PARTIES SUCH AS COMPETITORS AND REGULATORS

The fifth type of situation under consideration focuses on third parties, such as competitors, alliance partners and regulators, and seeks to comprehend the systemic characteristics of complex systems/networks. In this setting, the new element to be considered is the handling of multiple relations between buyers and sellers, which differs from type four as it takes third parties, such as the competitors of the focal firm, customers' other suppliers, suppliers' other customers, regulators, and trade unions into account. These sets of interdependent and interconnected relationships have indirect effects. Hence, through this network effect, interaction between Companies A and B can have an influence on Company C. Figure 4.5 illustrates the situation where complex systems/networks include third parties.

Mouritsen and Thrane (2006) and Thrane (2007) showed how different formalised interfirm networks were mediated by a variety of external relations with third parties. In one example, an agreement was reached about the joint selling and marketing of a newspaper, and the horizontal relationships of which the network was comprised were able to induce change, as well as bring about conflict. In the papers, the maintenance of well-functioning working relations is an issue, although the role of accounting therein differs, depending on whether the technology concerned made use of orchestration (technologies used to change resource profiles such as competency accounts) or self-regulation mechanisms (technologies used to enable frictionless cooperation, e.g., transfer prices).

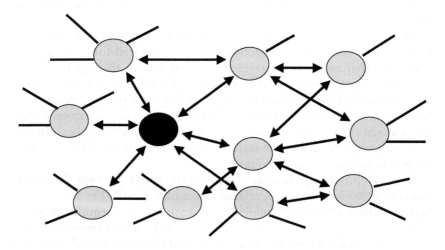

Figure 4.5   Complex systems/networks including third parties such as competitors and regulators.

Håkansson and Lind (2004) illustrated how accounting is involved in the coordination and development taking place between companies and units within a network including third parties, such as competitors. They focused on a central dyad, Ericson and Telia, but also included Nokia and other competitors. They showed how accounting was a central feature within the companies under investigation in the formation of relationships when it was used to shape units with overlapping accountability. However, accounting was also used to shape "new" units with overlapping accountability that did not follow the firm's boundaries, but crossed them instead. In this way, accounting "helped to establish a structure that is not a solution to the coordination problems, but rather, is a base facilitating a process that can lead to continuous adaptation of the 'solutions'" (p. 67). Accounting is a key ingredient in creating an unstable and dynamic network structure. In this network structure, problems, conflicts, and contradictions were distributed across various interfaces between the firms and units involved.

The value of measuring direct and indirect effects in the inter-organisational relationships was noticed by Lind and Strömsten (2006). They observed that three types of relationships, ranging from classical arm's-length relationships to intensive collaborative relations, were profitable in their own right. In these three types of relationships, a firm just needs to measure the direct effects and, as such, focuses on the relationships as dyads. However, the last type, the connective customer relationships, creates new demands on the company. Connective customer relationships are characterised by a high level of adaptation of products and production facilities and considerable investments in time and resources. However, the large investments in the customer are not associated with dedicated customer units and large revenue streams from the customer. Hence, a connective customer relationship will be viewed as "unprofitable" if it is evaluated on the direct revenues and on the costs associated with the relationship. A connective customer relationship must contribute with indirect benefits, such as channelling important knowledge, knowledge that can be leveraged in other relationships or act as a bridge to other potentially important relationships. Thus, the customer accounting technique associated with connective customer relationships should extend beyond the annual time period and it should incorporate the indirect benefits of connected relationships. This is easier said than done.

These thoughts were further developed by Christner et al. (2008) in their study of customer relationships and customer accounting in Holmen in a period during which large operational changes were taking place. Holmen is one of Europe's largest manufacturers of printing paper. Christner et al. (2008) illustrate how the firm measured indirect effects to justify some of the customer relationships when it shut down a paper machine. The research by Lind and Strömsten (2006) and Christner et al. (2008) gives an indication of how a certain accounting technique can be adapted to measure indirect effects in a network setting. However, this work mainly considered how a company can handle several counterparts in one direction.

Frances and Garnsey (1996) revealed how supermarkets in England were made powerful though monopolising information in the system. Suppliers were increasingly dependent on supermarkets and were able to use relations with suppliers in other countries to put pressure on their local suppliers. Furthermore, they illustrated the entire system of relations between supermarkets, labour markets, consultants, and international suppliers. In this analysis, accounting and information are key drivers of change in the overall system.

Miller and O'Leary (2007) studied how Moore's law predicting a doubling in capacity of computers every two years shaped investment decisions in the PC industry. They conceptualised the industry as a techno-economic network and illustrated how Moore's law, in conjunction with road maps constructed in industry associations, enabled the industry to become aligned by shaping capital budgeting decisions in a network of suppliers and manufacturers.

Contributions at this level have illustrated how accounting is implicated in the production of system structures. Accounting is a central ingredient able to induce conflict, destabilisation, dynamics, and change within the complex mixture of interconnected relationships a firm needs to handle. Other studies present attempts made to understand how indirect effects can be taken into account within the accounting system.

7   DISCUSSION

This chapter identifies five different types of situation that firms need to handle in relation to counterparts in a network setting. These situations have been discussed along with the relation between the type of situation and key managerial issues and type and role of accounting. This chapter is a first attempt to conceptualise some of the findings in the literature on accounting in an inter-organisational setting by considering different forms of structural setting. This has made it possible to interpret and shed some light on some of the conflicting findings in previous empirical studies. Further, it has also provided the opportunity to identify interesting avenues for future research. Table 4.1 presents the key findings of the paper.

The different types of situations result in a certain conceptualisation of the inter-organisational setting, which emphasises the importance of particular managerial issues and the type and role of accounting most relevant to these issues. Type five, with a network situation, emphasises other key managerial issues and the role of accounting, which is in stark contrast to type one, with its focus on one relationship which, in most studies, is viewed as an isolated dyadic island. At type one there are often clear relations, and recommendations between structure and control, and owing to the lower number of elements to take into consideration at this setting, consistent and rigorous frameworks are often developed in studies of this type of situation. The theories based on TCE argue that control patterns and governance are directly associated with structure.

Table 4.1   Types of Situation, Managerial Issues, and the Types and Role of Accounting

Type	Situation considered	Key managerial issues	Types and roles of accounting
1	One relationship	Make-or-buy decisions, control mix of the dyadic relationship. Information sharing and incentive-related issues in the relationship	Detailed cost information about own operations. Aligning control pattern to relationship. Management control systems that support information diffusion. Inter-organizational control system mitigating opportunistic behaviour.
2	Serial relationships in a chain	Maximising profits across the value chain through relocation of activities. Choice of position in the value chain.	Detailed cost information for activities in the value chain. Cost driver analysis in the value chain.
3	Several counterparts in one direction	Segmentation of suppliers or customers. Control as dependent on relationship depth (e.g., trust and ownership). "Outsourcing" of control to suppliers.	Rank-based rewards, inter-organizational cost management techniques, and heterogeneous customer accounting techniques.
4	Multiple counterparts in two directions	Prioritisation between different product supply chains. Chain-wide optimisation problems, e.g., how do customer relationship dynamics affect suppliers?	Accounting (e.g., target costing, customer accounting, and supplier accounting) that facilitates the simultaneous handling of heterogeneous customer and supplier relationships.
5	Complex systems/ networks including third parties such as competitors and regulators	Indirect effects, dynamics, and learning. Risk and opportunities in the wider chain: How are our suppliers involved with our customers, what are the risks from our suppliers' suppliers?	Overlapping accountability, accounting information about direct and indirect effects, and risk analysis. How does accounting shape network dynamics?

At situation type four and five, the relationships are less clear and the relation between control and structure either acts in two directions or is the opposite of what was anticipated, which we refer to as being bidirectional and reversed, respectively. A bidirectional relationship is clear in, for example, Thrane and Hald (2006), where the implementation of control and the structure that grows up are the outcome of complex processes where structural factors affect governance and control, and interactions between different control elements produce a pattern of simultaneous fragmentation and integration. A reversed relationship is also evident in Frances and Garnsey (1996), where accounting is one of the elements shaping the restructuring of the retail industry in the UK. The type of situation and the associated conceptualisations of the inter-organisational setting for types four and five are not as good at predicting specific outcomes for type and role of accounting as type one and two situations.

The framework developed, with the five types of relationships with counterparts in a network setting, shows that the field of accounting in inter-organisational relationships is highly nuanced. The framework indicates that, to some extent, the findings of an empirical study can be explained by the type of situation being considered. Hence, a critical issue when a study's findings are to be analysed is to compare and contrast the findings with those of previous studies from a similar inter-organisational setting. The different types of situations are also associated with different theories, where studies on situation types four and five are framed by theories such as institutional, techno-economic network, industrial network, and complexity theories. Studies on situation types one and two are mostly inspired by theories such as TCE and agency theory.

This chapter is a first step to understanding how accounting could be related to more complex inter-organisational structures and conceptualisations. So far, little systematic knowledge has been established about the type and role of accounting within these settings and, in our view, more research should be carried out on these settings. Such research should focus on managerial issues, considering, for example, prioritisation between different supply chains, indirect effects, and risk and opportunities in the interconnected links in the network. In addition, it appears that some of the most promising managerial issues for future investigation concern the dynamics of the connections between customer and supplier relationships and dynamics and learning throughout the wider network. Empirically, this strand of research will need to be comprised of in-depth field studies that can capture the complexities. Longitudinal field studies ought to be conducted to capture dynamic aspects.

However, in our view, more research on the first type of situation, with its dyadic conceptualisation of the inter-organisational setting, is still an important avenue for research, in particular in conjunction with the examination of theories that capture the bidirectional relationship between the organisations studied and between accounting and the inter-organisational setting. This type of theorisation of single relationships will provide opportunities to discover new key managerial issues and to better comprehend the type and role of accounting in dyadic settings.

Further aspects that could be explored in future studies are how actors are conceptualised within a network setting. In this chapter and, indeed, in most of the published papers, firms are understood as actors that have relations with other firms (Tomkins 2001; Dekker 2004; Kajüter and Kulmala 2005). An alternative definition of actors and a more detailed conceptualisation of the inter-organisational setting (Håkansson and Lind 2004; Thrane and Hald 2006) would entail inclusion of relations between departments and individuals within and beyond the firm.

8   CONCLUSION

This chapter has developed a framework for the consideration of different types of situations that a firm needs to manage in a network setting. In addition, for each situation considered in the framework, key managerial issues and the type and role of accounting have been identified. Application of the framework to a literature review revealed that the bulk of the literature in the field of accounting in an inter-organisational setting represents either of the situation types, one or three, in the developed framework (Håkansson and Lind 2007). These studies conceptualise the setting as a dyadic relationship between two independent firms or a chain of firms, where the focus is on make-or-buy decisions or on developing bureaucracy-based, market-based, and trust-based accounting "patterns". In addition, it is worth noting that the published literature mainly applies frameworks that are inspired by an economic theories view of the subject.

The literature on the situations represented by types four and five situations is less normative than type one situations and has been inspired by a number of different theories, including institutional theory, actor network theory, the industrial network approach, and complexity theory. Research into management accounting and control could benefit from investigating supply chains and networks with more complex conceptualisations of their researched inter-organisational setting. Such a research programme would be much more interested in the dynamics of complex systems incorporating a supplier, customers, and third parties and should attempt to conceptualise indirect effects, learning, and unintended effects of control in networks. Such an endeavour would probably move research closer to the real-life complexity observed in supply systems and networks, but it would also make clear normative frameworks less useful. This would point towards a more interesting but less managerialist research agenda.

NOTES

1. The different types of situations, it could be argued, show an increase in complexity from the simple dyad to the complex network. Tomkins, e.g., compares dyadic relations with networks in the following way: "a network

involves more than one alliance/relationship with high trust intensity and so the negotiation of roles, risks and profit-sharing will be more complex" (Tomkins 2001, p. 183). While we definitely agree on this, at least one qualification is necessary: studies on, e.g., the dyadic level need not be "simple" if, for example, they draw on or focus on complexity in other respects such as by focusing on differentiation within the two cooperating firms. See also Harland (1996) for different conceptualisations of networks and chains.

BIBLIOGRAPHY

Anderson, J., Håkansson, H., and Johanson, J. 1994. Dyadic relationships within a business network context. *Journal of Marketing* 58: 1–15.
Anderson, S. W., Glenn, D., and Sedatole, K. L. 2000. Sourcing parts of complex products: Evidence on transactions costs, high-powered incentives and ex-post opportunism. *Accounting, Organizations and Society* 25: 723–749.
Baiman, S., and Rajan, M. V. 2002. Incentive issues in inter-firm relationships. *Accounting, Organizations and Society* 27: 213–238.
Carlsson-Wall, M., Kraus, K., and Lind, J. 2009. Accounting and distributed product development. *IMP-Journal* 3: 2–27.
Carr, C., and Ng, J. 1995. Total cost control: Nissan and its U.K. supplier partnerships. *Management Accounting Research* 6: 347–365.
Christner, H., Lind, J., Strömsten, T., and Almgren, A. 2008. Kundstrategier och kundlönsamhetsbedömninar—en studie av Holmen Paper. In *Redovisning i fokus*, ed. Jennergren, P., Lind, J., Schuster, W., and Skogsvik, K. 111–128. Lund, Sweden: Studentlitteratur.
Cooper, R., and Slagmulder, R. 2004. Interorganizational cost management and relational context. *Accounting, Organizations and Society* 29: 1–26.
Dekker, H. C. 2003. Value chain analysis in interfirm relationships: A field study. *Management Accounting Research* 14: 1–23.
Dekker, H. C. 2004. Control of inter-organizational relationships: Evidence on appropriation concerns and coordination requirements. *Accounting, Organizations and Society* 29: 27–49.
Dekker, H. C., and Van Goor, A. R. 2000. Supply chain management and management accounting: A case study of activity-based costing. *International Journal of Logistics: Research and Applications* 3: 41–52.
Frances, J., and Garnsey, E. 1996. Supermarkets and suppliers in the United Kingdom: System integration, information and control. *Accounting, Organizations and Society* 21: 591–610.
Gietzmann, M. B. 1996. Incomplete contracts and the make or buy decisions: Governance design and attainable flexibility. *Accounting, Organizations and Society* 21: 611–626.
Gulati, R., and Singh, H. 1998. The architecture of cooperation: Managing coordination costs and appropriation concerns in strategic alliances. *Administrative Science Quarterly* 43: 781–814.
Håkansson, H., and Lind, J. 2004. Accounting and network coordination. *Accounting, Organizations and Society* 29: 51–72.
Håkansson, H., and Lind, J. 2007. Accounting in an interorganisational setting. In *Handbook of management accounting research*, ed. Chapman, C. S., Hopwood, A. G., and Shields, M. D. 885–902. Oxford: Elsevier.
Harland, C. M. 1996. Supply chain management: Relationships, chains and networks. *British Journal of Management* 7: 63–80.

Herget, M., and Morris, D. 1989. Accounting data for value chain analysis. *Strategic Management Journal* 10: 175–188.

Hopwood, A. G. 1996. Looking across rather than up and down: On the need to explore the lateral processing of information. *Accounting, Organizations and Society* 21: 589–590.

Kajüter, P., and Kulmala, H. I. 2005. Open-book accounting in networks: Potential achievements and reasons for failures. *Management Accounting Research* 16: 179–204.

Kaplan, R. S., and Cooper, R. 1998. *Cost and effect.* Boston: Harvard University Press.

Kulp, S. C. 2002. The effect of information precision and information reliability on manufacturer-retailer relationships. *The Accounting Review* 77: 653–677.

Langfield-Smith, K., and Smith, D. 2003. Management control systems and trust in outsourcing relationships. *Management Accounting Research* 14: 281–307.

Lind, J., and Strömsten, T. 2006. When do firms use different types of customer accounting? *Journal of Business Research* 59: 1257–1266.

Lind, J., and Thrane, S. 2005. Network accounting. In *Accounting in Scandinavia—The Northern Lights*, ed. Jönsson, S., and Mouritsen, J. 115–137. Malmö, Sweden: Liber & Copenhagen Business School Press.

Miller, P., and O'Leary, T. 2007. Mediating instruments and making markets: Capital budgeting, science and the economy. *Accounting, Organizations and Society* 32: 701–734.

Mouritsen, J., Hansen, A., and Hansen, C. Ø. 2001. Inter-organizational controls and organizational competencies: Episodes around target cost management/functional analysis and open book accounting. *Management Accounting Research* 12: 221–244.

Mouritsen, J., and Thrane, S. 2006. Accounting, network complementarities and the development of inter-organizational relations. *Accounting, Organizations and Society* 31: 241–275.

Porter, M. 1985. *Competitive Advantage—Creating and sustaining superior performance.* New Your: Free Press.

Seal, W., Cullen, J., Dunlop, A., Berry, A., and Ahmed, M. 1999. Enacting a European supply chain: A case study on the role of management accounting, *Management Accounting Research* 10: 303–322.

Shank, J. K., and Govindarajan, V. 1989. *Strategic cost analysis: The evolution from managerial to strategic accounting.* Homewood, IL: Irwin.

Shank, J K., and Govindarajan, V. 1993. *Strategic cost management—The new tool for competitive advantage.* New York: The Free Press.

Speklé, R. F. 2001. Explaining management control structural variety: A transaction cost economics perspective. *Accounting, Organizations and Society* 26: 419–441.

Tomkins, C. 2001. Interdependencies, trust and information in relationships, alliances and networks. *Accounting, Organizations and Society* 26: 161–191.

Thrane, S. 2007. The complexity of management accounting change: Bifurcation and oscillation in schizophrenic inter-organisational systems. *Management Accounting Research* 18: 248–272.

Thrane, S., and Hald, K. H. 2006. The emergence of boundaries and accounting in supply-fields: The dynamics of integration and fragmentation. *Management Accounting Research* 17: 288–314.

Van der Meer-Kooistra, J., and Vosselman, E. G. J. 2000. Management control of interfirm transactional relationships: The case of industrial renovation and maintenance. *Accounting, Organizations and Society* 25: 51–77.

5 The Role of Management Accounting in Joint Venture Relationships

A Dynamic Perspective

Jeltje van der Meer-Kooistra and
Pieter E. Kamminga

1 INTRODUCTION

When, in October 1997, Philips and Lucent combined their mobile telephone activities in a joint venture (JV), expectations ran high for what was presumed to be a win-win situation. The cooperation with Lucent provided Philips with the opportunity to enter the American market, where Lucent had well-developed distribution channels and strong brand names. Furthermore, Philips would gain access to Lucent's renowned research institute, Bell Labs. For Lucent, a JV relationship with Philips seemed to be just what it needed for its consumer product activities. As one of the three split-offs of AT&T, Lucent had become responsible for AT&T's consumer products. However, Lucent had no expertise in or affinity with consumer products as its actual ambitions were directed toward the business-to-business market. So, when Philips, which did have experience in the field of consumer products and, moreover, had a strong position in Europe, asked Lucent to combine their consumer product activities in a JV, Lucent agreed. It was decided to set up a 'shared subsidiary' with the ambition of achieving a 'top three position' on the mobile phone market by 2000.

In the last two decades, because of a growing globalisation of business activities, we have observed ever more companies, such as Philips and Lucent in the preceding example, collaborating with each other in order to gain access to new markets and thereby strengthen their position worldwide. By establishing a JV relationship, companies can more easily and much more quickly achieve their aim of gaining access to new markets than they could by operating on their own. They can share their knowledge and expertise of local markets and use each other's sales infrastructure and business and institutional networks. Other important reasons for establishing a JV relationship are risk reduction, economies of scale and scope, access to technological knowledge and expertise, production capacity and/or capital, bypassing trade barriers, and preventing governmental pressures (see, e.g., Contractor and Lorange 1988; Kemp 1999; Van der Meer-Kooistra and Kamminga 2008).

A JV relationship, such as that of Philips and Lucent, established in 1997, is a well-known form of inter-organisational relationship. We define a JV relationship as a long-term relationship between at least two independent companies, which is established as a new legal entity, of which the independent companies are the owners. The owners or parent companies share the ownership of the new entity, called an equity JV, as well as its management control.[1] Conversely, JV management control is the management control of the JV relationship exercised by the parent companies. If a JV is located in a country other than that in which one of the parent companies is located (i.e., the seats of the companies' headquarters), the literature (see, e.g., Yan and Zeng 1999) speaks of international joint ventures (IJV). The main difference between a JV relationship and other inter-organisational relationships, such as outsourcing, supplier-buyer, long-term contractual, and franchising relationships, is that, in a JV relationship, the collaborating companies establish a new, jointly owned entity.

Was the JV relationship established by Philips and Lucent able to achieve the parent companies' aim of realising a top three position on the worldwide mobile phone market? It was not. Quite soon after its establishment, the JV found itself in a troublesome situation, and, within one year, the cooperation between Philips and Lucent came to an end. The JV encountered a number of problems. First of all, conflict arose within the top management of the JV. As a result, a large number of the managers with a Philips background left, whereas the Lucent managers remained. Then, second, an external factor, which had a major impact, was the beginning of the strong competition that was emerging between the different network standards being used on the mobile telephone market. Whereas in Europe the national governments had all chosen the GSM standard, in the U.S., the choice was left to the market. Unfortunately for the JV under consideration, the final victor was not GSM, in accordance with which the JV had attuned its activities, but CDMA. A final problem concerned the product development activities of the JV. Whereas competitive companies introduced new telephones each week, the JV needed much more time to develop new products than had initially been expected. This delay was expressed in the financial results: while huge amounts of money were invested in the JV's activities, the JV's turnover remained very modest and the financial statements of the JV merely revealed losses.

The interesting aspect of the aforementioned example is that it clearly illustrates the different sides of a JV relationship. On the one hand, by jointly setting up a JV, the parent companies may attain results that would be much harder to achieve alone. For instance, Philips had access to both the American market and Lucent's technological know-how, and Lucent had the opportunity to gain a foothold in the European market as well as being able to benefit from Philips' experience in the field of consumer products. But the other side of a JV relationship is that its management control is rather complex because the ownership and management control of a JV are shared by the parent companies (Geringer and Hebert 1989; Yan and Gray 1994; Groot and Merchant 2000; Kamminga and Van der

Meer-Kooistra 2007). Hence, in a JV relationship, two types of relationships can be distinguished: a shared hierarchical one between a parent company and its JV and a hybrid (or lateral) one between two (or more) parent companies.[2] In the hierarchical relationship, a parent company has, in principle, the right of veto, so that it is able to impose its will. But because two parent companies share the JV ownership and each parent company must control the hybrid relationship with its partner, without having a right of veto in this relationship, exercising its right of veto may worsen the hybrid relationship with its partner and thereby create tension in the JV relationship.

Management control complexity is also created by dynamics within JVs, which may make a particular relationship rather unstable (Beamish and Delios 1997; Van der Meer-Kooistra and Kamminga 2008)—see, for instance, the preceding example in which we observed how the dynamics of the JV led to the deterioration of the relationship between Philips and Lucent. Dynamics within JVs can be caused by developments in their immediate environment, such as the introduction of new technology or increasing competition in the market a JV is operating in, but also by changes within the JVs, or changes within the parent companies. Moreover, external and internal developments and changes could interact and thereby create dynamic processes which unfold over the life of JV relationships. For example, the strategic motives for (initially) establishing a JV could change in response to environmental developments, or parent companies may lose their interest in the JV and decide to terminate it; or parent companies might lose interest in the JV because of its poor performance, which could be caused by an increase in the competition in the market; or the JV relationship between the parent companies could deteriorate because of opportunistic behaviour on the part of the partner.

Kamminga and Van der Meer-Kooistra (2007) discuss various forces that can cause dynamics within JVs, a topic that had been considered by several other authors previously and since (see, e.g., Killing 1983; Yan and Gray 1994; Yan 1998; Yan and Zeng 1999; Inkpen and Currall 2004; Kamminga et al. 2008). These forces relate to the situation within and behaviour of the parent companies (e.g., strategic motives, financial situation, and opportunistic behaviour), the JV (e.g., bad performance, key individuals, and learning), and the (institutional) environment (e.g., legal and governmental regulations, technology, and market conditions). Tensions in the JV relationship caused by these forces can sometimes be relieved by changing the JV management control, as we will see later, but these changes have to be approved by both of the parent companies. If a parent company is no longer interested in the JV, it will not be prepared to change the JV management control; indeed, it might decide to terminate the JV relationship instead of implementing change.

The literature on inter-organisational relationships distinguishes three main issues or problems associated with these relationships (see also Section 2). First, a coordination-related one (see, e.g., Das and Teng 2001;[3] Gulati and Singh 1998) concerning the coordination of the activities, processes, and transactions of the collaborating parties. Tomkins (2001) speaks of the need to master events, by which he means the planning of the input of physical and nonphysical resources (e.g., knowledge) and the execution of the activities, processes, and transactions that have to be geared to one another. The complexity of the coordination task depends on the type of interdependencies between the parties, the differences between each of the parties' own activities, processes, information systems and expertise, and dynamics. Management control theory (see, e.g., Simons 1995; Merchant and Van der Stede 2003; Anthony and Govindarajan 2004) addresses the coordination issue, albeit with a focus on intra-organisational relationships. In the 1990s, management control theory broadened its scope to encompass inter-organisational relationships (see, e.g., Otley 1994; Hopwood 1996; Gietzmann 1996). Second, a problem of opportunistic behaviour (see, e.g., Williamson 1996[4]), which relates to the different and even conflicting interests the parties may have with respect to their inter-organisational relationship. Such differences in interests create opportunities for opportunistic behaviour. Opportunistic behaviour can harm the other parties' interests and decrease the value that these parties attach to the relationship. Therefore, this problem of opportunistic behaviour creates a need to align the parties' interests in the relationship. Transaction cost economics (Williamson 1985, 1996) argues that alignment of interests can be achieved by developing credible commitments at the start of an inter-organisational relationship and writing them into the contract. The third issue is a relational one referring to the atmosphere of the relationship between the parties. A good relational atmosphere encourages them to cooperate and to align their commitment to the relationship over time (see, e.g., Lindenberg 2000; Van der Meer-Kooistra and Vosselman 2008; Vosselman and Van der Meer-Kooistra 2009). If the parties' commitments are aligned, they will trust the other parties to act in a cooperative way even in uncertain circumstances. If the parties trust each other, the parties have positive expectations regarding each other's competencies, intentions, and integrity. In particular, relational approaches (e.g., Parkhe 1993; Ring and Van de Ven 1994) focus on the relational aspects of inter-organisational relationships; aspects that, according to various researchers (e.g., Granovetter 1985; Ghoshal and Moran 1996), are underexposed by transaction cost economics. As we will discuss later, these three issues are interrelated.

In this chapter we aim to study the role of management control in addressing the three issues of inter-organisational relationships introduced earlier, with a specific focus on JV relationships. We will investigate how JV management control can be designed and used over the life of a JV relationship to deal with the issues of coordination, opportunistic behaviour, and relational atmosphere. In this respect, however, it should be noted that Kamminga and Van der Meer-Kooistra (2007) have argued that, especially when JVs are surrounded by uncertainty and the JV's activities and/

or output can hardly been planned and measured, JV management control focusing on the JV's activities and output cannot be used and parties have to rely on trust. Nevertheless, management control is still of considerable importance, as Tomkins (2001) and Vosselman and Van der Meer-Kooistra (2009) have pointed out the role that management control can play in trust building. In addition, Kamminga and Van der Meer-Kooistra (2007) have discussed JV management control, focusing on the context of the JV relationship. In this chapter we wish to expand upon the role of management control in building trust between the JV parties (i.e., parent companies and JV management) and in creating a good relational atmosphere over time.

The remainder of this chapter is organised as follows. In Section 2, we will give an overview of the main findings of the literature investigating the management control of JV relationships. In Section 3, we will discuss in more depth the issues of coordination, opportunistic behaviour, and relational atmosphere, all of which JV parties face and can cope with through the development of adequate JV management control. Next, in Section 4, we will elaborate on the role that management control can play in building trust between the JV parties. In Section 5, we will focus on JV dynamics over the life of a JV and the implication for JV management control and the JV relationship. Finally, in Section 6, we will round out the chapter by drawing conclusions about the role of management control in JV relationships and by discussing some avenues for research in the future.

2   LITERATURE REVIEW OF JOINT
VENTURE MANAGEMENT CONTROL

In the management accounting literature, the topic of JV management control has received little attention. Although some management accounting researchers (Foster and Young 1997; Shields 1997) called attention to this topic, until now only a few studies, mainly published in *Accounting, Organizations and Society*, have dealt with it (Groot and Merchant 2000; Chalos and O'Connor 2004; Emsley and Kidon 2007; Kamminga and Van der Meer-Kooistra 2007). In other fields, however, the topic of JV management control has had a longer research tradition.[5] In particular in the field of international business, but also in the field of management and organisation, a reasonable number of studies has been made. Therefore, in reviewing the literature on JV management control, we will take into account multiple disciplines.

A seminal paper on JV management control was written by Geringer and Hebert (1989), who define JV management control (p. 286) as 'the process by which the parents influence, to varying degrees, the behaviour and output of the JV through the use of power, authority, and a wide range of bureaucratic, cultural, and informal mechanisms'. Furthermore, they argue that three dimensions comprise JV management control, namely, the focus of the control, its extent or tightness, and the mechanisms or structures used to exert control. Almost all of the subsequent studies on JV management control have distinguished between these three dimensions.

With respect to *the focus of JV management control*, the literature has discussed three main foci. First, JV management control can be focused on coordination issues between the JV parties (i.e., the parent companies and the JV management). Mjoen and Tallman (1997) pointed out how JV management control should ensure the effective application and usage of a parent company's contributions to the JV. In particular, if a parent company's contributions involve tacit knowledge, it is crucial that this company is actively involved in the transfer of this knowledge (Choi and Beamish 2004). Control could also be needed to coordinate the contributions of the parent companies to the JV. This is especially relevant when the parent companies contribute different types of resources; in this instance, coordination is crucial. According to Kamminga and Van der Meer-Kooistra (2007), in such a situation, there is a considerable need for consultation between the parent companies. In some JVs, the parent company might need to focus its control on the coordination of the JV's activities with its own. For instance, if a JV and the parent company sell similar products, there will be a risk of unfavourable competition between the company's and the JV's products (Hennart 1991). This could harm the overall result of that parent company and require coordination measures.

Second, JV management control can be focused on preventing opportunistic behaviour of the JV parties. In the literature, several examples of such risks of opportunistic behaviour have been discussed. If the resources contributed to the JV involve a parent company's competitive advantage, for instance, its knowledge, this parent company runs the risk of losing its competitive advantage to another parent company (see, e.g., Mjoen and Tallman 1997; Chalos and O'Connor 2004). In addition, if a parent company's contribution involves a trademark, it risks a debasement of its trademark (Hennart 1991). By taking JV management control measures, the risks of opportunistic behaviour are likely to be reduced. For instance, to reduce the risk of leakage of knowledge, Lorange and Roos (1992) and Lorange (1997) suggest to develop a 'black box' strategy, which means that a parent company preserves some of its unique know-how and propriety skills in a black box. Such a black box can be created by not giving away too much information at the outset. However, if, over time, information does leak, a black box position has to be maintained by developing new competencies in the parent company. These new competencies should, deliberately, be signalled to the partner to underline the need for an ongoing relationship and discourage opportunistic behaviour.

Third, JV management control can be focused on creating trust and a good atmosphere between the JV parties. If the level of uncertainty surrounding the JV's activities is high, it will be difficult to conclude complete JV contracts. If contracts are incomplete, situations may arise that had not been foreseen, which may give rise to opportunistic behaviour. Kamminga and Van der Meer-Kooistra (2007) and Emsley and Kidon (2007) argue that, in such a situation, the likelihood of opportunistic behaviour taking place can be reduced by applying context-based management control structures. Such structures aim at creating a trustful relational context in which unforeseen problems can be discussed openly, and in which the JV parties take into account each other's interests. Examples of these structures include personal meetings and social events.

The second dimension of JV management control, that is, *the extent or tightness*, refers to the tightness by which the parent companies are involved in the activities and the decision-making processes of the JV. On the basis of this tightness, the literature has distinguished between different types of JV relationships: the dominant parent JV, in which one parent company plays a dominant role in the decision-making process; the shared-management JV, in which all parent companies play an equal role in the decision-making process; the independent JV, in which all parent companies maintain a certain distance and the JV management has a high level of autonomy; and the split control JV, in which different parent companies exercise dominant control over different activities of the JV (Killing 1983, 1988). In the literature, a number of factors have been discussed which may influence the tightness of JV management control. Some authors refer to the level of information asymmetry between the parent companies and the JV management and the level of uncertainty in which a JV operates (Kumar and Seth 1998; Kamminga and Van der Meer-Kooistra 2007). Physical distance between a parent company and a JV, cultural differences between the countries in which they operate, and differences in knowledge and expertise could give rise to information asymmetry between a parent company and its JV. In the event of a strong information asymmetry, tight control by a parent company will be at the expense of the JV management's flexibility. In particular, in environments with a high level of uncertainty, this loss of flexibility could be detrimental, as the ability to react quickly is crucial in such cases. Therefore, in dynamic environments, it could be desirable for parent companies to give autonomy to the JV management and exercise loose control.

Naturally, the extent to which a parent company can exercise tight control over its JV also depends on it being able to do so. Various researchers have associated this ability with the relative bargaining power of the parent companies (e.g., Harrigan 1986; Blodgett 1991; Yan and Gray 1994). In this respect, the extent to which a parent company can exercise control over its JV is regarded as the outcome of a bargaining process between the parent companies. A parent company can derive power from different sources. On the one hand, contributions to the JV may give a parent company power; Yan and Gray (1994) call such sources resource-based sources of bargaining power. On the other hand, the bargaining power of a parent company is associated with the degree to which a parent company is dependent on the JV relationship and with the availability of alternatives for the parent company to realise its goals. While a parent company's dependence decreases its bargaining power, the alternatives available to it increase it. Yan and Gray (1994) call these sources of bargaining power context-based.

With respect to the third dimension of JV management control, *the mechanisms or structures*, a wide range of structures has been identified in the literature by which a parent company can exercise control over its JV. While the earlier literature mainly considered JV management control as a synonym for the possession of equity and voting rights (e.g., Stopford and Haberich 1976), over time, more and more attention has been paid to other control structures, including the right of veto, representation in management bodies, staffing, contracts, and financial reports. The most extensive study of management control structures undertaken to date was that conducted by Schaan (1983, 1988). He distinguished between positive and negative control structures. Whereas parent companies deploy positive control structures to promote certain types of behaviour, they use negative ones to stop or prevent the JV from implementing certain activities or decisions. Positive control structures involve informal techniques for exerting influence, such as staffing and participation in the planning process. Exercising these control structures is an ongoing process. Negative control structures, on the other hand, rely on bureaucratic mechanisms, such as formal agreements, requirement for approval, and the use of a board of directors. Exercising these negative control structures is what Killing (1983) calls the exercise of raw power. Kamminga and Van der Meer-Kooistra (2007) distinguished two groups of management control structures by taking into account the orientation of the structures, namely, content-based management control structures and context-based management control structures. As the name would suggest, content-based management control structures focus on the content of a JV's activities and output, while the context-based ones focus on the relationship between the JV parties and the creation of a suitable relational context or atmosphere.

Having distinguished three dimensions of JV management control, Geringer and Hebert (1989) conclude that these dimensions (the mechanisms or structures, the tightness, and the focus) are not incompatible. On the contrary, they are 'complementary and interdependent' (Geringer and Hebert 1989, p. 241). The implication of the complementarity and interdependence of these dimensions is that the JV management control structures, and the tightness by which they are exercised, have to be interconnected to the focus of JV management control. Previously, we discussed how the literature has paid attention to three main JV management control foci: (1) the issue of coordination, (2) the issue of opportunistic behaviour, and (3) the issue of creating a relational atmosphere. In the next section, we will elaborate on these three issues.

3   COORDINATION, OPPORTUNISTIC BEHAVIOUR, AND RELATIONAL ATMOSPHERE

In this section we will discuss how the parent companies can use JV management control to manage the coordination of their input of resources and to control the activities, processes, and output of the JV, to prevent opportunistic behaviour by any of the parties concerned (i.e., the parent companies and the JV management), and to create a relational atmosphere in which these parties signal their commitment to the JV relationship. Furthermore, we will discuss the basis of the legitimacy for the use of JV management control in coordinating the JV's activities, processes and transactions, preventing opportunistic behaviour, and stimulating the creation of a good relational atmosphere.

Coordination

Parent companies have various strategic motives for establishing a JV relationship. Strategic motives mentioned by Contractor and Lorange (1988) are: risk reduction, economies of scale, complementary technologies, blocking competition, overcoming government-mandated investment, and access to all kinds of resources, including capital, materials, knowledge, and experience. Depending on their strategic motives, the parent companies contribute specific resources to the JV. The input of these resources has to be coordinated in terms of time, place, quantity, and quality; such coordination needs specific arrangements and procedures, the nature of which will depend on the type of resources under consideration. For example, the input of tacit knowledge requires frequent face-to-face cooperation and consultations between the JV parties (personnel from the parent companies and the JV) because this knowledge is embedded in the minds of people and, by nature, cannot be written down. Thus, when tacit knowledge is to be conveyed, JV management control has to facilitate frequent face-to-face encounters between the individuals possessing the relevant knowledge. General management control structures that contribute to the coordination of physical resources are planning and budgeting of the input of resources, quantity and quality checks on supplies of resources, planning and budgeting of the production processes for intermediate and final products, planning and budgeting of production outputs, measurement of production outputs, variance analyses, and so on. As these management control structures focus on the content of the JV's activities and output, Kamminga and Van der Meer-Kooistra (2007) speak of content-based management control structures. In such management control structures, accounting information derived from (formal) accounting information systems plays an important role. Kamminga and Van der Meer-Kooistra argue that content-based management control structures can only be used if the JV's activities and/ or output can be planned and measured. Then the parent companies can prescribe and tightly control the JV's activities and/or output. The parent companies will write content-based management control structures into the contract agreed at the outset of the JV relationship. Thus, the contract is the legitimate basis for the use of these management control structures.

In addition to content-based management control structures, Kamminga and Van der Meer-Kooistra (2007) identify context-based management control structures that focus on the context of the JV relationship. The information associated with context-based management control structures is not usually derived from formal accounting information systems, but is exchanged between the parties when they meet face to face and is often tacit in nature. Such an exchange of information depends on the parties' willingness to share their knowledge and experience with one another. Although context-based management control structures will be written into the contract so that the legitimacy of their use is ensured by the contract, the exchange of information resulting from the use of context-based management control structures is voluntary because of the tacit nature of the information. As mentioned earlier, this type of information exchange is required when the planning and measurement of the JV's activities and/or output are likely to be problematic as a result of environmental uncertainty and information asymmetry between the parent companies. Information asymmetry between the parent companies is likely to occur when they have different (but complementary) interests and contribute different resources to the JV.

Tomkins (2001) elaborates on the relationship between being able to coordinate the joint activities, or what he calls mastering events, and the building of a trusting relationship. Being able to master events implies that the parties have the required competencies and, moreover, receive the accounting information required to plan and coordinate their joint activities and to respond to environmental changes. Tomkins suggests that, particularly, in the early stage of a relationship, management control may stimulate trust building because the accounting information exchange that follows from the use of management control structures may produce more positive expectations about future contributions to the relationship. Child (2001) also points to the importance of experience with and knowledge about how to manage inter-organisational coordination. Tomkins (2001) argues that mastery of events could be realised purposively by making suitable contractual arrangements in the form of a package of management control structures at the start of an inter-organisational relationship or, if uncertainty makes it impossible to plan the activities beforehand, during the course of the relationship (see also Emsley and Kidon 2007). Hence, the design of JV management control is not limited to the start of a JV relationship, but can also be developed over time when the JV's activities and output become clear. In such a situation, the parent companies will negotiate framework contracts at the start of the JV relationship, agreeing upon and incorporating more general content-based management control structures, and will develop more precise procedures and arrangements over time.

Opportunistic Behaviour

Under circumstances of uncertainty, opportunities to behave opportunistically are highly likely to occur. Opportunistic behaviour leads to transaction costs, as is argued by transaction cost economics (Williamson 1985, 1996). The risk of opportunistic behaviour is related to three features of transactions between parties: (1) the degree of asset specificity; (2) the degree of uncertainty; and (3) the volume/frequency of transactions. The greater the asset specificity, uncertainty, and volume/frequency of specific transactions, the higher the risk of opportunistic behaviour will be. Opportunistic behaviour can be mitigated by putting in place adequate management control structures aimed at providing the JV parties incentives to stimulate their cooperation and monitoring and constraining their actions and thereby safeguarding against potential opportunistic behaviour (Williamson [1996] called the management control structures that are intended to prevent or mitigate opportunistic behaviour credible commitments). These management control structures are written into the contract the parent companies agree upon at the start of the JV relationship and are intended to align the parties' interests and make the behaviour of all parties more predictable and transparent.

Lindenberg (2000) claims that taking adequate measures by developing management control structures at the outset of a JV relationship compensates for legitimate negative expectations about the other JV parties' future behaviour. Negative expectations arise when the JV parties' interest in the relationship is neither similar nor complementary. If their interests are not aligned (i.e., similar or complementary), none of the JV parties can be expected to keep to the agreements when specific opportunities arise since no one can be expected to act against their own self-interests. Then the negative expectations are legitimate. Aligning the JV parties' interests by means of contractual arrangements in the form of management control structures ought not to threaten the relationship, as any 'reasonable party' will be prepared to take such measures. If one of the JV parties is not prepared to make suitable contractual arrangements, but, instead, is only willing to promise not to act opportunistically, it can signal untrustworthy behaviour. As this promise is 'blatantly against his self-interest' (Lindenberg 2000, p. 12) the other parties do not believe the promising party and expect that it will not act against its well-understood self-interest. This mistrust of the promises made is irrespective of the party's true intentions. Mutual cooperation will be stimulated by developing adequate management control structures and writing them into the contract because opportunities to defect will be limited and incentives to behave opportunistically will be reduced. Furthermore, the JV parties can agree to compensate a partner's loss if the opportunity to defect nevertheless arises and a party takes it.

Various management control structures, both content-based and context-based, can be used to prevent opportunistic behaviour of the JV parties. For example, if a parent company contributes proprietary technological knowledge to the JV, it can prevent leakage of this knowledge to competitors by claiming a majority share in the JV and, in the case of leakage of knowledge, by claiming substantial compensation for suffering the loss of knowledge. Alternatively, a parent company can prevent the JV from becoming a competitor to its own business by limiting the JV's sales activities to a specific geographical area. The structures mentioned in these examples restrict the JV parties' actions or punish them for inappropriate behaviour. Other structures can be more stimulating by rewarding cooperative behaviour, for example, by being prepared to broaden the scope of the JV's activities if the venture proves to be a success. Accounting information derived from formal accounting information systems can play a role in preventing opportunistic behaviour by, for example, augmenting the parent companies' knowledge of the JV's activities and output, thereby decreasing information asymmetries between the JV parties.

Research shows that the institutional environment can support the management control structures to prevent opportunistic behaviour (Luhmann 1979; Bachmann 2001). By means of legislation, regulations and the norms, values, and rules of business and social networks the institutional environment puts pressure on JV parties to ensure that they behave in an appropriate manner. Vosselman and Van der Meer-Kooistra (2009) point to the role that credible voice threats and exit threats can play, which can be derived from the institutional environment. The credibility of voice threats depends on the existence of trustworthy business networks through which reputations of members of that network are affected. Negative experiences with a specific member will be voiced to the network and will be penalised by the other members, for example, by avoiding establishing JV relationships with this member. Because of this, the network creates incentives to prevent incompetent and malevolent behaviour. The legal environment of JV relationships can also create credible voice threats if there is trust in the regulations and the legal system developed by regulatory bodies and the legislature. These regulations and legal rules create certainty that incompetent and malevolent behaviour will be punished. The credibility of exit threats requires trust in the working of markets, enabling a party to threaten to switch to other parties. For example, a parent company could decide to leave the JV relationship in response to the opportunistic behaviour of its partner and establish a new JV relationship with another party.

Regulations, legislation, and the norms, values, and rules of business and social networks are sources of trust that increase the enforceability of contractual arrangements, including management control structures. However, Kamminga and Van der Meer-Kooistra (2007) show that legal rules and regulations can only play such a role if they are clearly defined and well understood by the JV parties. If the legal rules and regulations are in a state of flux and the JV parties do not know how they are to be formulated, the institutional environment will create uncertainty, and the JV parties themselves have to implement management control measures to deal with this uncertainty. If the institutional environment is highly uncertain and causes the JV's activities and/or output to be unpredictable and hardly measurable, the JV parties cannot use content-based management control structures and will have to rely more on context-based management control structures to prevent opportunistic behaviour.

Relational Atmosphere

Though parent companies can take management control measures to prevent opportunistic behaviour and write them into the contract, there is no full guarantee that opportunistic behaviour will not occur in the course of a JV relationship. Over time, opportunities to defect may occur which could not be foreseen at the start of the relationship. In particular, if the JV is surrounded by a high level of uncertainty and if the parent companies are not able to fully plan and measure the JV's activities and/or output, the contract agreed upon at the start of the JV relationship will be incomplete (see, e.g., Van der Meer-Kooistra and Vosselman 2000; Kamminga and Van der Meer-Kooistra 2007). Incomplete contracts cannot be easily enforced and will limit the meaning of contracts (Macauley 1963; Blumberg 2001; Vosselman and Van der Meer-Kooistra 2006). The parent companies will be confronted with new opportunities created by environmental and technological changes. A trustworthy relationship between the JV parties (including the parent companies and the JV management) will facilitate their ability to jointly respond to new situations and thereby to act in the interests of the JV relationship. Therefore, it is important that the JV parties work on building a trustworthy relationship.

In a trustworthy JV relationship all of the parties concerned have aligned their commitments to the relationship and signal to the other parties that they are willing to behave in a cooperative way (Lindenberg 2000; Chaserant 2003). In particular, when a party might be tempted to defect, it needs to signal to the other parties that it will not take unilateral advantage of the opportunity, but, instead, show solidarity with the other JV parties. Lindenberg (2000) called these situations in which the JV parties voluntarily signal their cooperative behaviour solidarity situations. Such relational signals stimulate positive expectations about the competencies, benevolence, and integrity of the JV parties. Larson (1992) also described the need for continuous effort to show the parties' norms of fairness, honesty, and reciprocity. She argued that this would give 'confidence that the other side could be relied upon . . .; confidence that the relationship would not be exploited by the other side . . .; confidence that extra effort would be made consistently . . .' (Larson 1992, p. 96). Management control can play a role in relational signalling. As we will explain following, JV parties can use accounting information, for example, about costs, sales, and product quality, to signal a solidarity situation and to reveal their voluntary response to such a situation.

Lindenberg distinguishes five categories of solidarity situations. In the first, the common good situation, the parties produce a common good and by contributing to this good, even though there is a possibility of free riding, each party signals its willingness to behave in a cooperative way. In the second, the sharing situation, one of the parties has the power to divide the joint benefits and costs, and could decide to maximise its own results, but instead, this party decides to take a fair share and so shows that it wants to behave in the interests of the JV relationship. The disclosure of accounting information about the benefits and costs and the individual parties' share in the results signal the propensity for sharing behaviour. In the third, the need situation, one party helps the other in times of need. Accounting information could be of help in analysing the situation or in finding solutions. In the fourth, the breach situation, one of the parties will not act against the other's interests even at a cost to itself. An example of a breach situation is described by Kamminga and Van der Meer-Kooistra (2007, p. 152). One of the parent companies of a JV relationship which focused on the marketing and sale of gas on the British market was prepared to postpone part of the JV's gas purchase obligations and to lower the price of the JV's overall purchase portfolio in order to support the JV's results during a period in which the gas price fell drastically. Thus, this parent company wanted to demonstrate its desire for a smooth collaboration and to show that it was willing to act in the other JV parties' interests. In the fifth, the mishap situation, one party which unintentionally harms the other makes amends by apologising for the harm done and offering to make good the damage, thereby showing its real intentions. Furthermore, there might be occasions when a party cannot keep to the agreement, but as it intends to act in a cooperative way, it warns the other party in advance that it will act against the agreement. In both mishap situations, accounting information can disclose the resultant cost of the damage or loss.

The parties can use (formal) accounting information to measure the (financial) implications of solidarity situations for the individual parties and to divide the possible losses or benefits in a fair manner. Vosselman and Van der Meer-Kooistra (2009) argued that such a use of JV management control structures is not legitimated by the contract, but is based on the JV parties' cooperative behaviour and is of their own volition. A voluntary use of JV management control will only take place if the parties concerned trust each other.

In Summary

So far we have discussed the main issues of JV relationships and the role that management control, including accounting information, can play in managing them. We argued that the parties in a JV relationship will set up management control structures to manage coordination issues and to identify possible problems related to opportunistic behaviour at the start of the JV relationship and write them into the contract. But because the contracts are incomplete, additional management control structures will be developed over the life of a JV relationship when new situations occur and the parent companies feel a need to respond to them in a structural way. It is the contract, including the additional contractual arrangements agreed over time, which enables the parties to use JV management control structures. The enforceability of the contract, and thus the use of management control structures written into the contract, is strengthened by the credibility of the institutions in which the relationship is embedded, such as the legislation, regulations and norms, values and rules of business, and social networks.

In addition, we argued that, over time, solidarity situations could occur that lead to relational signals through which the JV parties signal their commitment to the relationship. These signals result from the parties' willingness to behave in a cooperative way and demonstrate that the parties will refrain from opportunistic behaviour. The JV parties will only be prepared to signal cooperative behaviour if they trust one another or, in other words, if they have built a good relational atmosphere.

Because trust between the JV parties is an important relational device, in particular under circumstances of internal and external uncertainty, we will describe the relationship between management control and trust building in greater depth in the next section, and discuss how the interplay of management control and trust reduces uncertainty in JV relationships.

4   MANAGEMENT CONTROL AND TRUST

The core of trust is the willingness to accept vulnerability. Positive expectations about the competencies, benevolence, and integrity of the other party underlie this willingness, whereas risk taking in the relationship is the outcome of this willingness and is the behavioural manifestation of trust. In the literature, various terms have been used to embody this concept of trust (i.e., the willingness to accept vulnerability), for example, goodwill trust (Sako 1992), relational trust (Rousseau et al. 1998) or thick trust (Nooteboom 2002). Trust reduces uncertainty. In its turn, uncertainty can be created by the (institutional) environment of a JV relationship, but it can also be found inside the JV relationship and be created by the behaviour of the JV parties during the course of their relationship. In particular, opportunistic behaviour exercised by one of the JV parties creates uncertainty, for it can harm the other parties and may result in the other parties behaving opportunistically and so create a relational atmosphere of distrust. The more environmental uncertainty, the more scope the JV parties have for behaving opportunistically, as the contract is unlikely to cover all eventualities and, if the JV is to hold together, the parties need to rely on each other's willingness to behave cooperatively and to show commitment to the JV relationship over the life of the JV.

Lindenberg (2000) claimed that trust can only be created when the JV parties have aligned their interests (i.e., have similar or complementary interests) at the outset of the JV relationship. If their interests are not aligned, none of the parties can be expected to keep to the contractual arrangements when specific opportunities arise over time. This also implies that, when establishing a new JV relationship, interests have to be aligned, even though the parties already trust one another because of previous or ongoing inter-organisational relationships. Hence, the JV parties have to develop effective management control structures able to align their interests; otherwise it will not be possible to create trust. This is one of the major findings of the study by Mayer and Argyres (2004) of inter-organisational relationships in the personal computer industry, which showed that the easier it is for the parties in an inter-organisational relationship to take contractual measures to avoid misunderstandings and to clarify each party's role and responsibilities, the easier the creation of trust becomes. These results were also supported by Blumberg (1997), who found no relation between the social embeddedness of the partners (i.e., a trusting relationship between the partners) and the interest aligning measures in their contracts; in other words, although the partners trusted one another, they nevertheless had written measures into the contract that were intended to align their interests.

Tomkins (2001) claimed that being able to coordinate the JV's resources, activities, and output or, as he puts it, mastering events supports processes of trust building. Being able to master events implies that the JV parties have the required competencies and receive the required information to plan and coordinate their activities and for an appropriate response to environmental changes. In addition, the JV parties demonstrate that they are prepared to develop adequate management control structures. This stimulates positive expectations about the future of the JV relationship and reduces uncertainty. Moreover, Tomkins stated that having a trusting relationship furthers the parties' ability to master events over time.

Both Lindenberg and Tomkins assumed that management control and trust are complementary—adequate management control stimulates trust building, and a trusting relationship supports the development of adequate management control. Other scholars argue that trust can substitute for management control (see Van der Meer-Kooistra and Vosselman 2000; Kamminga and Van der Meer-Kooistra 2007). These scholars argued that in JV relationships characterised by transactions of a high complexity and surrounded by high uncertainty, trust replaces management control, because the parties have difficulty developing and using management control structures, and therefore have to rely on trust. So, in these types of relationship trust is the alternative means by which to manage and control these relationships and to reduce environmental and behavioural uncertainty.

However, Vosselman and Van der Meer-Kooistra (2009) went beyond the complementary and substitution perspectives and argued that the 'rather simple "and/or" or "and/and" debate on the relationship between control and trust downplays the dynamics between trust and control' (p. 3). They claim that management control and trust interact in reducing uncertainty and stimulating positive expectations about the future behaviour of the JV parties. Management control is required to coordinate the input of resources, activities, processes, and transactions and to align the parties' interests to prevent opportunistic behaviour. Management control structures make the parties' interests transparent and their behaviour more predictable, and create foundations on which trust can be built through relational signalling in solidarity situations. Management control structures can be used in relational signalling and so support the building up of trust. On the other hand, trust strengthens the credibility of the management control structures. Hence, management control does not only have a direct effect on the trust built up, but also an indirect one.

Table 5.1 illustrates the differences between management control structures developed for JV relationships of less and more complexity, respectively. It gives an overview of the management control structures used in two JVs, Delesto and Gas Sales (see Kamminga and Van der Meer-Kooistra 2007). Delesto is owned by the parent companies Akzo Nobel (a Dutch chemical multinational) and Essent (a Dutch multi-utility company). The transformation process of Delesto is straightforward and transparent, so that its activities and output are measurable and can be readily assessed. The environment in which the JV operates is stable and well-understood and there is no information asymmetry between the JV parties. Gas Sales is an IJV owned by an American utility company, American Corp., which has an English subsidiary called α Gas, the managers of which are involved in Gas Sales; and an English electricity supplier, Electricity Corp. Gas Sales, experiences high environmental uncertainty and a great deal of ambiguity about the development of governmental regulations. The parent companies' input of resources, in particular knowledge and experience, differs, and exchanging and sharing knowledge is required to operate the JV. There is a high degree of information asymmetry between the parent companies as well as between the JV management and the parent companies.

A comparison of the data provided in Table 5.1 shows that the parent companies of Delesto use more *formal* management control structures that

Table 5.1 Overview of Management Control Structures in Two JV Relationships (Kamminga and Van der Meer-Kooistra 2007, p. 154)

Management Control Structures and Focus	Delesto	Gas Sales
Personnel	• Chief executive appointed by Akzo Nobel • Management of the operational activities by Akzo Nobel • JV personnel detached by Akzo Nobel • Equity holders committee: two from Essent and two from Akzo Nobel	• Board of directors: 5 appointed by Electricity Corp. and 1 by American Corp. • Staff, including management, from Electricity Corp. • Personnel training programme provided by Electricity Corp. (electricity market) • Initial training programme by a Gas (on gas infrastructure)
Financial mechanisms	• 50–50 equity share • Off-balance financing	• 75–25 equity share (Electricity Corp. 75% and American Corp. 25%) • Price and conditions of delivering gas to the JV by a Gas • Prices of the gas shipping services and supply point administration delivered by a Gas
Formal information	• Accounting principles used those of Akzo Nobel • Three-year investment, finance and exploitation budget • Annual report: investments, production activities, liquidity, costs, financial results • Quarterly reports • Monthly reports: expenditure of gas, supply of electricity and steam, staffing, environmental safety, number of accidents, lost-time injuries, near misses, balance sheet, income statement, yields, variance analyses	• Accounting principles used those of Electricity Corp. • Monthly reports • Annual report
Meetings and personal contacts	• Equity holders meeting (at least twice a year): to discuss reports and environmental developments	• Quarterly meetings of the board of directors: statutory compliance, strategy, accounts, JV performance, market changes • Operational meetings: operational issues, supply point administration, gas purchases and balancing, data transfer from the JV to a Gas • Personal contacts between the managers of a Gas and Electricity Corp. • Social activities

focus on the content of the JV relationship, that is, the production activities and output, than Gas Sales. In contrast, the parent companies of Gas Sales choose to use more *informal* management control practices, such as meetings, personal contacts, and social activities, which focus on the context of the JV relationship, that is, the relational atmosphere and norms and values of the JV parties. These meetings and personal contacts facilitate the exchange of proprietary, often tacit knowledge between the JV parties, which is required to enable them to operate the JV in a new market with considerable uncertainty about the governmental regulations. The social activities contribute to a better understanding of the other parent company's cultural background and norms and values, and support the development of attachments between individuals involved in the JV.

The complexity of JV management control is not only caused by the dynamic relationship between management control and trust discussed earlier but also by external and internal forces that shape the JV dynamics and give rise to changes in the JV management control over time. In the next section, we will discuss these forces and their influence on JV management control.

5   MANAGEMENT CONTROL AND JOINT VENTURE DYNAMICS

Various causes of JV dynamics have been discussed in the literature (see, e.g., Parkhe 1993; Inkpen and Beamish 1997; Yan 1998; Yan and Zeng 1999), where JV dynamics correspond to the definition of Van der Meer-Kooistra and Kamminga (2008), who define JV dynamics as changes in the JV relationship and JV management control over the life of a JV. They argue that JV management control has to be geared to the characteristics of the relationship, which take three forms: transactional, relational, and environmental (see also Kamminga and Van der Meer-Kooistra 2007). The transactional characteristics of JV relationships comprise uncertainty, asset specificity, and the measurability and knowledge of the JV's activities and/or output; the relational characteristics encompass parental differences, information asymmetry between the parties, relative bargaining power, and the level of trust between the parties; the environmental characteristics include the uncertainty of the institutional environment (i.e., associated with governmental regulations and business networks) and the local norms and values. These characteristics influence the character of the JV management control, which implies that changes in these characteristics will need changes in JV management control. If changes in JV management control do not take place, the JV relationship will be threatened. Next we will discuss the forces that can bring about changes in the characteristics of the JV relationship and, consequently, changes in the JV management control, and thereby shape the dynamics of JVs. We will start by discussing forces within the JV relationship, such as one parent company learning from the other, the JV's performance, and changes within the parent companies, and then elaborate on the influence of forces external to the JV relationship, such as market developments, changes in technology, and changes in governmental regulations.

Internal Forces of Change

Learning

Inkpen and Currall (2004) distinguished two types of learning. The first is how to cooperate with a partner (see also Kale et al. 2000). Williamson (1985, 1996) discussed how learning between transacting parties can increase the level of human and procedural asset specificity. By means of repeated transactions over an extended period, the parties learn the specifics of the transactions and each other's procedures, and this enables them to acquire the skills needed to coordinate activities better and to improve the measurement of the output. Such learning in JV relationships increases the measurability of the JV's activities and output, and decreases the information asymmetry between the parent companies and the JV's management, as a result of which, content-based control structures can be put in place (Kamminga and Van der Meer-Kooistra 2007). Furthermore, the parties can better understand their partner's norms and values, and each can learn whether their partner is committed to the relationship or is primarily interested in pursuing its own interests. Learning about how to cooperate with the JV parties will enable the parent companies to develop a JV relationship they trust and to set up adequate JV management control. This should strengthen the JV relationship.

A second type of learning, which may cause JV dynamics, is learning about the other partner's contributions to the JV (e.g., Hamel 1991; Inkpen and Beamish 1997; Yan 1998; Kale et al. 2000; Inkpen and Currall 2004). An important strategic motive for participating in a JV could be that of gaining access to the knowledge possessed by another party, for instance, in the form of technological know-how. Once such knowledge is acquired, the first party may be able to 'eliminate its dependency on its partner' (Inkpen and Beamish 1997, p. 184). Moreover, it may even be able to conduct the JV's activities itself (Yan and Gray 1994; Inkpen and Beamish 1997) and, consequently, lose interest in the JV. Hence, it is likely that learning from another partner's contributions will weaken the JV relationship and may even lead to its termination. This is especially so if the strategic motive for establishing a JV relationship was to gain access to the knowledge of the other partner as the strategic motive for initiating the joint venture has been satisfied, and no ongoing motive remains.

Key Individuals

Because the management of JV relationships requires specific skills and experience (Schaan and Beamish 1988), changes in the key individuals involved may have consequences for the relationship (Seabright et al. 1992; Inkpen and Currall 1998). If the individuals brought in lack experience in cooperating in long-term relationships with other independent partners, or, more particularly, if they have difficulty cooperating with the representatives of other parent companies, this could strain the relationship. Over time, through learning how to cooperate, the relationship between the key individuals may improve and the JV relationship may become stronger, but if such learning does not take place, the JV relationship will be weakened. This latter scenario could have severe consequences, in particular where JVs face high environmental uncertainty, where the activities and output are difficult to plan and/or measure, and where there is information asymmetry between the parent companies (Kamminga and Van der Meer-Kooistra 2007). In JV relationships with these characteristics, parent companies have to be prepared to exchange (often tacit) knowledge and experience in face-to-face meetings, which requires that the key individuals trust one another. If they are not able to develop an appropriate level of trust, the parent companies need to be willing to replace their key individuals with others with a more cooperative attitude; otherwise it is likely that these JV relationships will not survive for long.

However, if the JV is characterised by a stable environment and its activities and output are transparent, the key individuals do not need to have such extensive trust in one another for the JV to survive, because there is no information asymmetry and the parent companies are able to rely fully on the (written) accounting information they receive about the JV's activities and its output. Thus, in JV relationships with these transactional, relational, and environmental characteristics, a cooperative attitude of key individuals is less crucial, and the JV relationship will hardly be threatened because of the appointment of key individuals with a less cooperative attitude.

Financial Situation

According to Killing (1983), a JV facing substantial financial problems over an extended period can easily fall into a 'failure cycle'. Because of the financial problems, the parent companies may question the competence of the JV management. The loss of trust in the competence of the management may, in its turn, lead to tighter parental control over the activities, processes, and output of the JV. However, the tightened control is likely to slow down and possibly even confuse the decision-making processes, leading to yet worse performance and even tighter parental control. Ultimately, this cycle can lead to a major crisis (Killing 1983, pp. 82–83). On the other hand, good JV performance can increase trust in the competence of the JV management and, consequently, encourage the parent companies to give it great autonomy, thereby improving the JV's responsiveness and leading to further success (Killing 1983).

According to Killing's 'failure cycle', however, bad JV performance could have other consequences, depending on the characteristics of the JV relationship. According to Kamminga and Van der Meer-Kooistra's model of JV management control (2007), three types of JV relationship, each with a specific management control pattern, can be distinguished. The consequences of poor JV performance will differ for these types: In JV relationships where the control is straightforward, the environment stable, and the parent has tight control (the management control pattern is content-based), poor JV performance will not affect the existing tightness of the parent companies' control. In such relationships the 'failure cycle' will not occur. In contrast, in JV relationships where the control is highly complex, because of high environmental uncertainty and the lack of transparency of the transformation process, the parent companies are unable to control the JV tightly and have to give a substantial amount of autonomy to the JV management. Moreover, the parent companies will have put in place context-based management control structures facilitating the development of a good relational atmosphere between the JV parties (and thus, the management control pattern is context-based). If the parent companies of such JVs decide to control their JV tightly as a response to encountering substantial financial problems, the effects described by Killing will occur. Finally, in JV relationships with medium control complexity, which have a transparent transformation process but face substantial differences in terms of the parent companies' interests and/or contributions, the parent companies need to exchange their knowledge and experience in consultation with one another and will use a mixture of content-based and context-based management control structures (and therefore the management control pattern is consultation-based). If such JVs face substantial financial problems, a shift to tight JV control may also result in a negative spiral, albeit less radical than the one just discussed. At least, such a response by the parent companies to poor JV performance will weaken the JV relationship.

An equivalent line of reasoning can hold for good JV performance. If the parent companies control their JV relationship according to a content-based management control pattern because of the characteristics of the JV relationship (stable environment and transparent transformation process), good JV performance will not change the management control pattern and the parent companies will continue to control their JV tightly and use content-based management control structures. But, if the parent companies have developed a consultation-based or context-based management control pattern, giving the JV management more decision-making autonomy, good JV performance will increase the JV management's responsiveness, and may further stimulate the success of the JV. As a result, the relationship will be strengthened.

We have discussed the implications of the financial situation of a JV earlier; however, changes in the financial situation of a parent company could also affect the JV relationship and its management control. Changes in the financial situation of a parent company may be caused by environmental developments. For instance, a worse market situation may create financial problems for a parent company and, if its JV performs badly as well, there is no longer any justification for that parent company to put much effort into the relationship. When the parent company needs to reassess its business strategy, it is likely that it will reconsider its strategy towards the JV and look for ways of withdrawing from the relationship (see also Hennart et al. 1999).

However, if a parent company has financial problems and its JV performs well, the JV relationship will become more important for that parent company and it is likely that its interest in the JV relationship will increase and strengthen it.

Strategic Motives

Over time, either of the parent companies' strategic motives for establishing a JV relationship might change, altering the similarity or complementarity of the motives. This may result in differences in the parent companies' view on how to develop the JV relationship, and lead to protracted discussions between the parent companies, delaying decision making. This will threaten the effectiveness of the JV's operations and diminish the level of trust in the JV relationship, thereby weakening the JV relationship.

Organisational and Legal Structure of a Parent Company

Van der Meer-Kooistra and Kamminga (2008) described how a change in the organisational structure of a parent company can cause deterioration in the relationship with its JV partner. They produced an example of a parent company that had changed its business unit structure into a matrix structure that distinguished between various product groups. In this new structure, its JV partner had to deal with more managers from the restructured company. This was confusing to its partner because the managers had different ideas from one another. In addition, the partner had difficulty building trusting relationships with all these managers. Thus, the partner lost confidence in the JV relationship, which weakened the relationship.

Another complication in this JV relationship was attributable to the legal structure of the parent company, which was a cooperative. The members of the cooperative are the owners of the company and have a substantial influence on decision making by the executive board of directors. As, in this case, the interests of the owners conflicted with those of the JV, the executive board of directors had difficulty in persuading the owners to invest in the JV relationship. This hindered the development of the JV because the owners were reluctant to make additional investments in the JV. This also created tension in the relationship between the parent companies.

External Forces of Change

The literature points to a number of different ways in which environmental developments may shape JV dynamics. First, some may be due to changes in the institutional environment, which affect the JV's activities and the relationship between the parent companies (Yan 1998; Yan and Zeng 1999). Second, other environmental developments may be due to the nature of the market in which the JV operates or to advances in the technology used by the JV (Harrigan and Newman 1990). Third, environmental developments may influence internal forces, as discussed earlier, and subsequently shape the JV dynamics. Following we will discuss these three types of environmental developments.

Developments in the Institutional Environment

Developments in the institutional environment of a JV may increase or decrease the level of uncertainty in which a JV operates. On the one hand, the establishment of legal, governmental, or industrial regulations can create a level of certainty, because such regulations direct the behaviour of organisations as well as their employees. But constantly changing regulations can itself create uncertainty (Kamminga and Van der Meer-Kooistra 2007). If a JV operates in such a market, the JV management will need substantial autonomy to respond rapidly and appropriately to new situations (Kumar and Seth 1998; Merchant and Van der Stede 2003). This decision-making autonomy places the parent companies at a distance, and creates information asymmetry between the parent companies and the JV management. The increasing uncertainty and the information asymmetry–induced need for more intensive information exchange between the JV parties make the use of context-based management control structures crucial. In those instances where the parent companies had initially set up content-based management control, developments in the institutional environment like those under consideration would require a shift of management control pattern. Thus, as Kamminga and Van der Meer-Kooistra (2007) argued, a content-based or consultation-based management control pattern would have to be replaced by a context-based one. Moreover, the key individuals in a JV would need to develop and display a cooperative attitude and be prepared to invest in personal relationships. If, however, the parent companies are unable to change the control pattern, for example, because the parent companies are not prepared to facilitate the building of personal relationships and organise face-to-face meetings for the exchange of (tacit) information, the JV relationship will suffer.

If developments in the institutional environment decrease the level of uncertainty and give the parent companies better insights into the JV's activities and its output, they can tighten their control of the JV relationship by means of content-based management control structures (see Kamminga and Van der Meer-Kooistra 2007).

Environmental Developments Leading to Changes
in (the Importance of) Strategic Motives

Environmental developments may lead to changes in the parent companies' strategic motives for the initial establishment of a JV relationship. For instance, if new opportunities arise in the market, a parent company may change its strategy. Such a strategic change could change the motives for wanting to participate in a JV and remove the similarity/complementarity of the strategic motives of the parent companies (Harrigan 1986; Harrigan and Newman 1990), thereby weakening the JV relationship.

In addition, technological developments may change the strategic importance of the JV's activities for one or both of the parent companies. For example, an important strategic motive for a JV relationship may be to gain access to the specific knowledge and experience of another partner. Over time, however, this knowledge may diffuse through the market to become less company-specific, even to become common knowledge (Spender 1989; Kamminga and Van der Meer-Kooistra 2007). As a result, the original strategic motive will no longer be relevant, and this will weaken the JV relationship and may even lead to its termination.

Environmental Developments Leading to Learning

Previously, we discussed how learning about how to cooperate with the JV parties can increase a parent company's understanding of the JV's activities and its output and enable the parent company to improve its measurement of and control over the JV's activities. A similar effect can be achieved by learning from external technological developments. Such technological developments may give all the JV parties better insights into the JV's transformation process (Johnson and Kaplan 1987). If these developments also make the environment less uncertain, JV management control will shift to a more content-based pattern.

Environmental Developments Changing the Financial Situation of a JV

Developments in the market can affect a JV's financial position. A worsening market could change a successful JV into a loss maker, whereas an improving market could have an opposite effect. Such market changes, affecting a JV's financial position negatively, could weaken the JV relationship (while an improved financial position could strengthen it) (Williamson 1985; Hennart et al. 1999).

Previously we have discussed how internal and external forces cause changes in the transactional, relational, and environmental characteristics of a JV relationship, affecting the JV relationship and JV management control, thereby creating JV dynamics. We have also pointed to the interconnection between (the strength or weakness of) the JV relationship and JV management control. Furthermore, we have described the influence of JV dynamics on the level of trust. Kamminga and Van der Meer-Kooistra (2007) analysed how internal and external forces can cause transitions between the three management control patterns they distinguished. Table 5.2 is derived from their study of JV management control and illustrates the effects of learning (both internal and external) and environmental changes on transitions between JV management control patterns (Kamminga and Van der Meer-Kooistra 2007, p. 143). The reader is advised to read their work for a detailed description of these effects on JV management control.

Table 5.2 Transitions between JV Management Control Patterns (Kamminga and Van der Meer-Kooistra 2007, p. 143)

		Content-based	*Consultation-based*	*Context-based*
(1)	external learning, internal learning → measurability ↑	←		●
	information asymmetry between parents and JV ↓			
(2)	external learning, internal learning → measurability ↑	←	●	
	information asymmetry between parents ↓			
(3)	external learning, internal learning → measurability ↑		←	●
	information asymmetry between parents and JV ↓			
	(environmental uncertainty is high)			
(4)	environmental developments → information	●	→	
	asymmetry between parents ↑			
	parental differences ↑			
(5)	environmental developments → measurability ↓	●		→
	information asymmetry between parents and JV ↑		●	→

6 CONCLUSIONS AND AVENUES
FOR FUTURE RESEARCH

JV relationships are known for the complexity of their management control, which is caused by their multifaceted and dynamic character. In this chapter we have studied how parent companies can use management control to govern their JV relationship throughout the life of the JV. We have focused our study on the issues of coordination and opportunistic behaviour, and on the relational atmosphere the parent companies have to deal with. Reflecting on our study, we can draw the following conclusions.

First, JV management control is not a static concept, but develops over the life of a JV. If a JV is in an uncertain environment, the parent companies will not only develop management control structures at the outset of the relationship, but also continue to do so over time. Continued development takes place when the parent companies have had the opportunity to learn about the JV's activities and output, and once they know how best to coordinate their input of resources. Because the contract is unlikely to encompass all eventualities, opportunistic behaviour may be possible. However, preventing such behaviour can, to some extent, be achieved by developing and implementing adequate management control structures at the start of the relationship, but also by adapting these structures over time as the JV parties learn to recognise opportunities for opportunistic behaviour and understand how best to cope with them.

Second, the enforcement of contracts, including management control structures, is supported by an institutional environment that creates stability and enables the JV parties to punish opportunistic behaviour. Such a supportive environment can be considered to exist if the JV parties trust the legal rules and regulations issued by the legislature and other regulatory bodies, but business and social networks contribute to the formation of such an environment with their shared norms and values.

Third, because unforeseen opportunities arise over time, trust in each other's cooperative behaviour is required before being prepared to accept vulnerability. Management control structures can be used to build trust over time and to reduce behavioural uncertainty. We argued that, to enable the JV parties to build trust, adequate contractual arrangements have to be put in place to enable events to be mastered and to prevent foreseeable opportunistic behaviour by aligning the parties' interests. These arrangements structure the relationship between the JV parties and provide the foundation on which trust can be built. On the other hand, trust between the JV parties strengthens the enforceability of the contractual arrangements and facilitates the use of management control structures. Therefore, we argued that trust and management control interact dynamically to reduce environmental and behavioural uncertainty and to stimulate the willingness to accept vulnerability.

Fourth, trust building takes place through relational signalling. Such signalling in solidarity situations can be facilitated by management control structures that enable the parties to measure the (financial) implications of such situations and to divide the losses or benefits in a fair manner. We argued that this use of management control structures is voluntary, whereas the use of management control structures for aligning the JV parties' interests and coordinating the JV's input, activities, and output is based on the contract.

Fifth, we discussed a number of internal and external forces that can influence JV management control and the JV relationship over time. We argued that tension in the JV relationship can sometimes be relieved by changing JV management control. These changes can be on the level of specific management control structures, without leading to a transition to another management control pattern, but they can also be more radical and involve such a transition. Both types of changes point to the role that JV management control can play in coping with forces of change. JV management control facilitates adaptation by the parent companies to changing circumstances and new opportunities. However, if JV management control cannot play this facilitatory role, and one of the parent companies loses its interest in the JV, or both do, the relationship will be terminated.

Avenues for Future Research

Although ever more attention is being paid to how to govern JV relationships, much more has to be done to deepen our insight into this complicated issue. This is particularly the case for the management accounting literature, which has paid remarkably little attention to the management control of JV relationships: Whereas management control of inter-organisational relationships has received a considerable amount of attention, only a few studies have specifically focused on JV relationships. This is despite the fact that, in practice, the JV relationship has proved to be a popular form of inter-organisational relationship. There are various avenues for future research.

Kamminga and Van der Meer-Kooistra (2007) have developed three management control patterns and assume that the choice depends on the characteristics of the JV relationship. They argue that, if JV management control does not match the characteristics of a JV relationship, the mismatch will weaken the relationship. It would be interesting to conduct an in-depth study of the effects of a mismatch of JV management control on the functioning of a JV relationship and on the collaboration between the JV parties.

Much more attention could be paid to differences in managing and controlling JV relationships when there are two, three, or even more parent companies. Will the JV management control become more complicated when there are more than two parent companies? Will a larger number of parent companies lead to more autonomy for the JV management or to one of the parent companies occupying a dominant position in order to handle the larger number of hierarchical and lateral relationships?

Another interesting issue is that of the character of JV contracts and the role these contracts play over the life of a JV relationship. Will the role of contracts differ depending on the nature of the relational atmosphere between the JV parties?

Much remains to be discovered about the interaction between management control and trust, and the foundation of management control structures enabling trust building. The question of whether there is a threshold across which more management control leads to mistrust may be asked.

So far, the literature on JVs has taken a rather static approach and has paid little attention to the dynamics of a JV relationship over its lifetime. As JV relationships are known to be unstable and are very susceptible to changes in their environment, as well as to changes within the JV relationship itself, there is a need to increase our understanding of the processes of JV dynamics and of the role management control can play in such dynamics and in making the JV relationship more stable. We suggest conducting in-depth, longitudinal case research to examine the unfolding of JV dynamics. Such research could provide greater insight into how forces of change, in combination, cause JV dynamics and clarify how management control and trust influence these processes and strengthen or weaken the JV relationship. In this research, specific attention could be paid to the influence of changes within parent companies on JV dynamics.

NOTES

1. In this chapter, management accounting comprises the design, implementation, and use of management accounting systems, including both financial and nonfinancial information, and their effects on the behaviour of participants. Usually such a broad definition of management accounting is covered by the term 'management control' and this is, therefore, the term we will use in this chapter.
2. For convenience, in the remaining text we assume that there are just two parent companies.
3. Das and Teng (2001) speak of performance risk due to factors such as the parties' lack of competence, new entrants, demand fluctuations and changing government policies.
4. Gulati and Singh (1998) and Dekker (2004) speak of appropriation concerns, whereas Das and Teng (2001) call the potential for opportunistic behaviour by one of the parties relational risk.
5. Usually these studies use the term 'control'.

BIBLIOGRAPHY

Anthony, R. N., and Govindarajan, V. 2004. *Management control systems.* 11th ed. New York: McGraw-Hill.
Bachmann, R. 2001. Trust, power and control in trans-organizational relations. *Organization Studies* 22: 337–365.

Beamish, P. W., and Delios, A. 1997. Improving joint venture performance through congruent measures of success. In *Cooperative strategies: European perspectives*, ed. Beamish, P. W., and Killing, J. P. 103–127. San Francisco: The New Lexington Press.

Blodgett, L. L. 1991. Partner contributions as predictors of equity share in international joint ventures. *Journal of International Business Studies* 22: 63–78.

Blumberg, B. F. 1997. *Das Management von Technologiekooperationen.* Amsterdam: Thela Thesis.

Blumberg, B F. 2001. Cooperation contracts between embedded firms. *Organization Studies* 22: 825–852.

Chalos, P., and O'Connor, N. G. 2004. Determinants of the use of various control mechanisms in US-Chinese joint ventures. *Accounting Organizations and Society* 29: 591–608.

Chaserant, C. 2003. Cooperation, contracts and social networks: From a bounded to a procedural rationality approach. *Journal of Management and Governance* 7: 163–186.

Child, J. 2001. Trust—the fundamental bond in global collaboration. *Organization Dynamics:* 29: 274.288.

Choi, C.-B., and Beamish, P. W. 2004. Split management control and international joint venture performance. *Journal of International Business Studies* 35: 201–215.

Contractor, F. J., and Lorange, P. 1988. In *Cooperative strategies in international business*, ed. Contractor, F. J., and Lorange, P. 3–30. Lexington, MA: Lexington Book Co-operation.

Das, T. K., and Teng, B.-S. 2001. Trust, control, and risk in strategic alliances: An integrated framework. *Organization Studies* 22: 251–283.

Dekker, H. C. 2004. Control of inter-organizational relationships: Evidence on appropriation concerns and coordination requirements. *Accounting, Organizations and Society* 29: 27–49.

Emsley, D., and Kidon, F. 2007. The relationship between trust and control in international joint ventures: Evidence from the airline industry. *Contemporary Accounting Research:* 24: 829–858.

Foster, G., and Young, S. M. 1997. Frontiers of management accounting research. *Journal of Management Accounting Research* 9: 63–77.

Geringer, J. M., and Hebert, L. 1989. Control and performance of international joint ventures. *Journal of International Business Studies* 20: 235–254.

Ghoshal, S., and Moran, P. 1996. Bad for practice: A critique of the transaction cost theory. *Academy of Management Review* 21: 13–47.

Gietzmann, M. B. 1996. Incomplete contracts and the make or buy decision: Governance design and attainable flexibility. *Accounting, Organizations and Society:* 21: 611–626.

Granovetter, G. 1985. Economic action and social structure: The problem of embeddedness. *American Journal of Sociology* 91: 481–510.

Groot, T. L. C. M., and Merchant, K. A. 2000. Control of international joint ventures. *Accounting, Organizations and Society* 25: 579–607.

Gulati, R., and Singh, H. 1998. The architecture of cooperation: Managing coordination costs and appropriation concerns in strategic alliances. *Administrative Science Quarterly* 43: 781–814.

Hamel, G. 1991. Competition for competence and inter-partner learning within international strategic alliances. *Strategic Management Journal* 12: 83–103.

Harrigan, K. R. 1986. *Managing for joint venture success.* Lexington, MA: Lexington Book Co-operation.

Harrigan, K. R., and Newman, W. H. 1990. Bases of interorganisation cooperation: Propensity, power, persistence. *Journal of Management Studies* 27: 417–434.

Hennart, J.-F. 1991. The transaction cost theory of joint ventures: An empirical study of Japanese subsidiaries in the United States. *Management Science* 37: 483–497.

Hennart, J.-F., Roehl, T., and Zietlow, D. S. 1999. 'Trojan horse' or 'workhorse'? The evolution of U.S.-Japanese joint ventures in the United States. *Strategic Management Journal* 20: 15–29.

Hopwood, A. G. 1996. Looking across rather than up and down: On the need to explore the lateral processing of information. *Accounting, Organizations and Society* 21: 559–560.

Inkpen, A. C., and Beamish, P. W. 1997. Knowledge, bargaining power, and the instability of international joint ventures. *Academy of Management Review* 22: 177–202.

Inkpen, A. C., and Currall, S. C. 1998. The nature, antecedents, and consequences of joint venture trust. *Journal of International Management* 4: 1–20.

Inkpen, A. C., and Currall, S. C. 2004. The coevolution of trust, control, and learning in joint ventures. *Organization Science* 15: 586–599.

Johnson, H. T., and Kaplan, R. S. 1987. *Relevance lost: The rise and fall of management accounting.* Boston, MA: Harvard Business School Press.

Kamminga, P. E., and Van der Meer-Kooistra, J. 2007. Management control patterns in joint venture relationships: A model and an exploratory study. *Accounting, Organizations and Society* 32: 135–158.

Kamminga, P. E., Van der Meer-Kooistra, J., and Scapens, R. W. 2008. Dynamic aspects of joint venture relationships. Working paper.

Kale, P., Singh, H., and Perlmutter, H. 2000. Learning and protection of proprietary assets in strategic alliances: Building relational capital. *Strategic Management Journal* 21: 217–237.

Kemp, R. G. M. 1999. *Managing interdependence for joint venture success: An empirical study of Dutch international joint ventures.* Dissertation. Groningen, Netherlands: Datawyse.

Killing, J. P. 1983. *Strategies for joint venture success.* Kent, UK: Croom Helm.

Killing, J. P. 1988. Understanding alliances: The role of task and organizational complexity. In *Cooperative strategies in international business,* ed. Contractor, F. J., and Lorange, P. 55–67. Lexington, MA: Lexington Book Co-operation.

Kumar, S., and Seth, A. A. 1998. The design of coordination and control mechanisms for managing joint venture-parent relationships. *Strategic Management Journal* 19: 579–599.

Larson, A. 1992. Network dyads in entrepreneurial settings: A study of the governance of exchange relationships. *Administrative Science Quarterly* 37: 76–104.

Lindenberg, S. 2000. It takes both trust and lack of mistrust: The workings of cooperation and relational signaling in contractual relationships. *Journal of Management and Governance* 4: 11–33.

Lorange, P. 1997. Black-box protection of your competencies in strategic alliances. In *Cooperative strategies, European perspectives,* ed. Beamish, P. W., and Killing, J. P. 59–73. San Francisco: The New Lexington Press.

Lorange, P., and Roos, J. 1992. *Strategic alliances, formation, implementation and evolution.* Cambridge: Blackwell Publishers.

Luhmann, N. 1979. *Trust and power.* Chichester, UK: Wiley.

Macauley, S. 1963. Non-contractual relations in business: A preliminary study. *American Sociological Review* 28: 55–66.

Mayer, K. J., and Argyres, N. S. 2004. Learning to contract: Evidence from the personal computer industry. *Organization Science* 15: 394–410.

Merchant, K. A., and Van der Stede, W. A. 2003. *Management control systems, performance measurement, evaluations and incentives.* Harlow, UK: Prentice Hall.

Mjoen, H., and Tallman, S. 1997. Control and performance in international joint ventures. *Organization Science* 8: 257–274.

Nooteboom, B. 2002. *Trust: Forms, foundations, functions, failures and figures.* Cheltenham, UK: Edward Elgar.

Otley, D. T. 1994. Management control in contemporary organizations: Towards a wider framework. *Management Accounting Research* 5: 289–299.

Parkhe, A. 1993. Messy research, methodological predispositions, and theory development in international JVs. *Academy of Management Review* 18: 227–268.

Ring, P. S., and Van der Ven, A. H. 1994. Developmental processes of cooperative interorganizational relationships. *Academy of Management Review* 19: 90–118.

Rousseau, D., Sitkin, S., Burt, C., and Camerer, C. 1998. Not so different after all: A cross-discipline view on trust. *Academy of Management Review* 23: 387–392.

Sako, M. 1992. *Prices, quality and trust: Interfirm relationships in Britain and Japan.* Cambridge: Cambridge University Press.

Schaan, J.-L. 1983. *Parent control and joint venture success: The case of Mexico.* Unpublished PhD thesis, University of Western Ontario.

Schaan, J.-L. 1988. How to control a joint venture even as a minority partner. *Journal of General Management* 14: 4–16.

Schaan, J.-L., and Beamish, P. W. 1988. Joint venture general managers in LDCs. In *Cooperative strategies in international business,* ed. Contractor, F. J., and Lorange, P. 279–299. Lexington, MA: Lexington Book Co-operation.

Seabright, M. A., Levinthal, D. A., and Fichman, M. 1992. Role of individual attachments in the dissolution of interorganizational relationships. *Academy of Management Journal* 35: 122–160.

Shields, M. D. 1997. Research in management accounting by North American in the 1990's. *Journal of Management Accounting Research* 9: 3–61.

Simons, R. 1995. *Levers of control: How managers use innovative control systems to drive strategic renewal.* Boston, MA: Harvard Business School Press.

Spender, J.-C. 1989. *Industry recipes: An enquiry into the nature and sources of managerial judgement.* Oxford: Basil Blackwell.

Stopford, J. M., and Haberich, K. O. 1976. Ownership and control of foreign operations. *Journal of General Management* 3: 141–167.

Tomkins, C. 2001. Interdependencies, trust and information in relationships, alliances and networks. *Accounting, Organizations and Society* 26: 161–191.

Van der Meer-Kooistra, J., and Kamminga, P. E. 2008. Dynamics in joint ventures: The influence of changes within parent companies. Working paper.

Van der Meer-Kooistra, J., and Vosselman, E. G. J. 2000. Management control of interfirm transactional relationships: The case of industrial renovation and maintenance. *Accounting, Organizations and Society* 25: 51–77.

Van der Meer-Kooistra, J., and Vosselman, E. G. J. 2008. Management control, path dependencies and trust building in interfirm transactional relationships. Working paper.

Vosselman, E. G. J., and Van der Meer-Kooistra, J. 2006. Efficiency seeking behaviour in structuring management control in interfirm transactional relationships: An extended transaction cost economics perspective. *Journal of Accounting and Organizational Change* 2: 123–143.

Vosselman, E. G. J., and Van der Meer-Kooistra, J. 2009. Accounting for control and trust building in interfirm transactional relationships. *Accounting, Organizations and Society* 34: 267–283.

Williamson, O. E. 1985. *The economic institutions of capitalism: Firms, markets, relational contracting.* New York: The Free Press.

Williamson, O. E. 1996. *The mechanisms of governance.* Oxford: Oxford University Press.

Yan, A. 1998. Structural stability and reconfiguration of international joint ventures. *Journal of International Business Studies* 29: 773–798.

Yan, A., and Gray, B. 1994. Bargaining power, management control, and performance in United States–China joint ventures: A comparative case study. *Academy of Management Journal* 37: 1478–1517.

Yan, A., and Zeng, M. 1999. International joint venture instability: A critic of previous research, a reconceptualization, and directions for future research. *Journal of International Business Studies* 30: 395–412.

6 Accounting in Inter-Organisational Relationships within the Public Sector

Kalle Kraus and Cecilia Lindholm

1 INTRODUCTION

This chapter is about accounting in inter-organisational relationships within the public sector. Its purpose is to thoroughly review previous research on the subject as well as to provide novel empirical and theoretical insights. During the past few decades, public sector organisations have been subject to several significant and parallel trends. In isolation, each transformation accentuates the complexity and heterogeneity of these organisations. In combination, though, these transformations are indicative of the major challenges facing actors aiming to govern, control, and account for public sector activities, as the trends are contradictory when it comes to the definition and articulation of organisational boundaries.

The first trend, associated with a need to reduce organisational boundaries, is the response to an explicit request to create inter-organisational cooperation within the public sector. The second trend, frequently labelled "the New Public Management" (NPM) in the research literature, promotes the market and the privately owned business enterprise as a role model for public sector organisations. Public sector organisations are required to consider financial targets, cost-efficiency, and performance-based payments on a daily basis. In contrast to a development towards inter-organisational cooperation, however, the NPM movement emphasises the need to maintain organisational boundaries, because it is necessary to distinguish the specialised units within organisational hierarchies in the public sector. However, the incongruence of the creation of specialised units with separate budgets and the emphasis on the need for cooperation is creating considerable and interesting tensions. Public sector organisations are simultaneously required to meet "the drive to calculate activities of various professionals in terms of a single financial figure and the drive to reform public services by various forms of cooperative working." (Kurunmäki and Miller 2006, p. 88).

Inter-Organisational Cooperation

Since the 1990s there has been increased attention on cooperation as a means to achieve more effective and efficient public sector services, both in financial terms and in terms of quality (Jones 1999; Deakin 2002; Klijn 2002; Kurunmäki and Miller 2006; Lambert and Lapsley 2006; Miller et al. 2008). Boyne et al. (2001) described the importance of the joining up of public units within the same hierarchy and between public units from different hierarchies. According to Miller et al. (2008), different terms for governments, such as "joined up", "connected", and "networked", and even "whole-of-government", have given voice to widely shared political aspirations to resolve diverse problems within the areas of health and social care.

The need for inter-organisational cooperation has been justified in several ways and various arguments have been presented with the intention of promoting inter-organisational solutions. A frequently expressed notion favouring inter-organisational cooperation is based on a need to increase the efficiency of society's overall use of its resources. It is considered highly inefficient that two care providers perform the same tasks simultaneously, for example. Another important argument is that inter-organisational cooperation is particularly vital when it comes to the care of those citizens who are most vulnerable, such as the frail elderly and those with mental illnesses. These people often have complex needs requiring both health and social care, and it is unacceptable that they, or their relatives, "find themselves in the no man's land between health and social services" (Miller et al. 2008, p. 959).

Intra-Organisational Efficiency

In accordance with the NPM movement, decentralisation, specialisation, financial targets, and performance-based payments have become a prominent part of everyday life for managers and their personnel in the public sector (Hood 1991). It is also evident that savings and budgets have been shrinking at an accelerated rate and that the climate and discussions in the public sector are increasingly dominated by financial issues and a need for thriftiness and that more weight has been given to achieving a balanced budget when evaluating the performance of public units (Olson et al. 2001). In effect, there has been an increase in the use of intra-organisational accounting-based controls in the public sector (Hood 1991; Olson et al. 1998; Abernethy et al. 2007). A study of NPM systems in eleven different nations revealed that the implementation and experiences of NPM reforms differed between countries (Olson et al. 1998) with differences in national traditions and characteristics giving rise to a wide diversity of practice. Comparative studies show that Sweden, New Zealand, Australia, and the UK are countries where NPM

ideas have had a large impact (Hood 1995; Laughlin and Pallot 1998).
Hence, with respect to national differences, the development in the public sector has been towards more specialised units with separate budgets,
with the NPM reforms being interpreted as attempts at constructing public sector units and organisations with clear boundaries (Brunsson and
Sahlin-Andersson 2000).

Accountability and Professions

In addition to the parallel and incongruent requests for inter-organisational cooperation and intra-organisational efficiency, we recognise that
actors engaged in performing operative and professional tasks in many
public sector organisations are guided by norms and values that are, on
the whole, developed outside organisational hierarchies and within nonaccounting professions. Studies have shown that actors within health and
social care are, to a large extent, governed by fundamental ideas about
what constitutes good and legitimate health and social care. As members
of different professions, they perceive themselves to be accountable to
such ideas, particularly when it comes to balancing competing obligations, including moral ones (Sinclair 1995; Boland and Schulze 1996).
The connection between understanding the construction of accountability and the ability to govern and control activities within a highly professionalised context is vital.

With this in mind, in addition to a literature review, the chapter will
further elaborate on the construction of three different forms of accountability within domestic health and social care for the elderly. To enhance
the understanding of this elusive concept, we will use an in-depth case
study of domestic care of the elderly in Sweden, illustrating the construction of *professional accountability, managerial accountability,
and inter-organisational accountability.* Professional accountability is
the sense of duty that one experiences as a member of a professional or
expert group (Sinclair 1995, p. 229); it is mainly governed by professional norms and values. The construction of managerial accountability,
in contrast, emanates from the focus on intra-organisational efficiency.
Finally, inter-organisational accountability considers the need for inter-
organisational cooperation between health and social care providers. By
studying the construction of these three separate, but interconnected,
processes of accountability, we will draw upon a previously expressed
interest in the accountability literature, stressing that the need to study
the construction of accountability is accentuated as the development of
new business practices takes place (Munro and Hatherly 1993) or as
novel organisational forms spring up (Lindkvist and Llewellyn 2003).

It is worth emphasising that the parallel focuses on inter-organisational cooperation and intra-organisational efficiency as well as
the importance of professions and accountability have implications

for the discussion on accounting in inter-organisational relationships within the public sector. It becomes vital to study the simultaneous operation of, as well as the linkages between, intra- and inter-organisational accounting (Mouritsen et al. 2001). Kraus and Lind (2007) have argued that research on intra- and inter-organisational accounting has mainly been developed independently and that there is a need for integration.

We will now continue this chapter with a literature review on accounting in inter-organisational relationships within the public sector. In the third section, we elaborate on the distinctive character and conditions of public sector organisations, drawing particularly on the academic discussion on professions in general, and on different forms of accountability in particular. The fourth section presents novel empirical findings in a case study of domestic care of the elderly and the final section presents conclusions and implications.

2 LITERATURE REVIEW ON ACCOUNTING IN INTER-ORGANISATIONAL RELATIONSHIPS WITHIN THE PUBLIC SECTOR

The work reviewed here is from a significant set of accounting journals, but it does not cover the public management and administration journals. The reviewed journals are: *Accounting, Auditing and Accountability Journal; Accounting Forum; Accounting, Organizations and Society; British Accounting Review; Critical Perspectives of Accounting; European Accounting Review; Financial Accountability and Management;* and *Management Accounting Research.* We review these journals from 1990 to 2008. In total, thirty-five articles fall into our area of interest. The articles are grouped in Table 6.1.

The overall themes in the articles were related to different ways of organising the public sector and different approaches to delivering public sector services. Most of the articles, thirty-one in total, discussed the outsourcing of public sector services. Essentially, the plan is to retain public financing of welfare services, but the system of service provision is to be changed through outsourcing and the creation of public-private partnerships (PPP). Outsourcing and PPP are both in line with the ideas underlying the NPM reforms, with the private sector becoming more involved in provision of public sector services because the public sector was seen as being too large, inefficient, ineffective, and unresponsive to change. Thus, the size of the governing bodies should be reduced through privatisation and the outsourcing of many public services to private firms wherever possible.

Four of the articles discussed the straightforward outsourcing of public sector services to the private sector (Roodhooft and Warlop 1999;

Johnsen et al. 2004; Smith et al. 2005; Barton 2006). Roodhooft and Warlop (1999), for example, used an experiment with hospital managers to analyse the role of sunk costs and asset specificity in the outsourcing of catering for patients in Belgian hospitals. Barton (2006) examined the motivation for and operation of commercial-in-confidence outsourcing contracts in Australia. He focused on the reasons why governments engage in outsourcing of the provision of public sector services. All four studies focused on the decision to outsource and the role of the contract. Another aspect that these articles had in common was the fact that they paid no attention to the connections between intra- and inter-organisational accounting, or to how inter-organisational accounting was used in the ongoing inter-organisational relationships that were being established when public sector services were outsourced.

Table 6.1 The Reviewed Articles

Theme	Number of Articles	Authors
Outsourcing	4	Roodhooft and Warlop (1999); Johnsen et al. (2004); Smith et al. (2005); Barton (2006)
Public-private partnerships	27	Broadbent et al. (1996); Froud et al. (1998); McSweeney and Duncan (1998); Shaoul (1998); Broadbent and Laughlin (1999); Hodges and Mellett (1999); Mayston (1999); Froud and Shaoul (2001); Torres and Pina (2001); Broadbent and Laughlin (2002); Grimsey and Lewis (2002); Baker (2003); Broadbent et al. (2003); Broadbent and Laughlin (2003a, b); Edwards and Shaoul (2003); English and Guthrie (2003); Froud (2003); Heald (2003); Newberry and Pallot (2003); Rutherford (2003); Broadbent and Laughlin (2005); Shaoul (2005); English (2007); Broadbent and Guthrie (2008)
Network-like structures	2	Jones (1999); Newberry and Barnett (2001)
Inter-organisational cooperation between different types of professions in the public sector	2	Kurunmäki and Miller (2006); Miller et al. (2008)

Public-Private Partnerships

One special form of outsourcing is the PPP. This is an agreement whereby public sector bodies enter into long-term contractual arrangements with private sector entities to deliver public services. A total of twenty-seven of the articles reviewed dealt with the issue of PPPs. Broadbent and Laughlin (2003b, p. 334) defined the PPP as "an approach to delivering public services that involves the private sector, but one that provides for a more direct control relationship between the public and the private sector than would be achieved by a simple (legally-protected) market-based and arms-length purchase." In essence, this means that the PPP is not pure outsourcing, as described by Roodhooft and Warlop (1999), Johnsen et al. (2004), Smith et al. (2005) and Barton (2006). The service provision in a PPP needs to be long-term and relational. Each PPP involves the private sector supplying services to the public sector in exchange for a stream of payments over an extended period, often between twenty-five and sixty years (Lambert and Lapsley 2006). Underpinning the partnership will be a framework contract, which sets out the rules of the game; the government retains ultimate responsibility.

PPPs are a refinement of the private financing initiatives (PFI) for infrastructure that started in the UK in the early 1990s as an explicit attempt to engage more extensively with the private sector.[1] PFI and PPP are often used interchangeably in the literature. Lambert and Lapsley (2006) reviewed the literature on PPPs, examining their ontological and epistemological underpinnings, as well as reporting the central issues dealt with in the articles. They noted that the appraisal process for PPPs is a central issue in the literature, with the focus being on value for money issues and affordability. Another important concern is that of accounting disclosure, that is, whether the PPP project should appear on the balance sheet of the purchaser, the operator, both, or neither. PPP has promoted the public sector delivery of services by the private sector, but as Broadbent and Guthrie (2008) noted, while it is said that the services are achieved in partnership, in practical terms the essence of the approach is that the private sector is contracted to deliver public services that are funded by taxation revenue. In this way, partnerships can be seen to be a method by which the government can procure public sector services. This means that the government is increasingly perceived as procurers and regulators of services, rather than as the providers (Edwards and Shaoul 2003). The same is also true of the individual government agencies. Thus, there is often little by way of a partnership element and, consequently, the studies give limited details of day-to-day cooperative work practices.

Network-Like Structures

Two of the reviewed articles discussed network-like structures and compared them to traditional bureaucratic ways of organising the public sector

(Jones 1999; Newberry and Barnett 2001). Jones (1999) discussed the introduction of the internal market to the NHS (National Health Service). This created a hybrid form of market, where formerly integrated functions were decoupled and transformed to become the partners of inter-organisational relationships. The author proposed that aspects of the internal market and functioning within hospital units were suited to a network style of organisation. He analysed differences between hierarchy and network organisational forms, in terms of structure/culture, nature of outputs, and resource allocation and control. He also described inter-organisational networks in the NHS on the basis of a case study of a large UK acute general hospital and found that continuity of personnel and informal networks bridged the purchaser-provider market. However, as a result of the former close relationship between particular districts and hospitals, and their mutual interest in supporting and developing quality health care in particular districts, it was natural to organise the treatment of patients within the area, almost regardless of the existence of lower prices in less convenient locations. The quasi-market function did not, therefore, work as expected. In this respect, Jones (1999, p. 170) noted: "However, prior interpersonal relationships continued to be persuasive in, if not dominate, the selection of provider." He also found informal clinical networks that exercised an important role in inter-organisational networks and remained essentially outside direct management control.

After reviewing thirty-three of the thirty-five articles in Table 6.1, we note that lots of effort is put into investigating ex ante decisions such as whether to outsource and ex post evaluations of whether a particular cooperation has been efficient and effective. It is noteworthy that there is little discussion of ongoing day-to-day cooperation between interdependent public sector units/organisations and the role of accounting therein. The delivery of many public sector services is interdependent. Elderly people, for example, have needs spanning organisational and professional boundaries and, in the provision of these services, different organisations need to cooperate. The last two articles deal with this type of inter-organisational cooperation.

The Modernising Government Agenda and Cooperation between Health and Social Services

Kurunmäki and Miller (2006) and Miller et al. (2008) used the same empirical material to discuss the Modernising Government agenda. They first described the aspirations of the reformers and subsequently explored how the agenda has been articulated and made operable in a range of locales, based on fieldwork in five sites. The aim of the reformers was to promote intense and innovative cooperative working as a way of replacing the existing fragmented public sector service provision. In the two articles, the cooperation between health and social services, with separate histories and professional identities, was analysed. The Health Act 1999 aimed to strengthen formal working in partnerships, both within the NHS and between the NHS and local authorities. The aim was to strengthen the partnership working between health and social care, and to encourage innovative, cross-sectoral working. Three ways for better inter-organisational relationships were specified, called "flexibilities": the pooling of budgets, the delegating of commissioning responsibilities to a lead organisation, and the integrating of health and social service provider functions. The use of the "flexibilities" requires the partners to make formal notifications to the department of health, in which they specify the intended aims, objectives, and targets of the partnership project, as well as its governance arrangements. There is a requirement to establish systems for the measurement of governance and performance that provide an account of the improved performance provided by the arrangement.

Pooled budgets allow the health and social services to bring together resources, from different budgets in a discrete fund, to pay for services when a combination of health and social care is required. This means that, at the outset, the organisations need to agree upon the full range of services to be purchased and provided from the fund. Lead commissioning allows either authority to take responsibility for commissioning a range of services and therefore ensures that one authority or the other has the responsibility for the coordination and management of the services for a certain groups of clients. Integrated provision implies that services are provided under a single management structure, thereby offering integrated services from just one provider rather than many. In addition, a new organisational form was introduced, that of the "Care Trust", for partnership working. Care Trusts are used to form legal bodies to commission and take responsibility for all local health and social care.

From the case studies reported in Kurunmäki and Miller (2006) and Miller et al. (2008), it can be seen that cooperation was difficult to implement in practice. The choice of appropriate measures and interpretation of their results was complicated. There was disagreement between service providers and policymakers about whether the monitoring should be focused on the use of formal partnership arrangements or on the outputs and outcomes for the users of the cooperative working. Even though many service providers wanted outcome measures, defined as benefits to users, it proved to be very difficult to develop joined-up performance measures across organisational boundaries. There was also tension between social services staff and health care representatives about the appropriate use of resources and the means of reporting outcomes; there was a conflict between different professional identities. An additional complicating factor was that national targets were almost exclusively focused on function, that is, they were set for individual organisations. This made local development slow as a new approach was required at a national level. One important conclusion was that policymakers on a national level wanted more cooperation, but they still measured the organisations separately. In addition, how the cooperation might be achieved in detail was never specified, nor was the way that appropriate joined-up performance measures might be designed. These factors explained the difficulty in achieving well-functioning cooperation at a local level.

Conclusions from the Literature Review

A recurrent theme in our literature review was the role of accounting and management control in new forms of organisational structures for delivering public sector services, namely, outsourcing, PPP, and networks. In total, thirty-three of the thirty-five articles are concerned with describing and analysing the organisational structures and the implications that the adoption of such structures has for accounting. However, little attention is paid to how inter-organisational accounting is used in the ongoing inter-organisational relationships that are created when public sector services are outsourced. Further, linkages between intra- and inter-organisational accounting are not examined and the studies do not elaborate on the distinctive characteristics of public sector organisations, such as the existence of strong professions.

The two recent studies by Kurunmäki and Miller (2006) and Miller et al. (2008) can be seen as attempts to start to fill these gaps. These authors observed conflicts between different professional identities, manifested in a tension between social services staff and health care representatives about the appropriate use of resources and the means of reporting outcomes. They also touched upon linkages between intra- and inter-organisational accounting and the difficulty of developing seamless performance measures across organisational boundaries when national targets were almost exclusively set for individual organisations. However, the main focus in the two studies is on a general policy level. There are no detailed accounts of day-to-day inter-organisational work practices and no attempts were made to theorise about the observed conflicts between different professional identities.

We conclude that there is a need for in-depth empirical descriptions of inter-organisational accounting practices and their connections to actual work practices. This conclusion is supported by recent reviews of accounting in inter-organisational relationships that show that, almost without exception, the empirical material comes from the private sector (Håkansson and Lind 2007; Kraus and Lind 2007). These empirical descriptions should include an appreciation of the connections between intra- and inter-organisational accounting. In addition, there is little attempt to theorise about the working of inter-organisational accounting in public sector organisations and the notion of professions, for example, by focusing on different forms of accountability. There has been particular interest in how special characteristics of public sector organisations have implications for the understanding of management accounting within the organisations (see, e.g., Hofstede 1981; Anthony and Young 1988; Abernethy et al. 2007). There is reason to believe that these special characteristics also have implications for the understanding of accounting in inter-organisational relationships within the public sector.

In an attempt to fill these empirical and theoretical gaps as well as stressing the connection between the use of accounting and actors' construction of accountability within the public sector, the rest of the chapter will be spent on providing novel empirical and theoretical insights on the subject.

3   THEORETICAL ADVANCEMENTS— INTER-ORGANISATIONAL COOPERATION, ACCOUNTABILITY, AND PROFESSIONS IN HEALTH AND SOCIAL CARE

Emphasising the need for inter-organisational cooperation in health and social care to enhance efficiency and quality is not a controversial standpoint. Creating methods and procedures to manage and control such cooperation, on the other hand, is much more troublesome. Therefore, recognition of the connection between the intra- and inter-organisational means of control and actors' construction of accountability is crucial to enhancing understanding and knowledge of health and social care.

From an academic point of view, health and social care represent some of society's most complex fields. They are politically sensitive in the extreme and are governed by multiple and often conflicting goals, such as achieving a "high level of safety" and "good quality of care" along with "cost-efficiency" goals that are sometimes as hard to define and evaluate as they are to combine. Another most vital characteristic is that dominant professions, particularly the medical profession in health care, control complex core operating processes empowered by the professionals' autonomy and knowledge (Abernethy et al. 2007). In the literature, these characteristics are used to explain why health care organisations are particularly challenging to manage and control. In an inter-organisational context, these challenges are further accentuated as actors' behaviour is guided not only by professional norms and values, but also by norms developed within different organisational cultures (Empson 2004).

Construction of Accountability

Theoretical discussions on accountability offer almost as many definitions as there are authors engaged in the debate. Most of the definitions emanating from the work of sociologists and ethnomethodologists recognise a need or willingness as well as a capacity for human actors to explain and justify their actions and decisions (Garfinkel 1967;

Silverman 1975; Silverman and Jones 1976; Munro and Hatherly 1993; Boden 1994). Thus, accountability involves both how the actors perceive different and often competing obligations, including moral ones, as well as the ways and methods used to explain conduct with a story understood and accepted by other actors within and outside an organisation (Boland and Schulze 1996). In this 'process view', the construction of accountability is continuous and perpetual, that is, explaining and giving accounts is what everyday activities are all about. Accountability is "a chronic feature of daily conduct" (Giddens 1979, p. 57; Roberts and Scapens 1985, p. 448).

Accounting researchers have further elaborated on this definition, focusing on the connection between the accounting system and the construction of accountability (Roberts and Scapens 1985; Sinclair 1995; Ahrens 1996a, 1996b; Boland and Schulze 1996; Ahrens and Chapman 2002). In an early contribution, by making a distinction between the accounting system and the system of accountability, Roberts and Scapens (1985) established that accounting is not merely a technique to calculate and measure financial resources and financial outcomes. The most intriguing perspective on accounting derives from its capacity to transform and construct the way actors perceive one another, the environment, and themselves (see, e.g., Hopwood and Miller 1994; Munro and Mouritsen 1996).

The majority of the academic debate on accountability pivots on an analysis of different methods used to explain and justify daily conduct, that is, of the methods used to assist in decision making and the actions taken that are visible to other actors. In the literature on this topic, the ability to use numerical accounts is considered more powerful than the use of narrative accounts (Miller and O'Leary 1987; Roberts 1991; Munro 1996). That means that an actor who can substantiate his/her arguments with, for example, accounting figures is considered to be more convincing than the actor using narrative accounts alone. In this respect, Munro (1996, p. 3) claims that "we appear as a society obsessed with targets and outcomes". In some research traditions, mainly based on the work of Foucault, accounting calculations have also been found to be important means to discipline and control actors in organisations as well as society (Miller and O'Leary 1987).

Despite the obvious focus on different methods of creating and ensuring visibility, it is important to notice that the mere creation of visibility by the production of accounting figures is a necessary but not sufficient procedure in different processes of accountability. The construction of accountability, the way an actor perceives obligations and demands, presupposes that accounting numbers are activated, that is, used and drawn upon in social interactions and relations. Accounting figures have to be interwoven with narrative accounts if they are to be incorporated in an actor's construction of accountability (Robson 1992; Munro 1993). Munro (1993, p. 256) argues that "accounting data is brought to life through accountability".

That means that there is an interplay between visibility and accounting on the one hand and accountability and social conduct on the other.

Professions and Professional Accountability

The concept of professional accountability is associated with the sense of duty that one has as a member of a professional or expert group, and thus, conversely, a sense of duty is pivotal to the construction of professional accountability; professional accountability requires expertise and professional integrity (Sinclair 1995, p. 229). The concept of "membership" is intrinsic to accountability (Garfinkel 1967; Munro and Hatherly 1993), as explanations and justifications of daily conduct made with the express purpose of legitimising actions and decisions are often directed towards members of the same groups (Roberts 1991; Jönsson 1996; Panozzo 1996). Membership is often at stake in accountability processes, as the inclusion and exclusion of actors is one method by which members of different groups are able to sanction others (Munro 1996, p. 4). In professional contexts, the connection between membership, both formal and informal, and accountability is of particular interest.

According to Abernethy and Stoelwinder (1995, p. 5), a person with a high professional orientation is one who primarily identifies with his/her professional group, is committed to developing and retaining the power and prestige of the profession, develops an abstract knowledge system, and looks to professional colleagues both within and outside the organisation for support. Abbott (1988, p. 8) defines professions as "exclusive occupational groups applying somewhat abstract knowledge to particular cases". According to this fairly general definition, a number of occupational groups within health care and the social services, such as nurses and paramedics, are considered "professions" or "semi-professions", in addition to the traditionally strong medical profession. During the past few decades, social work has strengthened its position as a recognised profession (Abbott 1988; Llewellyn 1998).

Professional knowledge is based on a systematic, scientific theory and the profession collectively, and the professional individually possesses a body of knowledge and a repertoire of behaviours and skills. Preparation for and induction into the profession is provided through a long-term and standardised education accompanied by practical training as the professional learns to perform complex tasks independently, gaining experience and expertise (Abernethy and Stoelwinder 1995). It is through this training that professional actors are socialised into the professional community where norms and values are created and shared. Within highly professionalised contexts, such as hospitals, behaviour is based on established codes of ethics and conduct as well as professional cultures (Abbott 1988). Furthermore, decisions and actions are governed by professional knowledge, which, where ongoing controls are concerned, makes the professional actor autonomous to some degree in relation to organisational rules and regulations. The degree of this autonomy is dependent upon the strength of the profession in relation to other professions (Abbott 1988).

Different Forms of Accountability in Health and Social Care

Professional accountability may come into conflict with other forms of accountability, however, for example, when professional actors are located within a hierarchy in which a superior calls to account a subordinate for inadequate performance of delegated duties (Sinclair 1995, p. 227). In the literature, this is sometimes referred to as a conflict between managerial and professional accountability (Sinclair 1995), a conflict between the professional model of control, discussed earlier, and administrative and bureaucratic control systems (Abernethy and Stoelwinder 1995). A professional actor has to make professional decisions and still pay respect to rules and regulations imposed on the actor within the accounting system, including control, budget restrictions, and ensuring that decisions make economic sense. Accounting systems are implicated in the relationship between professionals and organisations because these systems are designed and implemented to achieve intra-organisational criteria of efficiency; they are also often implemented with little concern for the unique aspects of the professional character of the actor's perceived duties (Abernethy and Stoelwinder 1995).

The NPM literature demonstrates that there are a number of ways to describe the competition between hierarchies and different forms of expertise. The tension between managerial and professional accountability has already been mentioned. Other ways to describe the conflict are that it is a battle between "costing and caring in the social services" (Llewellyn 1998) or the tension between the notions of professional and financial capital in the field of health care (Kurunmäki 1999). Traditionally, some norms and values are considered fundamental to the way professional actors construct accountability. In the medical professions, it is not considered to be acceptable or legitimate to make decisions that negatively affect people's health on the basis of financial considerations. Despite that, the NPM debate shows a number of examples where even a traditional profession like the medical one has been transformed to the extent that it sometimes is referred to as being "hybrid" (Kurunmäki 2004).

A particular source of conflict and competition between different forms of accountability is to be found in the fact that health care organisations are highly politicised. Politicians are assumed to take actions according to democratic rules and principles. The public, that is, the voters, have the opportunity and the obligation to affect the use of public resources through democratic methods (Rose 1991; Hood 1995). The organisation of health care and the social services is a political issue of enormous public concern. In this perspective, it is a prerequisite for democracy that the public has reliable methods of determining whether political decisions have had the intended effect or not.

To provide such methods, part of the construction of managerial account-ability includes the designing of accounting and control systems to measure performance and the implementation of political decisions.

Different forms of accountability are to be found in health and social care for different groups of actors, as well as for individual actors in dif-ferent roles. Sinclair (1995) discusses five forms of accountability that she identifies as guiding the actions of the chief executives of public sector organisations. Her study shows that these political, public, managerial, professional, and personal forms of accountability create multiple mean-ings for certain key concepts, like efficiency and quality of service, giving rise to conflict. She advocates the need for a new conception of account-ability and new approaches to enhancing it. We agree. In Section 4, we sub-stantiate the need for studies on the construction of accountability within an inter-organisational context, by illustrating with a case study.

Intra- vs. Inter-Organisational Accountability

Previous studies on the connection between accountability systems and the construction of accountability have focused on intra-organisational pro-cesses of accountability. Roberts and Scapens (1985) even argued that the concept of a 'system of accountability' was one way by which to define the boundary of an organisation: "To be part of an organisation is to be subject to that organisation's system of accountability: a customer is not account-able to someone within an organisation in the same way that an employee is accountable" (p. 448).

Later research within the same tradition is pivoted around the construc-tion of accountability within organisational boundaries. Ahrens (1996b) discussed the novel concept "style of accountability" as a heuristic device to explain notions of "good management" to which organisational members hold themselves and each other accountable, and developed two frame-works to relate management accounting to organisational processes of accountability. Ahrens and Chapman (2002) studied processes of account-ability by examining the performance measurement systems of a single organisation, and Conrad (2005) considered organisational change within the gas industry.

A discussion within the academic debate on accountability emanates from the distinction made by Roberts (1991) between hierarchical and socialising forms of accountability, relating, respectively, to work and inter-action. The request for alternatives to hierarchical accountability has some-times been referred to as horizontal (Gray et al. 1987) or as lateral (Munro and Hatherly 1993). They emphasise the need to study the construction and development of different forms of accountability within an intra-organisa-tional setting. Other researchers (see, e.g., Boland and Schulze 1996; Lind-kvist and Llewellyn 2003), developing and criticising Roberts's dichotomy, have also focused on intra-organisational processes. However, it has also been stressed that organisational development creates a need to explore the construction of new forms of accountability, sometimes referred to as a "new commercial agenda" (Munro and Hatherly 1993) or as new "organizational forms or contexts" (Lindkvist and Llewellyn 2003).

Our aim is to explore such novel forms of accountability and develop new insights to the construction of accountability within both intra- and inter-organisational settings. Like Ahrens and Chapman (2002), who studied micro-processes of accountability within an organisation, we are studying day-to-day interaction within and between two public sector organisations as a financial crisis develops.

4 EMPIRICAL ADVANCEMENTS—INTER-ORGANISATIONAL ACCOUNTING, ACCOUNTABILITY, AND DAY-TO-DAY COOPERATIVE WORK PRACTICES IN DOMESTIC CARE OF THE ELDERLY[2]

Care of the elderly is an area constantly increasing in importance as the number of older people in the population is growing continuously. At the same time, the elderly is a highly heterogeneous group and the needs of individuals for care and assistance in daily life vary enormously from one individual to another. In Sweden, public policy explicitly states that the elderly should be able to continue living independently in their own homes for as long as possible and, to achieve that goal, a range of services is provided by the public sector. Many public sector services are decentralised to the local government at the county and municipality level, which organises the services for the citizens (Olson and Sahlin-Andersson 2005).[3] Domestic care of the elderly involves both the municipality and the county, that is, two separate hierarchical organisations with separate but partly overlapping responsibilities are involved in the provision of care to the elderly, as well as having responsibility for their own financial management. Although counties are responsible for health care and municipalities are responsible for social care, inter-organisational cooperation between these two organisations is both an explicit requirement under Swedish law and a frequently expressed political aim, corresponding to the desire to enhance effectiveness in the use of the overall resources and to increase quality of life, both for the elderly and their relatives.

Domestic Health Care for the Elderly Provided by the Counties

Many elderly people living in their own homes need help with certain, sometimes quite specific, aspects of *health care*, for example, collecting and taking their medicine, taking eyedrops, and caring for wounds. Domestic health care is the responsibility of the county and is carried out by different health centres. Health care per se is characterised by professional groups of varying professional status, which, in their daily practices, are governed by norms and standards developed within the professions. In the health centres, assistant nurses, nurses, and doctors work with the provision of domestic health care for the elderly. The doctors are responsible for medication and make some home visits, but they do not normally have daily contact with the elderly. As one would imagine, nurses constitute a higher ranked professional group than assistant nurses and have responsibility for allocating the different tasks to be done to themselves or the assistant nurses. The assistant nurses can take a patient's pulse and a blood test, measure blood pressure, bandage wounds, and give insulin injections. In addition to being able to conduct the aforementioned tasks, which they can delegate, nurses can give injections, judge whether a pensioner needs to be sent to hospital or not, prescribe aids, and handle medicine.

Domestic Social Care for the Elderly Provided by the Municipalities

The municipality is responsible for providing domestic *social care* to the elderly. Pensioners might, for example, need help with personal hygiene, shopping for groceries, laundry, and cleaning. During the past fifteen years, several market-based forms of governance have developed. One prominent example of this is the purchaser/provider model. Aiming to increase efficiency, the purchaser unit and the provider units charged with home help services have separate budgets and income statements. The providers of social care are organised into a number of separate home help units, where each unit manager is responsible for his/her personnel and for keeping their activities within budgetary limits. In this process, the social care contract is vital. The social care service purchaser discusses the elderly person's social care needs with him or her and, thereafter, writes a social care contract. Based on the contract, the purchaser orders services from the home help unit. This unit gets a social care contract from the social care service purchaser specifying what help the pensioner is entitled to have and stating the total duration of the service. The payments to the home help units from the purchasers are calculated on the estimated duration of each operational activity in the social care contract. The intra-organisational relationship between the purchaser and provider uses the contract as a foundation to plan domestic care activities. The domestic social care is provided by home helps, a professional group characterised by a shorter than average education and a lower professional status than more traditional professions.

Organising Domestic Care for the Elderly—
A Cooperation between Health Care and Social Care

Domestic care of the elderly is not just a matter of how the health centre and the home help unit arrange the separate performance of their tasks. There are also important interdependencies in many work practices involving the pensioners' care because pensioners often have complex needs involving both health and social care, so the two units need to coordinate their tasks and cooperate. The boundaries of the two specialised units become blurred as representatives from different professional groups from the two different organisations deliver services in the pensioners' homes, often in interaction with the pensioners.

Politicians and top managers alike underscore the importance of inter-organisational cooperation in the domestic care of the elderly; as a result of which, the two organisations have reached an explicit agreement on the arrangement of such cooperation. The overall goals of the inter-organisational relationship have been agreed upon and are the same, no matter what hierarchical level is concerned. The goals are to use public financial resources efficiently and to increase the quality of care for the elderly by increasing the security and dignity of elderly people. One part of the agreement is to increase cooperation in the inter-organisational relationship between the home help unit and the health centre.

There are a number of inter-organisational work practices in the domestic care of the elderly. Firstly, some of the operational activities involved in the delivery of care to pensioners are interdependent because, for example, the tasks need to be conducted in a certain order. These work practices depend on home helps, assistant nurses, and nurses, and cooperation is required because the personnel involved need to coordinate and agree on the schedule for performing the tasks. This is the case with, for example, insulin injections (which are the responsibility of the assistant nurse) and assistance with meals (which is the responsibility of the home help) because meals need to be served shortly after an insulin shot has been given.

Secondly, certain inter-organisational work practices should be performed according to an inter-organisational agreement—a formal means of imposing inter-organisational control—between the municipality and the county. An important example is provided by the guidelines for authorisation. In the provision of domestic care to the elderly, authorisation is required for tasks delegated to a person who does not have the formal competence, but does have the actual competence needed to perform certain tasks. Authorisation is given by a person who has both the formal responsibility for and actual competence required to perform or supervise a task to the person who is to perform it. This means that the home helps are able to perform certain health care tasks in the pensioners' homes, such as giving medicine and ear- or eyedrops. A nurse from the health centre is responsible for writing the authorisation for the home help. The idea is that such authorisations will increase the quality and efficiency of the domestic care of the elderly, because the home helps can give the aforementioned treatment on authorisation when they are in the pensioners' homes providing social care. This means fewer people are required to visit the pensioners' homes because the assistant nurses do not need to come.

Thirdly, activities commonly referred to as grey-zone activities constitute an important part of the inter-organisational relationship between the provision of domestic health services and social care. In the inter-organisational relationship between the health centre and the home help unit, there are often operational activities that need to be performed, but no one really knows who is responsible for getting them done. Thus, grey zones are areas where the division of tasks and responsibilities between the home help unit and the health centre is vague. Picking up medicine from the pharmacy is the most common example.

We will now describe and analyse three periods of a real event which represent the stages of an intra-organisational financial crisis experienced within the home help units within the last ten years. The first period is before the economic crisis. The second one covers the time when a financial crisis was experienced by the home help units and people feared for their jobs and for the survival of the units, resulting in an increased focus on intra-organisational matters. The third period is after the economic crisis was over; the home help units have made it and the situation now is said to be stable.

Period 1—Before the Financial Crisis

During this period, work practices in the pensioners' homes were governed by professional norms and an explicit aim of increasing the quality of care provided for the elderly. To the professionals involved in the domestic care of the elderly, organisational membership played a secondary role. Instead, they expressed a feeling of accountability towards the pensioners as well as to other professionals.

Intra- and Inter-Organisational Accounting

During this period, accounting and other financial discussions were described as being rare where the domestic care of the elderly was concerned. Many interviewees described this period as "the good old days", and home help unit managers and home helps alike explained that financial aspects were not the focus of attention. This was so, despite the fact that the home help units had large budget deficits. The managers of the health centres and the home help units were not involved in coordinating the inter-organisational activities. "The coordination of the inter-organisational activities was normally solved by those working with the pensioner", one health centre manager said. This statement was supported by the other managers; the inter-organisational domain was not the concern of the managers. The managers from the home help units and the health centres did not meet to discuss cooperation, and the only formal means of ensuring inter-organisational control were the general guidelines for authorisation.

Daily activities involving interaction between different occupational groups were governed by professional norms and a notion that the needs of the elderly were prioritised whatever the expense. As one home help put it: "We home helps, assistant nurses and nurses discussed with each other the fact that we were a team taking care of the pensioners." One nurse explained: "It was a good feeling when we talked with the home helps. We all focused on the pensioners." The interviewees all stressed a general feeling of the important role played by the nurses. "The nurses were considered to see the whole picture, and to know what should be done and who should do it", one home help stated. The home helps all claimed that there was an unwritten code that reinforced the importance of seeing the nurses as informal managers who had the right to tell the home helps and assistant nurses what to do. One home help stated: "We should listen to the nurses and look up to them. This was often discussed by us and the assistant nurses." In terms of accountability, the home helps and the assistant nurses felt accountable to the occupational group with the highest professional status, the nurses.

Inter-Organisational Work Practices

All interviewees described the cooperation between the health centre and the home help unit as well-functioning. The home helps, assistant nurses, and nurses felt free to solve the cooperation issues in the pensioner's home, and discussed cooperation when they saw each other or solved problems over the phone. Daily coordination of interdependent tasks was said to function smoothly because the home helps largely adjusted their work to accommodate the nurses' wishes. For example, if a wound was to be bandaged by the nurse, a home help had to shower the pensioner before; and for this to happen, the nurse and the home help needed to agree on a time. One home help explained: "We often had pensioners with sores. Then I needed to cooperate with the nurse. I had to shower the pensioner before the nurse put on a new bandage. For this, we needed to agree on a time. I always adjusted my schedule so it matched the nurse's schedule. It functioned well."

Nurses and auxiliary staff all described the way that the nurses acted as "informal managers" in the performance of tasks. Nurses often grabbed home helps in the pensioners' homes and told them to go and get prescriptions for medication, even if it was an emergency prescription and the responsibility of the health centre, and they also frequently told the home helps to accompany the elderly people to the hospital. The home helps did not find the situation strange because they considered the nurses to be authorities who knew what should be done in the pensioners' homes.

The grey-zone activities were not described as problematic. "There were never any discussions. No one cared about who should do what", one home help said. Nurses and auxiliary staff all pointed out that everyone saw to the best interests of the patient and did what needed to be done in the pensioner's home. If something needed doing, it did not matter if it was written down on a social care contract or not, or whose responsibility it was. One home help said: "We did not find the grey zones to be problematic. It was not a question of our duty or the nurses' duty. We thought of the pensioner. If the pensioner needed salve, I just picked it up and saw to it that the pensioner used it."

Nurses and auxiliary staff described how the grey-zone activities were solved without problems because the nurses often decided who should do what. "This was not an issue; we could just ask the nurse who should do it and they told us", one assistant nurse said. The home helps claimed that the writing of authorisations did not always function well. Frequently the nurses were late with the annual renewal of the authorisations and they were often slow to write authorisations for new home helps. The home helps were giving medication[4] to the pensioners anyway, because the home helps did these tasks even if they had not yet received the authorisation. Everything worked smoothly. One home help explained: "If a pensioner needed medicine and we did not give it just because we had not yet received the authorisation, the pensioner would have to wait for it. And that would not have been good for the pensioner, of course, so we gave the medicine anyway."

Constructing Professional Accountability

This period is characterised by the way the actors perceive themselves to be accountable to the professional norms developed in interaction with different professional groups, regardless of organisational membership. The intra-organisational relationship between the home helps and the management level was of secondary importance, and daily activities were governed by professional norms as well as perceived obligations towards the individual pensioner. Financial discussions were not an issue within the intra-organisational relationship even though the home help units faced considerable financial deficits. Hence, the professional actors did not express accountability for financial performance or income statements as the budget was not claimed to be of importance within the intra-organisational relationship.

Daily operations within the provision of domestic care for the elderly were governed at the operative/professional level and demonstrate the way the professional actors construct accountability—in terms of professional norms and beliefs. An important part of the development of professional accountability arose from the ranking and status of different occupational groups. In practice, the nurses acted as informal managers and the other professional actors adapted their activities to facilitate the nurses' work. The most obvious example is that both the home helps and assistant nurses adapted their time schedules to fit in with the nurses' requirements.

The overall professional norm governing the actors' construction of accountability is explicitly stated as being the well-being of the pensioners. This is a moral obligation constantly referred to in the explanations and justifications given by the nurses and auxiliary staff in discussing their conduct during this period. The same norm is even used to justify the fact that home helps occasionally exceeded their authority and gave the pensioners their medicine without a formal written authorisation from the nurses. The pensioners' best interests were stated to be the common goal governing all professional actors during this period.

At this time, no particular attention was directed towards the fact that the professional actors were members of different organisational hierarchies, or that cooperation between the county and the municipality constitutes an inter-organisational relationship. Organisational boundaries were not articulated and were of much less importance than professional status. This becomes particularly clear when it comes to handling grey-zone activities. Both home helps and assistant nurses perceived themselves to be accountable to the higher ranked professionals.

Period 2—During the Financial Crisis

In contrast to the first period, this second one was characterised by a strong focus on financial matters and a shortage of financial resources in the municipality. Over time, the professional actors, in interaction with politicians and the top management levels within the intra-organisational relationship, constructed a system of managerial accountability, articulated organisational boundaries, and introduced a means of accounting and of measuring financial performance. The budget progressively became the dominant means of control within the intra-organisational relationship governing and controlling domestic care of the elderly.

Intra- and Inter-Organisational Accounting

After some time with increasing budget deficits, the politicians acted. They wanted change. At that time, the home help unit managers and home helps recognised this to be an economic crisis within the domestic care of the elderly. There was a need to take drastic actions to achieve balanced budgets. The newly appointed top manager described the new perspective as follows: "For our part, it was all about having a balanced budget for the district. A balanced budget was the issue; with lots of focus on attaining this. There was no talk about developing something new, that had to come later." In discussing how her performance was evaluated, one home help unit manager explained: "The three most important parameters when our performance was evaluated? Budget, budget, budget. . . ." The managers had monthly meetings with the home helps where they discussed how the unit was doing financially. The home helps were provided with a document on which they could see the actual revenues and costs for the unit so far during the year, and the prognoses for the whole budget year. The managers tried to stress the connection between the revenue for the home help unit and the home helps' salaries and explained how the revenue came from the purchasers in the social care service and was based on the social care contracts. In discussing the situation, one home help unit manager explained: "The home helps had to understand that 300 000 [Swedish kronor] taken away was one less home help in our unit. This connection between the budget and their salary was important. They also had to know that it is the social care contracts that give us the revenue. In this way the home helps had been forced to become interested in financial issues."

The health centre managers and the home help unit managers did not issue any formal means of inter-organisational control of their own. There was only the general inter-organisational control of providing authorisations. The home help unit managers wanted to have meetings with the health centre managers, but argued that it was hard to find time for such meetings because they had to concentrate so much on their own financial situation. Issues related to cooperation were not in the picture. "We wanted to meet with the managers of the health centre, but nothing happened", one home help unit manager said. The health centre managers also talked about the need to have meetings with the home help unit managers. "But the relationship was so frosty and they were focusing so much on their internal activities", one health centre manager argued.

Home helps, assistant nurses, and nurses stated that there were two clear groups in the pensioners' homes. The home helps comprised one group, and the assistant nurses and nurses the other. It was clear that the two groups had different organisational loyalties. The home helps belonged to the home help unit and felt responsible for social care; the assistant nurses and nurses belonged to the health centre and felt responsible for health care. One home help explained: "In our home help group we said to each other that we should help the nurses by giving medicine on authorisation, but we should not take orders from them or run errands, or adjust our schedule all the time. We felt responsible for social care and not health care."

Inter-Organisational Work Practices

All interviewees from both the health centres and the home help units described the existence of a negative atmosphere between the home helps on the one hand and the assistant nurses and nurses on the other. There were often discussions about what the respective responsibilities of the home help unit and the health centre were. Both home helps and nurses emphasised the difficulty of coordinating interdependent activities. There was often disagreement on setting up a suitable time frame if a sore was to be bandaged by the nurse. One home help said: "The disagreements about the schedules created a bad climate between us and the nurses all the time.

And it was bad for the pensioner. Sometimes tasks were not carried out because we could not agree on a suitable time. But the nurses had to take their responsibility; we could not adjust our schedule all the time."

Nurses and auxiliary staff all gave examples of pensioners not getting their sores taken care of properly because of bad coordination. Sometimes pensioners who needed to take insulin ate breakfast too late because of a breakdown in the communication between the nurses and the home helps.

The grey zones were described as problematic and a source of annoyance. In particular, getting medicine from the pharmacy did not work well. "This had been a grey zone for such a long time", one home help claimed. Both home helps and nurses argued that the grey-zone tasks were often not carried out on time, and could even be delayed for many days. Pensioners sometimes had to wait for important medicine and salves. One assistant nurse explained: "It was really bad. Sometimes a pensioner did not get medicine on time because no one fetched it: We did not talk to each other, or there was a misunderstanding. We must communicate better with the home helps and we needed guidelines for the grey zones. We blamed them and they blamed us."

Everyone wanted clearer guidelines about responsibilities so that the grey zones could be eliminated. The authorisations were described by the home helps as being problematic. The writing of authorisations was often done too late and they claimed that giving medication sometimes took a considerable amount of time. The home helps gave medication, but they could be inflexible if something went wrong. The home helps claimed that they often denied the right to give medication if the pensioner had messed up the doses. One home help described: "If something was wrong with the medicine, we told the nurses—they had to fix it. It was not our responsibility." The assistant nurses and nurses emphasised that the home helps were not flexible. If the sign-off list was missing, or if something was wrong with the medicine, the home helps sometimes decided not to give the medication, and often without telling the nurses.

Constructing Managerial Accountability

This period was characterised by explicit articulation of organisational boundaries and the increasing importance of the intra-organisational relationships between the professional and management levels within the municipality. The management increased its control of daily activities performed by the professionals, and of major importance in this process is the construction of a new form of accountability by the nurses and auxiliary staff—managerial accountability focusing on budgetary issues and financial awareness.

Within the intra-organisational relationships, arguments emanating from the vocabulary used in accounting and finance were frequently used. The case description shows a distinct shift in use of language as the concepts and categories developed within the accounting system and used in the interaction between the professional and managerial level were pushed further down the organisation. The most obvious example is how the budget and the need to fulfil its requirements became the main argument in the interaction between home helps and their managers. It is also striking how the managers enhanced the home helps' understanding of the financial situation by using concepts they could easily relate to—their own salaries.

At this time the social care contract became an important account that, for control purposes, came to be used in conjunction with the budget in the intra-organisational relationship. The management emphasised the fact that the contract was the basis for the receipt of revenue. An important aspect of the construction of managerial accountability was that the professional actors perceived themselves to be accountable to the contract and to the explicit orders given within this document. If the home help unit received more social care contracts from the purchasing unit, this meant an increase in revenue, which could easily be translated into salaries and new employees. A budget deficit, on the other hand, was easily translated into reductions in the service that could be given and redundancies.

From an inter-organisational point of view, the actors' construction of managerial accountability resulted in the enforcement of organisational boundaries and in their use as a means of satisfying budget requirements and for avoiding financial shortfalls. Obviously, the best way to reduce expenditure was to lay the tasks to be performed at the door of the other organisation. Clear manifestations of the changes in accountability during this second period are to be found in the way that professional actors handled activities defined as being in the grey zones, as well as in the transformation of the nurses' role. Their previous role as informal managers changed as the home helps started to follow formal rules and "go by the book". During the financial crisis, the aim of protecting their own financial situation outweighed the advantages of cooperation and of attempting to identify more flexible solutions. As a consequence, even the well-being of the pensioners came second. Pensioners were sometimes left without their medication as the home helps struggled to gain control of their working hours. Time is considered a valuable resource within health and social care because it easily translates into monetary terms.

As the organisations started to pay attention to their boundaries, the willingness for inter-organisational cooperation decreased; this was particularly the case in the grey zones, where the allocation of tasks and scheduling had previously been solved by finding informal solutions and making adaptations. The grey zones become increasingly problematic. In this period, as well as the previous one, there was no interaction between the top management levels of the two organisations, albeit for different reasons. During the first period, there was no need for top-level interaction, as daily activities were conducted smoothly by finding informal solutions on an operational and professional level. In the second period, the interviewees expressed a lack of interest in inter-organisational matters. One important exception, illustrating conflicting forms of accountability, was the professional actors' request for formal guidelines and an inter-organisational agreement on how to handle the grey zones. The conflict is to be found in the actors' construction of professional accountability, focusing on the well-being of the individual pensioner, and the construction of managerial accountability, focusing on the need to reduce the home help unit's expenditure. An inter-organisational agreement emanating from higher levels of the organisational hierarchies was claimed to be the way to resolve this moral dilemma.

Period 3—After the Financial Crisis

This period was characterised by achieving a balanced budget in both organisations and an increasing interest in the inter-organisational relationship. Once again, daily coordination worked well and the different professional groups made mutually convenient adjustments to their schedules and helped each other. Formal means of control and clear routines were developed within the inter-organisational relationship and the professional actors expressed accountability towards the inter-organisational relationship. The outcome in this period illustrates the construction of inter-organisational accountability.

Intra- and Inter-Organisational Accounting

For some time now, the district as a whole had had a balanced budget, including the services responsible for the domestic care of the elderly. "This is very important. If the budget is unbalanced, there will always be a dark cloud hanging over you, taking all your time and energy", one controller argued. Everyone stressed how hard work was required to continue to maintain balanced budgets. As one home help put it: "We have survived our financial crisis and now things have stabilised. But for how long?" The managers of the health centres and the home help units had jointly agreed on a number of formal means of imposing inter-organisational control, to complement the general guidelines for authorisation. In addition, a task group was set up, which all managers mentioned as being positive for the inter-organisational relationship. The task group, comprised of managers and nurses from the health centres and managers from the home help units, had meetings approximately four times a year. These meetings provided a forum for discussing problems affecting the relationship, and gave the managers a chance to exchange important information. Here, too, issues falling between the health centres and the home help units were discussed, that is, the grey zones. A summary of the discussions held and the decisions taken during the meetings were written down and distributed to the nurses and auxiliary staff. One home help unit manager said: "The task group has developed very well. It is important that we introduce this throughout the entire district since health centres work with different home help units. Even though we have some grey zones left, the task group improves cooperation."

This was supported by the health centre managers; as one of them put it: "The task group is very interesting. Our health centre works with two districts, and we only have a task group in one. In this area we have an effective structure, working very well and, in addition, my nurses meet the home helps regularly. It is very important to have cooperation. The task group is very beneficial, and, importantly, I think this is the key to why the cooperation works so much better in this district."

The managers also required the home helps and nurses to meet once a month at the home help unit. Each nurse should talk to the home helps that attended to his/her domestic health care patients and both the home helps and the nurses were instructed to inform each other in advance about which pensioners they wanted to discuss so everyone could come prepared. Any changes in the condition of the pensioners that either the nurse or the home helps had noticed was to be discussed; for example, it could be the case that a pensioner had started to lose weight.

In addition, the managers required the nurses to use a common authorisation form throughout the district. This specified the different types of authorisation in a systematic and easily readable way so that the home helps knew what they were required to do. There were also specified routines for the authorisation procedure. The home help unit managers were required to call the nurses when a new home help had been hired and needed to be instructed by the nurses. A few nurses at each health centre were responsible for writing these authorisations and for instructing the home helps, which was done at the health centre. In addition, there were routines for the annual renewal of authorisations. A nurse should then come to the home help unit and renew the authorisations for a number of home helps at the same time.

Home helps, assistant nurses, and nurses all expressed that a common understanding had been developed between them and said that cooperation should be important when taking care of the elderly. There was pressure to be flexible and a need to be willing to help one another. One home help explained: "I feel the pressure from my fellow home helps and from the nurses to help the assistant nurses and nurses. It is vital for the pensioner that cooperation works well." The assistant nurses and nurses agreed and stressed that there was a general feeling in the group that cooperation was important and should be handled in a helpful and flexible manner. "Everyone seems to believe that cooperation is a pleasure and important. I often talk to my colleagues about this and we all agree", one assistant nurse said. The home helps said they did not feel that the nurses pushed them around, or pointed out that they were better educated. Rather, there was a norm that reinforced the importance of helping each other and of not thinking too much about who belong to which organisation. One home help claimed: "It feels like we all care for the pensioners; we do different things. We deal with the social care and they take care of the health care, but they do not look at us as if we were lesser professionals, as I have heard is the case in many districts."

Inter-Organisational Work Practices

The inter-organisational relationship was described as functioning well by all nurses and auxiliary staff. The key to good cooperation was said to be the willingness to give and take and to help each other. One nurse said: "We have a really good cooperation with the home helpers. They adjust their schedules, as do we." Coordination of inter-organisational activities was often discussed at the meetings between the nurses and home helps. Times were set for interdependent activities. One home help explained: "It works really well; we help each other. The nurses and assistant nurses call us—it is easy to agree on a time and I feel like they often adjust to us as well. Sometimes we are nice and reschedule, and sometimes they do the same thing. There is a good atmosphere."

Unexpected events that required coordination were solved by nurses and auxiliary staff who undertook some of the tasks that, on paper, were the responsibility of the other unit. One example was with patients who took insulin. The assistant nurses and nurses often gave the pensioners a snack after the insulin shot so the home help could save some time. The monthly meetings were said to be crucial for the well-functioning daily coordination of interdependent tasks. The meetings were considered to be valuable for deciding on times for joint home visits and for setting times for interdependent tasks that needed to be coordinated. The meetings also made the home helps feel more secure because they could discuss concerns with the nurse.

It was claimed by home helps, assistant nurses, and nurses that the grey-zone tasks were solved in a helpful spirit. As one home help put it: "Everyone helps one another; that way it is less important what is the responsibility of the health centre and what is our responsibility." One nurse said: "Some other districts are very strict. We, on the other hand, want to help each other, to meet halfway. One has to think what is best for the individual pensioner. One should not be too picky." The atmosphere in the relationship was described as being characterised by give and take. It was argued by nurses and auxiliary staff that, in spite of there being grey zones, things worked out well because everyone was flexible and helpful. Even though they did not always know who should do what, they solved it over the phone or in the pensioner's home.

The writing of authorisations was described as functioning well by both nurses and home helps. "Authorisation works perfectly, even if they change personnel", one nurse said. Both home helps and nurses suggested that this was largely due to the common authorisation form issued by the task group. "Standardisation is very good; we know exactly how we should write authorisations and the home helps know what to expect. In this way, the authorisation procedure can be very quick and everyone is satisfied", one nurse said. One home help described the cooperation saying: "We have a well-functioning routine. The new home helps go to the health centre to get an authorisation. For annual renewals, the nurses create a big group and do the authorisations for everyone at the same time. Then the nurses come to us. You see, there is give and take. The authorisation form is also very easy to understand."

Constructing Inter-Organisational Accountability

During the third period, the need to enhance inter-organisational coop-eration was of great importance. The short-term focus on the budget and the financial restrictions within the intra-organisational relationship were reduced, as both organisations managed to balance their budgets and develop new forms of inter-organisational control. The informal control described in the first period was replaced by a formal means of controlling the cooperation as the managers put the inter-organisational relationship on the agenda. Thus, inter-organisational cooperation became part of the intra-organisational relationship between home helps and the management.

The development is characterised by an explicit formalisation of the inter-organisational relationship. One striking example is that the encounters between nurses and home helpers, previously characterised by the nurses acting as informal managers, have been formalised, with the participants being required to notify one another in advance of which cases they wish to discuss in the scheduled monthly meetings. The professional accountability guiding the actors' behaviour in the first period was modified to correspond to the perceived obligation to develop and protect inter-organisational cooperation, as well as to find a means of managing and controlling these interactions. The actors constructed a form of accountability towards the inter-organisational relationship, incorporating a means of coordination and control within the relationship. The importance of the difference in status between professional groups has decreased. Instead of home helps and assistant nurses adjusting their activities to the nurses' schedule, mutual adaptation is the norm, and the atmosphere is one of give and take.

5   CONCLUSIONS AND IMPLICATIONS

The purpose of this chapter was to conduct a review of the previous research on accounting in inter-organisational relationships within the public sector, as well as to provide novel empirical and theoretical insights on the subject. Two significant trends have been introduced to address the major chal-lenges facing the actors aiming to govern, control, and account for public sector activities. The first of these emphasises an explicit request to create inter-organisational cooperation between service providers within the public sector, whereas the second, labelled "the New Public Management", stresses the fact that public sector organisations are required to consider financial targets and cost efficiency in their everyday life. The establishment of specialised units with separate budgets and the stress on cooperation take place in parallel, but are incongruent, as a result of which considerable tensions are created. This has to be taken into account when describing and analysing accounting in inter-organisational relationships within the public sector. It becomes important to study the simultaneous operation of, as well as the linkages between, intra- and inter-organisational accounting.

After reviewing a significant set of accounting journals, we conclude that the overall themes in the articles were related to different ways of organising the public sector and of delivering public sector services and to the role of accounting and management control in these new forms of organisational structures. The vast majority of the articles concentrated on describing and analysing the new organisational structures, namely, outsourcing, PPPs, and networks, and on assessing the implications for accounting. There is little discussion of ongoing day-to-day cooperation between interdependent public sector units/organisations and the role of accounting therein. For example, no attention has been paid to how inter-organisational accounting is used in the ongoing inter-organisational relationships that are created when public sector services are outsourced. Further, linkages between intra- and inter-organisational accounting were not examined, and the studies did not theoretically elaborate on the distinctive characteristics of public sector organisations, such as the existence of strong professions.

The two recent studies by Kurunmäki and Miller (2006) and Miller et al. (2008) are exceptions. They observed conflicts between different professional identities, manifested in tension between social services staff and health care representatives about the appropriate use of resources and the means of reporting outcomes. They also touched upon linkages between intra- and inter-organisational accounting in the difficulty of developing performance measures suitable for use across organisational boundaries when national targets were almost exclusively set for individual organisations. However, the two studies consider general policy rather than attempting to provide detailed accounts of day-to-day inter-organisational work practices or to theorise about the observed conflicts between different professional identities.

Based on the literature review, we concluded that there is a need for in-depth empirical descriptions of inter-organisational accounting practices and to examine their connections to actual work practices. These empirical descriptions should include an appreciation of the linkages between intra- and inter-organisational accounting. In addition, little attempt has been made to theorise about the working of accounting in inter-organisational relationships within public sector organisations and to examine the notion of professions, for example, by focusing on different forms of accountability. In an attempt to fill these empirical and theoretical gaps, we have also presented empirical and theoretical advancements on accounting in inter-organisational relationships within the public sector in this chapter. Empirically, we have drawn on an in-depth case study of the domestic care of the elderly in Sweden and, theoretically, we have used the notion of accountability. The empirical material gave us the opportunity to follow the construction of accountability in three separate but connected periods, which has enabled us to enhance the understanding of accountability as an ongoing process, as a sequence of events and actions unfolding over time.

The case study shows that there is a strong connection between the forms of accountability as perceived by the professional actors and the articulation of organisational boundaries. In the first period, the professional actors' statements and actions indicate that organisational boundaries were hardly recognised, much less considered to be of any great importance in the actors' daily work. Instead, the boundaries were felt to lie between the different professions, created in the actors' minds. The relative status and ranking of professions were mainly attributable to the fact that tacit knowledge governed an infinite number of day-to-day interactions in health and social care. Hence, we conclude actors' perceptions of boundaries are necessary to create a structure for the execution of daily activities and for stability to ensue. Therefore, boundaries constitute important prerequisites for the construction of accountability. This case study strongly supports the idea that a feeling of membership, in this case in a professional group, is vital for the construction of accountability.

Our case study further illustrates the widely recognised connection between the construction of accountability and the use of an accounting system. As organisational actors start to refer to rules and categories within the organisational accounting system, the nurses and auxiliary staff perceived themselves to be accountable to previously unacceptable norms and values. In a situation where the activities within domestic care were made visible by the use of concepts emanating from accounting and finance, and therefore with a vocabulary alien to the health and social services, the interaction between the different professionals started to transform. The difference in the methods used to create visibility during the first and the second period is striking. The second period was characterised by the use of numerical accounts and the professional actors constructed the accountability by referring to measures such as financial income and revenue. The use of these measures was legitimated by converting them into comprehensible requirements in the professional world, such as the ability to hire an additional home help, or the necessity of losing one. This way to create visibility contrasts sharply with the methods used during the first period, where narrative accounts or tacit knowledge guided the way the professional actors constructed the accountability in terms of professional norms and values. As the management level started to accentuate the use of accounting figures, the actors' perceptions of professional accountability were transformed. This is partly because of the difficulty of making professional activities visible when using numerical accounts, because of the difficulty of comparing concepts and categories directly with the figures emanating from the accounting system, such as the budget.

We conclude that the specification and activation of an organisation's accounting system leads to the articulation of organisational boundaries, at least in periods characterised by a shortage of financial resources. It is interesting to note that the accounting system showed budget deficits during both the first and the second periods, but with one difference that determined the actors' construction of accountability. During the first period, budget deficits were not discussed, nor were they prominent on a political or management level. Consequently, the importance of balancing the budget and of ensuring that there was intra-organisational cost efficiency did not play a part in the actors' construction of accountability. In periods characterised by a stable financial situation, politicians and managers may justify a budget deficit by referring to the need to provide security and to ensure quality, for example. In financially challenging situations, however, the precise numerical accounts produced by the accounting system constitute convincing arguments for the politicians, who are themselves answerable to the voters and whose future will be determined in the next election.

The initial and final periods in the case study illustrate that the professional actors' construction of accountability is not limited to the consideration of an intra-organisational relationship because all of the situations where human actors interact are characterised by a need to explain and justify actions taken and decisions made. Thus, accountability becomes an important part of all interaction. The third period revealed that accountability came to be constructed through the inter-organisational relationship. By developing rules and regulations that can be recognised by different groups of actors, inter-organisational interaction was controlled and formalised. The actors expressed accountability towards norms developed within an inter-organisational setting, such as the need for all actors to modify their behaviour and timing to suit one another from time to time. Though it is worth noticing that the forms of control developed all concerned the actors' behaviour; no output controls had been put in place to measure inter-organisational performance and therefore to encapsulate the inter-organisational relationship. This raises an interesting question: what will happen during the next financial crisis? Is it possible for these formal means of inter-organisational control, based on controlling the actors' behaviour, to be strong enough to prevent the organisations from closing their organisational boundaries once again?

To sum up, we see great potential for future research on accounting in inter-organisational relationships within the public sector. Relevant literature is thin on the ground, and we advocate future research that provides a grounded account of day-to-day public sector cooperative work practices and the role of accounting therein. One fruitful avenue for future studies is the creation of new performance measurements to make inter-organisational activities visible to different groups of actors. Being able to measure long-term efficiency may reduce the risk of opportunistic and short-term decisions being made. Such measurements would constitute valid arguments for inter-organisational cooperation in public sector operations. Another area for future research concerns the need for detailed empirical and theoretical discussions of linkages between intra- and inter-organisational accounting in public sector organisations. Finally, we can see great potential for including studies of inter-organisational relations in the academic discussion on accountability. Inter-organisational cooperation constitutes a new form of accountability; including consideration of the construction of accountability in the studies of inter-organisational relationships may add new insights to this debate.

NOTES

1. See Broadbent and Laughlin (2003b) for a historical overview of the PFI/PPP.
2. The case description is based on that in the PhD thesis of Kraus (2007), for which 78 persons working with elderly care were interviewed, including home help unit managers, health centre managers, home helps, assistant nurses, and nurses. In addition, documents in the form of meeting protocols, work descriptions, and financial documents have been used.
3. A more thorough discussion of the structure and characteristics of the Swedish public sector than is given in this chapter can be found in Olson and Sahlin-Andersson (2005).
4. When we say *medication*, we refer to medicine and ear- and eyedrops.

BIBLIOGRAPHY

Abbott, A. 1988. *The system of professions. An essay on the division of expert labor.* Chicago: University of Chicago Press.
Abernethy, M. A., and Stoelwinder, J. U. 1995. The role of professional control in the management of complex organizations. *Accounting, Organizations and Society* 20: 1–17.
Abernethy, M. A., Chua, W. F., Grafton, J., and Mahama, H. 2007. Accounting and control in health care: Behavioural, organisational, sociological and critical perspectives. In *Handbook of management accounting research*, ed. Chapman, C. S., Hopwood, A. G., and Shields, M. D. 805–829. Oxford: Elsevier Ltd.
Ahrens, T. 1996a. Financial and operational modes of accountability: Differing accounts of British and German managers. In *Accountability: Power, ethos and the technologies of managing*, ed. Munro, R., and Mouritsen, J. 149–163. London: International Thomson Business Press.
Ahrens, T. 1996b. Styles of accountability. *Accounting, Organizations and Society* 21: 139–173.
Ahrens, T., and Chapman, C. 2002. The structuration of legitimate performance measures and management: Day-to-day contests of accountability in a U.K. restaurant chain. *Management Accounting Research* 13: 151–171.

Anthony, R. N., and Young, D. W. 1988. *Management control in nonprofit organizations*. Homewood, U.S.: Richard D. Irwin.

Baker, R. 2003. Investigating Enron as a public private partnership. *Accounting, Auditing and Accountability Journal* 16: 446–466.

Barton, A. 2006. Public sector accountability and commercial-in-confidence outsourcing contracts. *Accounting, Auditing and Accountability Journal* 19: 256–271.

Boden, D. 1994. *The business of talk: Organisations in action*. Cambridge: Polity Press.

Boland, R. J., and Schulze, U. 1996. Narrating accountability: Cognition and the production of the accountable self. In *Accountability: Power, ethos and the technologies of managing*, ed. Munro, R., and Mouritsen, J. 62–81. London: International Thomson Business Press.

Boyne, G., Kirkpatrick, I., and Kitchener, M. 2001. Introduction to the symposium on new labour and the modernization of public management. *Public Administration* 79: 1–4.

Broadbent, J., Dietrich, M., and Laughlin, R. 1996. The development of principal-agent, contracting and accountability relationships in the public sector: Conceptual and cultural problems. *Critical Perspectives on Accounting* 7: 259–284.

Broadbent, J., Gill, J., and Laughlin, R. 2003. Evaluating the private finance initiative in the National Health Service in the UK. *Accounting, Auditing and Accountability Journal* 16: 422–445.

Broadbent, J., and Guthrie, J. 2008. Public sector to public services: 20 years of 'contextual' accounting research. *Accounting, Auditing and Accountability Journal* 21: 129–169.

Broadbent, J., and Laughlin, R. 1999. The Private Finance Initiative: Clarification of a future research agenda. *Financial Accountability and Management* 15: 95–114.

Broadbent, J., and Laughlin, R. 2002. Accounting choices: Technical and political trade-offs and the UK's private finance initiative. *Accounting, Auditing and Accountability Journal* 15: 622–654.

Broadbent, J., and Laughlin, R. 2003a. Control and legitimation in government accountability processes: The private finance initiative in the UK. *Critical Perspectives on Accounting* 14: 23–48.

Broadbent, J., and Laughlin, R. 2003b. Public private partnerships: An introduction. *Accounting, Auditing and Accountability Journal* 16: 332–341.

Broadbent, J., and Laughlin, R. 2005. The role of PFI in the UK government's modernisation agenda. *Financial Accountability and Management* 21: 75–97.

Brunsson, N., and Sahlin-Andersson, K. 2000. Constructing organizations: The example of public sector reform. *Organization Studies* 21: 721–746.

Conrad, L. 2005. A structuration analysis of accounting systems and systems of accountability in the privatised gas industry. *Critical Perspectives on Accounting* 16: 1–26.

Deakin, N. 2002. Public-private partnerships, a UK case study. *Public Management Review* 4: 133–147.

Edwards, P., and Shaoul, J. 2003. Partnerships: For better, for worse? *Accounting, Auditing and Accountability Journal* 16: 397–421.

Empson, L. 2004. Organizational identity: Managerial regulation and member identification in an accounting firm acquisition. *Accounting, Organizations and Society* 29: 759–781.

English, L. 2007. Performance audit of Australian public private partnerships: Legitimizing government policies or providing independent oversight? *Financial Accountability and Management* 23: 313–336.

English, L., and Guthrie, J. 2003. Driving privately financed projects in Australia: What makes them tick? *Accounting, Auditing and Accountability Journal* 16: 493–511.

Froud, J. 2003. The Private Finance Initiative: Risk, uncertainty and the state. *Accounting, Organizations and Society* 28: 567–589.

Froud, J., Haslam, C., Johal, S., Shaoul, J., and Williams, K. 1998. Persuasion without numbers? Public policy and the justification of capital charging in NHS trust hospitals. *Accounting, Auditing and Accountability Journal* 11: 99–125.

Froud, J., and Shaoul, J. 2001. Appraising and evaluating PFI for NHS hospitals. *Financial Accountability and Management* 17: 247–270.

Garfinkel, H. 1967. *Studies in ethnomethodology.* Cambridge: Polity Press.

Giddens, A. 1979. *Central problems in social theory.* London: Macmillan.

Gray, R. H., Owen, D. L., and Maunders, K. T. 1987. *Corporate social reporting: Accounting and accountability.* Hemel Hempstead, UK: Prentice-Hall.

Grimsey, D., and Lewis, M. 2002. Accounting for public private partnerships. *Accounting Forum* 26: 245–270.

Håkansson, H., and Lind, J. 2007. Accounting in an interorganizational setting. In *Handbook of management accounting research*, ed. Chapman, C. S., Hopwood, A. G., and Shields, M. D. 885–902. Oxford: Elsevier Ltd.

Heald, D. 2003. Value for money tests and accounting treatment in PFI schemes. *Accounting, Auditing and Accountability Journal* 16: 342–371.

Hodges, R., and Mellett, H. 1999. Accounting for the Private Finance Initiative in the United Kingdom National Health Service. *Financial Accountability and Management* 15: 275–290.

Hofstede, G. H. 1981. Management control of public and not-for-profit activities. *Accounting, Organizations and Society* 6: 193–211.

Hood, C. C. 1991. A public management for all seasons? *Public Administration* 69: 3–19.

Hood, C. C. 1995. The new public management in the 1980s: Variations on a theme. *Accounting, Organizations and Society* 20: 93–119.

Hopwood, A., and Miller, P. 1994. *Accounting as a social and institutional practice.* Cambridge: Cambridge University Press.

Johnsen, Å., Meklin, P., Oulasvirta, L., and Vakkuri, J. 2004. Governance structures and contracting out municipal auditing in Finland and Norway. *Financial Accountability and Management* 20: 445–477.

Jones, C. S. 1999. Hierarchies, networks and management accounting in NHS hospitals. *Accounting, Auditing and Accountability Journal* 12: 164–187.

Jönsson, S. 1996. Decoupling hierarchy and accountability: An examination of trust and reputation. In *Accountability: Power, ethos and the technologies of managing*, ed. Munro, R., and Mouritsen, J. 103–117. London: International Thomson Business Press.

Klijn, E.-H. 2002. Governing networks in the hollow state, contracting out, process management or a combination of the two? *Public Management Review* 4: 149–165.

Kraus, K. 2007. *Sven, inter-organisational relationships and control—a case study of domestic care of the elderly.* PhD thesis, Stockholm School of Economics: EFI.

Kraus, K., and Lind, J. 2007. Management control in inter-organisational relationships. In *Issues in management accounting*, ed. Hopper, T., Northcott, D., and Scapens, R. 3rd ed. Harlow, UK: Prentice-Hall.

Kurunmäki, L. 1999. Professional vs. financial capital in the field of health care—struggles for the redistribution of power and control. *Accounting, Organizations and Society* 24: 95–124.

Kurunmäki, L. 2004. A hybrid profession—the acquisition of management accounting expertise by medical professionals. *Accounting, Organizations and Society* 29: 327–347.

Kurunmäki, L., and Miller, P. 2006. Modernising government: The calculating self, hybridisation and performance measurement. *Financial Accountability and Management* 22: 87–106.

Lambert, V., and Lapsley I. 2006. Redefining the boundaries of public sector accounting research? *The Irish Accounting Review* 13: 85–105.

Laughlin, R., and Pallot, J. 1998. Trends, patterns and influencing factors: Some reflections. In *Global warning—debating international developments in new public financial management*, ed. Olson, O., Guthrie, J., and Humphrey, C. 376–399. Oslo: Cappelen Akademisk Forlag.

Lindkvist, L., and Llewellyn, S. 2003. Accountability, responsibility and organization. *Scandinavian Journal of Management* 19: 251–273.

Llewellyn, S. 1998. Boundary work: Costing and caring in the social services. *Accounting, Organizations and Society* 23: 23–47.

Mayston, D. J. 1999. The private finance initiative in the National Health Service: An unhealthy development in new public management. *Financial Accountability and Management* 15: 249–274.

McSweeney, B., and Duncan, S. 1998. Structure or agency? Discourse or meta-narrative? Explaining the emergence of the financial management initiative. *Accounting, Auditing and Accountability Journal* 11: 332–361.

Miller, P., Kurunmäki, L., and O'Leary, T. 2008. Accounting, hybrids and the management of risk. *Accounting, Organizations and Society* 33: 942–967.

Miller, P., and O'Leary, T. 1987. Accounting and the construction of the governable person. *Accounting, Organizations and Society* 12: 235–265.

Mouritsen, J. 1997. *Tællelighedens regime*. København: Jurist- og Økonomforbundets forlag.

Mouritsen, J., Hansen, A., and Hansen, C. Ø. 2001. Inter-organizational controls and organizational competencies: Episodes around target cost management/functional analysis and open book accounting. *Management Accounting Research* 12: 221–244.

Munro, R. 1993. Just when you thought it safe to enter the water: Accountability, language games and multiple control technologies. *Accounting, Management and Information Technologies* 3: 249–271.

Munro, R. 1996. Alignment and identity work: The study of accounts and accountability. In *Accountability. Power, ethos and the technologies of managing*, ed. Munro, R., and Mouritsen, J. 1–19. London: International Thomson Business Press.

Munro, R., and Hatherly, D. 1993. Accountability and the new commercial agenda. *Critical Perspectives on Accounting* 4: 369–395.

Munro, R., and Mouritsen, J. 1996. *Accountability. Power, ethos and the technologies of managing*. London: International Thomson Business Press.

Newberry, S., and Barnett, P. 2001. Negotiating the network: The contracting experiences of community mental health agencies in New Zealand. *Financial Accountability and Management* 17: 133–152.

Newberry, S., and Pallot, J. 2003. Fiscal (ir)responsibility: Privileging PPPs in New Zealand. *Accounting, Auditing and Accountability Journal* 16: 467–492.

Olson, O., Guthrie, J., and Humphrey, C. 1998. International experiences with New Public Financial Management (NPFM) reforms: New world? Small world? Better world? In *Global warning—debating international developments in new public financial management*, ed. Olson, O., Guthrie, J., and Humphrey, C. 17–48. Oslo: Cappelen Akademisk Forlag.

Olson, O., Humphrey, C., and Guthrie, J. 2001. Caught in an evaluatory trap, a dilemma for public services under NPFM. *The European Accounting Review* 10: 505–522.

Olson, O., and Sahlin-Andersson, K. 2005. Public sector accounting reforms in a welfare state in transition: The case of Sweden. In *International Public Financial*

Management Reform, Progress, Contradictions and Challenges, ed. Guthrie, J., Humphrey, C., Jones, L. R., and Olson, O. 223–245. Greenwich, CT: Information Age Publishing.

Panozzo, F. 1996. Accountability and identity: Accounting and the democratic organization. In *Accountability. Power, ethos and the technologies of managing,* ed. Munro, R., and Mouritsen, J. 182–195. London: International Thomson Business Press.

Roberts, J. 1991. The possibilities of accountability. *Accounting, Organizations and Society* 16: 355–368.

Roberts, J., and Scapens, R. 1985. Accounting systems and systems of accountability—understanding accounting practices in their organisational contexts. *Accounting, Organizations and Society* 10: 443–456.

Robson, K. 1992. Accounting numbers as "inscription": Action at a distance and the development of accounting. *Accounting, Organizations and Society* 17: 685–708.

Roodhooft, F., and Warlop, L. 1999. On the role of sunk costs and asset specificity in outsourcing decisions: A research note. *Accounting, Organizations and Society* 24: 363–369.

Rose, N. 1991. Governing by numbers: Figuring out democracy. *Accounting, Organizations and Society* 16: 673–692.

Rutherford, B. A. 2003. The social construction of financial statement elements under Private Finance Initiative schemes. *Accounting, Auditing and Accountability Journal* 16: 372–396.

Silverman, D. 1975. Accounts of organisations—organisational structures and the accounting process. In *Processing people: Cases in organisational behaviour,* ed. McKinley, J. B. London: Holt, Rinehart & Winston.

Silverman, D., and Jones, J. 1976. *Organizational work.* London: Collier Macmillan.

Sinclair, A. 1995. The chameleon of accountability: Forms and discourses. *Accounting, Organizations and Society* 20: 219–237.

Shaoul, J. 1998. Charging for capital in the NHS trusts: To improve efficiency? *Management Accounting Research* 9: 95–112.

Shaoul, J. 2005. A critical financial analysis of the Private Finance Initiative: Selecting a financing method or allocating economic wealth? *Critical Perspectives on Accounting* 16: 441–471.

Smith, J., Morris, J., and Ezzamel, M. 2005. Organisational change, outsourcing and the impact on management accounting. *The British Accounting Review* 37: 415–441.

Torres, L., and Pina, V. 2001. Public-private partnership and private finance initiatives in the EU and Spanish local governments. *European Accounting Review* 10: 601–619.

Part II
Accounting Techniques

7 Customer Accounting When Relationships and Networks Matter

Mikael Cäker and Torkel Strömsten

1 INTRODUCTION

Even if the quest for an increased customer focus has been strong in the management literature and is evident from research on contemporary business processes (e.g., Achrol and Kotler 1999), customer accounting (CA) as an academic subject has been largely neglected by management accounting scholars (e.g., Guilding and McManus 2002). This is one indicator of how management accounting as a subject is lagging behind marketing and management studies when it comes to the study of issues such as customer satisfaction (e.g., Anderson et al. 1994), the importance of creating strong and informational bonds and linkages with customers (Håkansson and Snehota 1995) with the intention of retaining customers and creating profitable relationships (e.g., Reichheld 1993). In this chapter, we try to remedy this somewhat by focusing explicitly on the role of customer accounting, albeit still in the context of the current trend of developing business relationships and managing in networks.

We have chosen to focus on financial information about customers produced in profit-driven organisations. Further, we view CA as an internal tool that firms use to measure and manage their customer relationships. CA will, thereby, be seen as an extension of classical management accounting. This view differs from other inter-organisational control and accounting techniques, which may focus on decision processes involving multiple organisations (e.g., target costing; see Chapter 8), or on accounting information produced in one organisation for use in others (e.g., open-book accounting; see Chapter 9).

The managerial and research literature on CA is dominated by papers that argue for an increased use of CA. Furthermore, articles within this literature also suggest how to do CA, that is, what techniques to use for calculating and presenting the information. However, research on how CA information is used is scarce, and papers on the effects of using CA are even more so. Nevertheless, there are still some interesting ideas and observations that can be drawn from this literature. The chapter is organised as follows. First, a brief historical background including motivations for choosing to use CA is presented. Next, we summarise and analyse the CA techniques presented in the literature. This is followed by a discussion of how CA is used in general and how it influences internal power struggles in organisations in particular. We then discuss the potential for CA when adopting an explicit dyadic and network perspective. Suggestions for further research will be outlined and the chapter then ends with tentative conclusions being drawn on the overall characteristics of the field.

2   A BRIEF BACKGROUND AND MOTIVATION

Early research on CA is primarily found in marketing and management journals (e.g., Anandarajan and Christopher 1987; Shapiro et al. 1987). Although still scarce, the research on CA has increased within the management accounting field in the last few years. Foster and Gupta (1994) discussed the interfaces amongst marketing, cost management, and management accounting. One of their observations is that customer profitability (CP), especially taking a long-term focus, has been the subject of little research (p. 56). Further, they welcomed research directed towards the retention of profitable customers rather than only creating sales. One argument supporting this motivation was that of Booth (1994); Booth's argument was for considering CP instead of product profitability because products may be sold at a loss as long as a customer is profitable to the organisation overall. This new "marketing environment" (Achrol and Kotler 1999) requires more effort to measure customers and their profitability. Foster et al. (1996), in their turn, identified a growing interest from practice, but a lack of research within the field of CA.

CA may, therefore, be seen as one of the developments within accounting that has followed a general change in the focus of business life (e.g., Chenhall 2008), exemplified by the concentration of relationships and networks within marketing since the 1990s (Anderson et al. 1994; Achrol and Kotler 1999) and the process orientation that grew up within the production and logistics literature at about the same time (e.g., Womack et al. 1991). Introducing a customer focus includes having a process-oriented approach to managing a firm, where the end-customers' demand should be the departure for all operational activities and, accordingly, the managing should be derived from interaction with customers (McNair 2007). Information about end-customers may have consequences many steps back along the value chain of a firm (e.g., Hergert and Morris 1989; Shank and Govindarajan 1992) and information about processes may be specific to one or each actor and motivate ongoing relationships, instead of focusing on each discrete transaction. Besides this managerial logic behind processes and relationships, research conducted within marketing in the 1960s and '70s showed that companies did choose to work with the same customers and suppliers in long-term relationships, long before the managerial literature was filled by calls for process orientation and a relationship focus (e.g., Håkansson and Östberg 1975; Johanson 1966).

Following on from this general development in business life and from the more specific changes in marketing and networks are two aspects that directly motivate the use of CA: resource heterogeneity and relationships. Penrose (1959) identified the importance of resource heterogeneity, which was subsequently developed using an industrial network approach (and by many other scholars). According to the industrial network approach (e.g., Håkansson 1982; Håkansson and Waluszewski 2002), linkages with customers and suppliers are important resources. These resources are to be seen as heterogeneous, reflecting the difference in their sizes, needs, volumes, and so on, but also taking into account their ability to be working partners, to develop processes and new products, and thereby using the heterogeneity in the physical and organisational resource interfaces (Strömsten and Håkansson 2007). An important consequence of the heterogeneity assumption is that each organisation or firm in a network must be able to prioritise between the potential customers and suppliers. Accounting information is critical in making these choices because CA is supposed to display how customers are different from each other and thereby how different customers affect costs and revenues in different ways.

Furthermore, heterogeneity may help to understand why relationships with customers may evolve and endure. Since customers differ, resources are needed to learn about and adapt to unique business partners. The cost for switching business partners provides the economic incentives to both customers and suppliers to continue their existing relationships instead of turning to the open market. Information about how expensive it might be to establish a new customer relationship and appreciation from the customers of well-functioning suppliers whose needs are fulfilled year upon year motivate the use of the relationship as the unit of analysis instead of focusing on individual transactions (Blois 1999).

Within the field of accounting, customers and their role as an object have developed strongly during the last fifteen years, with a few calls for research predating this period (e.g., Bellis-Jones 1989; Cooper 1989; Kaplan 1989a; 1989b; Foster and Gupta 1994; Mouritsen 1997; Guilding and McManus 2002; Cäker 2005; Lind and Strömsten 2006). McManus (2006) has traced the historical roots behind the development of CA and views CA as a part of the strategic management accounting context, with its external and long-term focus (see also Lord 2007).

The starting point of one of the more influential strands of CA within management accounting, the activity based costing-path (ABC), was a couple of case studies in which Kaplan and Cooper developed a new type of costing system (Kaplan and Cooper 1998). One of the cases examined the Swedish company Kanthal, a producer of electrical resistance heating elements and the company's development of an ABC analysis in relation to its customers (Kaplan 1989a, 1989b). The case illustrated how some customers contributed more than others to the firm's overall profit, and Kaplan made the point that some customers drive profit, while others actually destroy it. With the help of an ABC analysis, Kanthal was able to identify what kind of customer that was profitable and what kind that was not. The idea was to modify the behaviour of the unprofitable customers so that they could become profitable ones. Kaplan also developed the Manufacturers Hanover case (1990), where the company was facing "a new reality" after having conducted an activity-based costing analysis on its customers. What distinguishes this case is the fact that it emphasises an extended time horizon, as it involved measuring CP over several years.

3   CUSTOMER ACCOUNTING RESEARCH

Mulhern (1999) concluded that many different notions have been used to describe overlapping approaches within CA. These are customer profitability, lifetime value, customer lifetime value, customer valuation, customer lifetime valuation, customer relationship value, and customer equity. Pfeifer et al. (2005) argue that the use of different notions for the same phenomena and that different authors using the same concepts but meaning somewhat differing things are problematic to the advances within a field. They suggest that CP and customer lifetime value (CLV) should be used to describe two distinct and different approaches. CP is considered to be an accounting concept, where the difference between revenues and costs for a customer relationship is calculated for a specific time period. CLV is the present value of the future cash flow attributed to a firm's customer relationships. Jacobs et al. (2001) make a distinction between retrospective and prospective CP, where their interpretation of retrospective CP is almost equivalent to our CP, and represents the past financial influence of customers, while the prospective CP is intended to value future financial streams arising from specific customer relationships. Therefore, we have divided the literature on customer accounting depending on its emphasis on CP or CLV analyses.[1]

Research on Customer Profitability

CP analysis is the most widely used CA technique, according to Guilding and McManus (2002). The results from Kaplan's (1989a) study created high expectations on CP. From the study it was possible to read that "40% of . . . customers were profitable and these generated 250% of realized profits" (e.g., Kaplan 1989a). Claims like this one indicated that, by focusing on profitable customers' contributions, the firm's overall profit could be boosted. Thereby, the argument was, CP could help companies to create a more profitable business by directing attention towards the more profitable customers. Basically, information relating to CP should be used to clarify how each customer or customer segment contributed to a firm's profits.

The message from the normative literature considered is that action ought to be taken on the basis of CP information. Initially, since the literature on CP concentrates on past financial performance, long-term and cross-customer effects must be considered outside the calculations. If, even after these considerations, customers are still perceived to be unprofitable, it is suggested that CP information should be used to stimulate action in relevant inter-organisational relationships with the aim of making the relationships profitable or, if this is not possible, to end them.

Four main types of actions that can be taken in response to CP information can be traced from this literature (see Booth 1994; Innes and Mitchell 1995; Kaplan and Cooper 1998; Kaplan and Atkinson 1998), the first three of which involve:

- Protecting existing, highly profitable relationships to avoid future competition.
- Repricing products being sold to unprofitable customers.
- Negotiating with unprofitable customers to identify an alternative means of exchange or the choice of products, to lower costs or add value/services to customers.

And if unprofitable customers still remain after this, a firm should employ the fourth and final option, to:

- Stop selling unprofitable products to these customers or end the relationships.

The calculation of CP may appear to be straightforward but in reality, closer scrutiny reveals that it involves many complexities, in addition to which, the most suitable approach will vary for different industries and in accordance with other factors (Mulhern 1999). The main themes discussed in the literature and which will be summarised here are:

- The 'customer' as an object in the accounting system
- Cost allocation to the object 'customer'
- Models of customer-related processes

The Customer as an Object in the Accounting System

As with all objects in accounting systems, choices must be made about how and when to include them. In this respect, Mulhern (1999) suggested that we need to consider the following aspects:

a) What inclusion criteria should be used: Being a company, an SBU, or being located in a specific location are examples of alternative specifications that could be used. This question also relates to the segmentation of customers as we might group customers into clusters to enable them to be analysed as one object. The choice here regards how detailed the information we ought to register to attain a satisfactory balance between the quality attained and the cost of accounting.

b) A second choice regards when a customer should be viewed as an object. Should we require that customers have made their first purchase, or should the start be triggered when we spend money on attracting a specific customer?

c) Consequently, the next decision is: How long after the last purchase should we keep on analysing customers? Customers of potential value should probably be kept, but at the same time we want to base our accounting system on relevant factors, and therefore clear out inactive objects.

These questions reveal a need to work actively to uphold the relevance of an accounting system.

Cost Allocation to the Object 'Customer'

Within the literature on CP, the main advancements in calculating customer profitability have been produced by accounting researchers, which explains focus on cost, relative revenue. Traditionally, the tracing of customers' costs has been limited to direct selling costs, such as bonuses and discounts. A strong argument for developing CA resides in acknowledging that customers differ from each other, as discussed previously, and in recognising how this influences what has traditionally been labelled fixed costs. Kaplan and Cooper (1998) make an argument for considering the costs of selling, marketing, distribution, and administration as variable costs, based on the historical reflection that they have been constant or have increased in terms of the percentage of sales. Foster et al. (1996) consider these costs to be central to any calculation of CP.

The need to analyse individual customer relationships resides in the difference between them. Failing to appreciate how customers are able to influence cost risks decreasing the potential value of CA severely (Anandarajan and Christopher 1987). Hope (1998) claimed that many accounting systems used to report costs from functions and departments are ill-suited for identifying the influence of unique customers (see also Myer 1989). This is also an argument put forward by Shapiro et al. (1987), who argued that companies with poor cost accounting systems have problems determining CP (p. 1069). Payant (2003) notes that in the banking industry, the customer relationship management (CRM) systems that are used often base their CP calculations on standard product costs, which fail to recognise individual differences. As a consequence, the use of this information does not acknowledge the heterogeneity of customers.

Much of the literature on CP focuses on activity-based costing (ABC) and its application as a tool for enhancing analyses of customer costs (Connolly and Ashworth 1994; Ness et al. 2001). In this literature, it is suggested that one of the main benefits of ABC resides in its ability to analyse the influence of unique customers on a firm's overall profitability (Cooper and Kaplan 1991). Blois (1999) even suggested that it would be hard to make a CP analysis without an ABC system, and Goebel et al. (1998) developed an argument revealing how ABC can contribute to efficiency in marketing decisions on different customer levels. ABC as a technique is not only focused on products and production; the notions of activities and cost drivers are generic in the sense that they can be specified and developed for any part of an organisation's operations. For an empirical example from the service industry, see DeWayne (2004).

'Customers' are not, however, only objects about which an organisation may need financial information. 'Customers', as objects, can also support an analysis of a firm's costs (Foster and Gupta 1994). Certain costs are caused by establishing, developing, and supporting customer relationships (e.g., through visits to customer facilities, R&D work initiated by specific customers, implementation of information systems, and routines agreed upon in conjunction with specific customers). These costs might only be attributable to products on a general level, but they might be traceable to individual customers. Furthermore, some costs might be dedicated to multiple products, but easy to trace to one customer (e.g., costs associated with handling orders from or transport to one customer that include multiple products). Therefore, including 'customer' as an object in costing systems may increase the percentage of costs that are identifiable on a detailed level (Booth 1994; Cäker 2000). In ABC, it is suggested that customers and products are parallel objects in a cost hierarchy. To use two cost hierarchies (as suggested by Cäker 2000), one customer-related and product-related, would further enable the detailed analysis of both customers and products, because some costs may be attributable to both these objects on various levels within the respective cost hierarchy.

Models of Customer-related Processes

A number of suggestions have been made for general models and more specific listings have been published of how customers influence their suppliers' costs; these latter are often being accompanied by suggestions of how "less" and "more" costly customers tend to behave.[2] Two of the more general models in the literature are particularly worth a mention as they focus on the exchange process from either the relationship level or the transaction level:

- Ness et al. (2001) suggested four general activities in the process of managing a customer relationship that provide guidance in the analysis of customer-driven costs: acquisition, provision, service, and the act of retaining customers. The costs involved in building relationships and the providing of after-sales service are examples of the customer-driven costs that are emphasised in such a model, in contrast with classic cost accounting. This model emphasises the relationship level of customer cost.

- Smith and Dikolli (1995) recommend firms to analyse how different customers behave with respect to operational matters in the four categories: purchasing pattern, delivery policy, accounting procedures, and inventory holding. Such a model opens up the analysis of customers' influence on operational matters. For example, customers that buy few products in each order will augment administration costs, and customers with specific demands on how products should be packaged and delivered will introduce logistical costs. Operational models incorporating these principles will vary strongly from one industry to another.

The models of Ness et al. (2001) and Smith and Dikolli (1995), focusing on customer processes and operational processes, can be seen as examples of different levels of processes in the interaction with customers that both need to be considered by companies developing accounting systems. The models are thereby complementary to one other.

To sum up, previously we have identified and discussed some of the literature within accounting that focuses on customers, and where 'customers' are used as an object within accounting systems. What the articles included in this literature have in common are focus, whether explicit or implicit, on customer profitability measured over a specific period of time, that is, on accounting profitability. In the next section we look at the literature that more explicitly take into account a longer perspective on how to measure customer relationships, that is, customer lifetime value or valuation, CLV.

Research on Customer Lifetime Valuation

Whereas CP focuses on differences between revenue and cost for specific periods, CLV is within this literature (e.g., Jain and Singh 2002; Gupta and Lehman 2003) considered to be an extension to include 'everything' that is considered influencing value. In this section intra-relationship issues such as investment made in customers are discussed but also extra-relationship issues such as customers initiating valuable development work or acting as referral customers. CLV is primarily used to label techniques that aim to value customer relationships over a lifetime.

The main motivation to most CLV models is to support a long-term instead of short-term perspective on customer relationships and their profitability (Gupta and Lehman 2003). Customers need to be measured and managed as assets (Gupta and Lehman 2003) as loyal customers are assumed to generate high long-term profitability of firms (Jain and Singh

2002; Chenhall and Langfield-Smith 2007). Most research on CLV is conducted within the marketing discipline and two more specific motivations to the different models can be found:

- To direct marketing efforts to customers with high CLV. Jacobs et al. (2001, p. 362) says that "the prospective measurement of customer profitability [CLV in our terminology] is a necessary prerequisite to the efficient utilization of resources and vital to directing marketing efforts toward building customer value . . .". For example, Venkatesan and Kumar (2004) compares four different approaches[3] to analyse how to choose customers to focus on and claim (their version of) CLV to be superior.
- To enable communication of how valuable an organisation's customers are. To "value" customers can also be related to the idea that customer retention management also should help to create shareholder value (Rappaport 1986; Srivastava et al. 1998; Stahl et al. 2003). In this strand of literature, serving customers and managing customers is merely a way to help the organisation create shareholder value for its owners.

These two motivations differ in one central aspect to this review. The first motivation implies to differentiate customer (groups), while the second does not. The inter-organisational approach of this book highlights the need to acknowledge heterogeneity in a firm's customer base and to appreciate business opportunities with individual customers. Of course this perspective relates much better with the first than the second motivation of CLV. Some CLV models, focusing on the second motivation, are not aiming at establishing value per customer; instead, the accounting information is aggregated for different segments or all the customers of an organisation (see Rust et al. 2004; Kumar and Morris 2007) and their suitability for the broader complexity involved in transactions on the business-to-business market may be questioned. However, the first motivation of the CLV models and the general interest in valuing customers still makes the CLV literature a source to learn from for those interested in the inter-organisational perspective. This review of CLV literature is biased because it aims to review CLV regarding how we see it as it can potentially contribute to the inter-organisational field.[4]

Many of the authors claim that the interest in CLV is motivated due to their focus on relationships instead of single transactions (Berger and Nasr 1998; Reinartz and Kumar 2000). Both Berger and Nasr (1998) and Jain and Singh (2002) refer to four reasons from Reichheld (1993) to motivate the assumption that customer relationships are worth considering:

- revenues may increase when a company gets more well-known with the customer and is seen as a reliable supplier;

- better familiarity with supplier's products reduces demand for support,
- loyal customers may act as referrals; and
- in some industries price reductions decrease over time.

Therefore, a main theme in CLV literature is an increased focus on loyalty and relationships as a key to success. For example, Berger and Nasr (1998) take this as an argument to model that profitability from customers grows over time.

Most CLV papers develop mathematical models, in which some parameters are frequently reoccurring as important influences on customer value. These are:

- *Acquisition and retention costs for building relationships*: It is suggested that it costs to build relationships. Increase in revenues from a focus on customer relationships is not seen as arising without an effort and is suggested to be balanced with (often up-front) costs for building relationships. To make this balance manageable and not presuppose that loyal customers are more profitable, Berger and Nasr (1998) and Kumar and Shah (2004), among others, suggest that CLV must be considered when focusing on loyal customers. In this work, consideration of costs for acquisition and retention are central (Jain and Singh 2002). Thomas (2001) shows how retention of customers is affected by resources put in acquiring customers. In a decision-focused model, Blattberg and Deighton (1996) aim to guide spending on acquisition and retention in order to maximise CLV.
- *Switching costs*: Switching costs for the customers are often seen as important in influencing CLV. Dikolli et al. (2007) claim that switching costs can be a leading indicator of CLV and calculations of CLV often include consideration of switching costs (Berger and Nasr 1998; Rust et al. 2004). High switching costs in an industry imply that it is likely that a customer is lost for good if the customer stops buying, while low switching costs imply modelling a customer that buys from another supplier to continue to partly continue to be a customer (Rust et al. 2004).
- *Value from specific customers*: Key aspects in models for valuing customers are expectations on financial contribution per customer (Berger and Nasr 1998; Jain and Singh 2002). In most cases, fixed costs are not allocated to customers (Mulhern 1999). In most articles on CLV, there is a lack of discussion of what is included in revenues and costs. A notable exception is Hopkinson and Lum (2002; see following).

However, to value customers requires considering many more aspects than these three, and a key debate within the area is how extensive the models should be. For example, McManus (2006) brings to our attention that CLV models focus on customer retention as the single most important factor. This is at the expense of other factors, such as service usage, cross buying, and positive referrals. Numerous suggestions on how to value customers have been made but they are also accompanied by numerous limitations on their "correctness" and usability. Many models are information intensive (Gupta and Lehman 2003) or dependent on strong assumptions, as the alternative that Gupta and Lehman themselves present. For example, they claim that for the ambition to value the total customer base, an average contribution per customer is acceptable.

Hopkinson and Lum (2002) suggest that the problems of CLV mainly reside in two dimensions. Firstly, to identify both direct and indirect influence from customers on their suppliers is problematic. Secondly, many factors that have been identified as influencing relationship value are inaccurately integrated into or left out of models that aim for prediction of value. Hopkinson and Lum (2002) propose a generic model for valuation of ongoing relationships. They suggest to focus on 1) purchases; 2) extra-relationship value, created within a relationship, from both transferable cost savings and development of knowledge; 3) cost to serve the customer; and 4) the anticipated rate of growth. They also suggest to consider risk in relationships and to handle this by relying on findings concerning the capital asset pricing model (CAPM). The authors find CAPM to be informative to managers because it points at imbalances between risk and profitability, but at the same time they point at aspects that differentiate financial markets, for which CAPM is developed, and customer relationships. Foremost, the prevalence of switching costs is seen as troubling. Further, Hopkinson and Lum suggest including 'extra-relationship' benefits, like cost-savings initiated in one relationship and realised in others, development of competencies, and know-how that can be used in other relationships. However, they also warn for double counting. If value from a relationship where it is realised is transferred to a relationship where it is initiated, it must also be subtracted from the relationship where it is realised.[5]

Summing Up on Research on Customer Accounting

We chose to organise our review of customer accounting research around two different levels of ambition. The first level, labelled CP, argues that a focus on product for analysing costs and profitability is not enough and that diversity in customer behaviour warrants analysing their specific contribution to organisations' profit. The second level builds on the same type of argument but extends the time horizon and/or broadens the scope in how to study customers' influence on an organisation's profit. In this literature, foremost the presence of customer relationships is highlighted but also valuation of how a specific customer influences value through driving product development or bridging to other customers.

The second level is of course a more sophisticated, holistic approach but at the same time relatively more information intense and subjective. The motivation of this move towards an advanced approach is of course to avoid rejecting customers that are long-term profitable but currently unprofitable. It is also interesting to notice that the main question regarding CP, tracing of how customers influence costs, is not seen as problematic or is at least not explicitly discussed in presentation of most CLV models that do include past customer profits as a parameter.

We can also note that these are two schools within the CA field that largely are unconnected. The CP studies are foremost conducted by accounting researchers with an interest in the customer interface where the method used is primarily case studies (e.g., Kaplan and Cooper 1998), whereas CLV studies in general have been carried out by marketing researchers, mainly with a focus on consumer markets. Here the use of quantitative methods dominates (e.g., Kumar and Shah 2004).

4   DESCRIPTIVE AND INTERPRETATIVE RESEARCH OF CUSTOMER ACCOUNTING

Researchers have studied CA from different perspectives, ranging from the pure managerial and/or instrumental to the more critical and pluralistic. We now move on to consider different settings, or perspectives, where CA is employed. First, we review and discuss the literature concerned with the use of CA on the organisational level. The following sections will emphasise the firm internal processes and the consequences of making the customer an "object". In Section 5 and onwards, we look at how CA is used where the perspective is explicitly inter-organisational. First we examine CA when the perspective is dyadic and then, lastly, we discuss the use of CA from a network perspective and consider how embedded relationships might influence both the design and use of CA techniques.

In What Way is Customer Accounting Used in Organisations?

On the whole, the evidence on the use of CA techniques in organisations is scarce, and the few articles that do discuss their use draw different conclusions. Berger et al. (2003, p. 40) note that "In spite, however, of all the mathematical models that have been developed to indicate formulas for calculating CLV, there is little, if any, detailed discussion in the literature of the actual applied calculations of CLV." Although many of the authors of the references given in this chapter are convinced about the necessity of measuring customer value and of analysing which relations to develop, Blois (1999) reveals social practices and 'gut-feeling' to be more important in deciding to build a customer relationship than calculations of CLV. For instance, Blois argued that "in those cases where they were quoting for additional business from existing customers very little attention was devoted to the link between the cost of continuing to obtain the business and its anticipated value" (Blois 1999, p. 94). Most of the twenty respondents comprising his study did not focus on any formal analyses of cost for individual customer accounts. However, implicitly many of the interviewees in Blois's study seem to act *as if* they conducted some kind of CLV analysis. For example, when it came to evaluate relationship value, one manager argued: "Overall, we attempt to think in terms of life-time value" (p. 95). Another manager claimed: "The value of a relationship is a judgement of the customer's future potential and an expectation that costs can be contained though they may grow" (p. 95). These quotes indicate that advanced CA techniques such as ABC and CLV seem to influence managers' thinking but are used informally and on an ad hoc basis (see also Lind and Strömsten 2006; Christner et al. 2008).

Guilding and McManus (2002) claim that there is widespread support for CA, based on a survey they conducted of the three hundred largest Australian companies. Three out of the five CA techniques that they asked questions about yielded means above the mid-point on their scale, varying from "not used at all—used to a large extent". They perceive their results to be surprisingly high compared to what has been claimed, in the ongoing debate, as an absence of CA information. The two practices that were not used to a great extent involved long-term considerations such as deploying CLV techniques. Guilding and McManus (2002) further claimed that the use of CA is more common in companies with a high market orientation and that companies that face intense competition are generally more likely to use CA.

These differing views concerning how frequently CA is used may be understood by considering different accounts of what CA is. The normative accounts reviewed in Section 3 claim that use of advanced cost allocation is necessary for useful CP information and point out the advantages of mathematical modelling of CLV. Although the interview study by Blois (1999) revealed that these formal models are not dominant, it still acknowledged that there is an interest in using information at hand to try to focus on getting profitable customers—even if they claim that the final decision is made on gut feeling. We do not know how formal or how advanced the models referred to in the report on the high use of CA by Guilding and McManus are; we only know that there was a high degree of consideration of CP and CLV techniques among the firms that answered their survey.

Our own empirical experiences tell us that companies' routine customer accounting is of a relatively simple kind, but that these routine analyses are complemented by a broader evaluation of customer value when needed. We can illustrate this with Ericsson (further discussed in Lind and Strömsten 2006). Ericsson is a major supplier of equipment and services to the telecom industry. It has a global presence and, between 2001 and 2004, it underwent substantial restructuring after the telecom crisis (Strömsten

2006). In Ericsson's annual report of 2007 (p. 151), one can read: "We are supplying equipment and services to almost all major network operators globally. We derive most of our sales from large, multi-year network build-out agreements with a limited number of significant customers. Out of a customer base of more than 425 network operators, the ten largest customers account for approximately 42 percent of our net sales, while the 20 largest customers account for approximately 58 percent of our net sales. Our largest customer accounted for approximately 6 percent of sales during 2007." Hence, Ericsson's customer base is very concentrated. This has much to do with the regulated history of the telecom market, where one state-owned company used to serve one country. Since the deregulation of the telecom industry, the structure has changed, but still there are relatively few customers for Ericsson to handle, when it comes to network operators. Moreover, from the annual report one can also read that Ericsson has to manage deals that span several years, which makes its customer accounting somewhat complicated.

Dealing with individual customer relationships is customary within Ericsson. Even at the board level, the development and profitability of individual customers are discussed. Reflecting this, Ericsson has organised its major customers in global accounts and key accounts, where the profitability of each customer, globally and on a local basis, is traced on an annual basis. Furthermore, in Ericsson's SAP system it is possible to evaluate all the individual customers over time. For each customer, Ericsson measures the net sales and cost of sales from which a gross margin is obtained. Then adjustments and reserves are subtracted from the gross margin, as are the cost of sales, general and administrative, whereupon further operational expenses are subtracted. From this, a customer contribution margin is given. These procedures may be compared with traditional management accounting but with a 'new' object, the customer, measured both annually and over time.

The customer analyses are complemented in various ways, but for most customers without formal and routine procedures being put in place. In, for example, discussions held by the board of directors, the financial implications of the customers' investment plans are discussed. The number of customers is limited and the knowledge about each and every customer is well developed. A long-term perspective is explicitly taken and might influence pricing decisions during tendering processes. However, there is a strong emphasis within Ericsson that each individual project must show profitability. Furthermore, if customers initiate large investments, cross-customer effects may also be considered, albeit on an ad hoc basis and not as part of a daily routine including calculating the CP or CLV.

Amongst many organisations, we have observed a tendency to produce customer profitability reports with differing ambitions of tracing customer specific costs on a regular basis, for short time intervals and otherwise, to do qualitative, informal analyses, which are supported by 'rough' calculations, when making decisions with long-term consequences. That long-term cross-customer effects are only considered in decisions of great importance would be one way to understand why fewer companies use more advanced forms of valuations, as claimed by Guilding and McManus (2002). Furthermore, a possible explanation for why it is hard to find examples of CLV methods, like those described in Section 3, despite Guilding and McManus having found a substantial number of respondents who claimed to have an interest in the lifetime value of customers, is the use of nonformal and nonroutine procedures for these matters, as illustrated by the Ericsson case just mentioned.

As we noted earlier, some consider "good" (as in reliable and high qualitative) customer cost information to be lacking in practice, as reported on so far. From an empirical study, Anandarajan and Christopher (1987) noted two explanations for this. Firstly, systems and procedures were not adequately developed to enable them to identify an individual customer's influence on costs. Foster and Gupta (1994) claim that, traditionally, cost management and production have been developed alongside one another while marketing costs have been considered to be discretionary and allocated on an arbitrary basis. Secondly, there was a lack of interest from controllers and marketing personnel to focus on these costs (see also Blois 1999). During the last twenty years, the interest in customer costs has increased, but even today we find evidence of both these dimensions of the problem. Hopkinson and Lum (2002) recognised the need for cooperation amongst accountants, strategists, and marketers as a problematic aspect. Van Raaij et al. (2003) specifically pointed out the lack of information from salespeople, who would be in possession of valuable pieces of information that would otherwise be hard to get. A third explanation comes from case studies from van Raaij et al. (2003) and Helgesen (2007), revealing that the CP, as is the case with other accounting figures, is developed in a balance reflecting the trade-off between accuracy and workload. Simplifying choices are made to enable calculations to be done without exceeding a reasonable amount of work. So far, we can see a discrepancy between the accounting information that, according to a more normative literature, ought to be in place and the accounting information that actually is in place and, therefore, put into use. In the next section, we turn to how the CA is both important *and* challenged within intra-organisational processes.

Customer Accounting Influencing Intra-Organisational Processes

Inclusion of the customer as an object in the accounting system and thereby increasing the prevalence of formal information in communication about customers within organisations is bound to affect intra-organisational processes. Further, introduction of CA as a source of information in internal managing processes does not enter a "clean slate". Mouritsen (1997), Vaivio (1999) and Cäker (2007) have all shown aspects of both the financial focus and the formalisation of management processes to have the potential to clash with earlier established horizontal and informal communication processes.[6]

Mouritsen (1997) showed how a quality programme ended up as a force in marginalising the customer, in direct contrast with the intention. In this study, obligatory scrutinization of the customer's financial performance took place, irrevocably influencing how the customer was perceived by some of the most powerful actors within the organisation under investigation. Mouritsen (1997, p. 17) further went on to interpret the customer as "a medium mobilized by the different parties in their internal struggles about how it looks, what its preferences and needs are and how it can be accommodated. The mastering of the definition of the customer is a prerequisite for being seen as organizationally competent". Without appearing to consider the customer, one does not have a strong position within contemporary organisations (see also Du Gay and Salaman 1992). Mouritsen continues, "Part of this mastery is the way it can be related to accounting performance." Therefore, and in line with this reasoning, CA can be seen as a means to gain power in intra-organisational processes.

Vaivio (1999) further elaborated this reasoning by showing how quantification of the customer brings the management accountants more actively into the arena of organisational members that try to give voice to what the customer wants. He revealed a struggle for power between the accountants and the salespeople. Vaivio (1999) interpreted the basis of the power of salespeople to be associated with a more heterogeneous picture of customers than that provided through accounting. This could be taken as an argument to support the call for CA to recognise the individual customer. However, probably one should not interpret Vaivo (1999) to have been claiming that a more developed CA would have fully resolved the issues in the organisation studied. The sales managers' knowledge of their customers may often be qualitative and hard to quantify and incorporate in accounting systems (see Blois 1999).

Another example of how internal processes and relationships might be affected by the use of CA can be taken from our research on Ericsson. Here we have seen that the customer focus and how Ericsson accounts for customers have the potential to create tensions between the firm's different business units. As Ericsson sells integrated solutions to its customers, there are many different functions and business units involved in the customer interface. In complex deals, up to ten different product areas (PA) can be involved. In these complicated deals, Ericsson might sell radio-based solutions, advanced switches, charging solutions, messaging, installation, consulting services, and so on. All of these different parts and components are active in making the deal happen. Further, all the organisational units responsible for the respective products want a piece of the profit generated by the deal with that customer. "Since we use a variable pay scheme, this is an important aspect for the various managers and people that work with a large customer deal", as one controller put it. During negotiations, the key account unit signing the deal works closest with the PA that has the greatest share of the deal. This is for practical reasons, but also because a good relationship with the PA unit is important for future deals. As a consequence, the units that are responsible for parts of less strategic value might get a smaller share financially than they otherwise would. For example, installation or consulting services might be given away as "free" or for a lower price during the negotiations with a customer. This creates problems with measurement: Where should the profit then be placed within the organisation? Further, from a control perspective, it might be demotivating for the units that not are rewarded in relation to their own perceived performance, depending on how the firm's CA system is designed. Ericsson has therefore increased the formal control of the sales process in order to satisfy the individual requirements from PAs and MUs.

Another example on how CA information is involved in intra-organisational processes is provided by Cäker (2007), who showed how the CA information is downplayed and counterbalanced by the existence of customer accountability. Financial accounting information was in his study not considered to have a prominent role in the managing processes, as it was not seen as particularly relevant for handling customer relationships. This was in the study demonstrated by the popularity of nonfinancial CA information and the general strong accountability to customers. Accounting information was considered to provide mixed messages and the conclusion of Cäker's article is that it is not necessary to incorporate all information within an accounting system—the balance between different aspects that is so often sought in contemporary management models (as emphasised in much of the literature on the Balanced ScoreCard, for example) does not always need to be expressed within the formal accounting system.

Vaivio (1999) and Cäker (2007) show how CA is challenged by other sources of information. Ogden (1997), on the other hand, shows what may happen when there is no alternative source of information about the customer. In the water-supply organisation that he studied, the voice of the customer was missing from the managing process. A (quantified) customer was able to contribute by increasing the awareness of the customers' interests (Ogden 1997). In the study, the CA information was incorporated as an established way of considering the customer through quantification and formalisation.

These studies pick up on two main aspects, that customers are objects over which the company has limited influence and that being a "customer" not only implies being an actor of importance to the organisation, but it has, in effect, become an obligatory passage through which everyone "must" pass if they are to have influence in a contemporary organisation. Hence, CA may be expected to be a powerful tool in influencing intra-organisational processes but also be interpreted by many actors with differing agendas.

5   INTER-ORGANISATIONAL PERSPECTIVES ON CUSTOMER ACCOUNTING

Previously, we have highlighted internal processes and effects that follow from bringing the customer into the organisation in general and from the utilisation of CA more specifically. However, measuring customers has explicit inter-organisational effects, too. In the following we examine how customer accounting can be approached from two related perspectives: a dyadic one, where the management of customers is of primary concern, and a network perspective, where the embeddedness of a firm and its relationships also is taken into consideration.

A Dyadic Perspective: Customer Accounting in Managing Customers

From a dyadic perspective, CA means that a firm will design and use accounting information in relation to specific customers and will manage these relationships on the basis of this information. Certainly, customers may not only be indirectly influenced by the supplier's CA, but also directly use their supplier's CA in various ways. However, these actions can be seen as an example of open-book accounting and will be covered in Chapter 9 in this volume.

As reviewed in Section 3, the literature gives some recommendations on "what to do" with respect to both profitable and, most importantly, unprofitable customers. Empirical descriptions of what companies actually use CA for are, however, difficult to find. Examples do exist in the field of inter-organisational control, though, and Thrane and Hald (2006) demonstrated how customer-related priorities are made on the basis of accounting information. Cäker (2000) provided some examples of changes in administrative and logistical routines that were based on CA information.

Otherwise, most of the detailed examples come from the same authors who provided the normative instructions on how to do CP, namely, Kaplan and Cooper. Kaplan and Cooper (1998) provide an example of a supply chain in a supermarket context. ABC information was used to differentiate pricing on the basis of how customers pursue their operations. Lower prices are to be expected if, according to the suppliers' ABC information, operations are efficient for the supplier. Accounting information, thereby, enters directly into the business negotiations, and the outcome stands out as being a win-win situation. This could be seen as a spin-off of the discussion that Bromwich (1990) initiated on attribute costs, in which it was suggested that companies could organise costing after different parts of offerings to customers in order to be able to match features of costs with the tastes of customers.

In the late 1980s, Kaplan developed a series of case studies on ABC, where some of these focused explicitly on CA. As mentioned before, one example of customer accounting is the Kanthal case (Kaplan 1989a, 1989b) that is still used in textbooks and for teaching (e.g., Kaplan and Atkinson 1998). In this case, Kanthal had problems knowing which customers were profitable and which customers were not. After having conducted an ABC analysis on its customers, the company introduced new routines, emphasised standard products, and charged customers that made small orders with a higher price because of their expensive purchasing behaviour. For some customers the increased costs meant that they had to search for alternatives to Kanthal and in some cases the relationship with Kanthal was terminated. In an ongoing study on Kanthal (conducted by one of the authors of this chapter), the Kanthal case is revisited. The following information was collected during an interview with a sales manager as he reflected on the time when the company introduced the ABC concept:

> The purpose with the ABC project was to turn the unprofitable customers profitable ones for us, but that did not happen. Instead, it was easier to just "fire" the unprofitable customers. Essentially, I don't think one should terminate customer relationships. Customers are our means of living and it is always possible to find new ways to work with them. The risk is, as was the case when we did this ABC project within Kanthal, that we indirectly "fired" customers that we should have kept . . . They [the customers] became disappointed and angry, and thought that we took advantage of our strong market position when we increased prices and introduced extra charges for small orders. Many of these customers started to search for alternatives and I believe that we "created" a new competitive situation for ourselves as we indirectly pushed away the customers by managing them the way we did. In the long run we lost market share due to this.

This quote gives another perspective of what happened after the introduction of customer ABC at Kanthal. Furthermore, it reflects a risky decision, that of changing the conditions in customer relationships that are financially questionable according to a certain CA technique. All accounting techniques, as is the case with different models of CP and CLV, present a simplified picture of reality. In the case of Kanthal the ABC model did not incorporate variables of, apparently, overriding importance. The sales manager from Kanthal would have preferred another solution, at least with hindsight.

One approach to the situation of Kanthal is to suggest that they would have needed to perform further analyses to obtain a more reliable assessment of the outcome. It seems that the CA technique did not encourage managers to take indirect aspects into consideration, or to take account of the embeddedness of Kanthal's relationships.

Further, all relationships seem to have been measured in the same way, irrespective of differences or of heterogeneity. Lind and Strömsten (2006) initiated a discussion about differentiating the techniques according to the different relationships, to point out that a company should take into account the fact that customers are different, with different needs, skills, and experiences, and that they engage in different types of behaviour, and so on. Essentially, one size does not fit all. In most papers on CA, the same CA technique is used in evaluating customers, and it is used in isolation (Lind and Strömsten 2006). For example, customers that account for less than 1 per cent of the firm's total revenues are analysed with the same CA technique as a customer that accounts for 25 per cent. Similarly, customers that are active in product development are evaluated using the same CA technique as a customer that only purchases standard products. Thus, firms account for their customers but do not differentiate between how they use different CA techniques and, hence, how they evaluate customers financially. Thus, the basic motivation for introducing CA, which was the claim that customers are heterogeneous, is not taken to its full length. Instead, Lind and Strömsten argue that some techniques are more suitable for a given relational context. In fact, the techniques chosen ought to be able to both influence and be influenced by the relationship and may also drive it in a certain direction. If the supplier considers a customer relationship to be close, it will evaluate the customer in a certain way, and it will probably have greater patience with this customer than with a customer that is perceived to be more distant or at arm's length.

Lind and Strömsten link the CA techniques identified by Guilding and McManus to four different types of customer relationships: transactional, facilitative, integrative, and connective. In two of the relationships, transactional and facilitative, CP analysis is used, while in the two others, integrative and connective, longer time horizons are needed to motivate the existence of the relationships. In the connective relationships, other relationship benefits are needed, too. Therefore, in these relationships, cash flows are used to approximate a CLV measure. Such an analysis could perhaps have given Kanthal a different view of their "unprofitable" customer relationships.

A Network Perspective: Customer Accounting as a (Dangerous) Orientation within Traditional Management Accounting?

A network contains at least three actors, which are connected to each other (Cook and Emerson 1978). However in a business-to-business setting, the network surrounding a firm is much more complex than this, as resource ties and activity links might span several organisational boundaries (Håkansson and Snehota 1995). The embeddedness of business relationships influences both parties within a relationship; it affects the possibility to perform activities effectively and to innovate, and influences the strategic position of a firm in the network. There is little published research on how organisations account for networks (Hopwood 1996; Mouritsen 1997; Håkansson and Lind 2004) even if this is an area that is receiving more attention nowadays

(Caglio and Dittilo 2008; Scapens and Van der Meer-Kooistra 2008). In this section, therefore, the network perspective on CA is adopted, that is, it is acknowledged that a firm is embedded in a wider network and that its customers are connected to a web of actors.

The literature reviewed in Section 3 is sophisticated when it comes to develop techniques for accounting for customers. Even if the importance of relationships and networks is sometimes acknowledged in this literature, there are few examples on how the CA can be used when a firm is embedded in a wider network of relationships that must be managed simultaneously. Most research within CA has been conducted with an intra-organisational focus and mostly concerns individual relationships with customers. This implies that the CA research reviewed in Section 3 fits nicely into the traditional management accounting literature, where organisational boundaries are of great importance. In this literature (implicitly and explicitly) interaction takes place between firms in competitive markets (Chandler and Daems 1979; Johnson 1981; 1983; Håkansson and Lind 2004). In this management accounting tradition, the company can be perceived to be making the transition from a situation where it is engaged in discrete market transactions to a situation encompassing vertical integration. In short, the information that traditional management accounting provides seems to support these two—hierarchy and market—coordination modes.

Hence, customer accounting research does not seem to fully acknowledge the complexity that exists in industrial relationships, certainly does not take account of how these relationships are connected and form organisational networks. Instead, just like traditional management accounting, CA seems to have been developed in line with the concept of a market-hierarchy dichotomy. This stands in sharp contrast with the development within marketing and in other fields of research, where relationships, and the organisational issues and problems related to relationships and networks, have been of considerable interest since the 1970s (e.g., Arndt 1979; Thorelli 1986; Powell 1990). However, since is appears that the techniques used only take into account the market, which provides a simplified and generalised view of customers, and the hierarchy, defining how to act and coordinate scarce resources, this might create problems when customers' relationships are heterogeneous and embedded in a wider network.

Lind and Strömsten (2006) found that their case companies perceived a need to consider network effects when they made customer accounting analyses in certain situations. In one type of relationship, coined *connective customer relationships*, the interfaces between the supplier and customer are characterised by a high technical interface and a low organisational interface. In such relationships, the products involved are adapted to each individual customer's needs, so the company invests a considerable amount of time and significant resources in the customer, including, where required, adapting its production facilities. Thus, the products and production facility interface get customised. However, the revenues in connective customer relationships are low. Thus, these relationships place special demands on a company because they create high direct costs but only bring low direct revenues. Hence, such a customer relationship needs to contribute indirectly to other relationships by, for example, being a lead user or acting as a bridge to other customers. Since these relationships are hard to motivate in themselves, there is a need to incorporate other relationships in their financial evaluation. Hence, indirect revenues and costs can be associated with these types of relationships, enabling them to be seen as assets, generating future cash flows, albeit through other, connected relationships.

Being embedded in networks implies that a firm is dependent, directly and indirectly, upon actors that it interacts with. As a consequence, this also means that the issue of management control becomes different and more ambiguous. Let us, therefore, shortly return to the Kanthal manager's quote: "... we 'created' a new competitive situation as we 'pushed away' the customers. ..." Kanthal used the information in the intended way and changed the content of the relationships with a number of unprofitable customers. However, according to the sales manager interviewed, Kanthal did not foresee the future effects on the network level as the customers created new relationships with third parties, and identified new suppliers, which became Kanthal's competitors. Kanthal thereby dismissed customers that might never have become profitable to them. But these customers still needed access to the resource, heating elements, and therefore new suppliers were actively sought out and, in a way, "developed". In some sense, therefore, Kanthal created its own competition. There is certainly a cost in a situation like this, but it is one that will never be revealed by traditional accounting systems. How, then, should one account for something that must not be allowed to happen, such as keeping unprofitable customers to prevent them from moving to competitors?

What this illustrates is a need for CA techniques that acknowledge indirect effects and, perhaps more specifically, acknowledge the issue of embeddedness (Granovetter 1985) in an industrial network setting (Håkansson and Snehota 1995). Another view of the traditional accounting techniques is that they must be adapted and take account of the "new reality" (Axelsson and Easton 1992) of industrial networks, which is in line with what Tomkins (2001) argued when he discussed inter-organisational control. Tomkins claimed that traditional techniques might well serve inter-organisational relationships; however, they must be adapted to match each new context in which they are used. The same goes for customer accounting techniques in situations where relationships and networks matter. Essentially, what this comes down to is the issue of embeddedness and the way that the different types of interdependencies between the resources in networks create blurred organisational boundaries. This, combined with accounting's need for closed boundaries, creates a "clash" that is both troublesome and interesting, and the Kanthal case is just one example of this. This takes us on to a section where we discuss what we believe could present challenges, as well as interesting research topics, within customer accounting research.

6 CUSTOMER ACCOUNTING:
AN AGENDA FOR FUTURE RESEARCH

Most studies so far have either been focused on the techniques of CA or have incorporated an intra-organisational perspective on the use of CA for relationships in a general or homogeneous mode. Hence, further research on CA may benefit from the investigation of the five issues presented next.

The Influence of Inter-Organisational Processes on Customer Accounting

First, since our perspective on CA in this chapter is that of traditional management accounting, external influence on CA has not been discussed. However, in outlining future research within the area, it is of interest to notice how intra-organisational processes, like the development of systems to provide CA information, are influenced by inter-organisational processes. Organisations may not always be free to design systems in accordance with their own interests. In business-to-business markets with strong and influential customers, there is evidence that the customer determines the agenda for inter-organisational control, which includes deciding on, or at least influencing, certain internal procedures affecting the suppliers (Dekker 2003; Seal ct al. 2004; Cäker 2008). One common example of this is how customers influence the choice of certain aspects of the firm's costing system. Open-book accounting procedures, implying that internal accounting information is used in an inter-organisational cooperation (Carr and Ng 1995; Mouritsen et al. 2001; Kajüter and Kulmala 2005) have been shown to be accompanied by demands from the dominated actors to understand how the costing systems are developed (Kulmala 2004). CA, thereby, becomes a means for dominated suppliers to control (to some extent) the information that is used as the input for the interaction between the organisations. Kulmala et al. (2002) claim that CA can play a central part in the management of inter-organisational relationships. Thereby it also has the potential to cause problems, as Kajüter and Kulmala (2005) exemplify in discussing problems related to understanding the information produced by the other party and how such problems create disputes over accounting practices. Future research in CA, related to, for example, the establishment of an internal routine will probably gain from acknowledging the role of external influence and dependence.

Customer Accounting in Networks

Second, we argue that approaching customer accounting from a network perspective is an interesting avenue for future research. There are several questions that could be asked when approaching CA from this perspective. To start with, what CA techniques are suitable when taking a network perspective? Each and every CP technique reviewed in Section 3 in this chapter has its ground in product costing, where, in fact, the most challenging task is to allocate indirect costs more accurately to individual products. The same logic is then transferred to another object, namely, the customer. It is questionable, however, if it is really possible to do this without, as Tomkins argued, adapting the concept to the new context. The only dimension that costing is concerned with is that of costs. This is natural, since the historical roots and tradition deal with identifying the right and relevant costs to associate with the different products that a firm manufactures. The revenue side is much more complicated, and we shall return to this later, but for now we can also note that when we bring networks into the equation, the issue of allocating costs to specific customers is more challenging than first thought. This is because relationships are connected in a wider network, and these relationships channel exchanges and resources so that costs travel through relationships, into organisations, and then further away into other exchange relationships. Eventually, a product is used and consumed by a user. However, before that occurs, there is a web of resource interfaces that must be understood if it is to be possible to conduct CA "properly" or "accurately".

In a network, each and every calculable customer relationship rests on another relationship. If we take away one relationship in a network, the situation will change in some dimension, which will also change the "costing" of the relationship and introduce a need for new CA information to be calculated to cover the new situation. The situation becomes even more complex if we add the revenue side. The existing CP literature only considers the measurement of past revenues, which is often quite straightforward. The CLV literature focuses on modelling revenues with the base in past revenues and then examines the impact of switching costs, length of relationship, and sometimes models changes in income or in the relationship. As Hopkinson and Lum (2002) noted, valuation of nonfinancial influences on revenues is rarely conducted at all. Instead, we know how important referrals are, and how important it is that firms work with, through, or even despite customer relationships (see, e.g., Ford et al. 2003). The normal state is to work through, or with the help of, others. The importance of others (Håkansson and Ford 2002) is more or less invisible in the studies reviewed in Section 3. The reason for this is probably that accounting researchers take the organisational boundaries more or less as given, while B2B-marketing researchers—almost by definition—look beyond the boundaries of any organisation. Further, in order to calculate the profitability of a product and a customer, one has to create boundaries, and the organisation is where the revenues and costs are allocated in the end. The legal or, at least, the formal business unit is the natural boundary for accounting researchers, and also for researchers interested in CA. Boundaries are, however, considered to be blurred for most researchers interested in inter-organisational research, but, interestingly, they are not for most of the CA researchers. In CA research, boundaries do not seem to be an issue;

instead, they are viewed as being rather straightforward. Therefore it is possible to calculate both the profitability and the value of a customer.

The Balance between Standardised Processes and Heterogeneous Relationships

Third, firms always strive to create more efficient processes. This is also true for the organisational routines involving accounting and management control and, as a consequence, for CA techniques. Standardisation of the use of different measurements and control techniques is beneficial for the firm because it facilitates the more "efficient" use of resources in these processes. However, as we highlighted in Sections 4 and 5, there is a fine balance between using standardised CA techniques and still continuing to acknowledge the heterogeneity of customer relationships. Further, the CA literature indicates that comparisons should be made between customers to find out which should be prioritised and which should not; there is a need for standardised methods to be obtained. Hence, the balance between the need for efficient internal CA processes and the heterogeneity of a firm's customer base and any possible tensions that might arise are interesting areas for research in the future. What would be interesting to see is how firms manage this balance between standardised CA techniques, in order to facilitate internal processes, but at the same time also use differentiated CA techniques in order to make them suitable in relation to heterogeneous relationships.

Customer Accounting: A Need for Further Case Studies Illustrating Use

A general issue for future research is the need for more in-depth studies on how organisations are using (and are exposed to) customer accounting in its various forms. There is a need for more fine-grained information about how organisational processes are affected and how they affect the design and use of CA techniques. What CA techniques are used in firms, and why, and how they come into practical use are relevant questions to ask for future research.

Research regarding CA, just as when it comes to inter-organisational research in general, is always a question of what perspective should be taken. Should the centre of attention always be on the organisation that is designing and using CA or should the customers also be incorporated in the study? Or should even third parties be studied to ensure that the network level is incorporated? Further, we believe that doing multiple case studies might serve the CA field well, especially if the purpose is to find out under what conditions a certain CA technique is used. Hence, the sampling should take relational or network characteristics into consideration when choosing cases.

Doing in-depth case studies on the use of CA information involves empirical and methodological challenges, because the information needed is in the customer interface, an area which is often sensitive for firms. A related challenge is the question of getting access to multiple organisations. Obtaining access to one organisation and conducting deep case studies is one thing, but gaining access to two organisations in order to fully understand a dyad, or even three or more organisations, in the ideal case, might be a great deal harder, but if networks and network effects are to be understood, this is probably what is needed. Certainly, this type of research design is challenging and would demand considerable resources; nevertheless, a study that incorporated several firms and their use (and considered how firms are exposed to CA) would open up new types of research questions within the field of inter-organisational accounting and control, where information and its effects flow (and continue to create organisational imprints) over organisational boundaries.

Exploring the Interface between Financial and Nonfinancial Customer Accounting

The focus of this chapter has been *financial* CA. As a consequence, an important piece and contribution from the accounting research field is missing, the *nonfinancial* CA research. Within the accounting literature, there has been extensive treatment of nonfinancial information (e.g., Kaplan and Norton 1996; Ittner and Larcker 1998; Olve et al. 2003; Chenhall and Langfield-Smith 2007). One of the motivations behind the development of this literature was to enhance the understanding of the value companies have by measuring the quality of different processes—among other things, customer satisfaction and interactions processes with customers. In conducting the work for this review, we have not come across any empirical descriptions of how practitioners explicitly use any of the numerous CLV techniques that have been suggested. The gap between CLV models and practice is interesting and to explore the role of nonfinancial information in valuing customers would be one approach to study this. Many CLV models have been developed with consumer markets in mind and the complexity of B2B markets may further call for less deductive, more qualitative approaches.

7 CONCLUSIONS

In this chapter we have addressed the issue of customer accounting when relationships and networks matter. The focus in this chapter has been to review and discuss customer accounting from a financial perspective. Two streams of research were identified, where the focus either was on customer profitability, and where customer profitability (CP) is measured on an accrual basis for a specific period of time, or on customer lifetime value (CLV), where cash flows is emphasised and where the time horizon is extended to capture value creation over several years. From the review it was possible to see that CP research mainly was undertaken by accounting researchers, while research on CLV was conducted primarily by marketing researchers and that there seems to be little interaction between the two literatures.

The CLV studies view customers as important assets, and argue that these assets must be properly managed. This side of the CA research often applies mathematical models of CLV and uses quantitative methods. Research from the accounting community on customer accounting, on the other hand, is limited so far, despite calls for research since the mid-1990s. Some accounting scholars work on developing general costing models to support customer analysis. The primary research method is case studies.

Furthermore, customer accounting from both an intra-organisational perspective and an inter-organisational perspective was discussed. There are a small number of studies that focus on how CA techniques are used intra-organisationally. Blois (1999) provides interesting results from his interview-based study on this subject. Many of the interviewees showed scepticism towards accounting and accountants in general. For example, CLV models, discussed earlier, were not actively used by the managers in Blois's study even if a long-term view of relationships often was taken. In the study, the managers firmly believed that they had built profitable relationships even if formal CA information to support this intuition often was lacking. In addition, CA research where a dyadic or network perspective is explicitly taken is still scarce; only a few studies are so far conducted. Different challenges of CA when taking an inter-organisational perspective were identified. One conclusion was the need to acknowledge embeddedness when evaluating customers and to adapt the formal CA techniques and models to an inter-organisational context where indirect effects (see also Chapter 11) should be taken into consideration.

We may conclude that even if some achievements have been made within the CA field, much more remains to be done before CA can contribute substantially to business. A research community which pursues different lines of research is useful in bringing different approaches to our attention. However, a conclusion is that the field of CA would benefit from reducing borders between different streams of research. We believe that this might happen sooner if the accounting and marketing disciplines acknowledge both the possibilities and limitations of their respective fields.

NOTES

1. Guilding and McManus (2002) and Lind and Strömsten (2006) use a typology of four notions, customer profitability analysis, customer lifetime profitability, customer valuation, and customer segment profitability. Both articles

178 *Mikael Cäker and Torkel Strömsten*

focus on use and not on the techniques per se. CLV, according to Pfeifer et al. (2005), would include both customer lifetime profitability and customer valuation. According to Mansour (2004), Guilding and McManus (2002) use lifetime customer profitability analysis to "extend customer profitability analysis into the future to forecast life-time profitability of the customer" and valuation of customers as "the idea of including the value of customer relationships on the balance sheet as an asset", i.e., this is more of a difference in use than a difference in accounting technique. Lind and Strömsten (2006) use customer lifetime profitability to describe the customer relationship in itself and customer valuation to include effects on other relationships and on general development. With this, they suggest that organisations that cannot justify a relationship on the basis of long-term effects internal to the relationship by using customer lifetime profitability should turn to customer valuation and study effects external to the relationship. Customer segment profitability groups individual customers or breaks down the total mass of sales into subgroups in an attempt to obtain a balance between the amount of information and the need to have detailed information.

2. These can be found in Shapiro et al. (1987); Myer (1989); Smith and Dikolli (1995); Foster et al. (1996); Kaplan and Cooper (1998); van Raaij et al. (2003).
3. The three approaches are, besides CLV, based on past revenues, past value, and estimation of future lifetime.
4. For a more complete "within-the-discipline" review, see Jain and Singh (2002), and for short descriptions of many of the relevant papers, see McManus (2006, pp. 49–57).
5. This regards if interest is in the total value. However, for the realisation of this value, both the initiating relationship and the realising relationship are needed, which points at a need to actually incorporate this value in both relationships in evaluating each relationship. We then end up in a situation where the sum is less than the parts.
6. These articles discuss both a financial and a nonfinancial form of customer accounting.

BIBLIOGRAPHY

Achrol, R. S., and Kotler, P. 1999. Marketing in the network economy. *Journal of Marketing* 63: 46–163.

Anandarajan, A., and Christopher, M. 1987. A mission approach to customer profitability analysis. *International Journal of Physical Distribution and Logistics Management* 17: 55–68.

Anderson, E., Fornell, C., and Lehmann, D. 1994. Customer satisfaction, market share, and profitability: Findings from Sweden. *Journal of Marketing* 58: 53–66.

Arndt, J. 1979. Toward a concept of domesticated markets. *Journal of Marketing* 43: 69–75.

Axelsson, B., and Easton., G., eds. 1992. *Industrial networks—a new view of reality.* London: Routledge.

Bellis-Jones, R. 1989. Customer profitability analysis. *Management Accounting* 67: 26–28.

Berger, P., and Nasr, N. 1998. Customer lifetime value: Marketing models and applications. *Journal of Interactive marketing* 12: 17–30.

Berger, P., Weinberg, B., and Hanna, R. 2003. Customer lifetime value determination and strategic implications for a cruise-ship company. *Database Marketing and Customer Strategy Management* 11: 40–52.

Blattberg, R., and Deighton, J. 1996. Managing marketing with the customer equity test. *Harvard Business Review* 74: 136–144.

Blois, K. 1999. Relationship in business-to-business marketing—how is their value assessed? *Marketing Intelligence and Planning* 17: 91–99.

Booth, R. 1994. When customers are more trouble than they're worth. *Management Accounting* 72: 22.

Bromwich, M. 1990. The case for strategic management accounting: The role of accounting information for strategy in competitive markets. *Accounting, Organizations and Society* 15: 27–46.

Caglio, A., and Ditillo, A. 2008. A review and discussion of management control in inter-firm relationships: Achievements and future directions. *Accounting, Organizations and Society* 33: 865–898.

Cäker, M. 2000. *Vad kostar kunden? Modeller för intern redovisning.* Department of Computer Science, University of Linköping, Sweden. Licentiate thesis.

Cäker, M. 2005. *Management accounting as constructing and opposing customer focus: Three case studies on management accounting and customer relations.* Department of Computer Science, University of Linköping Sweden. Doctoral thesis.

Cäker, M. 2007. Customer focus—an accountability dilemma. *European Accounting Review* 16: 143–171.

Cäker, M. 2008. Intertwined coordination mechanisms in interorganizational relationships with dominated suppliers. *Management Accounting Research* 19: 231–251.

Carr, C., and Ng, J. 1995. Total cost control: Nissan and its UK supplier partnerships. *Management Accounting Research* 6: 347–365.

Chandler, A. D., and Daems, H. 1979. Administrative coordination, allocation and monitoring: A comparative analysis of the emergence of accounting and organization in the USA and Europe. *Accounting, Organizations and Society* 4: 2–20.

Chenhall, R. 2008. Accounting for the horizontal organization: A review essay. *Accounting, Organizations and Society* 33: 517–550.

Chenhall, R., and Langfield-Smith, K. 2007. Multiple perspectives of performance measures. *European Management Journal* 25: 266–282.

Christner, H., Lind, J., Strömsten, T., and Almgren, A. 2008. Kundstrategier och kundlönsamhetsbedömninar—en studie av Holmen Paper. In *Redovisning i fokus,* ed. Jennergren, P., Lind, J., Schuster, W., and Skogsvik, K. 111–128. Lund, Sweden: Studentlitteratur.

Connolly, T., and Ashworth, G. 1994. Managing customers for profit. *Management Accounting* 72: 34–40.

Cook, K. S., and Emerson, R. M. 1978. Power, equity and commitment in exchange networks. *American Sociological Review* 43: 721–739.

Cooper, R. 1989. You need a new cost system when . . . *Harvard Business Review* 67: 77–82.

Cooper, R., and Kaplan, R. 1991. Profit priorities from activity-based costing. *Harvard Business Review* 69: 130–135.

Dekker, H. 2003. Value chain analysis in interfirm relationships: A field study. *Management Accounting Research* 14: 1–23.

DeWayne, S. 2004. Using activity-based costing to assess channel/customer profitability. *Management Accounting Quarterly* 5: 51–60.

Dikolli, S., Kinney, W., and Sedatole, K. 2007. Measuring customer relationship value: The role of switching cost. *Contemporary Accounting Research* 24: 93–132.

Du Gay, P., and Salaman, G. 1992. The Cult[ure] of the customer. *Journal of Management Studies* 29: 615–633.

Ford, D., Gadde, L.-E., Håkansson, H., and Snehota, I. 2003. *Managing Business Relationships*. London: Wiley.
Foster, G., and Gupta, M. 1994. Marketing, cost management and management accounting. *Journal of Management Accounting Research* 6: 43–77.
Foster, G., Gupta, M., and Sjöblom, L. 1996. Customer profitability analysis: Challenges and new directions. *Journal of Cost Management* 10: 5–18.
Goebel, D., Marshall, G., and Locander, W. 1998. Activity-based costing: Accounting for a market orientation. *Industrial Marketing Management* 27: 497–510.
Granovetter, M. 1985. Economic action and social structure: The problem of embeddedness. *American Journal of Sociology* 78: 481–510.
Guilding, C., and McManus, L. 2002. The incidence, perceived merit and antecedents of customer accounting: An explanatory note. *Accounting, Organization and Society* 27: 45–59.
Gupta, S., and Lehmann, D. 2003. Customer as assets. *Journal of Interactive Marketing* 17: 9–24.
Håkansson, H., ed. 1982. *International marketing and purchasing of industrial goods. An interaction approach*. London: Wiley.
Håkansson, H., and Ford, D. 2002. How should companies interact in business networks? *Journal of Business Research* 55: 133–139.
Håkansson, H., and Lind, J., 2004. Accounting and network coordination. *Accounting, Organizations and Society* 29: 51–72.
Håkansson, H., and Östberg. C. 1975. Industrial marketing—an organizational problem? *Industrial Marketing Management* 4: 187–123.
Håkansson, H., and Snehota., I. 1995. *Developing relationships in business networks*. London: Routledge.
Håkansson, H., and Waluszewski, A. 2002. *Managing technological development: IKEA, the environment and technology*. London: Routledge.
Helgesen, Ø. 2007. Customer accounting and customer profitability analysis for the order handling industry—a managerial accounting approach. *Industrial Marketing Management* 36: 757–769.
Hergert, M., and Morris, D. 1989. Accounting data for value chain analysis. *Strategic Management Journal* 10: 175–188.
Hope, J. 1998. Customers. *Management Accounting* 76: 20–23.
Hopkinson, G., and Lum, C. 2002. Valuing customer relationships: Using the capital asset pricing model (CAPM) to incorporate relationship risk. *Journal of Targeting, Measurement and Analysis for Marketing* 10: 220–232.
Hopwood, A. 1996. Looking across rather than up and down: On the need to explore the lateral processing of information. *Accounting, Organizations and Society* 21: 589–590.
Innes, J., and Mitchell, F. 1995. A survey of activity-based costing in the UK's largest companies. *Management Accounting Research* 6: 137–153.
Ittner, C. D., and Larcker, D. F. 1998. Are nonfinancial measures leading indicators for financial performance? An analysis of customer satisfaction. *Journal of Accounting Research* 36: 1–35.
Jacobs, F., Johnston, W., and Kotchetova, N. 2001. Customer profitability: Prospective vs. retrospective approaches in a business-to-business setting. *Industrial Marketing Management* 30: 353–363.
Jain, D., and Singh, S. 2002. Customer lifetime value research in marketing: A review and future directions. *Journal of Interactive Marketing* 16: 34–46.
Johanson, J. 1966. *Svenskt Specialstål på utländska marknader*. Department of Business Studies, Uppsala University, Sweden. Licentiate thesis.
Johnson, T. 1981. Toward a new understanding of nineteenth-century cost accounting. *Accounting Review* 56: 510–518.

Johnson, T. 1983. The search for gain in markets and firms: A review of the historical emergence of management accounting systems. *Accounting, Organizations and Society* 8: 139–146.

Kajüter, P., and Kulmala, H. 2005. Open-book accounting in networks: Potential achievements and reasons for failures. *Management Accounting Research* 16: 179–204.

Kaplan, R. 1989a. *Kanthal (A)*. Harvard Business School (9–190–002).

Kaplan, R. 1989b. *Kanthal (B)*. Harvard Business School (9–190–003).

Kaplan, R. 1990. *Manufacturers Hanover Corporation: Customer profitability report*. Harvard Business School (9–191–068).

Kaplan, R., and Atkinson, A. 1998. *Advanced management accounting*. Upper Saddle River, NJ: Prentice Hall.

Kaplan, R., and Cooper, R. 1998. *Cost and effect: Using integrated cost systems to drive profitability and performance*. Boston: Harvard Business School Press.

Kaplan, R., and Norton, D. 1996. *The balanced scorecard: Translating strategy into action*. Boston: Harvard Business School Press.

Kulmala, H. 2004. Developing cost management in customer-supplier relationships: Three case studies. *Journal of Purchasing and Supply Management* 10: 65–77.

Kulmala, H., Paranko, J., and Uusi-Rauva, E. 2002. The role of cost management in network relationships. *International Journal of Production Economics* 10: 33–43.

Kumar, V., and Morris, G. 2007. Measuring and maximizing customer equity: A critical analysis. *Journal of the Academy of Marketing Science* 35: 157–171.

Kumar, V., and Shah, D. 2004. Building and sustaining profitable customer loyalty for the 21st century. *Journal of Retailing* 80: 317–329.

Lind, J., and Strömsten, T. 2006. When do firms use different types of customer accounting? *Journal of Business Research* 59: 1257–1266.

Lord, B. 2007. Strategic management accounting. In *Issues in management accounting*, ed. Hopper, T., Northcott, D., and Scapens, R. Harlow, UK: Prentice Hall.

Mansour, R. 2004. Summary of Guilding and McManus, 2002. Retrieved 2008–08–03, from http://maaw.info/ArticleSummaries/ArtSumGuildingMcManus02.htm.

McManus, L. 2006. *An examination of customer accounting in an Australian context*. Department of Accounting, Finance and Economics. Griffith University, Gold Coast, Australia. Doctoral thesis.

McManus, L., and Guilding, C. 2008. Exploring the potential of customer accounting: A synthesis of the accounting and marketing literatures. *Journal of Marketing Management* 24: 771–795.

McNair, C. 2007. On target: Customer-driven lean management. In *Lean Accounting: Best practices for sustainable integration*, ed. Stenzel, J. Hoboken, NJ: Wiley.

Mouritsen, J. 1997. Marginalizing the customer: Customer orientation, quality and accounting performance. *Scandinavian Journal of Management* 13: 5–18.

Mouritsen, J., Hansen, A., and Hansen, C. 2001. Inter-organizational controls and organizational competencies: Episodes around target cost management/functional analysis and open book accounting. *Management Accounting Research* 12: 221–244.

Mulhern, F. 1999. Customer profitability analysis: Measurement, concentration and research directions. *Journal of Interactive Marketing* 13: 25–40.

Myer, R. 1989. Suppliers—manage your customers. *Harvard Business Review* 67: 160–168.

Ness, J., Schroeck, M., Letendre, R., and Douglas, W. 2001. The role of ABM in measuring customer value: Part two. *Strategic Finance* 82: 44–49.

Niraj, R., Foster, G., Gupta, M., and Narasimhan, C. 2008. Understanding customer level profitability implications of satisfaction programs. *Journal of Business and Industrial Marketing* 23: 454–463.

Ogden, S. 1997. Accounting for organizational performance: The construction of the customer in the privatized water industry. *Accounting, Organization and Society* 22: 529–556.

Olve, N.-G., Petri, C.-J, Roy, J., and Roy, S. 2003. *Making scorecard actionable: Balancing strategy and control.* Chichester, UK: John Wiley & Sons.

Payant, R. 2003. The challenges and opportunities of customer profitability analysis. *The Journal of Bank Cost and Management Accounting* 16: 41–47.

Penrose, E. T. 1959. *The theory of the growth of the firm.* Oxford: Basil Blackwell.

Pfeifer, P., Haskins, M., and Conroy, R. 2005. Customer lifetime value, customer profitability, and the treatment of acquisition spending. *Journal of Managerial Issues* 17: 11–25.

Powell. W. W. 1990. Neither market nor hierarchy: Network forms of organization. *Research in Organizational Behavior* 12: 295–336.

Rappaport, A. 1986. *Creating shareholder value: A guide for managers and investors.* New York: Free Press.

Reichheld, F. 1993. Loyalty-based management. *Harvard Business Review* 71: 64–73.

Reinartz, W., and Kumar, V. 2000. On the profitability of long-life customers in a noncontractual setting: An empirical investigation and implications for marketing. *Journal of Marketing* 64: 17–35.

Rust, R., Lemon, K., and Zeithaml, V. 2004. Return on marketing: Using customer equity to focus on marketing strategy. *Journal of Marketing* 68: 109–127.

Scapens, R., and Van der Meer-Kooistra, J. 2008. The governance of lateral relations between and within organisations. *Management Accounting Research* 19: 365–384.

Seal, W., Berry A., and Cullen, J. 2004. Disembedding the supply chain: Institutionalized reflexivity and inter-firm accounting. *Accounting, Organization and Society* 29: 73–92.

Shank, J. K., and Govindarajan, V. 1992. Strategic cost management: The value chain perspective. *Journal of Management Accounting Research* 4: 179–197.

Shapiro, B., Rangan, K., Moriarty, R., and Ross, E. 1987. Manage customers for profits (not just sales). *Harvard Business Review* 65: 1–9.

Smith, M., and Dikolli, S. 1995. Customer profitability analysis: An activity-based costing approach. *Managerial Auditing Journal* 10: 3–7.

Srivastava R. K., Shervani T. A., and Fahey, L. 1998. Market based assets and shareholder value: A framework for analysis. *Journal of Marketing* 62: 2–18.

Stahl, H. K., Matzler, K., and Hinterhuber, H. H. 2003. Linking customer lifetime value with shareholder value. *Industrial Marketing Management* 32: 267–279.

Strömsten, T. 2006. Ericssons turnaround: Styrning i kris och förändring. *Bonniers ledarskapshandbok.* Stockholm, Sweden: Bonnier.

Strömsten, T., and Håkansson, H. 2007. Resources in use: The embedded electricity. In *Knowledge and innovation in business and industry. The importance of using others,* ed. Håkansson, H., and Waluszewski, A. London: Routledge.

Thomas, J. 2001. A methodology for linking customer acquisition to customer retention. *Journal of Marketing Research* 38: 262–268.

Thorelli, H. B. 1986. Networks: Between markets and hierarchies. *Strategic Management Journal* 7: 37–51.

Thrane, S., and Hald, K. 2006. The emergence of boundaries and accounting in supply fields: The dynamics of integration and fragmentation. *Management Accounting Research* 17: 288–314.

Tomkins, C. 2001. Interdependencies, trust and information in relationships, alliances and networks. *Accounting, Organization and Society* 26: 161–191.

Vaivio, J. 1999. Examining "the quantified customer". *Accounting, Organization and Society* 24: 689–715.

van Raaij, E., Vernooij, M., and van Triest, S. 2003. The implementation of customer profitability analysis: A case study. *Industrial Marketing Management* 32: 573–583.

Venkatesan, R., and Kumar, V. 2004. A customer lifetime value framework for customer selection and resource allocation strategy. *Journal of Marketing* 68: 106–125.

Womack, J. P, Jones, D. T., and Roos, D. 1991. *The machine that changed the world: The story of lean production.* New York, NY: Macmillan Publishing Company.

8 Target Costing in Inter-Organisational Relationships and Networks

Martin Carlsson-Wall and Kalle Kraus

1 INTRODUCTION

This chapter is about target costing in inter-organisational relationships and networks. Originating in Japan, target costing has been the object of increased attention in the West since the 1990s and has become a central accounting practice vital for product development (Kato 1993; Ansari and Bell 1997; Cooper and Slagmulder 1997; Ansari et al. 2007). It is claimed that 70 to 80 per cent of product costs are committed during development, and target costing aims to reduce costs already "on the drawing board" (Cooper and Chew 1996). By linking cost management to technology investments, target costing has been claimed to be "the next frontier within strategic cost management" (Ansari and Bell 1997). According to Ansari et al. (2007), target costing was an important factor behind the turnaround of Caterpillar in the mid-1990s. Other successful adaptations include Toyota, Olympus, and Komatsu (Cooper and Chew 1996; Cooper and Slagmulder 1997, 2004). The starting point and underlying logic is captured in the target costing equation (Ansari and Bell 1997):

Estimated Selling Price—Desired Profit = Target Cost

The equation demonstrates how the target cost is the cost at which the company can afford to sell the product and still make enough profit to satisfy its owners (Cooper and Slagmulder 1997; Everaert et al. 2006). The estimated selling price is determined by what customers are willing to pay. Important considerations are how well the product satisfies customers' needs and the price of comparable products available from competitors. The target profit is determined by the return on capital requirements of the owners. By disciplining design engineers, the goal of target costing is to ensure that unprofitable products are never launched. Two combinatory factors have been put forward to explain the need to be certain that products are profitable from the day that they are launched: increasing development costs and shorter product life-cycles (Cooper and Chew 1996; Ansari and Bell 1997). For example, if development costs were to be increased from $5 to $10 million at the same time as a product's life cycle is reduced from four to two years, it would be very difficult to recover the development costs unless the products were to be profitable right from the launch of the product (Ansari and Bell 1997; Everaert et al. 2006).

Table 8.1 illustrates how target costing differs from traditional cost-plus costing. The primary difference relates to the starting point: For cost-plus costing, internal costs are the starting point and the price is set once the costs are known; in contrast, for target costing, the acceptable costs are determined by the price external customers are willing to pay. A second difference relates to the focus. For cost-plus costing, costs are reduced after design when the costs are known and the product is in production. In contrast, target costing starts during the design stage because the largest cost savings are achieved by not allowing some components to be made at all (Ansari and Bell 1997). A third and final difference relates to the temporal scope. For cost-plus costing, it is the immediate product costs that need to be considered. In contrast, target costing takes the perspective of the life cycle of the product and the effort is put into minimising the cost of ownership for both the company and its customers (Ansari and Bell 1997).

Traditionally, target costing has focused on intra-organisational activities (Ansari et al. 2007).[1] Development projects are organised using cross-functional teams, which analyze current costs to see if they can attain the target cost. When there is a mismatch, the teams are forced to seek alternative solutions. Individual components are investigated to ensure that customer preferences can be met within the limits imposed on the costs. If the target cost cannot be met, the company must choose between closing down the project or identifying other positive effects for the product portfolio or specific customers (Cooper and Slagmulder 1997).

However, despite the intra-organizational focus, recent studies point to the importance of involving suppliers in the target costing process (Mouritsen et al. 2001; Cooper and Slagmulder 2004; Carlsson-Wall et al. 2009). When key technologies and 60–70 per cent of costs are located outside firm boundaries, collaboration with suppliers becomes crucial for financial success (Carr and Ng 1995; Cooper and Slagmulder 2004;

Table 8.1   Comparing Cost-Plus Costing with Target Costing

Costing Themes	Cost-Plus Costing	Target Costing
Starting point	Internal costs	Customer price
Focus	Production	Design
Temporal scope	Immediate product focus	Life-cycle perspective

Agndal and Nilsson 2009). In this respect, it is interesting to note that a recent review of target costing by Ansari et al. (2007, p. 522) concluded: "Since target costing originated in the automobile and assembly industries where a major portion of the costs come from suppliers, the process of involving suppliers in the target costing efforts is a major topic of interest."

This inter-organisational dimension of target costing is therefore the focus of this chapter, which starts off with a literature review of target costing in inter-organisational relationships and networks.[2] The literature is organised into three threads: a managerial, a structural, and a process one. For each of these, the empirical base, methodological considerations and use of theory are discussed. From this literature review, a number of issues regarding target costing in networks are discussed. A central argument is that new exiting avenues for target costing research can open up by explicitly theorising the product development process. Drawing on a case study of target costing in the development of industrial robotic systems, empirical advancements are thereafter presented followed by conclusions and suggestions for future research.

2   LITERATURE REVIEW ON TARGET COSTING IN NETWORKS

The literature review commences with an examination of the information obtained from the databases Business Source Premier, Emerald, JStor, Sage Publications, and ScienceDirect. In addition the three books, Cooper and Slagmulder (1997, 1999) and Ansari and Bell (1997), have been included. A total of seventeen articles and books were drawn upon, with the inter-organisational dimension of target costing being a theme that was common to them all. However, the approaches to target costing differ. As mentioned earlier, the articles can be divided into three threads: a managerial, a structural, and a process thread. These are discussed following.

The Managerial Thread

The first thread concerns normative studies primarily directed towards managers. Two main themes within this line of thought are positive effects and managerial guidelines (Ansari and Bell 1997; Cooper and Slagmulder 1997, 1999, 2003a, 2003b; Swenson et al. 2003; Ansari et al. 2006). Among positive effects, Ansari and Bell (1997) describe the turnaround of Chrysler. Using target costing, revenues increased by 70 per cent and Chrysler's profit margin went from 0.33 per cent to 7.1 per cent. Describing the positive effects, Ansari and Bell (1997, p. 2) wrote: "The Chrysler story shows how a target costing process, when well executed, can improve a firm's competitive position by reducing costs, improving quality and reducing time to market. Nor is Chrysler the only success story in this respect."

Positive effects obtained from the implementation of target costing are often highly related to suppliers. Studying best practice at Toyota, Cooper, and Slagmulder (1997, p. 141) argued: "At Toyota, third-party suppliers are responsible for approximately 70% of the parts and materials required to produce the firm's automobiles. This high level of dependency on externally supplied items makes supplier relationships extremely critical to the firm's success."

Managerial guidelines are a second theme. According to Ansari and Bell (1997), success relies on three main supplier activities: characterisation, rationalisation, and involvement. To begin with, companies must characterise their supplier relationships. This involves classifying suppliers according to their 'distance' from the focal firm (i.e., determining whether they are tier-1 or tier-2 suppliers) and the level of design work suppliers do for the project (Ansari and Bell 1997). Secondly, companies must rationalise. Instead of having a large number of suppliers, successful companies like Chrysler (Ansari and Bell 1997) and Toyota (Cooper and Slagmulder 1997) work more intensively with a relatively small number of suppliers. In addition to the mutual adaptations, this decreases procurement costs (Ansari and Bell 1997; Cooper and Slagmulder 2003a). Thirdly, companies involve suppliers during the conceptual design of their products (Ansari and Bell 1997; Cooper and Slagmulder 1997). Since 70–80 per cent of costs are committed before the product is in production, supplier feedback is needed as early as possible (Ansari and Bell 1997). However, managerial guidelines also include many subtechniques. Describing best practice at Boeing, Caterpillar, and DaimlerChrysler, Swenson et al. (2003) highlighted advantages to be gained from value engineering/analysis, design for manufacturing assembly, paper kaizen, and lean manufacturing. Even though all subtechniques contribute to attaining the target cost, value engineering is the most frequently discussed (Ansari and Bell 1997; Cooper and Slagmulder 1997, 2003a, 2003b; Swenson et al. 2003; Ansari et al. 2006). Describing value engineering in the development of the Chrysler Neon, Ansari et al. (2006, p. 22) wrote: "An early art rendering of Chrysler's Neon, a small car aimed at the low price segment showed a car with a front of a Maserati and the back of a Volvo . . . Clearly, this ambitious combination of features was scaled down to match the strategic position of the car. However, even after the repositioning, a significant gap usually remains. This gap is closed using value engineering."

According to Ansari et al. (2006), value engineering is accomplished in three steps. Zero-level value engineering concerns major technologies and customer features. This is followed by first-level value engineering, which focuses on product design, and second-level value engineering, where only modest refinements are possible (Ansari et al. 2006). Cross-functional teams are vital to the success of value engineering, as mentioned previously (Ansari and Bell 1997; Cooper and Slagmulder 1997). By including project members from marketing, engineering, production, and logistics, different technical options can be evaluated. The suppliers are involved to some extent in the first-level engineering, but are integral to the second-level engineering. By adapting technical specifications to suppliers' product portfolios and production processes, costs can be further reduced (Cooper and Slagmulder 2003b). Target costing and value engineering have also been extended to supplier networks (Cooper and Slagmulder 1999, 2003a, 2003b). In a conceptual article, Cooper and Slagmulder (2003a, p. 12) argued: "The primary benefit of chained target costing systems lies in their ability to transmit the competitive pressure faced by the firm at the top of the chain to other firms in the chain."

Cooper and Slagmulder (1999, 2003a, 2003b) differentiate between three types of supplier networks: kingdoms, baronies, and republics. In a kingdom, the network is ruled by a dominant king who pushes down orders to suppliers. In a barony, there are several core companies, but, together, they are powerful enough to influence suppliers. Finally, within a republic, there is no core company in the network. According to Cooper and Slagmulder (1999, 2003a, 2003b), a kingdom or barony is necessary for the successful implementation of target costing in a supplier network. Within a republic, network parties have too many individual wills, and it is difficult to create the required climate for mutual improvements to be brought about.

To summarise, the managerial thread focuses on positive effects and managerial guidelines. Empirically, best practice from large automotive and consumer electronics companies is described. Common examples include Toyota and Chrysler. Because of the managerial focus, there is limited theoretical and methodological discussion within this thread.

The Structural Thread

A second line of research concerns structural studies directed at an academic audience (Carr and Ng 1995; Gietzmann 1996; Ellram 2000, 2002, 2006; Cooper and Slagmulder 2004), where a central issue is the empirical and theoretical investigation of supplier dyads. An early example is that of Gietzmann (1996). Studying Japanese companies and drawing on agency theory and transaction cost economics, Gietzmann proposes three types of supplier dyads. The first of these is for standard off-the-shelf components. Without customisation, interaction is minimal and traditional accounting involving price comparisons is suitable. However, when supplier dyads include product development, price alone is inadequate and information sharing needs to be more sophisticated and intense. The second and third types, therefore, involve a higher degree of joint design. Complex components are developed in "design approved" relationships, which are long-term ones characterised by high levels of trust. Even though Gietzmann (1996) is often overlooked within the target costing literature, he (p. 619) particularly emphasises the importance of target costing and value engineering: "Of particular interest is DA [drawings approved] suppliers, which have been less prevalent in Europe and the USA . . . by using value engineering and target costing procedures, the assembler can forgo much of the development cost of component parts for new vehicle models while still maintaining an influence on final specification and cost."

A similar, but more detailed, study is provided by Cooper and Slagmulder (2004). When they, too, used transaction cost economics, they found that supplier dyads are linked to target costing clusters. Starting with standard components, a first cluster is called "Functional-Price-Quality Tradeoffs". This cluster involves a modest interaction which is associated with a fairly restricted ability to affect the design. Typically, costs are reduced by just 0–5 per cent. Continuing with more complex components, major suppliers use "Inter-organizational Cost Investigations" (Cooper and Slagmulder 2004). Here, the interaction is more intense and there is a greater scope for development. For example, a close relationship is established between the product design and the production processes, with the result that costs are typically reduced by 5–10 per cent. Finally, suppliers can be considered to be family members which belong to a cluster called "Concurrent Cost Management" (CCM). Family members are long-term suppliers characterised by high levels of interaction and trust. Typically, costs are reduced by 10–15 per cent. Cooper and Slagmulder (2004) describe the usage of CCM by the Japanese manufacturer Komatsu and its supplier Toyo. The challenge was enormous: to increase product capacity by 40 per cent, while only allowing costs to increase by 18 per cent. To succeed, Toyo, a single-source supplier, was invited to participate at a stage when it was possible for the technical design to be changed. In contrast to situations exemplifying lower levels of involvement, Komatsu set a target cost for the entire cooling system and then let Toyo decide the target cost for individual components. Because of the long-term focus, both parties shared strategic information about future products and borrowed key resources from one another. Cooper and Slagmulder (2004) also described two ways of conducting CCM, which they termed parallel or simultaneous engineering. During the initial design phase, or when there was a need for intense interaction, simultaneous engineering was used, with, as the name indicates, the two companies engaging in simultaneous activity. However, the normal stage is that of parallel engineering, where the two companies decide about the allocation of responsibilities and then each company conducts its own design activities for its respective tasks.

Ellram (2000, 2002, 2006), too, highlights the need to differentiate between types of supplier dyads. However, in contrast to Cooper and

Slagmulder (2004), the purchasing function is the centre of attention of her investigation. Studying eleven American companies, she argued that purchasing is especially important for close supplier relationships and that, when purchasers are responsible for supplier relationships, the most important activities are the identification, qualification, and handling of financial issues (Ellram 2000). Since close relationships involved both cooperation and conflict, Ellram (2002) described how purchasers handle "the business issues", while engineers focus on technical problem solving and, by showing these complementary roles, one of the major conclusions Ellram draws is the importance of cross-functional teams (Ellram 2000, 2002, 2006). Also emphasising the role of cross-functional teams, Carr and Ng (1995) demonstrated the link to strategic business plans in a study of Nissan UK. They illustrated how target costs for the Nissan Micra also included the sales volumes and profit margins on other products. According to Carr and Ng (1995), this holistic way of thinking shows how target costing is more than an isolated costing technique.

To summarise, the structural thread focuses on supplier dyads and the linkages between target costing and relationship complexity. Multiple case studies from Japan and America are frequent, but compared to the managerial thread, the companies concerned cover a wider spectrum of industries. Transaction cost economics is the most commonly used theory and, because of its academic focus, methodology discussions are of greater depth than they are for the managerial thread.

The Process Thread

A third thread concerns process studies, which are directed towards an academic audience (Nicolini et al. 2000; Mouritsen et al. 2001; Agndal and Nilsson 2009; Carlsson-Wall et al. 2009). In contrast to the managerial and the structural thread, product development is not seen as a rational process.[3] Instead, target costing is problematised and a key issue is to identify and explore challenges and tensions associated with target costing.

Studying UK construction, Nicolini et al. (2000) investigated information quality in supplier relationships. Using an action study approach, the researchers introduced target costing in two Ministry of Defence projects to build army training facilities. Based on normative guidelines, the projects start with the contractor writing a strategic brief. This is followed by functional requirements and discussions about particular requirements in the service. However, tensions quickly appeared. A first challenge is the difficulty of setting a target cost. The main contractor does not have a standard building to benchmark with, and each customer wants something special. Together with inadequate costing information, this creates a "Catch 22" situation: Without cost data, it is difficult to finalise a design, but without a detailed design, it is difficult to provide an estimate of costs. Problems with information quality further make it difficult to estimate life-cycle costs. With simple cost systems, few suppliers have cost data on durability and maintenance. It is therefore problematic to gather the data required to conduct a life-cycle analysis. A second challenge is that the discounted cash flow (DCF) model favours existing solutions. It is difficult to assess the future value of innovation when so many elements are unknown. As the finance manager says (Nicolini et al. 2000, p. 313): "In the project we considered the possibility of a very innovative maintenance-free aluminium swimming pool. However, once the data was inputted in the cost model, it appeared that more traditional solutions performed better when a DCF model is used. The DCF ends up hampering innovation and investments . . . it focuses on the here and now."

While Nicolini and his coauthors problematise information quality, Mouritsen et al. (2001) focus on the unpredictable effects of target costing. Using actor-network theory, they followed a Danish company called NewTech. After outsourcing product development, NewTech experienced a lack of control. Suppliers did not want to adapt or learn about interdependencies in relation to NewTech's other products. To regain control, functional analysis was introduced. By specifying the functional requirements, interaction between NewTech and its suppliers increased. However, solving one tension created another because increased control tended to reduce the speed at which development occurs. NewTech therefore complemented its functional guidelines with a purchasing budget. This way, suppliers learnt which functionality NewTech wanted as well as how much they were willing to pay for it. The result was an improved ability to identify "the right solution". According to Mouritsen et al. (2001), this shows how functional analysis simplifies a situation and creates a consensus about important interdependencies. Another unexpected effect concerned intra-organisational activities within NewTech. When functional analysis was introduced, it did not only improve inter-organisational coordination; NewTech also began to analyse what was taking place within the company. Over time, this led to substantial changes in terms of the core competence, organisation, and use of technology. Instead of developing products internally, NewTech became a 'systems integrator', learning about customers' needs and coordinating a network of suppliers.

Agndal and Nilsson (2009) use the industrial-network approach and highlight the supplier's perspective of target costing. Since the supplier often has most knowledge of the actual costs, it is difficult for the customer to determine an accurate cost. Instead, cost reduction is a more interactive process. The customer sets a preliminary target cost, which is then updated when the technical solution changes. Criticising previous target costing literature for being too focused on individual firms, Agndal and Nilsson (2009, p. 99) conclude: "Many authors argue that target costing is especially appropriate in the case of selecting suppliers for complex components that require a great deal of R&D. To the contrary, our findings indicate that this situation presents serious difficulties when attempting to apply the 'pure' target costing logic, since neither party can specify the component in detail at this stage. Consequently, pushing the market-derived price further up the supply chain is almost impossible."

Also using the industrial-network approach, Carlsson-Wall et al. (2009) further problematise the spatial dimension of target costing. They argue that one shortcoming in the previous literature on target costing is that supplier relationships are viewed in isolation. Based on a case study of ABB Robotics, they demonstrate how product development is a puzzling process where companies are embedded in a complex network of relationships. During some stages, the development process is characterised by hierarchical planning, that is, ABB Robotics dictates the conditions for their suppliers. However, during other stages, the development process is characterised by collective improvisation, where ABB Robotics, together with its suppliers and the suppliers' suppliers, works out pragmatic compromises to unexpected problems. Such complexity in the inter-organisational product development has implications for the understanding of target costing. Target costing has numerous roles in inter-organisational product development. During hierarchical planning, ABB Robotics takes on a dominant buying role controlling the suppliers through gate models, quality audits, and functional analysis. The development process has clear goals and, thereby, target costing has a disciplining role, helping ABB Robotics to see how the different functions met subtarget costs, deadlines, and technical specifications. However, when collective improvisation occurs, the target costing process is more interactive and nonhierarchical. Target costing plays a role in guiding the problem solving, thereby facilitating and directing knowledge integration between Robotics and its network of suppliers. Sometimes target costing forms the basis for rejecting technically well-functioning solutions, because they are determined to be too expensive. On other occasions, target costing is used to search for possible solutions that represent compromises between improved technological content and additional costs (Carlsson-Wall et al. 2009).

Summary of the Literature Review

To summarise, Table 8.2 describes the three research threads in terms of empirics, theory, and methods.[4] Overall, this shows how target costing in networks has grown considerably during the past ten years.

Starting with *the managerial thread*, important contributions are to describe positive effects and propose detailed managerial guidelines (Ansari and Bell 1997; Cooper and Slagmulder 1997). Directing efforts towards managers, this line of research has been instrumental in diffusing target costing among practitioners. Empirically, the focus has been on best-practice companies such as Toyota and Chrysler, and the research conducted has illustrated how these global consumer companies used target costing in corporate turnarounds; a situation in which the positive effects are highly visible. Placing the focus on managers means that there is less theoretical or methodological discussion than there would otherwise be.

Within *the structural thread*, a main contribution is from the theoretical and empirical investigation of supplier dyads. Drawing mainly on transaction cost economics and a wider spectrum of Japanese and American companies, this line of research has linked target costing with relationship complexity (Gietzmann 1996; Cooper and Slagmulder 2004). However, to realise large cost reductions, companies are dependent on close supplier relationships characterised by trust and a long-term focus. Another contribution has also been to describe the importance of cross-functional teams (Carr and Ng 1995; Ellram 2000, 2002, 2006). In particular, the numerous roles played by the purchasing function have been illustrated. Within the structural thread, multiple case studies are the preferred method.

Finally, within *the process thread*, a significant contribution is the theoretical and empirical problematisation of target costing. By breaking with product development as a rational process, challenges to target costing are discussed. Empirically, small, midsize, and large European companies are investigated. In contrast to describing target costing on an organisational level, daily practice on a project level is highlighted (Nicolini et al. 2000; Carlsson-Wall et al. 2009). Theoretically, actor-network theory (Mouritsen et al. 2001) and the industrial-network approach (Agndal and Nilsson 2009; Carlsson-Wall et al. 2009) are used and single as well as multiple case studies are used to gather empirical data.

Table 8.2 Summarising the Three Lines of Research Identified in the Literature

Characteristics	Managerial Thread	Structural Thread	Process Thread
Contribution	Positive effects, managerial guidelines	Structure of supplier dyads	Problematisation, tensions and challenges
Empirical	Toyota, Chrysler, and other best-practice companies	Large Japanese and American companies from different industries	Various European companies and projects from different industries
Theoretical	N/A	Agency theory, transaction cost economics	Actor-network theory, the industrial-network approach
Method	Best-practice illustrations	Multiple case studies	Single and multiple case studies

3 TARGET COSTING IN NETWORKS—INCORPORATING PRODUCT DEVELOPMENT THEORIES

From our literature review, we conclude that most studies on target costing in networks rarely discuss assumptions about product development. This is surprising because product development conceptualisation can be assumed to impact on the way that target costing is described and analysed. In the following, we will address this issue by linking target costing in networks to theories of product development in both time and space.

Time: Basic Assumptions of the Product Development Process

One important dimension when theorising about product development is how the characteristics of the process are viewed. We conclude that the majority of studies (implicitly) consider product development to be a *rational process* (Carr and Ng 1995; Gietzmann 1996; Ansari and Bell 1997; Cooper and Slagmulder 1997, 1999, 2003a, 2003b, 2004; Ellram 2000, 2002, 2006; Ansari et al. 2006). This implies that the product development process can be broken down into a predictable series of well-defined steps where a key issue is to minimise the uncertainty by planning and follow-ups. Planning and implementation are considered separately and the managers direct their employees and suppliers.

The adoption of a rational view of product development in the majority of studies on target costing is surprising because the rational model has been highly criticised in the product development literature. Since the mid-1990s, product development researchers have argued that the rational model of product development is deficient in that it fails to capture the importance of improvisation, discovery, and learning in product development processes (Brown and Eisenhardt 1995, 1997; Kamoche and Cunha 2001). In today's highly complex and turbulent environments, it is impossible to foresee the result of a predictable series of development steps. Instead of planning, the central issue is to absorb uncertainty and react to changes. A *flexible model* of product development can be considered to be the opposite of the rational model (Kamoche and Cunha 2001). It considers uncertainty to offer opportunities rather than being something that should be reduced, and emphasises how the product development process is an unpredictable journey. Learning and joint motivation rather than planning and follow-up are highlighted.

A few of the reviewed studies on target costing implicitly adopt a flexible view of product development (Nicolini et al. 2000; Mouritsen et al. 2001; Agndal and Nilsson 2009). Mouritsen and his coworkers' description of product development in NewTech and Nicolini and his coauthors' study illustrate the unpredictable nature of the development process. The importance of continuously adapting to new circumstances was particularly highlighted by Agndal and Nilsson (2009), who claimed that target costing in close relationships might be impossible without trial and error. Carlsson-Wall et al. (2009) is the only study with an explicit discussion of the assumptions of the product development process. They state that they adopt a flexible view of product development and find empirical support for this view. During the product development process in ABB Robotics, unexpected problems often occurred and temporarily valid compromises were reached that often failed to correspond to what had originally been planned. However, the empirical findings in Carlsson-Wall et al. (2009) also show the need to move away from the dichotomy of a rational and flexible view of product development. They found that the product development process corresponded to a rational view during some stages and to a flexible view during others.

Space: Inter-Organisational Unit of Analysis

Another important dimension when theorising about product development is how the inter-organisational relationships should be analysed: as *single dyads* or as part of a *larger network of companies* (Håkansson and Snehota 1995; Brusoni et al. 2001). Traditionally, the product development literature has focused on supplier dyads, but recently the importance of the network level has been stressed (Brusoni et al. 2001; Dubois and Araujo 2006). One reason is the complex interdependencies between components. Instead of developing new components, a major source of innovation and of cost reductions is to rearrange the architecture relating to how components are interconnected. Studying the development of Scania Trucks, Dubois and Araujo (2006) argued that architectural innovation is critical for overall customer functionalities such as "driver feeling" or "noise". According to Brusoni et al. (2001), one reason for adding a network level is that architectural innovation involves many unpredictable component interdependencies. Before the product is tested and embedded into the customer context, it is difficult to know how the components will function together.

From our literature review, it can be concluded that the majority of the studies on target costing in networks analyse isolated supplier dyads and, thereby, do not bring interdependencies between suppliers to the foreground (Carr and Ng 1995; Gietzmann 1996; Ansari and Bell 1997; Cooper and Slagmulder 1997, 2004; Ellram 2000, 2002, 2006; Nicolini et al. 2000; Mouritsen et al. 2001; Ansari et al. 2006; Agndal and Nilsson 2009). Only a few of the studies include the network level of analysis, and thus emphasise interdependencies between the inter-organisational relationships (Cooper and Slagmulder 1999, 2003a, 2003b; Carlsson-Wall et al. 2009). Cooper and Slagmulder (1999) describe how the automotive company Tokyo Motor works closely with the supplier Yokohama and the subsupplier Kamakura Ironworks. Emphasising the hierarchical aspects of target costing, a key issue is to form kingdoms and baronies.

This means that the top firm has a sophisticated market-driven target costing system which determines the target prices of the suppliers and subsuppliers. In contrast, Carlsson-Wall et al. (2009) consider the networks between customers and suppliers as being open, distributed, and unpredictable. Rather than having a formal network with one shared goal, a central issue is the process of combing target costing goals from multiple partners. For example, ABB Robotics both directs and listens to suppliers and subsuppliers. Often, the process of setting the target cost never stops because the technical content is never stable. Instead, preliminary target costs are set and then interactively revised when new interdependencies are discovered.

Summary and Future Research Opportunities

Our discussion of the importance of theorising product development can be summarised with a 2×2 matrix in which the reviewed literature on target costing in networks is mapped. On the vertical axis, we have the basic assumptions about the product development process, and on the horizontal one, we have the inter-organisational unit of analysis. As the majority of studies do not explicitly state the underlying theoretical assumptions made concerning the product development, future research could be improved by being more explicit on this matter.

As Figure 8.1 illustrates, the majority of the studies lie in the bottom-left cell of the matrix, with underlying theoretical assumptions about

	Dyadic relationships	Network of relationships
Flexible model (absorb uncertainty)	Agndal and Nilsson (2009) Mouritsen et al. (2001) Nicolini et al. (2000)	Carlsson-Wall et al. (2009)
Rational model (reduce uncertainty)	Ansari et al. (2006) Ansari and Bell (1997) Carr and Ng (1995) Cooper and Slagmulder (1997; 2004) Ellram (2000, 2002, 2006) Gietzmann (1996) Swenson et al. (2003)	Cooper and Slagmulder (1999, 2003a, 2003b)

Basic assumptions of the product development process

Inter-organisational unit of analysis

Figure 8.1   Basic assumptions on product development in the literature on target costing in networks.

product development that have been highly criticised.[5] Rather than focusing on planning in single supplier dyads, several authors have shown that understanding the development of multi-technology products requires a broader scope both in time and space (Brown and Eisenhardt 1997; Brusoni et al. 2001; Kamoche and Cunha 2001; Dubois and Araujo 2006). This proposed direction can also be seen in studies of target costing in an intra-organisational setting. Summarising the literature, Hansen and Jönsson (2005, p. 223) wrote: "The existing literature on Target Costing has primarily been *prescriptive* in the way that it has presented the target costing principles and focused on the benefits of pursuing them in companies (Cooper 1995; Cooper & Slagmulder 1997) or *descriptive* in terms of focusing on how the principles have been 'setup' in different companies—how the form gets content . . . Not much research has been *explorative* and addressing organizational complexities that arise when Target Costing principles are performed in practice (for exception, see Mouritsen et al. 2001)."

In the following section, therefore, we contribute with novel theoretical and empirical findings to target costing in networks. We will build on and extend the findings in Carlsson-Wall et al. (2009), where it has been shown, empirically, that the product development process had characteristics that corresponded to both the rational and the flexible view. These findings are in line with the recent literature on product development. For example, Kamoche and Cunha (2001) put forward a view of product development called "the improvisational model".[6] To manage both rational and flexible aspects, companies rely on minimal structures or templates. Without the structure, chaos easily occurs, but with too much structure, there is no role for improvisation and creativity. It therefore becomes crucial to manage uncertainty, including both reducing and absorbing uncertainty in time and space (Kamoche and Cunha 2001).

Product development is therefore seen as a continuous process of trying to freeze some design elements, while keeping others open, and of maintaining a balance between flexibility and structure (Kamoche and Cunha 2001; Dubois and Araujo 2006). Hence, product development occurs through a dialectic process involving constant redesign, where there is a need to unifying the rational and flexible view of product development. With this theoretical perspective, it becomes interesting to explore the multiple roles of target costing. What happens when disciplining occurs simultaneously with collective problem solving? If one target costing logic relies on details and routines, while another uses target costing as a guide, what happens? Novel empirical material from ABB Robotics, as is described in the case presented by Carlsson-Wall et al. (2009), is discussed. The empirical case study was conducted between 2002 and 2008 and involved, in total, ninety-three interviews, twenty-two days of participant observation, and more than two thousand pages of financial and technical documentation.

4   TARGET COSTING IN NETWORKS: THE CASE OF INDUSTRIAL ROBOTS

ABB Robotics (Robotics) is a global manufacturer of industrial robots with an annual turnover of about 1,500 million dollars. The robots are mainly sold to large automotive companies or their tier-1 suppliers, which together make up 60–70 per cent of Robotics' annual revenues. Sales to these customers are highly order-driven, customised, and often include a broad range of products and services. Robotics also sells robots to smaller customers from different backgrounds. These customers purchase only one or two robotic systems at a time and, although individually they are not important, they pay high prices and together they assure a steady volume. Robotics has about 200 suppliers, some of which involve relationships that are arm's-length; with others the relationships are close.

To exemplify the multiple roles of target costing, we describe ALFA, a four-year development project to develop the next generation of Industrial Control System[7] (ICS). ALFA was chosen for two reasons. First, the ICS is a multi-technology product (Brusoni et al. 2001) involving a large number of components and subcomponents developed in close cooperation with suppliers. Second, because of the technical interdependencies, the ICS is Robotics' most costly product. The ICS represents about 60–70 per cent of the cost of a robotic system, which means that target costing in the development of a new generation ICS is closely related to Robotics' overall cost management and profitability. In addition, the ICS has to communicate with the customer's production system and, since Robotics has more than twenty-five different types of large, small, and specialized robots, the ICS has to be adapted to past, present, and future functionality. To describe the multiple roles of target costing and how uncertainty and redesigns occur late in the development process, the description starts when ALFA has been going on for two years. At this point, Robotics had found three lead users: General Motors, BMW, and Volvo. Working with these companies not only enables Robotics to secure its target sales but also results in feedback on the technical functionality of the ICS.

Target Costing and Synchronising on a Network Level

The project manager described how the ALFA project was concentrated on reducing uncertainty, synchronising supplier development, and delivering on time: "The project changed from a development project to becoming a delivery project. As with all projects with small delays and other surprises, I had to make drastic cuts in the functionality. The product was not ready as a standard product. We did not have the time. Everything that was not absolutely crucial was moved to the next year. The cost control was also tough, because GM had imposed too low a margin."

To secure target sales volumes, Robotics delivered to General Motors, BMW, and Volvo. On the one hand, this gave feedback and direction. On the other hand, it reduced flexibility because Robotics was embedded in the customers' target costing logic. Target costing was, therefore, highly focused on synchronising deliveries on a network level. This corresponds to the lower right cell in the 2×2 matrix previously discussed. How could unexpected costs be avoided? What was needed to enable deliveries to take place on time? Were Robotics' suppliers acting according to plan?

To facilitate synchronisation, Robotics used gate models and formal quality audits as part of the target costing process. Since there were so many technical interdependencies, it was important that activities were not omitted. The goal at this point was clear—to deliver robots on time—and Robotics directed its suppliers in a hierarchical manner. Often, one of the central issues was checking how suppliers were doing and giving them feedback about how they were developing in relation to the other, parallel, sub-projects. Even though suppliers sometimes came up with new ideas or asked for more time, target costing was used to discipline suppliers and inform them that their financial future depended on the end-customers, General Motors, BMW, and Volvo. Target costing was further formalised to avoid unnecessary costs. If formal routines were followed, Robotics argued, it was easier to remember all the key activities. This also installed a sense of urgency. Instead of thinking "out of the box", suppliers had their sights fixed firmly on the next deadline and it became easier to get all suppliers to move in one direction.

Target Costing and Synchronising on a Relationship Level

The customer relationship with BMW was important in ALFA. Since it took more than one year to build BMW's production lines, a central issue was to understand the initial use to which they would be put. Describing the situation, the project manager said: "We knew that it would take one year before they [BMW] were ready. I mean, we were late. In the first deliveries, we were nowhere near ready. We asked them: 'What do you need the robot for?' Then we worked hard to ensure that that goal was met. Initially, they got very little software. However, they only needed the robots to integrate with cables and other production systems. Then we updated the hardware and software along the way to match their growing requirements. It was, however, really tight."

BMW's deadlines also put great pressure on DriveSys, one of Robotics' key suppliers. Being responsible for the drive system, the component that runs the motors in the robots, DriveSys was one of Robotics' closest suppliers. The relationship was long-lasting, depended on mutual trust, and to finish on time Robotics and DriveSys used simultaneous engineering. Since the drive system was one of the most technically advanced components, a central issue was to synchronise the testing of both hardware and software.

To speed up the process, senior engineers from Robotics directed the testing and DriveSys was allowed to borrow robotic systems from Robotics. The two companies worked closely together but when new ideas emerged, they were often abandoned because they would either increase the target cost or, possibly, imperil target sales through delayed customer deliveries. The role of target costing in this situation corresponded to that of the lower-left cell in the aforementioned matrix. Both temporally and spatially, there was a narrow focus where Robotics synchronised DriveSys' development and ensured time and quality goals were attained. Nonfinancial goals were an important way of managing the target cost. Deadlines were used to communicate the importance of large customer orders (target sales) and formal quality testing was used to avoid unnecessary target cost increases.

Target Costing and Guiding on a Network Level

However, parallel to the synchronisation with DriveSys, joint testing with BMW showed critical customer functionality was missing. To meet the target cost, Robotics had left out the option to run a seventh axis in the standard ALFA configuration. Since a robot has six axes, the introduction of a seventh one means that the Industrial Control System can run additional customer equipment in conjunction with the robot. In this case, BMW wanted ALFA to stand on a railroad where robots would conduct one arc welding operation, move a few meters on, and then conduct a new operation. However, since ALFA did not include a seventh axis, Robotics had to give BMW two Industrial Control Systems, which was very costly. Even though the initial goal had been to finish on time, interaction with BMW revealed the need to redesign. How could this be fixed?

When Robotics began to explore the problem, further investigations were conducted among other customers. Was this problem particular to BMW, or did other customers encounter related constraints? After discussing with specialists on arc welding, the seventh axis was determined to be an important functionality for many customers. In parallel with the discussions with its customers, Robotics turned to its suppliers to consider how a seventh drive could be included in ALFA. Most components had already been designed and tested. Indeed, with the time pressure being imposed by Robotics' customers, was there even enough time to implement a seventh drive? Describing the problem solving, the project manager said: "I guess you identify a problem and start grappling with it. First, you need to make it clear that it is a problem. Then you start searching . . . Is it possible to do anything at all? Well, kind of like that. I mean, initially, I did not know much. Then they [DriveSys] returned . . . we had an idea that might work . . . and then it gained momentum: It started off with: 'We have seen a possibility, is it interesting?'"

Parallel to DriveSys' investigation of their subsuppliers, Robotics considered potential network effects. For example, would a larger drive also increase the need for a larger transformer? The investigation was highly problem-oriented and collective as it involved DriveSys but also Robotics' other suppliers. If the transformer could be increased without additional cost, would the new drive and transformer physically fit in ALFA? Here target costing had a guiding role corresponding to the upper-right cell in the matrix. Unexpected problems occurred in the development project, so Robotics' customers and suppliers had an impact on the target costing process. Target costs were important for guiding collective problem solving and facilitating knowledge integration between Robotics and its network of interconnected suppliers. The guiding role of target costing meant that the target costs sometimes formed the basis for rejecting solutions that were technically acceptable, but too expensive, and on other occasions target costs directed the search for possible compromises on a network level between improved technological content and additional costs.

Target Costing and Guiding on a Relationship Level

How was the problem resolved? Did Robotics manage to finish the technical redesign? Reflecting on the situation, the project manager said: "Imagine if something were to go wrong. At GM, we were delivering to GM Trucks, which at that time made up 80% of GM's profit. At BMW, it was their new 3-series. Imagine just how much they wanted to delay their product launch! . . . It is just a fact, you finish on time. In ALFA, I had the upper hand. I was free to get what I wanted."

After discussing the pros and cons, target costing helped to find a compromise between technical suitability on an architectural level and the deadlines of key customers. Robotics worked closely with each supplier of components to accomplish this. After exploring different options, DriveSys had discovered a solution that could temporarily work. By redesigning the drive, a seventh axis could be included without requiring changes to other components, but if the customers wanted more than one external axis, the compromise was that they would have to buy an additional drive unit. However, the redesign was lifted out of ALFA. To avoid synchronisation problems with both customers and suppliers, it was decided DriveSys should begin when ALFA was finished. The new "add-on" project also meant a new contractual discussion with DriveSys. Because of the large technical changes, the target cost for ALFA did not include the redesign. On the other hand, close cooperation with DriveSys had identified a technical solution that avoided technical change to other components, so a cost increase for one supplier was offset by not being obliged to give customers two entire Industrial Control Systems.

Summary and Contributions to the Existing Literature on Target Costing in Networks

Figure 8.2 summarises the findings of ALFA where the development process had characteristics corresponding to all four cells in the matrix. Target costing

202 *Martin Carlsson-Wall and Kalle Kraus*

played numerous roles during the project. In the bottom-left cell, target costs were reduced by planning and by implementation on a relationship level. Unexpected events that might have increased the target costs during the project were not discussed as the project went according to plan. As the literature review highlighted, most studies in the managerial and structural streams are examples of this cell. Experience from ABB Robotics showed similar results to those of Cooper and Slagmulder (2004). Robotics and DriveSys worked closely together, but it was Robotics who directed the development. In addition, the empirics illustrated the role of target costing in rejecting technical solutions that would necessitate an increase in cost. When alternative technical solutions were proposed, they were abandoned or postponed whenever they meant the preset target cost would not be reached.

When adopting a rational view of the product development process, target costs can also be reduced by changing the product architecture on a network level. This happens in the bottom-right cell. A conceptual development of this cell is provided by Cooper and Slagmulder (1999, 2003a, 2003b), who discussed hierarchical supplier networks in the form of kingdoms, baronies, and republics. Even though the ALFA project changed over time, observation showed how Robotics acted as king, using target costing to synchronise suppliers to ensure that customer deadlines were met. In addition to providing an empirical description of how target costing can be linked to kingdoms, the concept of synchronisation might be suitable for further illustrating hierarchical target costing on a relationship and network level.

In the upper-left cell, we find the process thread on target costing. When problematising target costing in supplier dyads, these contributions

Flexible model (absorb uncertainty)	Target costing to guide pragmatic compromises with DriveSys	Target costing to guide pragmatic compromises on a network level
Basic assumptions of the product development process Rational model (reduce uncertainty)	Target costing to synchronise time and quality with DriveSys to avoid additional costs	Target costing to synchronise multiple suppliers to reach customer deadlines
	Dyadic relationships	Network of relationships

Inter-organisational unit of analysis

Figure 8.2 Target costing practices in the ALFA project.

show how product development often has unexpected effects (Mouritsen et al. 2001) or occurs interactively with suppliers (Agndal and Nilsson 2009). In the redesign with DriveSys, the goals and means changed over time. Both Robotics and DriveSys appreciated the need to discuss different solutions. Rather than Robotics dictating a target cost, both companies attempted to identify a suitable technical solution without grave financial consequences. Thus, they posed questions like: When did the seventh axis need to be finished? What alternatives did Robotics have? The companies entered into a joint process of trial and error, where target costing was used to guide the examination of which technical solutions were acceptable for both parties.

Finally, in the upper-right cell, target costs are reduced by redesigning the architecture (Carlsson-Wall et al. 2009). Owing to new customer requirements or large cost-reduction opportunities, development projects can become highly uncertain even during the later stages. Target costing had a guiding role in collective problem solving on a network level and facilitated knowledge integration between Robotics, its customers, and suppliers. Target costs sometimes formed the basis for rejecting technically acceptable, but too expensive, solutions; and on other occasions, target costs were used to direct the search for possible compromises on a network level where a balance needed to be found between improved technological content and additional costs.

Thus, we conclude from our case study that there is a need to dissolve the dichotomy between the rational view and the flexible view of product development, as well as the dichotomy between the dyad and the network: The four cells in the matrix complement each other in the same development project and target costing has numerous roles during the product development process.

5   CONCLUSIONS AND SUGGESTIONS FOR FUTURE RESEARCH

The first part of the chapter reviewed the literature on target costing in networks. A total of 17 articles and books were related to this chapter's area of interest. It was concluded that the approaches to target costing differed and the studies were divided into three lines of research: a *managerial thread*, a *structural thread*, and a *process thread*. The managerial thread described some of the positive effects of target costing and resulted in detailed managerial guidelines being proposed. The empirical focus was on best-practice companies, such as Toyota and Chrysler, and theoretical or methodological discussions were largely absent. The structural thread considered supplier dyads, and transaction cost economics was often used as the theoretical basis. The empirical material mainly consisted of Japanese and American companies and the importance of cross-functional teams was emphasised. Within the process line of research, target costing was theoretically and empirically problematised. By breaking with the traditional view that product development is a rational process, challenges to target costing were discussed. Theoretically, actor-network theory and the industrial-network approach were used.

We also concluded that most studies paid little attention to discussing the *underlying theoretical assumptions of product development*. The majority of the studies (implicitly) considered product development to be a rational process comprised of a predictable series of well-defined steps, despite the fact that this rational model has been highly criticised in the literature on product development (Brown and Eisenhardt 1995, 1997; Kamoche and Cunha 2001). Only a few of the studies had a flexible perception of product development, emphasising the unpredictable nature of the process and the importance of continuously adapting to new circumstances, rather than sticking to predetermined and outdated goals. In a similar vein, the majority of the studies focused on supplier dyads even though the recent product development literature has emphasised the importance of including interdependencies in a network of relationships. We summarised these findings in a 2×2 matrix where the vertical axis represented the basic assumptions of the product development process (i.e., rational or flexible) and the horizontal axis represented the inter-organisational unit of analysis (i.e., supplier dyads or a network of relationships). We argued for the need for more studies to be conducted on target costing in networks, adopting a flexible view of the product development process, and taking the network of interconnected relationships into consideration.

We also presented novel empirical findings from ABB Robotics, and one important conclusion was the need to dissolve the dichotomy between the rational view and the flexible view of product development, as well as between the dyad and the network. The justification for this is that the product development in Robotics had characteristics that corresponded to all four cells in the matrix. It was crucial to *manage uncertainty*, and this included both reducing and absorbing uncertainty. Product development was a continuous process of trying to freeze some design elements while altering others and, hence, maintaining a balance between flexibility and structure. This implied target costing had numerous roles. Target costing was used to manage time and quality with DriveSys on a dyadic level to attain preset goals, as advocated by the majority of the previous target costing studies. However, target costing also helped to synchronise suppliers on a network level (Cooper and Slagmulder 1999, 2003a, 2003b). In addition, it was used to arrive at pragmatic compromises with DriveSys when things did not go according to plan, and, in a similar vein, target costing guided pragmatic compromises on a network level because some unexpected problems arose involving a number of the suppliers and customers (Carlsson-Wall et al. 2009).

This chapter has pointed out a number of avenues for potential future research on target costing in networks. There is a need for in-depth case studies that explicitly theorise product development and the role of target costing therein, notably, for example, by extending target costing beyond dyadic relationships. To address architectural innovation, analysing *embeddedness* on the network level can add valuable insights. Moving beyond target costing, the network level has also been highlighted by several authors within the inter-organisational accounting literature (Tomkins 2001; Håkansson and Lind 2004; Mouritsen and Thrane 2006; Thrane and Hald 2006; Van der Meer-Kooistra and Vosselman 2006; Håkansson and Lind 2007; Kraus and Lind 2007; Thrane 2007). One conclusion from these articles is that the network level is particularly relevant to product development. For example, Håkansson and Lind (2004) show how the interaction between Ericsson and its key customers is more distributed and unpredictable during intense periods of product development. Still, recent reviews show that few articles have explicitly focused on inter-organisational product development within projects (Håkansson and Lind 2007; Kraus and Lind 2007; Caglio and Ditillo 2008). Most articles restrict themselves to the consideration of several functions and the organisational level. Thus, extending target costing to the *network level* would not only contribute to the target costing literature, but also to inter-organisational accounting literature in general.

Another research opportunity concerns *customer dyads*. Since target costing studies have mostly focused on global business-to-consumer companies, this dimension has been neglected or, as Nicolini et al. (2000, p. 320) observed, "The determination of the price acceptable by the 'market' for a unique item and a unique customer is a difficult and complex issue that will need further exploration." Researchers within the industrial-network approach have shown that interaction in close customer relationships is highly order-driven and based on trial and error (Håkansson and Snehota 1995; Ford et al. 2003). Research in customer dyads could develop the issue of chained target costing (Cooper and Slagmulder 1999, 2003a, 2003b). In one way, ABB Robotics was forced to accept the target cost of General Motors and BMW. However, because of the incomplete nature of the product development, the details of the technical content were not predetermined. ABB Robotics could choose to give BMW two Industrial Control Systems to handle the seventh axis functionality that had been overlooked. Understanding how target costing is affected by the customers being industrial ones rather than consumers (i.e., in a business-to-business setting, compared to a business-to-consumer one) would be interesting. For example, in contrast to Toyota, ABB Robotics is a midsize company, with several of its customers and suppliers being larger and having other customers and suppliers that are more important than Robotics. Using the terminology introduced earlier (Cooper and Slagmulder 1999, 2003a, 2003b), how does the relative difference in size affect the design of target costing systems and the target costing process when a company is neither a king nor a baron?

Finally, a third area for future research relates to the *"combinatory roles" of target costing in the process of networking.* The empirical description illustrated how Robotics interacted with BMW, DriveSys, and other customers and suppliers to continuously handle new problems and opportunities. Even though there was an initial target cost for ALFA, the process was far from linear. As far as the companies involved in the development were concerned, different customers and suppliers were involved at different stages, and the rhythm of the development changed frequently. Instead of considering the 2×2 matrix introduced as four cells, combining the cells in the same development project and investigating the linkages between cells will raise some intriguing questions for target costing. For example, are the cells complements or supplements? If they are both, how does this impact on the role of target costing during a project and, in the long run, between projects? Is there tension between the different logic implicit in target costing? What happens if two or more companies do not agree that an idea is sufficiently large to warrant architectural redesign? What compromises are made? We have shown that target costing had "combinatory roles" during the same product development project. Sometimes target costing was used to manage time and quality on a dyadic level to attain preset goals, but on other occasions target costing was used to arrive at pragmatic compromises where preliminary target costs were set and then interactively revised when new interdependencies, often on a network level, were discovered. These "combinatory roles" of target costing link to recent broader discussions in the literature on accounting in inter-organisational relationships (see, e.g., Caglio and Ditillo 2008; Van der Meer-Kooistra and Scapens 2008) and accounting in product development (see, e.g., Davila 2000; Bisbe and Otley 2004; Ditillo 2004; Jörgensen and Messner 2009).

Van der Meer-Kooistra and Scapens (2008, p. 382) concluded: "Thus, we need to move beyond simple notions of control—as a linear process in which objectives are formulated, targets set and performance monitored. A package of governance practices is needed to enable the parties in lateral relationships to handle the complex mix of hierarchical, market and relationship practices." In a similar vein, Ditillo (2004, p. 417), when discussing accounting and product development, stated: "As research advances, certainly better classifications, descriptions and roles of management control mechanisms can be developed as well as implications of combinations of controls and their interactive effects examined." By discussing the combinatory roles of target costing in the process of networking, target costing could be applied to consider broader issues within inter-organisational accounting and the field of accounting and product development.

Appendix 8.1   Overview of articles on target costing in networks.

Article	Empirical	Theory	Method
Ansari et al. (2007)	Review	Life-cycle	N/A
Managerial thread (7)			
Ansari et al. (2006)	N/A	Prescriptive	N/A
Cooper and Slagmulder (2003a)	N/A	Prescriptive	N/A
Cooper and Slagmulder (2003b)	N/A	Prescriptive	N/A
Swenson et al. (2003)	4 "best cases" companies; Boeing, Caterpillar, Continental Teves, DaimlerChrysler	Prescriptive	Multiple case studies
Cooper and Slagmulder (1999)	7 Japanese manufacturing companies	Target costing process	Multiple case studies
Cooper and Slagmulder (1997)	7 Japanese manufacturing companies	Target costing process	Multiple case studies
Ansari and Bell (1997)	7 American "best practice" companies from different industries	Target costing process	Multiple case studies
Structural thread (6)			
Ellram (2006)	11 American companies from different industries	Target costing process	Multiple case studies
Cooper and Slagmulder (2004)	7 Japanese manfacturing companies	Transaction cost economics	Multiple case studies
Ellram (2002)	11 American companies from different industries	Target costing process	Multiple case studies
Ellram (2000)	11 American companies from different industries	Target costing process	Multiple case studies
Gietzmann (1996)	21 responses from European tier-1 suppliers	Transaction cost economics	Survey
Carr and Ng (1995)	1 UK automobile company	Target costing process	Single case study

(*continued*)

Appendix 8.1   (continued)

Article	Empirical	Theory	Method
Process thread (4)			
Agndal and Nilsson (2009)	3 different customer-supplier dyads in Sweden	The industrial-network approach	Multiple case studies
Carlsson-Wall et al. (2009)	Product development projects in the Swedish industrial robot producer ABB Robotics	The industrial-network approach	Single case study
Mouritsen et al. (2001)	2 Danish high-technology companies	Actor-network theory	Multiple case studies
Nicolini et al. (2000)	2 UK construction projects within Ministry of Defence	Target costing process	Single case study

NOTES

1. Examples of target costing studies with an intra-organisational focus are: Cooper and Chew (1996); Nixon (1998); Davila and Wouters (2004); Hansen and Jönsson (2005) and Everaert et al. (2006).
2. "Target costing in inter-organisational relationships and networks" will henceforth be shortened to "target costing in networks".
3. Brown and Eisenhardt (1995) and Kamoche and Cunha (2001), two frequently cited reviews of product development, discuss different perspectives on product development, such as the rational view.
4. In Appendix 1, all of the reviewed articles are described according to empirics, theory, and method.
5. Two literature reviews that summarise the critique of the rational view are those of Brown and Eisenhardt (1995) and Kamoche and Cunha (2001).
6. The idea of an "improvisational model" is highly inspired by Brown and Eisenhardt (1997), who study how organisations continuously change through product innovation. Within the inter-organisational accounting literature, these ideas have recently been picked up and explored by Van der Meer-Kooistra and Scapens (2008).
7. The Industrial Control System is "the brain" of a robotic system. It calculates how the robot should move, directs the robot's arms, and then checks that the activity was conducted in the way it was supposed to be. The main functionalities of a robotic system are usually speed, accuracy, and payload (weight).

BIBLIOGRAPHY

Agndal, H., and Nilsson, U. 2009. Interorganizational cost management in the exchange process. *Management Accounting Research* 20: 85–101.
Ansari, S., Bell, J., and the CAM-I Target Cost Core Group. 1997. *Target costing—the next frontier in strategic cost management*. Chicago: Irwin.

Ansari, S., Bell, J., and Okano, H. 2007. Target costing: Uncharted research territory. In *Handbook of management accounting research,* ed. Chapman, C. S., Hopwood, A. G., and Shields, M. D. Oxford: Elsevier.

Ansari, S., Bell, J., and Swenson, D. 2006. A template for implementing target costing. *Cost Management* 20: 20–27.

Bisbe, J., and Otley, D. 2004. The effects of the interactive use of management control systems on product innovation, *Accounting, Organizations and Society* 29: 709–737.

Brown, S., and Eisenhardt, K. 1995. Product development: Past research, present findings and future directions. *Academy of Management Review* 20: 343–378.

Brown, S., and Eisenhardt, K. 1997. The art of continuous change: Linking complexity theory and time-paced evolution in relentlessly shifting organizations. *Administrative Science Quarterly* 42: 1–34.

Brusoni, S., Prencipe, A., and Pavitt, K. 2001. Knowledge specialization, organizational coupling and the boundaries of the firm: Why do firms know more than they do? *Administrative Science Quarterly* 46: 597–621.

Caglio, A., and Ditillo, A. 2008. A review and discussion of management control in inter-firm relationships: Achievements and future directions. *Accounting, Organizations and Society,* 33: 865–898.

Carlsson-Wall, M., Kraus, K., and Lind, J. 2009. Accounting and distributed product development. *IMP-Journal* 3: 2–27.

Carr, C., and Ng, J. 1995. Total cost control: Nissan and its U.K. supplier partnerships. *Management Accounting Research* 6: 347–365.

Cooper, R., and Chew, W. B. 1996. Control tomorrow's costs through today's designs. *Harvard Business Review* 74: 88–97.

Cooper, R., and Slagmulder, R. 1997. *Target costing and value engineering.* Portland, OR: Montvale.

Cooper, R., and Slagmulder, R. 1999. *Supply chain development for the lean enterprise, interorganizational cost management.* Portland, OR: Montvale.

Cooper, R., and Slagmulder, R. 2003a. Interorganizational costing, part 1. *Cost Management* 17: 14–21.

Cooper, R., and Slagmulder, R. 2003b. Interorganizational costing, part 2. *Cost Management* 17: 12–23.

Cooper, R., and Slagmulder, R. 2004. Interorganizational cost management and relational context. *Accounting, Organization and Society* 29: 1–26.

Davila, T. 2000. An empirical study on the drivers of management control systems' design in new product development. *Accounting, Organizations and Society* 25: 383–409.

Davila, T., and Wouters, M. 2004. Designing cost competitive technology products through cost management. *Accounting Horizons* 18: 13–26.

Ditillo, A. 2004. Dealing with uncertainty in knowledge-intensive firms: The role of management control systems as knowledge integration mechanisms. *Accounting, Organizations and Society* 29: 401–421.

Dubois, A., and Araujo, L. 2006. The relationship between technical and organisational interfaces in product development. *The IMP Journal* 1: 28–51.

Ellram, L. M. 2000. Purchasing and supply management's participation in the target costing process. *Journal of Supply Chain Management* 36: 39–51.

Ellram, L. M. 2002. Supply management's involvement in the target costing process. *European Journal of Purchasing and Supply Management* 8: 235–244.

Ellram, L. M. 2006. The implementation of target costing in the United States: Theory versus practice. *Journal of Supply Chain Management* 42: 13–26.

Everaert, P., Loosveld, S., Van Acker, T., Schollier, M., and Sarens, G. 2006. Characteristics of target costing: Theoretical and field study perspective. *Qualitative Research in Accounting and Management* 3: 236–263.

Ford, D., Gadde, L.-E., Håkansson, H., and Snehota, I. 2003. *Managing business relationships,* 2nd ed. Chichester, UK: Wiley.

Gietzmann, M. 1996. Incomplete contracts and the make or buy decision: Governance design and attainable flexibility. *Accounting, Organizations and Society* 6: 611–626.

Håkansson, H., and Lind, J. 2004. Accounting and network coordination. *Accounting, Organizations and Society* 29: 51–72.

Håkansson, H., and Lind, J. 2007. Accounting in an interorganisational setting. In *Handbook of management accounting research,* ed. Chapman, C. S., Hopwood, A. G., and Shields, M. D. 885–902. Oxford: Elsevier.

Håkansson, H., and Snehota, I. 1995. *Developing relationships in business networks.* London: Routledge.

Hansen, A., and Jönsson, S. 2005. Target costing and coordination—framing cost information sharing in new product development. In *Accounting in Scandinavia—the Northern Lights,* ed. Jönsson, S., and Mouritsen. Malmö, Sweden: J. Liber & CBS Press.

Jörgensen, B., and Messner, M. 2009. Accounting and strategising: A case study from new product development. *Accounting, Organizations and Society* (2009) doi: 10.1016/j.aos.2009.04.001.

Kamoche, K., and Cunha, M. 2001. Minimal structures: From jazz improvisation to product innovation. *Organization Studies* 22: 733–765.

Kato, Y. 1993. Target costing support systems: Lessons from leading Japanese companies. *Management Accounting Research* 4: 33–47.

Kraus, K., and Lind, J. 2007. Management control in inter-organisational relationships. In *Issues in management accounting,* ed. Hopper, T., Scapens, R. W. and Northcott, D. 269–296. Harlow, UK: Financial Times Prentice Hall.

Mouritsen, J., Hansen, A., and Hansen, C. Ø. 2001. Interorganizational controls and organizational competencies: Episodes around target cost management/functional analysis and open book accounting. *Management Accounting Research* 12: 221–244.

Mouritsen, J., and Thrane, S. 2006. Accounting, network complementarities and the development of inter-organizational relations. *Accounting, Organizations and Society* 31: 241–275.

Nicolini, D., Tomkins, C., Holti, R., Oldman, A., and Smalley, M. 2000. Can target costing and whole life costing be applied in the construction industry?: Evidence from two case studies. *British Journal of Management* 11: 303–324.

Nixon, B. 1998. Research and development performance measurement: A case study. *Management Accounting Research* 9: 329–355.

Swenson, D., Ansari, S., Bell, J., and Il Won, K. 2003. Best practices in target costing. *Management Accounting Quarterly* 5: 12–17.

Thrane, S. 2007. The complexity of management accounting change: Bifurcation and oscillation in schizophrenic inter-organizational systems. *Management Accounting Research* 18: 248–272.

Thrane, S., and Hald, K. 2006. The emergence of boundaries and accounting in supply fields: The dynamics of integration and fragmentation. *Management Accounting Research* 17: 288–314.

Tomkins, C. 2001. Interdependencies, trust and information in relationships, alliances and networks. *Accounting, Organizations and Society* 26: 161–191.

Van der Meer-Kooistra, J., and Scapens, R. W. 2008. The governance of lateral relations between and within organisations. *Management Accounting Research* 19: 365–384.

Van der Meer-Kooistra, J., and Vosselman, E. 2006. Research on management control of interfirm transactional relationships: Whence and whither. *Management Accounting Research* 17: 227–237.

9 Open-Book Accounting in Networks

Peter Kajüter and Harri I. Kulmala

1 INTRODUCTION

Cost data is one of the most sensitive pieces of information in firms and is, therefore, generally hidden from third parties such as customers and suppliers. With the emergence of manufacturing networks in recent years, however, organisational boundaries have become increasingly blurred. Major suppliers are, for example, involved in the product development process of manufacturing firms. In such close inter-firm relationships, information sharing between firms has become much more comprehensive. It may even include the disclosure of cost data that was traditionally kept secret.

The practice of disclosing and sharing cost information between firms is called open-book accounting (OBA) (Kulmala 2002; Kajüter and Kulmala 2005). Other terms used to describe the same phenomenon are open-book costing or open-book transparency. OBA plays a key role in inter-organisational cost management as it serves to identify additional cost reduction opportunities through collaborative efforts that could not be discovered by the individual firms acting on their own. Despite this potential, OBA introduces the risk that the disclosed cost information is misused by the supply chain partner. For this reason, the overall advantage of introducing OBA is not clear-cut and, consequently, firms are often reluctant to adopt it.

A Finnish heavy frame welding SME (Small and Medium size Enterprise), for example, was invited to increase the product design and prototype manufacturing business it did for a large customer in 2006. The customer wanted to see the cost structure of the current production, extract the product design and prototype manufacturing costs from the serial production costs, and move serial production to a low-cost country (Lappeteläinen 2007). The SME had to take a very hard decision regarding OBA: If they were to open up their cost structure, the customer might pay as much for the product design and prototype manufacturing per product as they had paid during the serial manufacturing times. This would, however, be insufficient to make the product design and prototype manufacturing profitable without the serial manufacturing as well. On the other hand, the product design and prototype manufacturing seemed to be more interesting as a business and would help in getting rid of the serial manufacturing problems and cost competition. So, should the SME open up or be careful to maintain its old, core business? As in most double-edged situations, the SME opted for a midway solution: They gave a semi-open calculation concerning the behaviour of the unit price of the prototype manufacturing to the customer, according to the prototype volumes and iteration rounds. However, they did not provide the customer with detailed cost structures for the existing product design and prototype manufacturing costs. In 2008, the SME was still a serial manufacturer, but their reliability, in the eyes of the customer, was slightly better than two years before.

The objective of this chapter is to discuss OBA in inter-firm relationships and to illustrate potential achievements and problems in both dyadic and network settings. The remainder of the chapter is structured as follows: Section 2 introduces the concept of OBA, outlines its application in dyadic and network settings, and discusses some benefits and failures of OBA. After that, Section 3 presents different theoretical perspectives for the analysis of OBA. The chapter concludes with a summary and discussion of the outlook in Section 4.

2   EMPIRICAL EVIDENCE ABOUT OPEN-BOOK ACCOUNTING

Open-Book Accounting in Dyadic Settings

OBA is still a fairly new practice, appearing with the spread of lean production and supply in the 1990s (Kajüter and Kulmala 2005). One of OBA's main objectives is to reveal cost savings through the joint actions of the buyer and supplier (Kulmala et al. 2002; Kajüter and Kulmala 2005). Such collaborative efforts in inter-organisational cost management are reported mostly for dyadic settings between customers and suppliers. A recent literature review (Möller and Windolph 2008) indicates that, in just under twenty years, about ten conceptual studies, less than twenty empirical case studies, and two surveys have been published relating to OBA. One of the first papers discussing techniques and behavioural issues related to OBA was that of Mouritsen et al. (2001). However, to date, little of the existing research has addressed the question of to what extent OBA affects performance (Möller and Windolph 2008). OBA can be a potential risk to inter-firm cooperation by increasing the buyer's opportunism. To elaborate on and summarise the field practices and earlier literature, the main aspects of OBA are outlined in the following from both the customer's and the supplier's perspective.

In *dyadic settings* a customer usually asks a supplier to present a detailed cost breakdown for any component or service that it sells and delivers to the customer. From the supplier's point of view, the motive of the customer may be either cooperative or opportunistic.

A customer with cooperative intentions:

- intends to search for potential cost reductions in the products/services bought from the supplier or in inter-firm processes between the two firms,
- has the willingness and enough capabilities to reorganise the processes to take advantage of the identified potential cost savings, and
- supports the supplier's accounting and development personnel to implement the necessary changes.

In an opportunistic case, however, the customer:

- intends to identify in which part of the overall deliveries the supplier's competitors have their lowest costs,
- has the willingness and enough negotiation power to put pressure on the supplier to achieve lower prices, and
- does not care about or does not analyse the business processes between itself and the supplier.

In both cases, the three issues listed summarise the potential and the risks of OBA. Since the understanding of the customer's good will is a key prerequisite for a supplier to participate, OBA is closely associated with trust. However, the consequences of the choice of whether to trust or distrust the customer cannot be seen in the supplier's decision about whether to engage in OBA or not. The supplier's motives, too, need to be taken into account, and these, in turn, define how much a customer can benefit from OBA.

In a cooperative case, the supplier:

- intends to utilise its customer's knowledge to improve its products or processes,
- provides the customer with high-quality and nonmanipulated cost data, and
- supports the customer's development personnel by openly participating in the development of mutual operations.

In an opportunistic case, the supplier:

- intends to hide most of the technical details regarding its products and processes,

- provides the customer with poor or manipulated cost data, and
- is not interested in analysing and developing any activity outside its own operations.

A customer's potential to benefit may be lost in the case of engaging in business with an opportunistic supplier. Hence, while OBA may be a powerful tool in specific circumstances, it is important to consider contextual factors that might fuel opportunistic behaviour. All dyadic case studies report about suppliers providing cost information to customers. This evidence can be explained by the cost reduction motive of OBA. It may also explain why OBA has not been reported in supplier dominant relationships.

Figure 9.1 visualises the business circumstances under which OBA may have the largest potential (Kulmala 2004). If the partners are, at least, inter-connected somehow over the long term and depend on each other to exploit the market opportunities, the environment is promising for OBA. In the opposite case, it is more likely that at least one of the partners would attempt to behave opportunistically. For example, a customer might be more inclined to impose cost reductions on suppliers if there is overcapacity in the market and suppliers can thereby be easily replaced.

Open-Book Accounting in Networks

OBA can not only be observed in dyadic settings but also in networks (Håkansson and Lind 2004). In both settings, the firms involved are

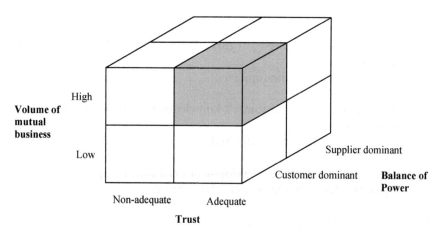

Figure 9.1   A framework for analysing the development potential of inter-organisational cost management in dyadic relationships. The shaded volume indicates the region with the highest potential for open-book accounting (adapted from Kulmala 2004, p. 75).

legally independent and pursue their individual objectives. As a consequence, they may behave in a cooperative or in an opportunistic manner. The latter can be assumed to be most likely if the firms' objectives are conflicting. Although opportunities and risks exist in dyadic and network relationships, they become more complex in the latter context. Previous research has only anecdotally analysed OBA in network settings (Kajüter and Kulmala 2005; Jarimo and Kulmala 2008). In most cases, networks have been perceived to be closed systems comprised of firms and their business relationships (Lambert and Cooper 2000; Harland et al. 2001). Networks are defined, in this case, by the end product that the network members produce and deliver to a customer. Networks are considered as single entities that compete against alternative end-product networks. Individual network members can, however, be part of several networks, even competing ones. In contrast to this view, networks can be perceived as an open system of business relationships (Håkansson and Lind 2004). In both cases, the network, in all its complexity, is a relevant unit of analysis for OBA.

In *network settings*, OBA means that companies multilaterally open some or all of their network-related cost data. However, owing to the multilateral relationships and the larger number of participants in a network than in a relationship with fewer parties involved, OBA practices and, especially, their motives and their consequences become more complex. This complexity also entails positive and negative aspects. Some positive aspects are:

- The potential to multiply the cost savings reached in one dyadic relationship increases.
- Network partners help a single member to increase its competitiveness and, in return, to benefit from the presence of a stronger and more cost-efficient partner.
- A company helps network partners to reduce their costs, and thereby improves the competitiveness of the overall network in the market.
- The speed of learning and innovation in an open network discussion is higher than for bilateral discussions.
- The network's incentive system rewards network-wide knowledge sharing.

Some negative aspects are:

- The partners' fierce competition may destroy the idea of sharing knowledge related to cost saving.
- A company is participating in OBA discussions with the sole intention of spying on competitors' solutions.
- A company presents poor or manipulated cost data in order to mislead competitors.

- Network partners use their negotiation power against one company in order to destroy its competitive position.
- Forced OBA destroys the possibility of discussing issues that would otherwise be on the agenda.
- The network's incentive system rewards "best-in-this-network" or postponement of cost saving ideas.

Similar to the dyadic setting, the opportunistic behaviour of a firm may destroy the potential benefits of OBA practice. In a network setting, however, this might have an impact on the other inter-firm relationships in the network, making OBA in multilateral relationships even more vulnerable. As illustrated in a Finnish assembly network, network-wide OBA can work as a multiplier or amplifier of process development and cost savings reached in dyadic settings (Jarimo and Kulmala 2008). At the other extreme, network-wide open-book demands may even destroy networks that would otherwise work at least to some extent (Kulmala 2006). However, there is no clear empirical evidence regarding improved performance in networks due to OBA (Möller and Windolph 2008).

In the literature on inter-organisational cost management it has been discussed whether extending cost management efforts across organisational boundaries requires new cost management tools, or whether inter-organisational cost management can be characterised as a practice of applying existing tools to a wider context. Tomkins (2001), for instance, argues that no new cost accounting tools but rather new practices in using the cost data are required within the network context. Empirical evidence of case study research in networks supports this view as regards target costing and cost accounting systems. The former had only been extended to the inter-organisational context, while the latter had not been changed at all (Kajüter and Kulmala 2005).

However, there is also empirical evidence that the firms in a network develop and apply specific tools to facilitate the disclosure of cost data within the network. This evidence, which runs contrary to Tomkins's view, relates to the Eurocar (Kajüter and Kulmala 2005) and the Offshore (Kulmala et al. 2007) networks.

The Eurocar network is a German car-manufacturing network. It can be classified as a hierarchical network supplying functional products. To identify cost reduction opportunities, Eurocar, the focal company of the network, has initiated OBA. In order to handle suppliers' concerns about potential disadvantages of cost data disclosure, Eurocar has introduced specific mechanisms that create an infrastructure for OBA. This infrastructure comprises cross-functional, cross-company teams, technical support for suppliers, as well as specific tools. The value chain flow chart is one of these tools (Figure 9.2). It presents the network members involved in the production of a particular component or system and the cost incurred at the different stages as the material flows through the network. The value chain flow chart was prepared by Eurocar in cooperation with the Tier 1 supplier, which in turn involves the Tier 2 and, on some occasions, Tier 3 suppliers.

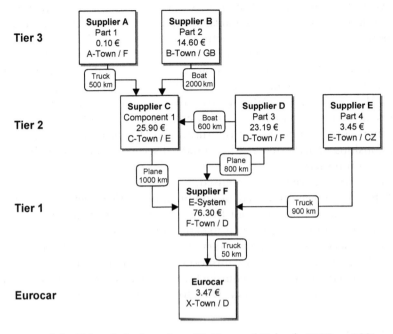

Figure 9.2 Value chain flow chart (Kajüter and Kulmala 2005, p. 188).

The value chain flow chart is complemented by specific worksheets that formalise the cost element disclosure at each stage of the network. It includes information about the major cost elements, as well as the profit margin. Figure 9.3 presents an example of such a worksheet prepared by the Tier 1 supplier. It shows the additional cost ("on-cost") that occurs at this firm for the production of the component under review.

A similar approach to developing specific tools for OBA was taken in the Offshore network (Kulmala et al. 2007). Offshore is a Finnish equipment provider for watercrafts. It holds a focal position in the hierarchical

Cost Element	On-Cost (€)	% of On-Cost
Raw Material	n/a	n/a
Direct & Indirect Labor	20.00	26
Manufacturing Overhead	31.00	41
Corporate Overhead	13.20	17
Packaging	1.50	2
Transportation	0.55	1
Warranty	2.95	4
Research & Development	3.70	5
Profit	3.10	4
Total	**76.30**	**100**

Figure 9.3 Worksheet for cost structure analysis (Kajüter and Kulmala 2005, p. 189).

network, like Eurocar, although the size of the two main contractors differs. While Eurocar is a large multinational company, Offshore is an SME. In both cases, however, the structured method for OBA turned out to be a critical success factor. The tools contributed to enhancing the suppliers' understanding of the OBA practice. This seemed to be particularly relevant for new suppliers that were not yet familiar with the procedure of disclosing cost data. Offshore also invested in the improvement of suppliers' accounting knowledge, which created an atmosphere in which the suppliers directly understood the future benefits of their other customer relationships. Furthermore, the standardised approach contributed to reducing transaction costs despite the fact that the cost accounting systems in the network were not harmonised.

While OBA was practiced in combination with target costing in the Eurocar network, this was not the case in the Offshore network. As the main purpose of target costing is to determine cost reduction requirements, OBA can serve as a complementary practice to identify opportunities to close the cost gap by inter-organisational cost management efforts. However, target costing is no prerequisite for OBA because cost reduction needs can also be determined in other ways, for example, by cost benchmarking.

Discussion

General

OBA describes the disclosure of a firm's cost data to another firm that would not have access to this data under normal circumstances. The firms are legally independent and do not belong to a group. Nevertheless, they may depend on each other economically. OBA is, above all, a means of dealing with cost information. It is based on a firm's cost accounting system and is thus not an instrument in itself. OBA can, but need not, encompass specific OBA tools. In addition to costs, other operational data (e.g., process times) can be subjected to OBA as well.

While the two previous subsections are empirically oriented and present examples of how events can unfurl, it should be remembered that the world is not black and white. The case examples open up the field in which OBA is practiced. Naturally there are variations in company behaviour, and, in the world of small numbers, opportunism may hit back hard.

Even though the data and the examples on which this chapter is primarily based have been collected from private business, several OBA activities take place in the public sector and at the public-private interface. Like life-cycle costing, OBA has some roots in military agreements. The traditional discussions between military and private suppliers have tackled the future annual change of unit prices. However, there are examples, both in U.S. and in Europe, in which military ordering is based on OBA carried out with many or selected suppliers (Kulmala et al. 2006). Even though the customer (the public) can define how OBA should be carried out in the phases concerned with offering services and delivering them, it cannot change definitions after writing them down, and it cannot in any way influence the supplier's accounting. This often leads to situations where prices are actually discussed, and the eventual cost decided upon might not have too much connection to prices: The organisation offering the lowest price gets the order, and subsequently tries to minimise costs, possibly eventually making a loss from the contract.

Research in OBA, especially in the network context, is still at an exploratory stage (Kajüter and Kulmala 2005). For this reason, it is not surprising that the empirical evidence is largely based on case studies and on interventionist research. Surveys providing descriptive empirical evidence on a large-scale basis have only been conducted in the UK (Munday 1992; McIvor 2001) and Germany (Möller and Windolph 2008). The empirical findings revealed, for example, that in the UK, 30 per cent of the suppliers of electronic components disclosed their product costs to customers and only 10 per cent did so with their subcontractors (McIvor 2001).

Most of the case study research analyses the practice and the problems associated with the implementation of OBA in dyadic buyer-supplier relationships (Carr and Ng 1995; Seal et al. 1999; Mouritsen et al. 2001; Dekker 2003; Kulmala 2004). Research dealing with OBA practice in networks is even sparser (Håkansson and Lind 2004; Kajüter and Kulmala 2005; Hoffjan and Kruse 2006). Owing to the constraints of research resources, or inability to gain access to firms, OBA is often only studied in networks from the perspective of the leading firm, a limitation that is also common in other empirical research on inter-organisational cost management.

Types of Open-Book Accounting

In practice, several different types of OBA have emerged. On the basis of the inter-firm relationship in which cost data is disclosed, dyadic and multilateral OBA can be distinguished. Dyadic OBA can often be observed in buyer-supplier relationships. If more than two firms are involved in disclosing cost data, then multilateral OBA takes place. This may be the case in networks.

The cost data that is disclosed can be actual costs or planned costs. For example, if the cost structure of an existing product is analysed, actual costs are used for the OBA. If suppliers are asked to disclose their product costing as part of their offer, then the OBA will be based on planned costs. In both cases, the extent of disclosure can vary. At one extreme, a firm provides detailed information about all elements of its product cost structure (known as full OBA). At the other extreme, information is only provided at an aggregated level or may only include selected cost items, for instance, direct material costs (referred to as limited OBA). Carr and Ng, for example, remarked that "Nissan's suppliers in the U.K. range from those that are 'totally open-book' to those that are 'downright awkward' about giving information" (Carr and Ng 1995, p. 359).

As regards the information flow, one-way and two-way OBA can be differentiated. In the former case, one firm only discloses its costs to the other firm involved and thus the disclosing firm (in most cases the supplier) receives no corresponding information from the other company (the customer). This, however, takes place in two-way OBA, where both firms exchange information.

Finally, the basis of the OBA can differ. As a result of the confidential and sensitive nature of the information disclosed, trust forms an important prerequisite for OBA. If there is no trust, OBA may be enforced by the dominant and more powerful firm, which is in a position to take advantage of the economic dependence of the other company. For example, the disclosing firm may fear that it will lose business and therefore feels obliged to meet the expectations of its customer. Table 9.1 summarises the various types of OBA.

Firms may have different intentions when applying OBA. As mentioned before, one major purpose is to reduce costs (Mouritsen et al. 2001; Dekker 2003, 2004; Cooper and Slagmulder 2004; Kulmala 2004). OBA enables firms to extend their cost management efforts beyond their own organisational boundaries. The cost transparency achieved by OBA can help to identify and exploit cost reduction opportunities that could not be identified and realised by the firms individually (e.g., by requesting design changes to purchased components by the supplier that facilitate the final assembly by the customer). OBA is thus an important practice in inter-organisational cost management. A purpose related to cost reduction is benefit sharing: Companies do not focus on cost savings in this case, and indeed, costs may even increase if, as a result, there is greater profit to be made. In these cases, OBA can be used as a method to analyse the benefit sharing potential beforehand or to calculate the actual benefits for each partner afterwards, according to calculation rules agreed beforehand (Jarimo and Kulmala 2008). The second purpose of OBA is to build trust in inter-firm relationships. Trust is not only a prerequisite for OBA. The disclosure of cost data

Table 9.1 Types of Open-Book Accounting

Characteristic	Types of Open-Book Accounting
Inter-firm relationship	dyadic—multilateral
Type of cost data	actual—planned
Extent of disclosure	full disclosure—limited disclosure
Information flow	one-way—two-way
Basis	trust based—power based

can also contribute to creating trust if firms believe that prices are calculated in a fair way and that confidential cost information is not misused.

Benefits

The potential benefits of OBA are closely linked to its purposes: cost reduction and trust building. Hence, the potential benefits are quite diverse. They include monetary aspects such as improved financial performance and intangible issues, notably, the quality of inter-firm relationships. As a result, it is difficult to provide an exact measure of the benefits that are realised by OBA practice. This is also the case for cost reductions: At Eurocar, for example, the cost reduction opportunities that were identified in conjunction with suppliers and that were selected for implementation were incorporated into a four-year action plan (Kajüter and Kulmala 2005). Nevertheless, it is not always clear-cut whether a measure is a result of OBA or of other inter-organisational cost management efforts. Despite these limitations, OBA was considered to significantly support inter-organisational cost management in the Eurocar network.

Empirical evidence from case study analysis also indicates positive effects on trust in inter-firm relationships. In a Finnish network, for instance, OBA was able to warrant calculative trust that was based on a potential increase in business volume (Kajüter and Kulmala 2005). This calculative trust, in turn, served as a means of using OBA for cost reduction purposes. Hence, the empirical findings suggest that OBA provides information that Tomkins (2001) classified as Type 1 (warranting trust) and Type 2 (revealing opportunities for joint cost savings).

OBA can not only provide benefits when being applied to physical products, but also when it is used in the marketing of services. For example, a Swedish conveyor manufacturer, Kellve AB, suggests full-scale OBA with their customers even in cases in which the customers do not ask for it. Since 2004, Kellve has doubled its order intake every year without endangering its profitability. This growth indicates both the increase of trust and experienced realisation of cost reductions. It may even be that, in some cases, the customer does not have as much control over Kellve as its other suppliers, because, through its OBA, Kellve ensures the existence of an atmosphere of reliable self-control. At the same time, Kellve demonstrates the potential for process change resulting in cost savings for their customers, and in addition to which, it demonstrates a desire for openness and transparency (Lappeteläinen 2007). This way of working might not be good marketing if every company were to implement it, but when only a few do, it seems to pay back.

In addition to the matter of which benefits might be associated with OBA, the related question of how financial benefits are shared among the network partners is important. To attain a long-term commitment, it is crucial that all partners gain some benefit from the practice of OBA. Hence, a win-win situation has to be achieved. This does not mean that the benefits always have to be shared equally among the partners (Christopher 1998). Empirical evidence suggests that, on average, suppliers benefit less from OBA than customers (McIvor 2001).

Networks, finally, also have to decide whether they want to define a general rule for sharing the benefits between the partners or whether this question is discussed case by case. A general rule might reduce transaction costs; however, it is noteworthy that, in the Eurocar network, it was felt that a general rule would be inappropriate because of "varying circumstances" (Kajüter and Kulmala 2005). Consequently, various agreements have emerged. They include equal sharing of the benefits, the allocation of benefits to the supplier alone in return for a promise not to increase the price, or the allocation of benefits to Eurocar alone if the supplier has benefited from Eurocar's technical support and can realise further cost savings with other customers.

Failure Risks

Several cases show that OBA often fails despite the potential benefits outlined earlier. This can be explained through the theoretical perspectives discussed in Section 3. Summarising the empirical results from three Finnish manufacturing networks, a list of six major reasons for the failure of implementing OBA can be compiled (see, e.g., Kajüter and Kulmala 2005):

1. *Suppliers experienced no extra benefit from the openness and main contractors did not offer win-win solutions.* Some suppliers expected OBA to change the way in which business with the main contractor was organised. If such a change was not forthcoming, and that usually meant a new measurable benefit from the suppliers' point of view, disclosure of accounting information was seen as a purposeless act. For example, the centralization of paint purchasing in Network A (Kajüter and Kulmala 2005) was needed to open up one of the SMEs.

2. *Suppliers thought that accounting information should be kept in-house.* Some suppliers wanted to limit the availability of cost information to the personnel or management of the firm. This way of thinking may have its origin in ideas of perfect markets, according to which sales prices include all the information, and in the desired independence of the entrepreneur. Suspiciousness towards cost, as a factor that determines the success of a firm or a network, also existed. The understanding of what the role of accounting information is in the management of a firm seemed to be low. An SME in a network built up for joint marketing in western Finland, for instance, left the whole network because of openness requirements (Kulmala 2006).

3. *Network members could not produce accurate cost information* and saw no sense in sharing poor cost data. The accounting system of

some suppliers was known to be poor or inadequate. At the same time, there was no desire to mislead main contractors by providing them with poor cost data for cost analyses. In instances where poor accounting information is provided, it may be reasonable to start from reorganising cost accounting and, only after that, turn to OBA. Many SMEs, for example, are talking about totally different concepts to their customers when they refer to an "activity cost" or a "unit cost". Having realised their lack of knowledge, some suppliers wanted to hide their limited accounting knowledge rather than to continue OBA discussions.

4. *Suppliers were afraid of being exploited* if they revealed their cost structure. It was felt that firms receiving cost data might use it against the firms that provided it. This might happen, for example, by demanding frequent competitive bidding or by conducting benchmarking and always selecting the lowest cost supplier, which might eliminate the possibility of creating a long-term partnership strategy. A recent history of bad experiences also explained this attitude. For example, fear was the reason for not fully opening the books in the heavy frame welding SME case mentioned in the introduction to this chapter.

5. *Suppliers did not have the capacity and were not provided with the requisite support from main contractors for the development of accounting systems.* Building and updating such accounting systems as were needed for reasonable open-book practice were expected to require more work than could be assigned, or more sophisticated competence than was available. Furthermore, some suppliers expected main contractors to help by supplying the human resources and providing the knowledge to the suppliers since the initial request to utilise open-book practices came from the main contractor. In the Offshore network, for instance, this problem was avoided through the investment of the main contractor.

6. *Network members could not agree on how open-book practice should be implemented.* Some suppliers had a conflict either with their main contractors or with other suppliers, with the result that their position and status in the network were uncertain. Agreement on how open-book practices should be organised and on what the "accounting rules" should be in the case of cost information disclosure could not be obtained. In these cases, the problem arose not only as a result of the suppliers' attitudes, but also because of the inflexibility of the main contractors. For example, the marketing network in western Finland (Kulmala 2006) eventually collapsed owing to this problem.

These six separate reasons for failures of OBA emerged in the case analysis and were repeated in later field experiences, but in other circumstances, they may also be interrelated, creating a very complex managerial problem.

3   THEORETICAL PERSPECTIVES OF OPEN-BOOK ACCOUNTING

Overview

There is no coherent theory of OBA, but several theoretical perspectives can be used to analyse it. Given the nature of OBA practice and the empirical evidence presented in the previous section, two theories seem to be particularly useful to gain a deeper understanding of OBA. First, *contingency theory* may contribute to explaining under which circumstances OBA can be applied successfully. Second, in view of the information asymmetries and conflicts of interest that may exist between suppliers and customers, *agency theory* might also provide a valuable theoretical framework. For example, the issue of trust that emerged in the cases presented in Section 2 can be analysed as a means of mitigating the agency problem. For this reason, OBA is analysed in more detail from the perspective of contingency theory and agency theory in the following two subsections.

It is important to note, however, that there are further theories that contribute to enhancing our understanding of OBA, such as the transaction cost economics, resource-dependence theory, game theory, or evolutionary theories. *Transaction cost economics* rests on similar assumptions to agency theory and can also be considered in explaining OBA practice. It was originally developed to determine the most efficient governance structure and thereby to define corporate boundaries (Williamson 1975). According to this theory, a firm can manage its business transactions through three different governance structures: markets, hierarchies, and hybrid organisations. Each of these structures gives rise to transaction costs. They comprise costs before and after the transaction: costs for searching and evaluating business partners (searching costs), costs for drafting and negotiating an agreement (contract costs), and costs for enforcing the contract and solving disputes (monitoring costs). The most efficient governance structure is the one that minimises the transaction costs. It depends, among other things, on the specificity of the asset that is the subject of the transaction. In the case of a high asset specificity, a hierarchy (known as vertical integration) is the preferred governance structure.

OBA can contribute by reducing transaction costs in buyer-supplier relationships and networks (i.e., hybrid organisations) because it facilitates the evaluation of suppliers and makes it possible to monitor the contract. From this perspective, customers have an economic incentive to ask suppliers to use OBA. Moreover, they also have an incentive to formalise or standardise OBA in order to reduce the transaction costs that are caused by heterogeneous practices within a network (Jarimo and Kulmala 2008).

The *resource-dependence theory* suggests that a firm's autonomy is reduced by its dependence on scarce resources (Pfeffer and Salancik 1978). Thus, firms aim to build relationships to avoid or reduce their dependence on these resources or seek to make other firms dependent on them. As OBA can serve to build trust into inter-firm relationships, it contributes to developing dyadic or network relationships. OBA may, therefore, be perceived as a means to reduce a firm's dependence.

Furthermore, *game theory* provides an analytical framework with which to study OBA practice (Hoffjan 2008). Game theory analyses situations in which at least two parties are involved and each of them makes decisions depending on the choices made by the other party. For example, a supplier decides on the disclosure of correct or misleading cost data based on the expected actions of the customer, which in turn chooses to embark on cooperative or opportunistic behaviour, depending on the expected quality of cost data disclosed by the supplier. The analysis of such situations would be based on narrow assumptions, but could nevertheless contribute to explaining cooperative or opportunistic behaviour in OBA applications.

Finally, it has been proposed to take an evolutionary perspective on inter-organisational cost management (Coad and Cullen 2006). *Evolutionary theories* refer to concepts such as institutionalisation, capabilities, and learning and change to explain the development of cost management practices in inter-firm relationships. From an evolutionary perspective, it could be argued that OBA is practiced in networks as a result of imitation and the replication of effective routines. Evolutionary theories, thus, seem to be a promising approach for studying the spread of OBA in networks.

Open-Book Accounting and Contingency Theory

Contingency theory was originally developed to explain the structure of organisations by particular circumstances (e.g., Lawrence and Lorsch 1967). It has been adopted and further developed by management accounting scholars to study the shape of management accounting systems within firms (e.g., Waterhouse and Thiessen 1978; Otley 1980; Chenhall 2003). According to contingency theory, there is no universal management accounting system that fits all situations. The application and design of management accounting systems rather depend on external and internal context factors (e.g., the degree of competition and size of the firm under consideration, respectively). Contingency theory can also be applied to networks. However, from a network's perspective there are a number of context factors that are neither firm-specific nor environmental but rather network-specific. As a consequence, network-specific factors constitute a third type of context factor that should be considered in a network-related contingency analysis (Kajüter and Kulmala 2005). An example for a network-specific factor is the level of trust or the type of network coordination.

Figure 9.4 presents a specified contingency model for open-book accounting in networks. From empirical observations, it mentions the determinants inducing open-book practice for each contextual factor in parenthesis. As regards exogenous environmental factors, it can be

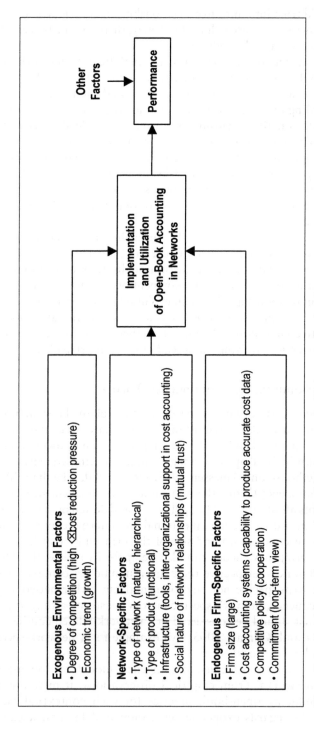

Figure 9.4   Contingency framework for OBA in networks (Kajüter and Kulmala 2005, p. 198).

assumed that OBA is fuelled by a high degree of competition (increasing the cost reduction pressure) and facilitated by economic growth of the economy (promising more business). With regard to network-specific factors, OBA takes place above all in hierarchical networks supplying functional products or services. Such networks are usually long-term oriented so that the partners can realise cost savings over an extensive period of time. This is particularly relevant for functional products, which require ongoing cost reductions, contrary to innovative products, for which flexibility and speed are critical. Moreover, an adequate infrastructure in terms of cost management tools and inter-organisational support for cost accounting facilitate OBA practice. In addition to this technical issue, the social nature of the network relationships can ease or impede OBA. Mutual trust is an enabling mechanism in this respect. Finally, firm size, cost accounting systems, competitive policy, and commitment are endogenous, firm-specific contingency factors relevant for OBA.

The abovementioned contingency factors could also be useful to explain differences in OBA practice that have been observed internationally. Empirical evidence suggests that Japanese firms seem to require far greater levels of detail in the cost data disclosure than Western firms (Munday 1992). In the UK, for example, most of the suppliers surveyed confirmed that they were not providing such information in all cases. At Nissan, only 25 per cent of the UK suppliers used open-book techniques in 1993 (Carr and Ng 1995). Similarly, case study research in Japan revealed significant differences in the extent to which OBA is applied (Cooper and Slagmulder 1999). Hopper et al. (1999) noted that none of the Japanese SMEs under consideration outside a "keiretsu" expressed any enthusiasm for sharing cost information with customers and suppliers. Hence, disclosure of internal cost data may be more common in Japanese firms because the principles of lean supply originate in the Japanese environment, but nevertheless, specific circumstances have to prevail in these firms, too, to make OBA work. Further research could apply a contingency framework to the study of national differences in OBA while controlling for other factors.

Moreover, little evidence exists so far regarding the potential positive effects of OBA on the firm or network performance (Möller and Windolph 2008). Future studies in this area could also build on a contingency framework and would require a large empirical basis.

Open-Book Accounting and Agency Theory

Agency theory takes a different perspective on OBA. In general, agency theory analyses the relationships between people or entities that arise when one person or entity (the principal) delegates certain tasks to another one (the agent) (Jensen and Meckling 1976). The agent disposes of specific competences and is better informed than the principal. Therefore, the principal can achieve a better performance by delegating the task. However, both the principal and the agent are assumed to be utility maximisers. Given the information asymmetry and the potential for conflicts of interest between them, opportunistic behaviour becomes likely. "If both parties to the relationship are utility maximisers, there is a good reason to believe that the agent will not always act in the best interests of the principal" (Jensen and Meckling 1976, p. 308). As a result, three types of agency problems may arise: hidden characteristics, hidden action, and hidden intention. Hidden characteristics may result in choosing the wrong agent (adverse selection), hidden action may lead to a poor performance of the delegated task (moral hazard), and hidden intention may become apparent if the agent exploits the dependence of the principal (holdup).

Dyadic and multilateral inter-firm relationships in supply chains are a typical setting in which the aforementioned agency problems arise. Thus, several examples of potential opportunistic behaviour in the course of OBA have been mentioned in Section 2. Agency theory suggests, however, that there are three mechanisms to reduce agency problems. A first one is control. It aims at avoiding opportunistic behaviour by reducing the information asymmetries. In this perspective, OBA can be seen as a control mechanism that contributes to avoiding adverse selection or moral hazard. The disclosed cost data serve to choose the right supplier or to monitor the supplier's operations. As the use of OBA as a control mechanism reflects a confrontational attitude, its use is usually based on power. Incentives are a second mechanism by which to reduce agency problems. They aim at reducing the conflicts of interest between the principal and the agent by creating win-win solutions. Incentives induce a cooperative approach to the agency problem that can be applied along with OBA if its benefits are shared among the partners. Finally, trust is a third mechanism for handling agency problems. It entails a cooperative approach, like the use of incentives. If the purpose of OBA is to create trust in inter-firm relationships, it can also be perceived as a means to mitigate agency problems. Hence, in terms of agency theory, OBA may be explained as both a control and trust building mechanism.

In the spirit of Laaksonen et al. (2008), trust and dependency are the co-evolutionary building blocks of partnerships. In the case of OBA, this means that the decent use of OBA in a suitable business environment may create a positive cycle of increasing trust. In this perspective, there is enough trust to start OBA discussions, some beneficial results emerge, and trust increases, with the result that OBA can be taken beyond what had been planned at the outset. In the negative case, OBA is used in a totally unsuitable business environment and/or with the wrong motives and methods. This may lead to ruining a normal customer-supplier relationship, which would have worked well otherwise. This shows that additional contingency factors have to be considered before using OBA as a trust-building mechanism in an agency relationship.

4 CONCLUSIONS

OBA in inter-firm relationships is still a fairly new phenomenon having emerged as organisational boundaries have become increasingly blurred in recent years. There are various types of OBA that can be observed in practice. However, it seems to be dangerous to assume that OBA is suited to all customer-supplier relationships. OBA can work if used systematically in certain well-analysed business contexts, but, like any other managerial tool, it does not work if it is only tried in an unsuitable business setting.

Research in this area is still in its infancy; however, several promising theoretical perspectives have been identified to pave the way for an in-depth analysis of OBA. Building on the existing exploratory case studies, future research could try to investigate OBA on a larger empirical basis. This might provide evidence about the actual adoption rate of OBA and offer the opportunity to test hypotheses. Moreover, experimental research could deliver interesting insights into OBA, for example, to test hypotheses derived from agency or game theory.

There are several potential research settings and questions that could be addressed in future OBA research. Firstly, it is important to know if OBA users perform better in their inter-organisational relationships than those not using it. And if so, to determine why. If OBA users performed better than nonusers, would this be evidence against networking? Or would it be proof against the traditional assumption that a market mechanism includes all the information on prices?

Secondly, most of the empirical OBA case studies reported so far are from Japan, Northern Europe, and Scandinavia. In Japan, there is the kei-retsu culture in which everything is led by the centre. In Europe, many markets are imperfect, so that there are only a limited number of potential suppliers/customers and everybody knows each other, in practice. Are these so-called "trust" cultures more suitable for OBA than the traditional trading culture typified by that of U.S.? Is OBA, then, a natural way to tackle the advantage of almost perfect markets, or is it process engineers' innovation against the continuous drawbacks of using market mechanisms repeatedly?

Thirdly, network settings may put suppliers into a difficult position. If they apply OBA with many customers, they may face situations in which OBA with one customer suggests process changes that it is extremely important to avoid for the OBA with another customer. The supplier has to select whom to serve best, or open the calculations to many customers, which, in certain circumstances, may even infringe competition laws.

Fourthly, the role of cost accounting in OBA is crucial. Cost accounting as such may show, for example, that minimum costs can be attained in certain relationships. If the actor's other relationships are not calculated or are calculated with different accounting parameters, the identified minimum might only be a local suboptimum, causing severe problems in other relationships. Since product or process costs can show anything depending on how the accounting parameters are selected, the only true way to prove benefits from OBA are by investigating the opinions of participating organisations and persons, preferably over an extended period of time.

Fifthly, why do we have so few empirical studies reporting the techniques and outcomes of OBA? Is it because companies do not use OBA, because they do not let researchers follow and report developments, or could it be that researchers are not interested in this topic? We know, at least, that the two last are true. According to our ten-year experience of OBA in the field, this topic is highly confidential. Only two of the tens of case companies analysed by us have been willing to have their names published. Many companies that suffer from problems try to make their failures "opaque" or deny that the published report concerns them. In the opposite case, success is often something that firms wish to keep quiet about to maintain their competitive advantage in the processes concerned. From a practical perspective, a result-oriented researcher facing this situation might prefer to select other topics to study. However, from a scientific point of view, a phenomenon that is relevant to management, but hard to analyse, should not be overlooked.

To summarise, there seem to be many opportunities for further research in this area of accounting in networks.

BIBLIOGRAPHY

Carr, C., and Ng, J. 1995. Total cost control: Nissan and its U.K. supplier partnerships. *Management Accounting Research* 6: 346–365.

Chenhall, R. H. 2003. Management control systems design within its organizational context: Findings from contingency-based research and directions for the future. *Accounting, Organizations and Society* 28: 127–168.

Christopher, M. 1998. *Logistics and supply chain management: Strategies for reducing cost and improving service*. London: Financial Times Management. Pitman Publishing.

Coad, A. F., and Cullen, J. 2006. Inter-organizational cost management: Towards an evolutionary perspective. *Management Accounting Research* 17: 342–369.

Cooper, R., and Slagmulder, R. 1999. *Supply chain development for the lean enterprise—interorganizational cost management*. Portland, OR: Montvale.

Cooper, R., and Slagmulder, R. 2004. Interorganizational cost management and relational context. *Accounting, Organizations and Society* 29: 1–26.

Dekker, H. 2003. Value chain analysis in interfirm relationships: A field study. *Management Accounting Research* 14: 1–23.

Dekker, H. 2004. Control of inter-organizational relationships: Evidence on appropriation concerns and coordination requirements. *Accounting, Organizations and Society* 29: 27–49.

Håkansson, H., and Lind, J. 2004. Accounting and network coordination. *Accounting, Organizations and Society* 29: 51–72.

Harland, C. M., Lamming, R. C., Zheng, J., and Johnsen, T. E. 2001. A taxonomy of supply networks. *Journal of Supply Chain Management* 37: 20–27.

Hoffjan, A. 2008. *Incentives to cost information sharing in supply chains: A game theoretical analysis of open book accounting.* Paper presented at the EAA Annual Congress, Rotterdam.

Hoffjan, A., and Kruse, H. 2006. Open book accounting in supply chains—when and how is it used in practice? *Cost Management* 20: 40–48.

Hopper, T., Koga, T., and Goto, J. 1999. Cost accounting in small and medium sized Japanese companies: An exploratory study. *Accounting and Business Research* 30: 73–86.

Jarimo, T., and Kulmala, H. I. 2008. Incentive profit-sharing rules joined with open-book accounting in SME networks. *Production Planning and Control* 19: 508–517.

Jensen, M. C., and Meckling, W. H. 1976. Theory of the firm: Managerial behavior, agency costs and ownership structure. *Journal of Financial Economics* 3: 305–360.

Kulmala, H. I. 2002. Open-book accounting in networks. *The Finnish Journal of Business Economics* 51: 157–177.

Kulmala, H. I. 2004. Developing cost management in customer-supplier relationships: Three case studies. *Journal of Purchasing and Supply Management* 10: 65–77.

Kulmala, H. I. 2006. *Purchasing from equal SME networks: The perspective of pricing and cost management.* 29th EAA Annual Congress Abstract Book, p. 216. Dublin, Ireland, March 22–24, 2006.

Kulmala, H. I., Kajüter, P., and Valkokari, K. 2007. Inter-organizational cost management in SME networks. Proceedings of the 8th Manufacturing Accounting Research Conference (CD-ROM), Trento, Italy, June 18–20, 2007.

Kajüter, P., and Kulmala, H, I. 2005. Open-book accounting in networks: Potential achievements and reasons for failures. *Management Accounting Research* 16: 179–204.

Kulmala, H I., Ojala, M., Ahoniemi, L., and Uusi-Rauva, E. 2006. Unit cost behaviour in public sector outsourcing. *International Journal of Public Sector Management* 19: 130–149.

Kulmala, H. I., Paranko, J., and Uusi-Rauva, E. 2002. The role of cost management in network relationships. *International Journal of Production Economics* 79: 33–43.

Laaksonen, T., Pajunen, K., and Kulmala, H. I. 2008. Co-evolution of trust and dependence in customer-supplier relationships. *Industrial Marketing Management* 37: (Forthcoming).

Lambert, D. M., and Cooper, M. C. 2000. Issues in supply chain management. *Industrial Marketing Management* 29: 65–83.

Lappeteläinen, I. 2007. *Profitability of supplier's specialization to prototype production* (in Finnish). MSc thesis, Tampere University of Technology. Tampere, Finland.

Lawrence, P., and Lorsch, J. 1967. *Organization and environment.* Irwin, U.S.: Homewood.

McIvor, R. 2001. Lean supply: The design and cost reduction dimensions. *European Journal of Purchasing and Supply Management* 7: 227–242.

Möller, K., and Windolph, M. 2008. The effect of open-book accounting on inter-firm cooperation's performance by means of relational factors. Paper presented at the 6th Conference on New Directions in Management Accounting, Brussels, Belgium, December 15–17.

Mouritsen, J., Hansen, A., and Hansen, C. 2001. Inter-organizational controls and organizational competencies: Episodes around target cost management/functional analysis and open book accounting. *Management Accounting Research* 12: 221–244.

Munday, M. 1992. Accounting cost data disclosure and buyer-supplier partnerships: A research note. *Management Accounting Research* 3: 245–250.

Otley, D. T. 1980. The contingency theory of management accounting: Achievement and prognosis. *Accounting, Organizations and Society* 4: 413–428.

Pfeffer, J., and Salancik, G. R. 1978. *The External control of organizations—a resource dependence perspective.* New York: Harper & Row.

Seal, W., Cullen, J., Dunlop, A., Berry, T., and Ahmed, M. 1999. Enacting a European supply chain: A case study on the role of management accounting. *Management Accounting Research* 10: 303–322.

Tomkins, C. 2001. Interdependencies, trust and information in relationships, alliances and networks. *Accounting, Organizations and Society* 26: 161–191.

Waterhouse, J., and Tiessen, P. 1978. A contingency framework for management accounting systems research. *Accounting, Organizations and Society* 3: 65–76.

Williamson, O. E. 1975. *Markets and hierarchies: Analysis and antitrust implications.* New York: Free Press.

Part III

Theoretical Perspectives on Accounting in Networks

Part III

Theoretical Perspectives on Accounting in Networks

10 Accounting in Networks— The Transaction Cost Economics Perspective

Shannon Anderson and Henri Dekker

1 INTRODUCTION

Transaction cost economics (TCE) is the dominant theory used to analyse the economics of inter-firm relationships. TCE's key predictions are that: 1) firm boundaries are the outcome of managerial decisions to lower the cost of doing business; and 2) firms use organisational design, governance, and management control choices to mitigate exchange hazards and to enhance transaction efficiency.[1] Exchange hazards arise between self-interested, profit-maximising transaction partners as a result of information asymmetry and uncertainty. When information asymmetry or uncertainty is present, it is too costly (or impossible) to write complete contracts that specify responses to all contingencies. As a result, transaction partners are exposed to the risk that a partner will behave opportunistically, exploiting private knowledge or the resolution of uncertainty at some future date to enhance their position at the expense of their trading partner.

Researchers use TCE theory for a variety of purposes, such as:

- identifying transaction characteristics (i.e., asset specificity, environmental uncertainty, measurement uncertainty, transaction frequency) that are associated with exchange hazards;
- explaining why firms employ close inter-firm relationships that are subject to exchange hazards instead of using other approaches (e.g., arm's-length market transactions, vertical integration of activities by the firm); and
- testing the contingency proposition that better performance outcomes for transactions are realised when specific approaches to governance and management control are aligned with transaction hazards.

Exchange hazards are described with a variety of labels: opportunism, relational risk, appropriation concerns, and transaction hazards. All of these terms express the concern that, by engaging in a transactional relationship, firms place valuable resources at risk by relinquishing some control over these resources to a partner whose interests may diverge from the interests of the firm. Accordingly, TCE posits that control mechanisms such as contracts, monitoring systems, and incentive/reward systems are needed to deter opportunistic behaviour and to align the transaction partners' interests (e.g., Dekker 2004; Vosselman and Van der Meer-Kooistra 2009). In recent years accounting researchers have shown increasing interest in TCE-based research, often complemented with other theoretical perspectives. For instance, studies have used TCE reasoning jointly with theory about strategic behaviour (Anderson and Dekker 2005) and organisational theory (Dekker 2004, 2008). In addition, the narrow calculus of self-interest is often expanded to include relational or trust-based perspectives and motivations (Van der Meer-Kooistra and Vosselman 2000; Langfield-Smith and Smith 2003; Cooper and Slagmulder 2004; Dekker 2004; Vosselman and Van der Meer-Kooistra 2009).[2]

In this chapter, we review the use of TCE in the study of inter-firm relationships. An extensive literature in economics and business strategy delves into inter-firm governance choices. In our review, we focus on accounting and nonaccounting studies to assess how TCE has contributed and can further contribute to the understanding of accounting and control in inter-firm settings. We structure this discussion according to the different stages of inter-firm relationships and highlight, for each stage, the importance of accounting and management control (Gulati 1998; Van der Meer-Kooistra and Vosselman 2000; Anderson and Sedatole 2003). For instance, accounting information may be used in the decision to commence a relationship (e.g., make-or-buy analyses), may inform the partner search-and-selection process (e.g., supplier evaluations), and may be implicated in the design of management control structures (e.g., specification of contract terms and provisions using accounting metrics). Moreover, adaptation of management control may be warranted as the transactional, relational, and/or business context change, and accounting information may be implicated in the dynamic adjustment process (e.g., when accounting information alters the level of trust in the exchange partner). In accounting research, TCE has been used in each of these stages to explain accounting and control choices. Thus, our discussion follows the stages: 1) alliance decision and choice of governance mode; 2) partner search and selection; 3) management control design; and 4) dynamic evolution and change.[3] In addition, we review other theoretical perspectives that complement TCE and have influenced TCE-based research.

We begin in Section 2 with reviewing the use of TCE in the analysis of choice of governance mode; in particular, the use of arm's-length market transactions, vertically integrated enterprises (i.e., hierarchy), or hybrid organisational forms such as alliances, partnerships, and joint ventures. Inclusion of hybrid organisational forms recognises that the traditional two-alternative, make-versus-buy decision neglects the rich middle ground between these extremes. In the next section, we continue this discussion by reviewing studies that examine the selection and choice of exchange partner, which follows from the decision to ally and may precede or be made jointly with choices of governance mode and structure. Section 4 examines TCE's contribution to explaining variety in design and use of accounting and control within the relationship formed with an exchange partner (i.e., within the governance mode chosen). We divide these broadly into studies about management control and about accounting techniques and use of accounting information. In Section 5, we explore developments in an area of TCE research that has received relatively limited theoretical and empirical attention: the dynamics of and change in inter-firm relationships, and the potential of TCE to inform research questions about the role of accounting in these dynamic adjustments. In Section 6, we discuss complementary perspectives to TCE-based reasoning, in particular the notions of value creation and the resource-based view of the firm, the influence of coordination requirements across firm boundaries, and the proposition that relational governance and trust offer alternatives to contracting and formal controls. We conclude with a discussion of how TCE theory may be used to extend and expand our understanding of accounting in inter-firm relations and provide for this purpose an agenda for future research.

Although this chapter is by design bounded by the particular theoretical lens of TCE, our own views on inter-firm accounting research are not. Thus, although we provide assessments of when TCE appears useful for theorisation, we also offer assessments of its limitations and suggest complementary perspectives that researchers should consider when basing their research on TCE. Finally, we identify what we believe to be a number of fruitful avenues for future TCE-based research into inter-firm relationships.

2 ALLIANCE DECISION—CHOICE OF GOVERNANCE MODE AND THE BOUNDARIES OF THE FIRM

A substantial literature examines the boundaries of the firm, taking as the point of departure Coase's (1937) proposition that boundaries reflect cost-minimising modes of organisation. Specifically, TCE's prediction, as informed by comparative economics, is that boundaries are chosen to minimise the sum of production and transaction costs (Williamson 1975, 1985, 1991). For example, a firm that considers the alternatives of making a distinctive manufactured component or obtaining it from an alliance partner might face the following comparison: higher costs of self-production with limited access to unique supplier capabilities but few transaction costs[4] versus lower production costs of a specialised supplier that has economies of scale and distinctive production competencies but higher transaction costs associated with the risk that the supplier will exploit its position as a supplier of a critical component in the future. In this analysis the traditional make-or-buy decision is reframed as the *make-buy-or-ally* decision to recognise the existence of hybrid organisational forms that often emerge in the presence of transaction uncertainty, asymmetric information and distinctive partner capabilities that are not widely available through arm's-length transactions (e.g., Geyskens et al. 2006).

Transaction Costs and the Make-Buy-Or-Ally Decision

Firms that decide to "buy" inputs, procure them from other firms in arm's-length market transactions, perhaps with the help of simple, relatively complete contracts (e.g., specifying price, quantity, and a delivery schedule). Firms that vertically integrate to "make" inputs take part in a broad range of activities that are frequently organised in separate strategic business units that transact with one another. In the hybrid or "ally" transaction mode, firms enter into formal arrangements with one another (or multiple others) using more complex and typically incomplete contracts than those found in arm's-length transactions. However, because contracts are incomplete, residual risks remain and are controlled through mechanisms that often resemble management controls within the vertically integrated firm. Examples of such management controls include measurement of actions as well as outcomes and collaborative work that enhances communication and provides opportunities for informal mutual monitoring. Thus, the hybrid is an intermediate form of governance that encompasses both the use of high powered market-driven incentives (though weaker than in 'pure markets') and the coordination and cooperativeness allowed by hierarchies (though these are weaker than in 'pure hierarchies') (Williamson 1991). Within the category of hybrid governance, more specific governance modes are distinguished, including contractual cooperation (which is closest to market transactions), minority equity alliances, and joint ventures (which are closest to vertical integration or "hierarchy") (Gulati and Singh 1998).

Although the basic TCE prediction is that the mode with the lowest sum of production and transaction costs will be selected, most empirical studies assume that both parties can produce at nearly identical production costs and focus on transaction costs.[5] Thus, the TCE prediction is often abbreviated to say that the selected governance mode is determined by the mode of organisation with the lowest transaction costs. Transaction costs, or the costs of exchange between firms, include *ex ante* costs such as partner search, negotiation and contract development, and *ex post* costs of monitoring, enforcing contract compliance, and dispute resolution (Williamson 1985; Joskow 1987; Milgrom and Roberts 1992).

Transaction costs arise as a result of the characteristics of the transaction. Key transaction characteristics that provide the circumstances under which concerns about opportunism can arise are asset specificity, uncertainty, and frequency/duration (Williamson 1985). These characteristics provide grounds for transaction costs to arise and influence decisions about governance modes, given two characteristics of human decision makers: bounded rationality and self-interest. Bounded rationality includes the notion that decisions need not be fully optimal if decision makers are limited in their ability or willingness (owing to the cost of data collection or computation) to incorporate all available information in their decisions, while self-interested behaviour can give rise to opportunism when individual interests are not aligned with the interests of the firm.

In addition to transaction costs and the characteristics of human decision makers, the make-buy-ally decision is also influenced by characteristics of the firms involved in the transactions. Key exchange partner characteristics that influence decisions about governance mode derive from Porter's (1980) literature on competitive advantage and include features such as partners' competitive position in their respective industries, bilateral power in negotiations, and each partner's alternatives to the transaction at hand (i.e., the opportunity cost of foregoing other transactions). In the discussion that follows, we focus on the specific predictions of TCE that are related to transaction characteristics, noting points of interaction with elements of strategic interaction, agency problems, and limits to cognition.

Asset specificity is the key cause of appropriation concerns and refers to the degree to which investments that have little alternative use outside the relationship are made specifically for the inter-firm relationship. TCE recognises different types of asset specificity as determined by the object of investments, including *physical assets* (e.g., specialised equipment), *human assets* (e.g., specialised knowledge, experience, training), *dedicated assets* (tools and dies for car models), *goodwill assets* (e.g., brand name), and *location* (e.g., colocation for just-in-time production) (Williamson 1991). High asset specificity causes parties involved in a transaction to have few alternatives in which the asset can be employed without loss of value, with the result that they become locked in to their relationship. This provides an opportunity for 'holdup' problems in which the investing party suffers losses as a result of exploitation of its vulnerability by an exchange partner.

TCE identifies two additional transaction characteristics that interact with asset specificity in determining exchange hazards: uncertainty and frequency. Uncertainty includes environmental uncertainty and behavioural uncertainty (Geyskens et al. 2006). The first type of uncertainty reflects the predictability of the environment in which the transaction is executed and the degree to which intended performance can be specified up front. The second arises from the difficulties that exchange partners experience in monitoring performance ex post. In particular, when specific investments are made in a situation characterised by uncertainty about the future state of events, adaptation-related problems can emerge when unanticipated contingencies arise which create scope to renegotiate the terms of exchange. TCE theorises that markets and hierarchies differ in the capacity to adapt to changing conditions, resulting in differences in transaction costs. Since bounded rationality causes contractual agreements between transaction parties to be essentially incomplete, and the cost of trying to specify and cover every possible future contingency is disproportionately high, uncertainty exacerbates concerns about appropriation generated by asset specificity. Accordingly, within TCE, firms are hypothesised to vertically integrate activities characterised by high asset specify and environmental uncertainty.[6] Similarly, high behavioural uncertainty following from monitoring problems is hypothesised to favour hierarchical modes of governance that offer better evaluation capabilities (Geyskens et al. 2006).

The frequency/duration of transactions reflects the volume and value of the transactions over time (Williamson 1985). This transaction characteristic influences exchange hazards and governance choices because specific transactions that take place frequently in a market setting would require the effort of constant monitoring. Transactions that occur only occasionally require less monitoring and therefore do not merit the costs of establishing a hierarchy (Williamson 1985; David and Han 2004). Accordingly, more frequent transactions allow investments in governance to be justified. Thus, in the presence of asset specificity, an increase in frequency makes hierarchical governance relatively more attractive to market governance (Williamson 1985).[7] As compared to asset specificity and uncertainty, this dimension has received relatively limited attention in empirical TCE-based research (David and Han 2004; Geyskens et al. 2006).

Figure 10.1 illustrates the basic TCE predictions on choice of governance mode. The figure illustrates that, for low exchange hazards, transaction costs favour the buy mode until exchange hazards reach a level, k_1, beyond which they favour the hybrid or ally mode of governance. When exchange hazards shift further to the level of k_2, governance costs reach a level favouring vertical integration. Thus, hybrid governance modes are anticipated when transaction hazards cause pure market exchanges to be insufficient (i.e., "market failures") but are not sufficiently large to warrant vertical integration (Williamson 1991).

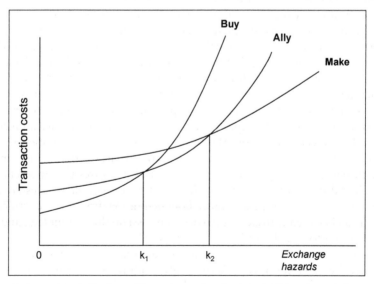

Figure 10.1   The choice between make, buy and ally (adapted from Gulati and Nickerson 2008)

Empirical Research into the Choice of Governance Mode

A substantial research literature, primarily outside accounting, has examined empirically TCE predictions about the boundaries of the firm (for comprehensive overviews of this empirical research, see Shelanski and Klein 1995; David and Han 2004; Geyskens et al. 2006). Empirical studies have particularly focused on the make-or-buy decision, although in recent years increasingly the ally decision has been included to expand the set of alternatives available for firms to consider (Geyskens et al. 2006). In contrast to internal organisation, alliances are argued not to 'suffer' from the high burden of bureaucratic costs and to retain some of the incentives provided by the market, while they provide better coordination and control than arm's-length governance (Williamson 1991; Oxley 1997). Within the category of alliances, between k_1 and k_2 in Figure 10.1, similar arguments are made for contractual alliances, minority equity alliances, and joint ventures. Contractual arrangements are used when exchange hazards are at or just beyond k_1. Contractual arrangements thus are considered to be closer to the market (buy) mode, with high-powered incentives but without shared ownership and an administrative structure. JVs are used when exchange hazards are at or just before k_2, and provide enhanced coordination and alignment of incentives around JV profit that are closer to the bureaucracy (make) mode (e.g., Oxley 1997; Gulati and Singh 1998). Minority equity alliances fall between these two alternatives.

Most empirical studies that aim to test TCE predictions examine whether firms' governance choices are consistent with hazards following from transaction attributes (i.e., following the logic of 'congruence fit'; Gerdin and Greve 2004). These studies use TCE to generate predictions based on the (explicit or implicit) assumptions that firms are in equilibrium and that competitive forces weed out inefficient choices. Accordingly, empirically observed governance choices are assumed to reflect "optimal" choices that have survived the test of competition. An extensive meta-analysis of TCE-based studies on firms' governance choices conducted by Geyskens and colleagues (2006) find broad support for the explanatory power of the theory in predicting the make-buy decision and the buy-ally decision, although it did not find asset specificity to have stronger predictive power than uncertainty.

While TCE literature expects convergence towards equilibrium in the long run, it also recognises that in the short run firms may make mistakes in their governance choices, and may, temporarily, be in a state of disequilibrium (Williamson 1985). Recognising this temporal disequilibrium provides TCE-based research with the possibility to examine the performance consequences of 'misfit' or 'misalignment'. However, relatively few studies have examined the effects of governance choices on performance in comparison to the effort that has been devoted to TCE-based equilibrium predictions (David and Han 2004; Geyskens et al. 2006). Disequilibrium studies take, as their point of departure, the proposition that the alignment (or 'fit') between governance choices and transaction attributes enhances exchange performance, which follows the logic of 'contingency fit'.[8] For example, Leiblein, Reuer, and Dalsace (2002) find that a firm's technological performance is contingent upon the alignment between its governance decisions (insourcing or outsourcing) and the degree of exchange hazards. Sampson (2004) examines how the governance of R&D alliances, viewed as the choice between pooling contracts and joint ventures, affects R&D outcomes. Following TCE reasoning, Sampson argues that pooling contracts should be used when exchange hazards are relatively low, and JVs when they are relatively high. When firms use pooling contracts under conditions of high exchange hazards, excessive uncontrolled hazards are expected to remain and firms are unlikely to effectively engage in innovation (e.g., because concerns about free riding limit their willingness to share knowledge). Similarly, when firms use a JV while exchange hazards are low, performance is likely to decline as the high bureaucracy dampens incentives to innovate. Sampson's findings are consistent with these expectations.[9] In their meta-analysis of TCE studies, Geyskens et al. (2006) summarise the empirical findings relating to the relation between 'fit' and performance, and conclude that choosing appropriate governance modes in response to transaction hazards is associated with increased performance.

Studies that examine determinants of firm boundaries have tended to be published in strategy, management, or economics journals rather than accounting journals.[10] Two studies that have been published in accounting journals, however, use TCE to test predictions about make-or-buy and outsourcing decisions in the professional accounting industry. Widener and Selto (1999) examine sourcing decisions for internal auditing activities (i.e., the choice between insourcing and outsourcing) and find support that in-house provision is positively associated with asset specificity and transaction frequency. Speklé et al. (2007) replicate the aforementioned study in a sample of Dutch firms and find additional confirmation for these relations.

Anderson et al. (2000) is a study that bridges the question of firm boundaries and the questions of partner selection and control system design that we take up in the next two sections of this chapter. They revisit sourcing decisions in the U.S. auto industry to test whether the early involvement of suppliers in product design and the use of new contracting provisions yield different results than in prior studies conducted in this industry. In contrast to prior studies that find that specific assets favour insourcing of complex parts (i.e., technical uncertainty and interdependence among related parts), they find that under the new collaboration and contracting regime, these conditions now favour outsourcing. In addition, more complex subassemblies are outsourced to fewer suppliers, providing evidence that colocating decision rights and making different supplier selection decisions reduce transaction costs caused by part interdependence. Thus, the Anderson et al.

paper goes beyond the traditional strategy and economics studies that focus on boundary choices, to illustrate that decisions about firm boundaries are taken jointly with decisions about the design of control systems to fulfil the TCE aim of selecting the "lowest cost" mode of transacting.

To summarise, TCE has been tested empirically in the business strategy, economics, and accounting literatures and has generally held up well as a theory that fits with the empirical regularities that describe firm boundaries.

3 PARTNER SELECTION—THE SEARCH FOR AND CHOICE OF EXCHANGE PARTNER

While the choice of governance mode has received broad attention in TCE-based research, the selection and choice of transaction partners, following from the decision to ally, has received less interest. Typically, studies take the selection of partners as given, without recognising that this choice is often coupled with the choice of governance mode discussed in the previous section and foreshadows the design of management controls that is discussed next in Section 4. Exceptions include studies such as that of Ireland et al. (2002), who identify partner selection as essential for transaction success and critical to alliance management, and those of Dekker (2008) and Dekker and Van den Abbeele (2010), who investigate how partner selection affects contract design and the use of control mechanisms in the management of transactions.[11] Gulati (1998) suggests that the availability of information about alliance partners (e.g., resulting from the selection process or prior ties) may influence cooperating firms' choice of structure for the alliance, as well as the key processes that drive the alliance's dynamic evolution.

Importantly, the choice of partner and the selection process employed are unlikely to be independent of the transaction characteristics, as increases in exchange hazards increase the importance of selecting a reliable partner to mitigate concerns about potential appropriation (Blumberg 2001; Dekker 2004; Li et al. 2008). Li et al. (2008) suggest that, in the context of R&D alliances, limiting the scope of an alliance or introducing even the most restrictive governance structures may be insufficient to reduce knowledge expropriation. Selection of a 'good' partner contributes to controlling the threat of expropriation and helps to protect core intellectual property.[12]

In a traditional buy mode, buyers face a competitive supplier market, supplier selection is price-based (i.e., relies on spot market prices), and partner identity is irrelevant to the exchange. When the transaction is associated with exchange hazards, however, the partner search-and-selection process gains importance as the identification of a suitable partner becomes more important. Van der Meer-Kooistra and Vosselman (2000), for instance, described how the selection processes in the contact phase of two complex and specific outsourcing arrangements emphasised the reliability, abilities, and competencies of contractors. For technology cooperation, Blumberg (2001) found that the effort invested in the search for a partner increased with exchange hazards associated with the size, specificity, and environmental uncertainty of the exchange. Dekker (2010) obtained similar results for transaction size and asset specificity in the context of IT exchanges by Dutch firms, and Dekker and Van den Abbeele (2010) found that the search time for IT exchanges by Belgium firms was influenced by transaction size, uncertainty, and task interdependencies.[13] In an analysis of the choice of partner type in relation to the potential loss of intellectual property versus the benefits of innovation, Li et al. (2008) examined the preferences for 'friends', 'acquaintances', and 'strangers'.[14] They conclude that choosing prior partners for a new R&D relation carries both risks and rewards. On the one hand, technology transfer may be facilitated, but on the other hand, a familiar partner may find it easier to appropriate the firm's technology. Based on these considerations, they predicted and found that when innovations are more 'radical' and opportunities for knowledge leakage are greater, the benefits of trust lead firms to prefer friends over both acquaintances and strangers. At the same time, the protective benefits of information asymmetry lead them to prefer strangers over acquaintances, because strangers experience more difficulty in appropriating the firm's knowledge. Jointly these studies provide support for TCE predictions with respect to the partner selection process and the type of partner chosen.

A critical question raised in this literature is how partner selection relates to subsequent management control choices. One argument voiced is that an extensive selection process and choice of a reliable partner can eliminate some need for control and are a substitute for the use of formal management controls. An opposing argument, however, is that partner selection and management controls act as complements; a more extensive selection process (following from anticipated exchange hazards) promotes learning and knowledge acquisition that can be embedded in the design of the management control structure. Empirical evidence in the setting of IT exchanges confirms this latter argument of complementarity, with learning during the selection process facilitating subsequent management control design (Dekker 2008; Dekker and Van den Abbeele 2010).[15]

4   MANAGEMENT CONTROL—DESIGN AND USE OF ACCOUNTING AND CONTROL MECHANISMS

In this section we make an important distinction between studies that use TCE to examine elements of *management control*, such as contract design and use of performance measures, and studies that use TCE to examine the more specific use of *accounting techniques,* such as collaborative or 'open-book' cost management (see Caglio and Ditillo [2008] for a general review of these issues). Conditional on the decision to use a mode of inter-firm collaboration rather than a make-or-buy governance mode, an important question is how firms engaging in relationships structure management controls (Van der Meer-Kooistra and Vosselman 2000). As noted by Gulati and Singh (1998, p. 782), "The same logic by which firms choose between the extremes of making or buying is also expected to operate, once firms have decided to form an alliance, in their choice of governance structure: when firms anticipate appropriation concerns, they are likely to organise alliances with more hierarchical contracts." Thus, research has been centred on the risks that remain after the choice of governance mode has been made, connecting this residual risk with the management control practices introduced to manage collaborative activity. These studies have focused on explaining two issues in particular: (1) management control choices, and (2) use of accounting techniques and accounting information.[16]

Management Control Choices in Inter-firm Relationships

Management control choices in inter-firm relationships include decisions concerning the structures, mechanisms, and practices used by exchange parties to gain control of their cooperative activities. Studies of management control choices have typically focused on control archetypes, which include definite mixes of control mechanisms, or on the design and use of specific management control mechanisms (Caglio and Ditillo 2008). While the first type of studies has aimed to develop taxonomies of control patterns used under different transactional conditions, the second type has typically focused on a subset of controls implemented to solve specific control problems. Multiple classifications of control mechanisms have been used in these studies, relating to the types and nature of controls (Gulati and Singh 1998; Groot and Merchant 2000; Van der Meer-Kooistra and Vosselman 2000; Dekker 2004; Anderson and Dekker 2005; Emsley and Kidon 2007; Kamminga and Van der Meer-Kooistra 2007), the objects and purposes of control (Dekker 2004; Reuer and Ariño 2007; Dekker 2008), and the tightness of control (Groot and Merchant 2000; Kamminga and Van der Meer-Kooistra 2007; Faems et al. 2008). Studies have also distinguished between formal and informal control mechanisms, and between contractual and noncontractual control (e.g., Smith et al. 1995; Dekker 2004). Formal control includes contractual obligations and organisational routines and practices for cooperation. Informal control (also referred to as social control) refers to the organisational cultures and systems that influence the members of an exchange. The differentiation between contractual and noncontractual control recognises that control mechanisms are often embedded in a legal contract that underlies cooperation but also often extend beyond the contract (e.g., Dekker and Van den Abbeele 2010). We first review TCE-based studies of contract design and then look at studies that examine the broader design and use of management control in inter-firm relationships.[17]

Ex ante contracts between exchange partners provide formal and legal arrangements in which accounting and control practices are embedded (Van der Meer-Kooistra and Vosselman 2000; Anderson and Dekker 2005; Dekker and Van den Abbeele 2010). Contracts are often viewed as frameworks in which cooperation between exchange parties proceeds (Gulati 1995). Accordingly, 'adequately developed' formal contracts are seen as key determinants of performance and a critical component of management control to be considered in empirical research. Contracts include clauses that align parties' interests and that facilitate coordination and adaptation, including the specification of controls to be used during the execution of transactions. Empirical studies tend to focus on the inclusion of specific clauses intended to induce desired behaviour (e.g., fixed or variable price agreements, and price adjustment method), or on the overall extensiveness of the contract in response to transaction hazards. Relatively little consideration has been provided to the content of the contract and the nature and structure of clauses.

Furlotti (2007) provides a review of the empirical contracting literature, and describes contracts in terms of their duration, complexity, specificity, and contingency planning. Reuer and Ariño (2007) examine 'contractual complexity' and identify two general functions of contractual provisions related to the *enforcement* and *coordination*. Faems et al. (2008) similarly describe structural perspectives of contracting (including TCE) to focus on the safeguarding and coordinating purposes of contracts. In particular, by specifying what is (and what is not) allowed and by imposing penalties for violations of specified behaviours, contract clauses limit partners' ability and incentives to act opportunistically (Parkhe 1993; Faems et al. 2008). In addition, such clauses facilitate coordinated action by specifying the division of labour and by providing guidelines to integrate partners' activities, thereby simplifying decision making and preventing disputes centred on how best to accomplish tasks (Dekker 2004; Reuer and Ariño 2007; Faems et al. 2008). Luo (2002) describes contracts used for international joint ventures in terms of their specificity and adaptability to contingencies. These dimensions provide a focus on the 'completeness' of contracts in controlling opportunism and their ability to incorporate unanticipated contingencies. Anderson and Dekker (2005) have analysed the dimensionality that underlies contract design in a large sample of IT transactions and identified four interdependent contract dimensions that are used for managing exchange hazards:

1. rights assignment provisions, including ownership rights, decision rights, and partners' responsibilities
2. product and price provisions, including the basic terms of the transaction, such as product descriptions, price level/change agreements, and delivery terms

3. after-sales service provisions, including agreements for ongoing support and service after product delivery
4. legal recourse provisions, including provisions covering liability, sanctions, arbitration, and termination.

These four contract dimensions exhibit similarities with control frameworks that have been developed to study intra-firm control, such as Jensen and Meckling's (1992) "three legs of the stool", that include allocation of decision rights and responsibilities, performance measurement and rewards, and sanctioning. Anderson and Dekker (2005) further find that the relation between transaction characteristics and contract design differs between transactions with and without large ex post problems, and that the latter are better aligned with transaction characteristics. These results support the contingency hypothesis that better aligned governance structures are associated with higher performance.[18]

Studies of management control design in inter-firm relationships often extend beyond the analysis of contractual control, to include broader notions of control. Anderson and Sedatole (2003), for instance, described how management control in alliances includes three broad dimensions: (1) alliance control, including the management of risk and trust, (2) the management of alliance performance through ongoing measurement and evaluation, and (3) the management of alliance evolution, including elements such as partner selection, termination, and the management of learning and incentives. In contrast to contract design, relatively few studies have examined how firms design management control mechanisms and use them to manage their relationships. This scarcity may be related to the relative difficulty of collecting data about actual management-control practices. Studies that have examined the design of control mechanisms typically employ Ouchi's (1979) framework, which classifies control mechanisms as outcome, behaviour, and social/clan controls (e.g., Langfield-Smith and Smith 2003; Dekker 2004; Emsley and Kidon 2007; Cäker 2008; Langfield-Smith 2008). Outcome controls specify and measure results to be achieved without interfering in the way that results are obtained. Examples of the use of these mechanisms by exchange partners to manage their transactions include target setting, performance evaluation, the rewarding and penalising of results, and provision of feedback (Dekker and Van den Abbeele 2010). In contrast, behaviour controls specify and measure desirable behaviours of exchange partners to achieve preset goals, without necessarily focusing on the extent of goal achievement. Examples of the use of these mechanisms are the extent to which partners engage in activity planning and programming, set rules and develop operating procedures, monitor the use of procedures, modify partners' procedures, require activity reports to be produced, reward the adequate following of guidelines, and develop dispute resolution procedures (Gulati and Singh 1998; Dekker and Van den Abbeele 2010).

One early study in this area was that of Van der Meer-Kooistra and Vosselman (2000), who used an archetypical approach to describe control in outsourcing arrangements in terms of the emphasis on market, bureaucracy, and trust-based patterns that differ systematically across transaction contingencies. They expect to find mixes of these "ideal types" in practice and predict and find that, in each stage of cooperation (namely, contact, contract and execution), characteristics related to the transaction, environment, and exchange parties cause one dominant control pattern to prevail. Studies have also focused directly on the use of (subsets of) management control mechanisms instead of archetypes (Caglio and Ditillo 2008). An example is a case study of a buyer-supplier alliance by Dekker (2004), who described how the partners in this alliance use a comprehensive mix of outcome and behaviour controls to align incentives and to facilitate coordination and collaboration.[19]

Several other frameworks have been used to study management control in inter-firm settings. These include the framework of Merchant and Van der Stede (2007), which identifies control structures as including results, action, personnel and cultural controls (e.g., Groot and Merchant 2000; Anderson et al. 2009), and the framework of Jensen and Meckling (1992), which describes control design as the interrelated choices of policies and practices that serve the functions of performance measurement, rewarding and sanctioning, and assigning rights and responsibilities (e.g., Anderson and Dekker 2005). One particularly important question concerns the adequacy of these extant management control frameworks for describing the management controls used to mitigate and manage risks in inter-firm relationships (Anderson et al. 2009), for, as Caglio and Ditillo (2008) observe, variables conceived for intra-organisational analysis have been transplanted to inter-firm settings without questioning their appropriateness. Inter-firm relationships have several unique features that may challenge the relevance of extant control frameworks, such as partners' overlapping but separate profit motives, the absence of a central authority and control through fiat, and the role of courts of law and third-party arbitration in severe cases of alliance failure (Williamson 1991; Menard 1995; Anderson et al. 2009). Anderson et al. (2009) used field and survey data to examine the descriptive validity of four control frameworks that have traditionally been developed and used in intra-firm settings, including COSO (1992), Simons (1995), Merchant and Van der Stede (2007), and Jensen and Meckling (1992). They concluded from the field research that risk management in strategic alliances may be construed as an adaptation of intra-firm controls to fit the setting of inter-firm collaboration. Consistent with that, the survey data identifies six groups of alliance controls that are used in response to different types of alliance risk and partnership characteristics and that fit well with the frameworks describing intra-firm control: partner selection mechanisms, asset safeguards, contractual outcome measures, termination provisions, financial review practices, and informal control mechanisms.

However, they also observe that, consistent with alliance partners being separate entities, there is a greater emphasis on preventive controls aimed at defining boundary conditions, selecting suitable partners, and allocating decision rights than would likely be present if the same activities were conducted within a single firm.

Accounting Techniques and Use of Accounting Information

In the literature, various roles have been identified for management accounting in inter-firm settings that relate to specific accounting techniques and different uses of accounting information. These roles include the use of financial and nonfinancial information in the (make-buy-or-ally) decision to engage in inter-firm relations, in the selection of potential partners with whom to collaborate, during the management of a cooperation, and in the monitoring and evaluation of collaborative activities (Seal et al. 1999; Tomkins 2001; Caglio and Ditillo 2008; Anderson and Dekker 2009a, 2009b). Importantly, Cooper and Slagmulder (2004) argue that one outcome of firms' increased propensity to engage in alliances is the development of cost management techniques that cross firm boundaries. Accounting researchers have described and analysed cost accounting techniques such as: total cost of ownership analysis, value chain analyses, target costing, collaborative cost management, and open-book accounting (Caglio and Ditillo 2008). Chapters 7, 8, and 9 in this volume describe several of these techniques in detail.

These formalised interactions, termed inter-organisational cost management (IOCM), are typically aimed at jointly reducing costs in the value chain. The potential benefits of introducing IOCM practices are better realised when these are associated with information sharing and open-book practices, in which partners share accounting information to identify opportunities for improvement (Seal et al. 1999; Dekker 2003; Kajüter and Kulmala 2005; Coad and Cullen 2006; Van den Abbeele et al. 2009). Although studies have found IOCM practices to have the potential to provide considerable benefits to collaborating parties, viewed from a TCE perspective, these practices can also confront firms with exchange hazards and expose them to risks. For instance, firms may fail to maximise potential gains because of their reluctance to share information needed for cost minimisation (Baiman and Rajan 2002), a reluctance that naturally follows from the sensitive nature of accounting information and from concerns about equity (Drake and Haka 2008). Caglio and Ditillo (2008) suggest that investigating firms' motivations may help explain why some firms are willing to open their books, and why open-book accounting has been associated with mixed results.

Prior research that has examined inter-firm accounting in conjunction with the issues of motivation and incentives underscores the importance of studying accounting in a broader control context. Cooper and Slagmulder (2004), for instance, described how the use of IOCM practices during product design is intertwined with concerns about relational risks and misaligned incentives. These concerns have implications for safeguarding partners' interests and putting in place adequate incentives when they engage in IOCM. Using TCE reasoning, Dekker (2003) described three concerns that may confront firms aiming to improve value chain efficiency through collaborative cost management and information sharing practices: (1) sharing of sensitive information, (2) sharing of costs and benefits following from realised improvements, and (3) investments in specific assets as part of value chain improvements. As before, these concerns may necessitate the adoption of management control practices with the intention of augmenting firms' willingness to engage in IOCM in the first place. Appropriate incentives and safeguards may be needed to stimulate active engagement by partners in cost reducing activities and to encourage them to share information. Studies of IOCM practices have frequently taken a value-creation perspective by focusing on the prospect of potential collaborative benefits. However, the adoption of a value-appropriation perspective may shed more light on why, in practice, the extent of collaborative cost management practices is more limited than could be expected when considering only the opportunities for value creation (e.g., Tomkins 2001). Similarly, a value appropriation perspective could provide further insight into the hazards that may be implied in the failure of such practices.

5   DYNAMIC EVOLUTION—CHANGE AND ADAPTATION OF MANAGEMENT CONTROL DESIGN

Inter-firm relationships are typically long-term arrangements, and over time can be subject to evolutionary processes and change. A recurrent critique of the explanatory power of TCE in the study of inter-firm relationships concerns its essentially static nature; it does not provide much guidance when examining relationship dynamics, processes, and change (Dekker 2004; Vosselman and Van der Meer-Kooistra 2006).[20] Indeed, the implementation of alliances has received much less attention than the initial decisions for their formation, despite the recognition that the success of alliances is strongly determined by their management and dynamics (Zajac and Olsen 1993; Ring and Van de Ven 1994; Das and Teng 2000; Anderson and Sedatole 2003; Ariño et al. 2008; Phua et al. 2009). Accordingly, recent studies have started to raise questions about the extent to which TCE can contribute to an understanding of dynamics, change, and evolution of alliances. Questions about dynamics that have been studied from a TCE perspective (though, typically, not exclusively from this perspective) include the role of initial conditions and learning processes (Doz 1996), effects of changes in transactional conditions on control changes (Kamminga and Van der Meer-Kooistra 2007), characteristics that make alliances more likely to experience or require contractual adjustments (Reuer and Ariño 2002; Reuer et al. 2002), and the adjustment of the relationship to any equity and efficiency concerns emerging over time (Ariño and de la Torre 1998). These questions reflect three dynamic issues that have been fruitfully explored in recent studies that employ TCE reasoning: (1) contract renegotiations, (2) control change and supplier switching, and (3) learning effects.

Examinations of contractual renegotiations are based on the recognition that, at the outset of a transaction, firms may design efficient and equitable governance structures. Nevertheless, governance mistakes do occur and, over time, changes may lead to inefficiencies and injustices (Ariño et al. 2008). These contractual renegotiations are inherently linked to dynamic alliance processes. Assessments of alliance performance and/or changes in the firms' strategies or environment cause alliance managers to perceive the need to adapt contract agreements (Bell et al. 2006). Accordingly, managers may renegotiate an alliance to alleviate inefficiencies stemming from the initial governance design, if this design no longer matches the alliance's needs. These arguments build on the notion of deviations from 'contingency fit' (see Section 1), which recognises that misaligned transactions may persist for some time. Firms may, for instance, have put in place excessive or inadequate contractual agreements for a particular transaction, which may result in excessive bureaucracy or high residual uncontrolled risks, respectively (Sampson 2004; Ariño et al. 2008). Reuer and Ariño (2002) have argued that the greater the degree of misalignment (leading to greater inefficiencies), the greater firms' incentives are to renegotiate. Furthermore, they argue that renegotiations are more likely when a firm has made significant transaction-specific investments, because its partner may recognise the opportunity for holdup and appropriating value through a renegotiation of the terms of trade. Following these arguments, Ariño et al. (2008) use a sample of small entrepreneurial firms to examine alliance dynamics and contract renegotiations that ensue when governance misalignment and holdup problems are evident. When imbalances caused by minor deviations add up, or when an important breach in efficiency or equity is detected, renegotiations are used to regain balance and to achieve justice.[21]

Related to these ideas of contractual renegotiations are studies that look at the dynamics of management control structures and, in particular, when and how adaptations in control structures take place, and how control structures established at the outset affect post-formation dynamics. Pernot and Roodhooft (2008), for example, used TCE to examine management control dynamics in a longitudinal case study of Volvo Car Company. Their study examines how changes in transaction characteristics give rise to incongruence between the transaction context and the design of management controls that, in turn, results in decreased performance and a need to adapt the control system. The case evidence shows how changes in the degree of fit between the control system and transaction characteristics are associated with variations in product quality over time. An incongruent control design temporarily diminishes performance, until controls are changed to fit the new contingencies and risks. Kamminga and Van der Meer-Kooistra (2007), too, argued that changes in control can follow from changes in the transaction environment, and provide case evidence that is consistent with this argument. Another approach to examine post-formation dynamics using TCE is used by Phua et al. (2009). Based on TCE's remediableness criterion (Williamson 1985), the authors hypothesised that initial control choices made in response to exchange hazards lead to the creation of exit barriers that reduce the ability of the firms concerned to switch to new suppliers. The case evidence collected in a broad sample of outsourcing relationships supports the claim that investments in control structures generate exit barriers that increase switching costs. These exit barriers are additional to the direct barriers imposed by exchange hazards. To summarise, these reviewed studies have fruitfully used TCE to study dynamic change in management control and how the initial control system design inhibits subsequent adaptation.

A third issue related to dynamic evolution that studies have examined concerns the effects of learning. At least two types of learning are identified in the alliance literature that may affect control choices and exchange performance: (1) learning to manage cooperation and exchange hazards, either with the same partner or from the collective experience of partnering, and (2) learning in the context of a specific transaction that resolves initial uncertainties and alters the profile of exchange hazards associated with the transaction. With respect to the first type of learning, studies have examined the effects of repeated ties that enable the development of alliance management skills. In a case study of eleven sequential contracts between the same two firms, Mayer and Argyres (2004) describe how learning from problems that arose during earlier contracts is associated with contract adaptations; evidence of learning across transactions that take place over time. Sampson (2005) similarly suggests that by engaging in repeated alliances, firms acquire skills to manage them better, and that these skills increase in importance with increasing exchange hazards (e.g., when uncertainty is high). These ideas are based on the learning curve, which suggests that experience helps firms make better inferences about good and bad practices. Although every additional alliance presents an opportunity to learn to manage better, this is particularly the case for firms with limited experience since, for these firms, an additional alliance represents a large proportion of their accumulated experience. With increasing alliance experience, however, firms experience diminishing returns to learning with additional alliance formation. Sampson's evidence, accumulated for alliances in the telecommunication industry, supports the claim that (recent) prior experiences are associated with governance choices for new alliances, which in turn are associated with improved performance (measured through patenting). This is particularly the case for alliances that face high uncertainty.[22] Dekker and Van den

Abbeele (2010) specifically considered learning in examining how prior transaction experiences provide outsourcing firms with partner information that contributes to the development of control structures for new transactions. Their results indicate that, while exchange hazards generate a need for control, prior exchange experiences provide buyers with fine-grained information about suppliers that facilitates management control design. Importantly, these learning effects may not only emerge from prior interactions with the same partner, but may also arise from interactions with other partners (Hoang and Rothaermel 2005), which may add up to firms' alliance capabilities (Kale and Singh 2007). From a TCE perspective, these types of learning may be expected to increase in importance when exchange hazards associated with transactions are more substantial and necessitate more extensive control.[23]

The second (related) type of learning concerns the resolution over time of uncertainties that are not sufficiently understood at the outset of the alliance to be incorporated in the initial contract. As mentioned earlier, at the start of a cooperative arrangement, managers face at least two types of related uncertainties: uncertainty about the future state of events and behavioural uncertainty about the partner's intentions (Ring and van der Ven 1994; Geyskens et al. 2006). Ring and van der Ven (1994) described the developmental processes that take place in alliances in terms of negotiations, commitments, and execution. These authors argued that, in the execution stage, parties become more familiar through interactions, and as the alliance matures, the initial uncertainties about the future state of events may be resolved. Doz (1996) examines how the learning in strategic alliances about the environment, task processes, skills, and goals mediates between the initial alliance conditions and their outcomes. His longitudinal case observations suggest that successful alliance projects are highly evolutionary and go through a sequence of interactive cycles of learning, reevaluation, and readjustment. In contrast, failing projects are inertial, with little knowledge being gained, or with divergent learning between cognitive understanding and behavioural adjustment, or frustrated expectations. Kamminga and Van der Meer-Kooistra (2007) argue that internal learning processes and learning from external technology development provide improved insight into collaborative activities. This insight can resolve measurement problems and improve knowledge of transformation processes, which in turn may impact on the design and use of outcome and behaviour control mechanisms.

Based on the studies reviewed in this section, we conclude that TCE does provide some scope for understanding the change and adaptation of control design in inter-firm relationships. In studying these questions, however, TCE appears most useful for identifying *when* changes can be expected, and less useful for providing researchers with the tools required to study how and through which processes change takes place (Kamminga and Van der Meer-Kooistra 2007).

6   COMPLEMENTARY PERSPECTIVES TO TRANSACTION COST ECONOMICS

In this section, we review theoretical perspectives that have influenced TCE-based analyses of governance and control in inter-firm relationships, both as complementary and rival perspectives to TCE. Specifically, we review perspectives that reflect on: (1) value creation and the resource-based view of the firm, (2) the influence of coordination costs, and (3) the emergence and influence of relational governance and trust. Although these three perspectives are by no means an exhaustive set of the frameworks and perspectives with which TCE has been compared, contrasted, and complemented, in the context of inter-firm transactions they represent some of the most influential ones.

Value Creation and the Resource-Based View of the Firm

Historically, TCE has dominated the debate on boundaries of the firm. However, more recently a second school of thought, the resource-based view (RBV), has been implicated in the analysis of inter-firm governance. The RBV has gained much prominence in strategy research and derives from Penrose's (1959) proposition that firm boundaries reflect strategic choices about how best to achieve competitive advantage from valuable, scarce, and inimitable resources (e.g., Combs and Ketchen 1999).[24] Modern RBV theory focuses on how distinct firm capabilities or resources define boundaries of the firm (Barney 1991; Madhok 2002; Jacobides and Winter 2005; Argyres and Zenger 2009). A key argument in this perspective is that firms perform internally those activities that they perform with greater capability than external providers (Argyres and Zenger 2009). Firm boundaries are defined by the sequence of decisions firms take in their dynamic search for opportunities to deploy resources in a manner that yields abnormal returns. Thus, with the passage of time, a unique sequence of deployment decisions for physical and intellectual capital would cause firms with identical initial endowments to end up with very different accumulations of wealth. Studies applying the RBV in an inter-firm context focus on the inimitable value of collaborative partnerships, the super-additive effects of networks on performance, and opportunities for shared learning to explain the new organisational forms (e.g., Lorenzoni and Baden-Fuller 1995).

In recent years, a substantial literature has emerged that aims to compare, contrast, and even reconcile TCE and RBV explanations of firm boundaries. Although the two theories differ in perspective, both assume that firms seek to maximise long run performance. Whereas TCE's primary interest lies with minimisation of transaction costs at a given point in time, the RBV emphasises the untradeability and immobility of valuable idiosyncratic resources (Zajac and Olsen 1993; Lorenzoni and Lipparini 1999). In contrast to TCE's more static approach of cost minimisation, the RBV admits the possibility that the act of transacting with external parties (or internalising the same work) dynamically changes the resources and capabilities that will be available in future periods. Accordingly, TCE and RBV are considered to be complementary perspectives for explaining boundary choices. Nonetheless, studies also point to differing expectations that arise from each theory, such as when resource constraints promote cooperation while exchange conditions favour another governance mode (Combs and Ketchen 1999). Argyres and Zenger (2009) argue that TCE and capability-based explanations of boundary choices are tightly intertwined, and that understanding the role of firm capabilities and resources requires a deeper integration of these theoretical perspectives, rather than treating them as rival theories.

The Influence of Coordination Costs

Another perspective that has gained significance in TCE studies of governance and control choices concerns the influence of coordination costs. Coordination costs arise as a result of the need to align, coordinate, and adapt activities across firm boundaries. Coordinating decisions and activities across firms is a significant challenge for managers, even when concerns about incentives and goal incongruence are well managed with appropriate governance and management control choices (Gulati and Singh 1998; Dekker 2004; Gulati et al. 2005; Vlaar 2008). The need for coordination follows from alliances' logic of value creation (Zajac and Olsen 1993). Key sources of coordination requirements are interdependencies between transaction partners, which reflect the degree to which the activities and outcomes of one partner provide the input for the other (Thompson 1967). Different logics of value creation provide different types and levels of interdependence between the partners. Task uncertainties (associated with the performance of nonroutine activities) further add to the need for adaptation and coordination. Recognising these concerns, Tomkins (2001) argues that establishing goals and methods to facilitate mutual planning may be a major contribution of inter-firm contracting.

Gulati et al. (2005) similarly argue that, additional to incentive conflicts, adaptation problems in exchange relationships arise as a result of insufficient responsiveness to changing conditions and from coordination failure. In other words, exchange failures can occur for reasons other than problems of misaligned incentives and/or holdups that are typically the focus of TCE research. This is more likely for complex and uncertain transactions involving highly interdependent tasks, or when at the outset of the transaction, the nature of interdependence cannot be assessed adequately (Gulati and Singh 1998; Dekker 2004; Gulati et al. 2005). Different governance modes, such as buy, ally, and make, differ in the capacity to respond and adapt to changing circumstances because they differ in the extent of their differentiation (Gulati et al. 2005). Differentiation is highest in the buy mode, while integration is highest in the make mode, with ally scoring in between on both dimensions. Indeed, an examination of component procurement by Ford and Chrysler by Gulati et al. (2005) indicates that exchange performance varies with the match between the governance mode chosen for the transaction and the need for adaptation in the exchange relationship, and not only the match between governance mode and exchange hazards. Similarly, within chosen governance modes, management control design may not only relate to exchange hazards, but also to task characteristics that present coordination requirements to exchange partners, even when problems of cooperation and misaligned incentives are completely absent (Dekker 2004). Since coordination, intended to align and adapt actions, can form an important second objective of inter-firm control, this can provide a useful additional lens in TCE-based examinations of appropriation and incentive concerns.[25]

The Influence of Relational Governance

Similar to the concerns expressed earlier about the ability of TCE to explain dynamics and change in inter-firm relationships, doubts have been raised about its ability to explain the emergence and use of relational modes of governance. Relational governance modes, in which "relationships" substitute for and augment other modes of management control, are based on the development of long-term relationships between exchange partners. Over time, "repeated ties" enable a different mode of coordinating and controlling exchanges. Relational governance is based on the elements of trust, cooperative norms, and information sharing (Gulati 1995; Poppo and Zenger 2002; Poppo et al. 2008), and includes both social and economic mechanisms that facilitate exchange. Repeated interactions provide firms with benefits such as mutual knowledge, ease of knowledge transfer, and trust (e.g., Gulati 1995; Li et al. 2008). The prospect of continued interaction helps align firms' incentives, ensuring that they are concentrated on mutually beneficial activities in the present to secure profits for the future (Heide and Miner 1992).[26]

The implications of repeated ties can be far-reaching. With respect to the choice between governance modes represented in Figure 10.1, for instance, Gulati and Nickerson (2008) examine how preexisting trust acts as a "shift parameter" that changes the way that exchange hazards affect governance choices of governance mode for new transactions. They find that, for similar exchange hazards, a higher level of preexisting trust increases the probability that a less formal governance mode is chosen. However, they also find that, regardless of the chosen governance mode, trust increases exchange performance. These results point to both substitutive and complementary relations between trust and control.

The question of whether (and when) relational governance and formal controls are substitutes or complements is one of the more complex and challenging questions that confront inter-firm researchers. Since the trust and mutual awareness that underlies relational governance may reduce transaction costs and behavioural uncertainties, this may substitute the use of formal control mechanisms. On the other hand, it has also been argued that relational governance may facilitate the (low-cost) development of more extensive control structures, in particular in response to coordination requirements (e.g., Poppo and Zenger 2002; Dekker 2004, 2008). In addition, the process of developing control structures helps to clarify partners' expectations, roles, and responsibilities, enhances expectations of cooperation, and can increase commitment to the relationships (Poppo and Zenger 2002; Mayer and Argyres 2004; Li et al. 2008; Vlaar 2008). To summarise, both complementary and substitutive effects between formal control and relational governance may exist, and we believe that TCE-based research can benefit from recognising perspectives that allow a wider assessment of the relational dimensions of inter-firm relationships.

7 CONCLUSION AND DISCUSSION OF DIRECTIONS FOR FUTURE RESEARCH

TCE has a long history in the economics, strategy, and management literature; however, its application in accounting research is more recent. Coincident with calls for accounting researchers to consider how accounting is applied in the modern context of inter-organisational collaboration (Otley 1994; Hopwood 1996; Kinney 2001), we have seen a renewed interest in questions about the design and use of management control practices as well as the use of novel approaches to cost management. TCE has been a key framework used in the analysis of these practices and approaches. Our review indicates several areas of research related to inter-firm governance, control, and accounting in which TCE has played a significant role. However, it also points to several limitations and to complementary perspectives that can help fill some of the gaps. As the newness of the literature that we have reviewed suggests, there is much about inter-organisational relationships that remains unexplored. Accordingly, in this section, we offer several ideas for how TCE theory can contribute to future research.

A first important area for future research concerns firms' use of accounting information in the extended make-or-buy analysis. In particular, research is needed into how firms use accounting information to decide about the structural alternatives of internal production, market transactions, and hybrid governance; and within the latter category, about the specific type of hybrids. From a TCE perspective, this enquiry could include how accounting information is used to assess the extent of exchange hazards that influence the choice between alternatives.

A second area where future research could make significant contributions involves the partner selection process, partner choice, and their effects on management control design and performance outcomes. As our review of the literature indicates, there is growing recognition that transaction characteristics and partner selection are intertwined. Future studies must examine questions such as:

- Whether exchange hazards induce firms to acquire information during partner search, and if so, to identify what type of information is sought;
- Whether information gathered in the partner search-and-selection process influences the management controls used in managing collaboration and transactions; and
- Whether information used in the search-and-selection process predicts better transaction and relationship outcomes.

In addition, other important questions about the search-and-selection process can be raised, such as how the type and 'quality' of chosen partners are associated with exchange hazards and with performance outcomes (Li et al. 2008).

A third area that we believe merits research relates to control choices for inter-firm relations, and in particular to interdependencies or complementarities among controls. The theoretical literature recognises that control structures usually consist of multiple interrelated controls, and that control choices are not made in isolation (e.g., Milgrom and Roberts 1992). Whereas most of the literature in this area relates to intra-firm settings, the same arguments hold for inter-firm ones. Anderson and Dekker (2005), for instance, examine the use of multiple contract dimensions that are descriptive of different types of contract clauses, and find evidence of interrelations in the use of these dimensions. Similarly, Dekker and Van den Abbeele (2010) note that use of more extensive contracts is associated with increased use of outcome and behaviour controls. That firms use multiple controls as a "package" has been posited for several decades (Otley 1980); however, this proposition has received limited attention in the empirical accounting literature. As an empirical issue, this proposition can pose serious concerns about model specification and analysis. For example, studies that relate the use of individual control mechanisms to transaction characteristics will suffer from omitted variables bias if other controls are used in conjunction to manage the same transaction. The failure to recognise such interdependencies in the design and use of different control mechanisms results in underspecified models and may generate flawed inferences about control choices. These questions may also be extended to interrelations and complementarities with other choices, such as partner search and selection.

A fourth research area in which some interest is already evident and which we believe has great potential for novel and interesting research concerns the dynamics of inter-firm relations, changes in management control over time, and the effects of learning. Studies that focus on the descriptive validity of TCE relative to other theoretical frameworks for explaining dynamic adjustments to firm boundaries and management control practices would do a great deal for advancing the static approach of relating cross-sectional differences in transactions to firm boundaries and management controls. Specific questions to be addressed include how management control responds to changes in transaction characteristics over time (Gulati and Nickerson 2008) and to changes in partners' goals and expectations (Gulati and Singh 1998). These studies may include assessments of contractual renegotiations (Reuer and Ariño 2002), switching decisions and how changes in control structures are made (Phua et al. 2009), and their effects on the cooperative relations, operations, and outcomes (Pernot and Roodhooft 2008). Substantial effects of partner experience on firms' 'learning to control' can also be predicted (Mayer and Argyres 2004; Sampson 2005). In this line of enquiry, important questions further relate to how accounting practices (e.g., cost allocations or performance evaluation results) may drive change and dynamics, such as renegotiations between partners.

Another issue related to learning that has received little inquiry from accounting researchers involves firms' use of dedicated alliance managers and departments that collect and distribute knowledge of current and prior alliances for use in the design and management of new alliances (Ireland et al. 2002; Kale and Singh 2007). Little evidence exists on the extent to which such processes take place in firms, how knowledge is efficiently transferred from one alliance to another, and how alliances are managed as a portfolio, in contrast to the focus on prior studies of how individual relationships or transactions are managed. This question is particularly relevant because firms are often involved in multiple relationships (Anderson and Sedatole 2003; Ding et al. 2009). With proper empirical tools that recognise the nested structure of transactions, partner relations, and the alliance portfolio (e.g., Anderson et al. 2000), TCE can be useful for examining expectations about how the value of alliance functions relates to the firm's exposure to exchange hazards at each level of analysis.

In settings in which disequilibrium may occur at any given point in time, studies that pursue the directions previously outlined could also make significant contributions by including analyses of the impact the alignment of governance, management control, and accounting choices with transaction characteristics have on performance (Anderson and Dekker 2005). Such analyses include identifying the various ways in which these choices are able to affect performance in different types of alliances, such as control benefits, but without neglecting negative effects such as reduced incentives to innovate (Sampson 2004).

Moving from governance and management control into inter-firm accounting, an important area that has received limited enquiry concerns the interrelations between accounting and control. Dekker (2003), for instance, found that firms' collaborative use of value chain analysis provided them with concerns about increased exposure to risk, and Cooper and Slagmulder (2004) found that inter-organisational cost management practices required different contextual and relational circumstances that involved different forms of control. Thus, the effectiveness of accounting techniques in inter-firm settings may well be dependent on effective management control design. This is a largely unexplored area that would benefit from closer scrutiny by researchers.

Finally, we believe that many important and interesting research questions emerge when shifting the focus from a dyadic relationship, which is the focus of most of the studies that we have reviewed, to network relationships involving more than two partners. Prior studies have viewed alliances with multiple relations to face greater exchange hazards and complexities (e.g., Gulati and Singh 1998), but much theoretical and empirical work is needed to learn how network relations differ in exchange hazards and complexities from dyadic relations, and to understand what the implications are for accounting and control. Recent accounting research has, however, started to engage in the analysis of network relations (e.g., Mouritsen et al. 2001; Håkansson and Lind 2004) and further work can be expected in this area.

To summarise, we believe that the field of inter-firm relationships provides accounting researchers with a broad agenda of interesting research questions in which TCE, complemented with other frameworks, can provide a useful framework for analysis.

NOTES

1. As described by Williamson (1985, p. 1), a transaction occurs when "a good or service is transferred across a technologically separable interface".
2. Although TCE is widely used in the analysis of inter-firm governance and control choices, it has also been used in the analysis of intra-firm control design, such as in transfer pricing decisions (Colbert and Spicer 1995), and management controls system design more generally (Speklé 2001).
3. This sequence of key events in the formation, governance design, and dynamics (cf. Gulati 1995) is similar to Van der Meer-Kooistra and Vosselman's (2000) description of the extended make-or-buy analysis, which includes the decision to purchase from third parties on a structural basis (instead of engaging in in-house production), the selection of exchange partner(s) with whom to cooperate, and the design of the relationship and control system.
4. Even in the case of vertical integration, transaction costs may emerge in the form of "loss of high powered incentives".
5. Studies also often assume that production costs and transaction costs are independent, although these are frequently related (Anderson et al. 2000).
6. The TCE literature distinguishes different types of uncertainty, which may have differential main effects on governance choices. Two important dimensions are *volume uncertainty* and *technological uncertainty* (Walker and Weber 1984). Volume uncertainty reflects the difficulty of predicting volume requirements in a relationship and favours hierarchical governance, since vertical integration should provide more efficient coordination of fluctuations in volume. Technological uncertainty reflects the difficulty of predicting technical requirements

and changes and favours market governance in order to retain flexibility, to avoid becoming locked in to obsolete technology and to facilitate switching to partners with better matching technological capabilities (Geyskens et al. 2006).

7. An alternative effect of frequency is to bond partners to one another so that future benefits are obtained. The expectation of future interactions, which provide both mutual benefits and opportunities for opportunistic behaviour, creates incentives for and expectations about cooperation. This effect, termed 'the shadow of the future' (Heide and Miner 1992), can induce firms to use less hierarchical governance structures than one would expect on basis of TCE arguments alone.

8. See Gerdin and Greve (2004) for a discussion of the differences between congruence fit and contingency fit.

9. Sampson's findings also indicate that the dampening of innovation by excessive bureaucracy is substantially more detrimental to performance than uncontrolled hazards associated with opportunism.

10. Although accounting researchers have been interested in questions about firm boundaries and governance decisions (e.g., Gietzmann 1996; Seal et al. 1999; Satorius and Kirsten 2005), empirical tests have remained scarce.

11. Most research in this area examines partner selection as it relates to the attractiveness of potential partners in terms of providing access to valuable resources (e.g., Geringer 1991; Hitt et al. 2004). Accordingly, to develop predictions, these studies often build on resource dependence theory or on the resource-based view of the firm.

12. From a value-creation perspective, it is similarly argued that transaction complexity and its effect on anticipated coordination requirements influences the importance of identifying and selecting partners who posses the right competencies (Dekker 2004, 2008).

13. Importantly, these studies also report a decrease in selection effort for firms with prior ties. Since prior ties allow trust and mutual knowledge to be built up, these can reduce concerns about potential opportunism and inadequate partner capabilities, and consequently limit the need for partner search for future transactions.

14. Li et al. (2008) characterise 'friends' by the existence of many prior interactions, lack of information asymmetry, and a high level of trust, 'acquaintances' by the existence of some prior interactions, some information asymmetry, and a semi-strong or weak level of trust, and 'strangers' by the absence of prior interactions, high information asymmetry, and a lack of trust.

15. The issue of learning also relates to Section 5 on dynamic adjustment of alliance transactions.

16. The effects of TCE problems and related problems of coordination and adaptation (also see Section 6) on the design and use of governance and control mechanisms are often framed in terms of *relational risk* and *performance risk* (Das and Teng 2001; Anderson and Sedatole 2003; Anderson et al. 2009).

17. We note that broad conceptions of management control also include elements such as partner selection and trust development (e.g., Dekker 2004; Anderson et al. 2009). These are more extensively reviewed and discussed in Sections 3 and 5, respectively.

18. Specifically, they find that as compared to poor performing transactions, transactions that experienced few *ex post* problems employed contracts that were well suited to the uncertainty and complexity of the transaction and used competition among suppliers to more effectively resolve potential opportunism. It remains challenging, however, to test whether weaker performing transactions are "off equilibrium". Firms experiencing more *ex post* problems may, for instance, have differential contracting skills (e.g., a higher

cost of contracting) or a different appetite for risk (e.g., be risk-seeking) that affects their contracting decisions.

19. Specific outcome controls included planning and goal setting, cost reduction monitoring, and financial incentives aimed at motivating innovation and forecasting accuracy. Specific behaviour controls included ordering procedures, activity programming, quality plans and audits, pre-action reviews and behaviour monitoring by the alliance board, and specification of intellectual property rights.

20. Other critiques raised involve TCE's singular focus on the notion of opportunism, while inter-firm governance structures may fulfil more purposes than mitigating opportunism and minimising transaction costs alone, and its limited recognition of organisational and social mechanisms of governance that facilitate exchange (Dekker 2004). Indeed, intertwined with alliance dynamics and change is the development of 'relational governance' and trust between exchange partners that interact repeatedly over time (e.g., Gulati 1995). We discuss these issues in Section 6 on complementary perspectives to TCE.

21. From their empirical work, Ariño et al. (2008) conclude that small firms are no more or less likely to renegotiate their contracts than larger firms. However, small firms tend to tolerate inefficiencies of two kinds in their collaborations: (1) they are less likely to adapt alliances in the presence of governance misalignments, and (2) they are more prone to make transaction-specific investments, which can stimulate ex post holdup in the form of contractual renegotiations.

22. The findings also underscore the presence of decreasing returns to scale and the learning benefits of more recent experiences. In particular, older experiences may have involved key managers that have left the firm and may concern outdated knowledge, since exploiting management techniques that proved successful in the past may even reduce performance for new situations (Sampson 2005).

23. In order to develop and capitalise on alliance capabilities, many large organisations nowadays use specific alliance management functions and departments (Ireland et al. 2002), which are focused on learning and are actively involved in knowledge acquisition, dissemination, interpretation, and storage for use in future alliances (Kale and Singh 2007).

24. See Crook et al. (2008) for a meta-analysis of empirical RBV-based studies.

25. Although managing concerns about appropriation and facilitating coordination have been suggested to be primary functions of alliance contracts, the literature has identified additional functions, such as signalling commitment (Klein Woolthuis et al. 2004), acting as knowledge repositories (Mayer and Argyres 2004), and handling uncertainty resulting from organisational change (Dekker 2004).

26. In addition to relational effects from prior interactions, ties to other network parties can also affect alliance decisions and outcomes. Gulati (1998) provides a structured analysis of the influence of social networks, arguing that firms' network position can provide them with informational and control benefits, which may impact on the alliance decision, choice of partner and governance mode, design of control structure, and on the evolution and outcomes.

BIBLIOGRAPHY

Anderson, S. W., Christ, M., Dekker, H. C., and Sedatole, K. L. 2009. *Risk management in strategic alliances: Field and survey evidence*. Working paper, Rice University. Houston, Texas.

Anderson, S. W., and Dekker, H. C. 2005. Management control for market transactions: The relation between transaction characteristics, incomplete contract design and subsequent performance. *Management Science* 51: 1734–1752.

Anderson, S. W., and Dekker, H. C. 2009. Strategic cost management in supply chains, part 1: Structural cost management. *Accounting Horizons* 23: 201–220.

Anderson, S. W., and Dekker, H. C. 2009. Strategic cost management in supply chains, part 2: Executional cost management. *Accounting Horizons* 23: 289–305.

Anderson, S W., Glenn, D., and Sedatole, K. L. 2000. Sourcing parts of complex products: Evidence on transaction costs, high-powered incentives and ex-post opportunism. *Accounting, Organizations and Society* 25: 723–749.

Anderson, S. W., and Sedatole, K. L. 2003. Management accounting for the extended enterprise: Performance management for strategic alliances and networked partners. In *Management accounting in the digital economy*, ed. Bhimani, A. 37–73. Oxford: Oxford University Press.

Argyres, N., and Zenger, T. 2009. Capabilities, transaction costs, and firm boundaries: A dynamic perspective and integration. *Strategic Organization* (forthcoming).

Ariño, A., and de la Torre, J. 1998. Learning from failure: Towards an evolutionary model of collaborative ventures. *Organization Science* 9: 306–325.

Ariño, A., Ragozzino, R., and Reuer, J. J. 2008. Alliance dynamics for entrepreneurial firms. *Journal of Management Studies* 45: 147–168.

Baiman, S., and Rajan, M. V. 2002. Incentive issues in inter-firm relationships. *Accounting, Organizations and Society* 27: 213–238.

Barney, J. 1991. Firm resources and sustained competitive advantage. *Journal of Management* 17: 99–121.

Bell, J., den Ouden, B., and Ziggers, G. W. 2006. Dynamics of cooperation: At the brink of irrelevance. *Journal of Management Studies* 43: 1607–1619.

Blumberg, B. F. 2001. Efficient partner search: Embedded firms seeking co-operative partners. *Journal of Mathematical Sociology* 25: 329–354.

Caglio, A., and Ditillo, A. 2008. A review and discussion of management control in inter-firm relationships: Achievements and future directions. *Accounting, Organizations and Society* 33: 865–898.

Cäker, M. 2008. Intertwined coordination mechanisms in interorganisational relationships with dominated suppliers. *Management Accounting Research* 19: 231–251.

Coad, A. F., and Cullen, J. 2006. Inter-organisational cost management: Towards an evolutionary perspective. *Management Accounting Research* 17: 342–369.

Coase, R. H. 1937. The nature of the firm. *Economica* 4: 386–405.

Colbert, G. J., and Spicer, B. H. 1995. A multi-case investigation of a theory of the transfer pricing process. *Accounting, Organizations and Society* 20: 423–456.

Combs, J. G., and Ketchen Jr., D. J. 1999. Explaining interfirm cooperation and performance: Towards a reconciliation of predictions from the resource-based view and organizational economics. *Strategic Management Journal* 20: 867–888.

Cooper, R., and Slagmulder, R. 2004. Interorganizational cost management and relational context. *Accounting, Organizations and Society* 29: 1–26.

COSO. 1992. *Internal control—integrated framework*. Jersey City, NJ: Committee of Sponsoring Organizations of the Treadway Commission.

Crook, T. R. Ketchen Jr., D. J., Combs, J. G., and Todd, S. Y. 2008. Strategic resources and performance: A meta-analysis. *Strategic Management Journal* (forthcoming).

Das, T. K., and Teng, B.-S. 2000. Instabilities of strategic alliances: An internal tensions perspective. *Organization Science* 11: 77–101.

Das, T. K., and Teng, B.-S. 2001. Trust, control and risk in strategic alliances: An integrated framework. *Organization Studies* 22: 251–283.

David, R. J., and Han, S. K. 2004. A systematic assessment of the empirical support for transaction cost economics. *Strategic Management Journal* 25: 39–58.

Dekker, H. C. 2003. Value chain analysis in interfirm relationships: A field study. *Management Accounting Research* 14: 1–23.

Dekker, H. C. 2004. Control of inter-organizational relationships: Evidence on appropriation concerns and coordination requirements. *Accounting, Organizations and Society* 29: 27–49.

Dekker, H. C. 2008. Partner selection and governance design in interfirm relationships. *Accounting, Organizations and Society* 33: 915–941.

Dekker, H. C. and Van den Abbeele, A. 2010. Organizational learning and interfirm control: The effects of partner search and prior exchange experiences. *Organizational Science* (forthcoming).

Ding, R., Dekker, H. C., and Groot, T. L. C. M. 2009. An exploration of the use of interfirm cooperation and the financial manager's governance roles: Evidence from Dutch firms. *Journal of Accounting and Organizational Change* (forthcoming).

Doz, Y. L. 1996. The evolution of cooperation in strategic alliances: Initial conditions or learning processes? *Strategic Management Journal* 17: 55–84.

Drake, A. R., and Haka, S. F. 2008. Does ABC information exacerbate hold-up problems in buyer-supplier negotiations? *The Accounting Review* 83: 29–60.

Emsley, D., and Kidon, F. 2007. The relationship between trust and control in international joint ventures: Evidence from the airline industry. *Contemporary Accounting Research* 24: 829–858.

Faems, D., Janssens, M., Madhok, A., and Van Looy, B. 2008. Toward an integrative perspective on alliance governance: Connecting contract design, trust dynamics, and contract application. *Academy of Management Journal* 51: 1053–1078.

Furlotti, M. 2007. There is more to contracts than incompleteness: A review and assessment of empirical research on inter-firm contract design. *Journal of Management and Governance* 11: 61–99.

Gerdin, J., and Greve, J. 2004. Forms of contingency fit in management accounting research—a critical review. *Accounting, Organizations and Society* 29: 303–326.

Geringer, J. M. 1991. Strategic determinants of partner selection criteria in international joint ventures. *Journal of International Business Studies* 22: 41–62.

Geyskens, I., Steenkamp, J. B. E. M., and Kumar, N. 2006. Make, buy or ally: A meta-analysis of transaction cost theory. *Academy of Management Journal* 49: 519–543.

Gietzmann, M. B. 1996. Incomplete contracts and the make or buy decision: Governance design and attainable flexibility. *Accounting, Organizations and Society* 21: 611–626.

Groot, T. L. C. M., and Merchant, K. A. 2000. Control of international joint-ventures. *Accounting, Organizations and Society* 25: 579–607.

Gulati, R. 1995. Does familiarity breed trust? The implications of repeated ties for contractual choice in alliances. *Academy of Management Journal* 38: 85–113.

Gulati, R. 1998. Alliances and networks. *Strategic Management Journal* 19: 293–317.

Gulati, R., Lawrence, P. R., and Puranam, P. 2005. Adaptation in vertical relationships: Beyond incentive conflict. *Strategic Management Journal* 26: 415–440.

Gulati, R. and Nickerson, J. A. 2008. Interorganisational trust, governance choice, and exchange performance. *Organization Science* 19: 688–708.

Gulati, R., and Singh, H. 1998. The architecture of cooperation: Managing coordination costs and appropriation concerns in strategic alliances. *Administrative Science Quarterly* 43: 781–814.

Håkansson, H., and Lind, J. 2004. Accounting and network coordination. *Accounting, Organizations and Society* 51: 51–72.

Heide, J., and Miner, A. 1992. The shadow of the future: Effects of anticipated interaction and frequency of contact on buyer-seller cooperation. *Academy of Management Journal* 35: 265–291.

Hitt, M. A., Ahlstrom, D., Dacin, M. T., Levitas, E., and Svobodina, L. 2004. The institutional effects on strategic alliance partner selection in transition economies: China vs. Russia. *Organization Science* 15: 173–185.

Hoang, H., and Rothaermel, F. T. 2005. The effect of general and partner-specific alliance experience on joint R&D project performance. *Academy of Management Journal* 48: 332–345.

Hopwood, A. 1996. Looking across rather than up and down: On the need to explore the lateral processing of information. *Accounting, Organizations and Society* 21: 589–590.

Ireland, R. D., Hitt, M. A., and Vaidyanath, D. 2002. Alliance management as a source of competitive advantage. *Journal of Management* 28: 413–446.

Jacobides, M., and Winter, S. 2005. The co-evolution of capabilities and transaction costs: Explaining the institutional structure of production. *Strategic Management Journal* 26: 395–414.

Jensen, M., and Meckling, W. 1992. Specific and general knowledge, and organizational structure. In *Contract economics*, ed. Werin, L., and Wijkander, H. 251–274. Oxford: Oxford Blackwell.

Joskow, P. L. 1987. Contract duration and relationship-specific investment: Empirical evidence from coal markets. *American Economic Review* 77: 168–185.

Kajüter, P., and Kulmala, H. 2005. Open-book accounting in networks: Potential achievements and reasons for failures. *Management Accounting Research* 16: 179–204.

Kale, P., and Singh, H. 2007. Building firm capabilities through learning: The role of the alliance learning process in alliance capability and firm-level alliance success. *Strategic Management Journal* 28: 981–1000.

Kamminga P. E., and Van der Meer-Kooistra, J. 2007. Management control patterns in joint venture relationships: A model and an exploratory study. *Accounting, Organizations and Society* 32: 131–154.

Kinney, W. R. 2001. Accounting scholarship: What is uniquely ours? *The Accounting Review* 76: 275–284.

Klein Woolthuis, R. J. A., Hillebrand, B., and Nooteboom, B. 2005. Trust, contract and relationship development. *Organization Studies* 26: 813–840.

Langfield-Smith, K. 2008. The relations between transactional characteristics, trust and risk in the startup phase of a collaborative alliance *Management Accounting Research* 19: 344–364.

Langfield-Smith, K., and Smith, D. 2003. Management control and trust in outsourcing relationships. *Management Accounting Research* 14: 281–307.

Leiblein, M. J., Reuer J. J., and Dalsace, F. 2002. Do make or buy decisions matter? The influence of organizational governance on technological performance. *Strategic Management Journal* 23: 817–833.

Li, D., Eden, L., Hitt, M. A., and Ireland, R. D. 2008. Friends, acquaintances, or strangers? Partner selection in R&D alliances. *Academy of Management Journal* 51: 315–334.

Lorenzoni, G., and Baden-Fuller, C. 1995. Creating a strategic center to manage a web of partners. *California Management Review* 37: 146–163.

Lorenzoni, G., and Lipparini, A. 1999. The leveraging of interfirm relationships as a distinctive organizational capability: A longitudinal study. *Strategic Management Journal* 20: 317–338.

Luo, Y. 2002. Contract, cooperation and performance in international joint ventures. *Strategic Management Journal* 23: 903–920.

Madhok, A. 2002. Reassessing the fundamentals and beyond: Ronald Coase, the transaction cost and resource-based theories of the firm, and the institutional structure of production. *Strategic Management Journal* 23: 535–550.

Mayer, K., and Argyres, N. 2004. Learning to contract: Evidence from the personal computer industry. *Organization Science* 15: 394–410.

Menard, C. 1995. Markets as institutions versus organizations as markets? Disentangling some fundamental concepts. *Journal of Economic Behaviour and Organization* 28: 161–182.

Merchant, K. A., and Van der Stede, W. A. 2007. *Management control systems: Performance measurement, evaluation and incentives.* Upper Saddle River, NJ: Prentice Hall.

Milgrom, P., and Roberts, J. 1992. *Economics, organization and management.* Englewood Cliffs, NJ: Prentice Hall.

Mouritsen, J., Hansen, A., and Hansen, C. Ø. 2001. Inter-organizational controls and organizational competencies: Episodes around target cost management/functional analysis and open book accounting. *Management Accounting Research* 12: 221–244.

Otley, D. T. 1980. The contingency theory of management accounting: Achievement and prognosis. *Accounting, Organizations and Society* 5: 413–428.

Otley, D. 1994. Management control in contemporary organizations: Towards a wider framework. *Management Accounting Research* 5: 289–299.

Ouchi, W. G. 1979. A conceptual framework for the design of organizational control mechanisms. *Management Science* 25: 833–848.

Oxley, J. E. 1997. Appropriability hazards and governance in strategic alliances: A transaction cost approach. *Journal of Law, Economics and Organization* 13: 387–409.

Parkhe, A. 1993. Strategic alliances structuring: A game theoretic and transaction cost examination of interfirm cooperation. *Academy of Management Journal* 36: 794–829.

Penrose, E. T. 1959. *The theory of the growth of the firm.* New York: John Wiley.

Pernot, E., and Roodhooft, F. 2008. *The impact of inter-organizational management control systems on performance: A longitudinal case study of a supplier relation in automotive.* Working paper, Katholieke Universiteit Leuven, Belgium.

Phua, Y. S., Abernethy, M. A., and Lillis, A. M. 2009. *Controls as exit barriers in multi-period outsourcing arrangements.* Working paper, University of New South Wales, Australia.

Poppo, L., and Zenger, T. R. 2002. Do formal contracts and relational governance act as substitutes or complements? *Strategic Management Journal* 23: 707–725.

Poppo, L. P., Zhou, K. Z., and Ryu, S. 2008. Alternative origins to interorganizational trust: An interdependence perspective on the shadow of the past and the shadow of the future. *Organization Science* 19: 39–55.

Porter, M. E. 1980. *Competitive strategy.* New York: The Free Press.

Reuer, J. J., and Ariño, A. 2002. Contractual renegotiations in strategic alliances. *Journal of Management* 28: 51–74.

Reuer, J. J., and Ariño, A. 2007. Strategic alliance contracts: Dimensions and determinants of contractual complexity. *Strategic Management Journal* 28: 313–330.

Reuer, J J., Zollo, M., and Singh, H. 2002. Post-formation dynamics in strategic alliances. *Strategic Management Journal* 23: 135–151.

Ring, P. S., and Van de Ven, A. H.. 1994. Developmental processes of cooperative interorganisational relationships. *Academy of Management Review* 19: 90–118.

Sampson, R. C. 2004. The cost of misaligned governance in R&D alliances. *Journal of Law, Economics and Organization* 20: 484–526.

Sampson, R. C. 2005. Experience effects and collaborative returns in R&D alliances. *Strategic Management Journal* 26: 1009–1031.

Sartorius, K., and Kirsten, J. 2005. The boundaries of the firm: Why do sugar producers outsource sugarcane production? *Management Accounting Research* 16: 81–99.

Seal, W., Cullen, J., Dunlop, A., Berry, T., and Ahmed, M. 1999. Enacting a European supply chain: A case study on the role of management accounting. *Management Accounting Research* 10: 303–322.

Shelanski H. A., and Klein P. G. 1995. Empirical research in transaction cost economics: A review and assessment. *Journal of Law, Economics, and Organization* 11: 335–361.

Simons, R. 1995. *Levers of control: How managers use innovative control systems to drive strategic renewal.* Boston: Harvard Business School Press.

Smith, K. G., Carroll, S. J., & Ashford, S. J. (1995). Intra- and interorganizational cooperation: Toward a research agenda. *Academy of Management Journal* 38: 7–23.

Speklé, R. F. 2001. Explaining management control structure variety: A transaction cost economics perspective. *Accounting, Organizations and Society* 26: 419–441.

Speklé, R. F., van Elten, H. J., and Kruis, A.-M. 2007. Sourcing of internal auditing: An empirical study. *Management Accounting Research* 18: 102–124.

Thompson, J. D. (1967). *Organizations in action.* New York: McGraw-Hill.

Tomkins, C. 2001. Interdependencies, trust and information in relationships, alliances and networks. *Accounting, Organizations and Society* 26: 161–191.

Van den Abbeele, A., Roodhooft, F., and Warlop, L. 2009. The effect of cost information on buyer–supplier negotiations in different power settings. *Accounting, Organizations and Society* 34: 245–266.

Van der Meer-Kooistra, J., and Vosselman, E. J. G. 2000. Management control of interfirm transactional relationships: The case of industrial renovation and maintenance. *Accounting, Organizations and Society* 25: 51–77.

Van der Meer-Kooistra, J., and Vosselman, E. J. G. 2006. Research on management control of interfirm transactional relationships: Whence and whither. *Management Accounting Research* 17: 227–237.

Vlaar, P. W. L. 2008. *Contracts and trust in alliances: Discovering, creating and appropriating value.* Cheltenham, UK: Edward Elgar.

Vosselman, E. J. G., and Van der Meer-Kooistra, J. 2006. Efficiency seeking behaviour in changing management control in interfirm transactional relationships: An extended transaction cost economics perspective. *Journal of Accounting and Organizational Change* 2: 123–143.

Vosselman, E. J. G., and Van der Meer-Kooistra, J. 2009. Accounting for control and trust building in interfirm transactional relationships. *Accounting, Organizations and Society* 34: 267–283.

Walker, G., and Weber D. 1984. A transaction cost approach to make-or-buy decisions. *Administrative Science Quarterly* 29: 373–391.

Widener, S. K., and Selto, F. H. 1999. Management control systems and boundaries of the firm: Why do firms outsource internal audit activities? *Journal of Management Accounting Research* 11: 45–73.

Williamson, O. 1975. *Markets and hierarchies: Analysis and antitrust implications*. New York: The Free Press.

Williamson, O. E. 1985. *The economic institutions of capitalism*. New York: The Free Press.

Williamson, O. E., 1991. Comparative economic organization: The analysis of discrete structural alternatives. *Administrative Science Quarterly* 36: 269–297.

Zajac, E. J., and Olsen, C. 1993. From transaction cost to transaction value analysis: Implications for the study of interorganisational strategies. *Journal of Management Studies* 30: 131–45.

11 Accounting in Networks— The Industrial-Network Approach

Håkan Håkansson, Kalle Kraus, Johnny Lind, and Torkel Strömsten

1 INTRODUCTION

Since the 1970s, a theoretical approach has been developed, called the *industrial-network approach*, the aim of which is to comprehend inter-organisational relationships in industrial markets, that is, in markets where both buyers and sellers are companies (Håkansson et al. 2009). The industrial-network approach has been developed through a large number of empirical studies of interaction between companies, especially in buying and selling processes. The results from the studies show that the interaction that takes place between companies is vital for their well-being (Håkansson et al. 2009). One important outcome of the interaction is the development of substantive inter-organisational relationships between the companies, relationships that are highly significant from an economic point of view (Håkansson and Waluszewski 2002). Thus, the companies tend to have some few highly significant customers and suppliers that are critical for the companies' development and survival with which they have well-developed relationships (Håkansson 1982; Turnbull and Valla 1986; Hallén et al. 1991). The relationships have an important role for the creative use of resources, as well as for creating efficient and effective production and supply chain structures (Dubois 1998; Håkansson and Waluszewski 2007). Consequently, the relationships are important economic activities as well as resources from the single company's point of view.

Another important result from studies using the industrial-network approach is that of embeddedness, meaning that each inter-organisational relationship is connected to the other relationships of both companies and, through these, the companies are linked to a web of other relationships in a wider network (Anderson et al. 1994; Håkansson and Snehota 1995). Thus, the inter-organisational relationship between, for example, a customer and a supplier will be affected by the customer's relationships with its own customers and with their other customers and suppliers (Anderson et al. 1994). The relationship will also be affected by the relationships between each of those suppliers and customers and their other customers and suppliers. Even companies that view each other as competitors can be connected because of the interdependence created through adaptations within individual business relationships to mutual customers or suppliers (Håkansson and Snehota 1995).

Analysing inter-organisational relationships through the lens of the industrial-network approach has implications for the understanding of accounting in networks and, in recent years, some case studies on this subject have been published (Dubois 2003; Håkansson and Lind 2004; Frimanson 2006; Lind and Strömsten 2006; Baraldi and Strömsten 2009; Carlsson-Wall et al. 2009). The existence of significant and interconnected business relationships challenges traditional intra- and inter-organisational accounting design and use that support hierarchical coordination as it disturbs the "boundary" of the company and the "boundary" of the inter-organisational relationship. Both intra- and inter-organisational accounting have been developed with the notion that the boundary separates what is controllable from a management point of view (Håkansson and Lind 2007). The resources within the boundary can be designed and exploited by the company (intra-organisational accounting) or by the two cooperating companies (inter-organisational accounting), whereas all those resources existing outside the boundary are given to or controlled by others.

However, with an industrial-network approach, resources within the boundary will be controlled, in part, by companies outside the boundary and resources existing in companies outside the boundary will, at least partly, be controllable from the company's point of view. The conceptualisation of a company's inter-organisational context through a value chain analysis centred on the focal company becomes too simple and homogeneous a description. Instead, a company will be part of a large number of value chains at the same time. These different value chains can even compete with each other. Another implication is that a single company cannot control a network of interconnected business relationships, although some companies may be more powerful than others.

The purpose of this chapter is to present the core ideas of the industrial-network approach and to explore how these ideas influence and challenge our understanding of the design and use of accounting in networks. As far as possible, previous research will be used, but as there is a limited amount of accounting research that uses the industrial-network approach, some topics remain to be explored from an empirical point of view (Håkansson and Lind 2007; Kraus and Lind 2007).

2   THE INDUSTRIAL-NETWORK APPROACH

The industrial-network approach was developed by the Industrial Marketing and Purchasing (IMP) Group. The IMP Group was formed in 1976 by researchers originating from the Universities of Uppsala, Bath, and Manchester (UMIST), and ESC Lyon and the Ludwig Maximilian University. Since then, the group has developed into a large informal network of researchers throughout the world, with annual conferences being held in Europe and Asia.[1] The industrial-network approach is based on the idea that business in industrial markets mainly is conducted through interaction between interdependent companies, whether they are customers, suppliers, development partners, or competitors (Håkansson 1982).

The origin of the industrial-network approach was a large-scale comparative study of buyer-supplier relationships within and across France, Germany, Italy, Sweden, and UK (Håkansson 1982). The study resulted in a new approach to industrial marketing, the interaction approach (Håkansson 1982). This early work focused on the interaction processes between industrial buyers and suppliers. The empirical results showed that industrial markets were inadequately characterised by the marketing research in existence at that time (Håkansson 1982). One of the most influential conclusions drawn was that, instead of being active in fast and fluid markets, industrial companies tended to interact with their customers much more closely and deeply. As a result of the initial studies, interaction and long-term business relationships emerged as key characteristics of industrial markets (Håkansson 1982). Since then, there have been an extensive number of empirical studies of inter-organisational relationships conducted and, gradually, a theoretical perspective— termed the industrial-network approach—of how business relationships and networks can be described and analysed has been developed.

The common ground of the researchers using the industrial-network approach is their aim to make sense of inter-organisational relationships between companies in the complex networks in which they operate as they buy from, sell to, and cooperate and compete with each other. The theory can be seen as a reaction to the traditional view of the active seller, a passive consumer, and atomistic markets (Ford et al. 2003). The industrial-network approach questioned some of the basic assumptions in the mainstream microeconomic model. The original work builds on over one thousand in-depth interviews (Håkansson 1982). The industrial-network approach has developed in an inductive way, by assimilating with managerial practice and identifying regularities in inter-organisational relationships (Håkansson et al. 2009). Over the years, the methodology has taken the form of a mixture of relationship and focal organisational surveys and case research (Dubois and Gadde 2002). The majority of the studies have used a case study methodology and involved a large amount of empirical work (Dubois and Araujo 2004). The focus on empirical data using in-depth case studies can, therefore, be seen as a characteristic of the industrial-network approach. The argument being that business relationships are complex phenomena which cannot be easily explained by surveys (Easton 2000).

Core Assumptions in the Industrial-Network Approach: Interdependencies and Resource Heterogeneity

One core assumption in the industrial-network approach is the recognition of the *interdependencies* between companies (Håkansson and Snehota 1995). When companies engage in inter-organisational relationships, they invest significant physical, financial, managerial, and developmental resources in establishing the basis for the relationship. But these mutually demanding investments are often made with a view to obtaining returns that can only be realised over a long period of time. These relationship-specific investments may lead to economies of scale for either or both of the companies. In addition, the investments made by one company may reduce or eliminate the other company's requirement for operational investments. Hence, the investments made by the companies lead to significant interdependencies between them (Håkansson and Snehota 1995).

These interdependencies, being an inevitable part of business in industrial markets, are multidimensional. First, there are links between the activities of the companies, for example, integrated production scheduling to minimise logistics (Håkansson and Snehota 1995). Second, there are ties between the resources of the companies, in the form of joint product or service development, or dedicated staff working with a specific counterpart (Håkansson and Snehota 1995). Third, there are bonds between the individuals in the companies, based on experience, friendship, and trust (Håkansson and Snehota 1995). The interdependencies can vary in form from just a single pair of companies consisting of one purchaser and one seller working together for their mutual advantage, to several interconnected companies engaged in a complex exchange of goods and/or services.

The existence of interdependencies makes it important for a single company to take part in a structuring of its own activities in relation to others (Håkansson and Ford 2002). It is still important that a company's own activities are designed in an efficient and effective way, but the efficiency and effectiveness are relative. The internal activities need to be designed and coordinated by linking the activities in relation to each other (Gadde and Håkansson 2001). One example can be that two companies can coordinate their activities together to mutual advantage, for example, production and quality control. The customer might demand some changes in the production activities, changes to the input resources, or that the overall process becomes more efficient. This coordination might be dependent upon what happens in a connected relationship, which means that the production process within the focal company is interdependent with, and embedded in, a wider activity structure.[2]

Another core assumption in the industrial-network approach regards the characteristics of the resources involved. The existence of *resource heterogeneity* affects their use and, thereby, their economic value (Penrose 1959). From an economic point of view, a resource is homogeneous if its value is not affected by the existence of the other resources with which it is combined (Alchian and Demsetz 1972). The industrial-network approach views resources as heterogeneous, meaning that the value gained from the use of one resource is dependent on what other resources it is combined with (Håkansson and Waluszewski 2002). This implies that, through relationships, a company can utilise the heterogeneity existing in resources that are controlled predominantly by another company. When relationships are formed, the existing resources in one company are combined with and adapted to those resources available in the other companies. Over time, through cooperation between a provider and a user, the knowledge about how to use and develop the resource will increase (Håkansson 1993). Every company has a set of resources that is mainly controlled internally, including, for example, technical resources, marketing resources, financial resources, and human resources. These resources are used internally but are also connected to those that are mainly controlled by other firms. For example, the value of a customer's production facility can be increased with the knowledge and experience that a supplier can provide (Gadde and Håkansson 2001). Furthermore, it is not uncommon for several companies to engage in the joint development of products or processes to bring about economics benefits for a mutual customer, with the consequence that this is beneficial for them, too.[3]

Building on the assumptions of interdependence and resource heterogeneity, the industrial-network approach gives a particular view of the *structure* and *process* of business in industrial markets that challenges conventional ideas (Ford and Håkansson 2006). The conventional view of the structure of business is of independent companies and anonymous markets. In contrast, the industrial-network approach views the structure of business as a network of significant relationships between interdependent companies (Ford and Håkansson 2006). Rather than considering a process based on the actions of independent companies, the industrial-network approach implies that business takes place through interaction between interdependent companies (Ford and Håkansson 2006).

The Structure of Business in Industrial Markets—Embeddedness And Variety

The industrial-network approach challenges the idea that the business world is comprised of companies that are more or less independent of each other and which are able to build and execute their own strategy (Håkansson and Snehota 1989). Instead, studies advocating this approach show the importance of *embeddedness* in industrial markets, that is, when each inter-organisational relationship is connected to the two companies' other relationships and, through these relationships, the companies are linked to numerous other companies in a wider network (Anderson et al. 1994; Håkansson and Snehota 1995). Hence, the notion of embeddedness implies that industrial markets consist of networks of relationships between interdependent companies (Håkansson and Snehota 1995; Håkansson et al. 2004). The networks of connections that stretch across the business landscape define the position of each inter-organisational relationship in a multidimensional space (Ford and Håkansson 2006). The research and results that have come out from the industrial-network approach imply that one cannot make sense of what happens in individual inter-organisational relationships by examining them in isolation; instead, they must be viewed within the wider network of relationships in which they are embedded (Anderson et al. 1994; Håkansson and Snehota 1995). Interdependencies between a multiplicity of companies render impossible the identification of factors that are external to business networks (Håkansson and Snehota 1995).

Business networks are difficult to define and delimit because they have no objective boundaries and there are no correct or complete descriptions of them (Ford and Håkansson 2006). From a research as well as a practical point of view, the networks to consider consist of all of the companies and other organisations that are significant for the particular issue being addressed (Ford et al. 2003).

Another important characteristic of the structure of business in industrial markets is that customers and suppliers vary widely in size, requirements, and importance (Håkansson and Snehota 1995). Some customers will be more important than others because, for example, they buy more or because their requirements are difficult to meet and are important for the company's future development (Ford et al. 2003). Similarly, some suppliers will be more important than others, for example, because they supply a large volume or because what they supply is critical for the success of the company (Håkansson et al. 2009). This results in a *world of variety* where the actions of the company are based on the company's interpretation of the previous action of specific customers and suppliers and on the company's anticipation of the possible reactions and re-reactions of those specific customers and suppliers (Ford and Håkansson 2006). The industrial-network approach acknowledges that the companies that surround a specific company are unique in their resources, problems, aims, and interactions. In addition, these companies cannot be categorised into neat homogenous groups with names such as suppliers, customers, or competitors (Ford and Håkansson 2006). A counterpart to a company could be classified within all these groups at the same time, delivering inputs to the company, buying the company's output and, simultaneously, be competing for the same customer. The existence of variety also implies that no company has sufficient resources to single-handedly satisfy the requirements of any customer, and therefore is dependent on the skills and resources and the actions and intentions of suppliers, distributors, customers, and competitors to satisfy those requirements (Ford et al. 2003).

The Process of Business on Industrial Markets— Interaction and Dynamics

The industrial-network approach challenges the idea that the process of conducting business on industrial markets consists of the independent actions of individual companies, directed towards a generalised group of customers, suppliers, or competitors. Instead, the process of business is considered to be a *dynamic process of interaction* between individually recognised, interdependent companies (Ford and Håkansson 2006). The change process is driven by interactions in inter-organisational relationships. Change is generated and carried out by actions, which, to some extent, are themselves always reactions to earlier actions. This means that stability and change become related to each other. Given this, a network of inter-organisational relationships can never be seen as a stable structure but, instead, must be considered to consist of inherently dynamic features, characterised by a continuous organising process (Håkansson and Snehota 1995).

The change in business networks is evolutionary. It does not tend to a stable equilibrium as hypothesised in the classic picture of the market mechanism. Nor does it follow a grand design established once and for all by some mastermind. Business networks are the result of a continuous collective organising process (Ford and Håkansson 2006). The situation, evolution, success, or value of a particular relationship can only be fully assessed in the context of the evolving network in which it is embedded (Ford and Håkansson 2006).

The evolution of an inter-organisational relationship has no predetermined direction and speed. It is beyond the complete control of either of the companies alone, and is subject to the aims of both of them, their investment in it, and to the interplay of the particular relationship under consideration with other relationships. There are always new ways to combine investments, creating new opportunities. As actors change their priorities, ways of performing activities, and how they combine resources, change is brought about in business networks. These changes, small as they might seem, can travel fast and have a substantial influence far away from the initial starting point. On the other hand, a radical innovation with great future prospects might fail just as easily because it is not well taken in the existing technical and social structure of a company's surrounding network. There are several empirical industrial-network approach studies where new technologies have been introduced with high hopes and with initial commercial and technical success (Håkansson 1987; Wedin 2001), but as they did not fit with the economic logic of the users or providers of resources, the "great product" eventually faded away and vanished (Håkansson and Waluszewski 2007).

Networking

Describing and analysing industrial markets in terms of embeddedness, variety, interaction, and dynamics have important implications for how "rational" both companies and the people within them can be. In most management textbooks, a company is perceived to be independent in relation to its environment and is therefore free to make strategic decisions, based on the information that it has collected and analysed. However, studies based on the industrial-network approach have shown again and again how this picture is not only wrong but also misleading and perhaps even dangerous (Håkansson et al. 2009). Instead, companies that are active in industrial markets take into consideration the interdependencies that exist, knowledge-wise, technically and financially. Companies try to improve their positions in their networks and even increase their control over critical resources and activities. However, this is done somewhat differently from the way that conventional business wisdom would have us believe. Companies are continuously struggling to use their experience and knowledge of the networks as well as their relationships with others to improve their position. This is termed *networking* and implies that companies constantly try to influence other companies in their networks in order to increase the value of their resources (Håkansson 1987). Even if a network can never be controlled, many actors may try to influence the evolution and direction of their immediate network. Networking involves identifying where there is scope for individual action and working within the constraints of business networks (Håkansson et al. 2009).

A company's position in business networks is based on its set of inter-organisational relationships and the reputation, rights, limitations on behaviour, and obligations that it has acquired through interactions within those relationships (Johanson and Mattsson 1992). The management process in any company is interactive, evolutionary, and responsive (Ford and Håkansson 2006). An individual company has limited freedom to act independently, and the outcome of its actions will be strongly influenced by the attitudes and actions of those with whom it has relationships (Ford et al. 2003). Management thereby involves lots of reacting to the actions of others, and successful management of inter-organisational relationships depends on understanding the nature of the dynamics of the wider network. Networking implies that strategy involves using a company's own resources as well as those with which it interacts and with which it is interdependent. A company's ability to be successful depends on its overall network position and its skills in managing and prioritising relationships with the aim of activating and combining technologies and to assess the problems and requirements of both customers and suppliers. Contrary to many other theoretical approaches to inter-organisational relationships, the more successful a company's suppliers and customers are, the better it is for the company itself. A company's interdependence with others is, therefore, not only a restriction on its operations: Instead, the relationships are a resource on which the company can build. An important way of creating value, and a core competence, for a company is to gain resources through long-lasting relationships (Ford et al. 2003; Håkansson et al. 2009).

3 USING THE INDUSTRIAL-NETWORK APPROACH IN THE STUDY OF ACCOUNTING IN NETWORKS

The industrial-network approach, with its assumptions of resource heterogeneity and interdependencies, and its view of industrial markets in terms of embeddedness, variety, dynamics, interaction, and networking has implications for the design and use of accounting in networks. It changes the perception of what should be included in the accounting, who should conduct it, and how accounting is to be used (Håkansson and Lind 2007; Kraus and Lind 2007). The accounting issues brought to the fore by applying the industrial-network approach differ from those that are prominent when the main focus of the activities of a company that is involved in inter-organisational relationships is to protect itself from opportunistic behaviour, given the effective allocation of resources (Van der Meer-Kooistra and Vosselman 2000; Baiman and Rajan 2002; Dekker 2004).

The industrial-network approach implies that the safeguards which lie at the heart of many other theoretical approaches (i.e., agency theory and transaction cost economics) to inter-organisational relationships, such as formal contracts and private ordering arrangements, are rarely of primary importance (Håkansson and Lind 2007). Contracts stipulate how the profit should be divided between two parties, but as the knowledge about resources is never absolute, as assumed in the industrial-network approach, there are always things to learn about how to combine resources and their interfaces, and hence there are good reasons for two or more parties to cooperate to increase the value of the resources exchanged (Håkansson and Waluszewski 2002). This is something that is hard to encapsulate in a contract, as a result of which, contracts can act as deterrents, reducing the incentives for joint development work, when struggles over sharing costs and revenues become the overriding issue.

Another implication for accounting concerns the conceptualisation of inter-organisational relationships. If an inter-organisational relationship is viewed as something that is built up in isolation by the two parties involved, then explanations for any events with implications for the relationships will be sought within the frame of the relationship itself. Such explanations will, most likely, focus either on the characteristics of the two parties or on the nature and characteristics of the interaction and development processes between them (Van der Meer-Kooistra and Vosselman 2000; Dekker 2004). In contrast, with an industrial-network approach, inter-organisational relationships, and hence interaction with others, provide a way to create and utilise resources in a better way. The focus is on the process of creating value and not on how to divide a given value between the firms involved (Håkansson and Lind 2007). When the inter-organisational relationship is viewed as part of a network of interdependent relationships, then explanations of what is happening in a certain relationship can be searched for, to some extent, in factors external to the relationship itself.

This has an important effect on all costs and revenues because it introduces a spatial dependence that did not exist before. Accounting needs to accommodate this new dimension, because indirect (network) effects need to be taken into consideration. The company needs accounting information to support networking, as well as accounting information for identifying and supporting new resource combinations within the company, in the dyadic inter-organisational relationships and in a wider network. Agreements on how to improve the links between activities and to exclude activities or to move them between companies in a network are also issues that are either directly or indirectly tied up with accounting issues. Furthermore, information on the counterparts' intra-organisational accounting systems is critical to enable the company to influence the design and use of these systems to ensure that they support and promote interaction. These issues are elaborated following under the headings "Accounting for Indirect Effects", "Accounting for Prioritisations", and "Accounting for Networking".

Accounting for Indirect Effects

The view of the structure of industrial markets inherent in the industrial-network approach necessitates a reinterpretation of the ideas underpinning accounting in networks. The interconnections and interdependencies that enmesh a company in a network connect it specifically and uniquely to individually significant inter-organisational relationships, as well as to a myriad other companies with entirely different operations and technologies. These interdependencies mean that operations, investments, cash flows, costs, and revenues are intimately connected between specific companies across a business network. Many relationships have similar requirements and a company may be able to combine relationships that can benefit from a single investment in facilities or knowledge (Gadde and Håkansson 2008). The outcome of investments in one relationship will often appear as decreased costs or increased revenues in other relationships. Accounting needs to be designed to capture both the direct effects of the company's decisions on the other company in the inter-organisational relationship and the indirect effects on the third and fourth parties (Lind and Thrane 2005; Baraldi and Strömsten 2008). As Tomkins (2001, p. 184) put it, "The essence of a portfolio problem is that it is inappropriate to assess individual components on a separate basis." Obtaining a complete model for all these direct and indirect effects is impossible, and the company needs to focus on the most important interconnections.

Some of a company's inter-organisational relationships are close, complex, and long-term, necessitating significant relationship-specific investments (Ford et al. 2003). Over time, these relationships can comprise important assets for the current and future problem solving of the companies involved, enabling them to exercise influence and to generate sales, and hence revenue, and to gain access to critical resources in an efficient way on the supply side (Gadde and Håkansson 2001). In many ways, relationships are the assets that bind together all of the other assets of a company and convert them into something of economic value (Jahre et al. 2006), rendering the economic structure more relational than the perceptions of the individual companies involved. The costs and potential value of relationship-specific assets are separate from the costs of individual purchases or the revenue from sales. However, the future "capital value" of a relationship as an asset is difficult to measure, and to manage, because the relationships are likely to involve complex and unique offerings by suppliers and important adaptations and investments by the customers. One important aspect of inter-organisational relationships as assets is that they have to be built up over time, through a process of incremental investment, through, for example, sales calls, technical liaison, or introducing a new logistical arrangement to cope with a supplier's location (Håkansson et al. 2009).

Lind and Strömsten (2006) developed a framework within which to consider the profitability analysis of customer relationships that accounts for long-term investment and indirect benefits. In their view, the use of customer lifetime valuation analysis shows a customer's contribution to the firm's long-term profitability. This is a customer accounting technique that measures the present value of the presumed future cash flows derived from the customer relationship. Hence, lifetime valuation is a customer accounting technique that extends beyond the annual time period typically used in accounting and incorporates benefits from connected relationships. However, measuring the investments and indirect benefits from all the firm's customer relationships will be a complex and expensive task. According to Lind and Strömsten (2006), however, it is not necessary to evaluate all customer relationships with a lifetime customer valuation, and they argue that only a few customer relationships need to be evaluated in this way.

Lind and Strömsten (2006) identified four different groups of customer relationships—transactional, facilitative, integrative, and connective—and it is only the connective customer relationships that are associated with lifetime customer valuation analysis. The four groups of customer relationships are categorised on the basis of how well developed the technical and organisational interfaces between the companies are. The connective customer relationships are characterised by less developed organisational interfaces (e.g., buying volumes are small) and a high integration of technical interfaces through adaptation of products and production facilities. These customer relationships impose specific demands on the firm's customer profitability evaluation because they create high direct costs but generate low direct revenues. Hence, the existence of these relationships is motivated in accounting terms by the revenues that these relationships can generate indirectly in and through other relationships, and by extending the time horizon to periods of multiple years for the relationship to become "profitable".

When it comes to the other three groups of customer relationships, it is not necessary to account for indirect benefits because they are profitable on a stand-alone basis. However, it is necessary to extend the time horizon to the lifetime of the relationships when integrative customer relationships are evaluated because these are characterised by large upfront investments in production facilities and joint technical development work. In contrast to the integrative customer relationships, the transactional and facilitative customer relationships are evaluated on an annual basis. Hence, the framework developed by Lind and Strömsten (2006) shows that different types of customer relationships will be associated with different types of customer accounting techniques.

Another study that describes and analyses accounting for indirect effects is that of Dubois (2003). In her case study of a large multinational company, she illustrated how accounting was used to support a "new" combination of resources within a network of business relationships, and for the purchasing of supplies for maintenance repair and operations. Her study shows the possibility of increasing the value of the resources exchanged through new combinations of the resources even when the exchange is one of commodity products. The buying firm and the key supplier formed a 'commodity team' with the goal of bringing about reductions in the purchasing costs. The team focused on the total cost of exchange, and one important role of accounting was to provide information about costs related to the network in which the inter-organisational relationship was embedded. The cost discussions included assorted requirements from the supplier's other customers; the supplier's suppliers also became involved. Dubois (2003, p 370) concluded: ". . . The definition of the total cost of the exchange was extended beyond the boundaries of the two firms, since price had become a matter of the suppliers' cost structures, which, in turn, were greatly influenced by the preferences and behaviour of their other counterparts." Accounting information helped the buying company understand that the costs in the inter-organisational relationship with a supplier were not only driven by the buying firm's costs and the supplier's costs, but also by how the relationship related to other relationships. Decisions on adding new products were, for example, analysed in terms of the consequences they would have on the companies' overall costs that mainly depended on what and how the supplier's other customers bought. This meant that the scope of the costs to include in the analysis was expanded to include the costs of embedded counterparts.

Dubois' (2003) study of ad hoc use of accounting to support problem solving and Lind and Strömsten's (2006) study of more frequent use of different customer accounting techniques are two illustrations of how firms use accounting to capture both direct and indirect effects. However, neither of these studies illustrates how accounting can be a mutual source of information on an ongoing basis that supports the interaction between the firms involved. The study of customer accounting is focused on just one firm and its evaluation of customer relationships. The accounting information in Lind and Strömsten's (2006) study gives firm advice on how it should act towards its customers. Should the firm invest more resources in the customer relationships, continue just as it is, or terminate the relationships with a particular customer? Dubois' (2003) study of purchasing illustrates how mutually available accounting information is used to change behaviour within the firm and its key suppliers and in the operations of some connected counterparts. However, the accounting is applied on an ad hoc basis within a project implemented with the sole or primary goal of enforcing change. No studies based on the industrial-network approach appear to exist that show how, on a frequent and ongoing basis, accounting can account for indirect effects, or that it is used to influence the interaction between the firms involved. However, Kajüter and Kulmala's (2005) study of the open-book accounting practices of a German car manufacturer is one empirical illustration of how a company and its suppliers and the suppliers' suppliers account for indirect effects in a formalised setting. It should be noted that Kajüter and Kulmala based their paper on contingency theory. The company used a value flow chart to provide a "network" picture of its interconnected inter-organisational relationships. The names and locations of upstream suppliers were shown on the value flow chart along with the connections between the suppliers, the flow of materials, and each supplier's added costs.

However, if the industrial-network approach were to be used to analyse the German car manufacturer and its network of suppliers, then it would be obvious that the open-book accounting system could only track direct linkages between the German car manufacturer and suppliers on different tiers. The open-book accounting system could not track indirect linkages such as the suppliers' deliveries to other car manufacturers. According to the findings presented in Dubois (2003), these indirect linkages to other customers and suppliers were a central ingredient when the company she studied was able to reduce its total cost of exchange through new resource combinations. This means that the industrial-network approach implies that information sharing via open-book accounting within one relationship is related not only to other direct relationships within the supply chain, but also to information sharing in connected relationships. Open-book accounting agreements can then be used to provide information useful for increasing the knowledge of the interconnections between the different relationships, as opposed to the "traditional" use of open-book accounting to increase the knowledge of each individual relationship.

All three of the aforementioned studies (i.e., Dubois 2003; Kajüter and Kulmala 2005; Lind and Strömsten 2006) have discussed how accounting for indirect effects is used in a deliberate way to create value, by incorporating the indirect effects in the intra-organisational accounting systems. However, in networks, indirect effects might appear as surprises and unintended effects as a large number of actors are involved, having their own, sometimes multiple, agendas and objectives. This is illustrated in the work of Baraldi and Strömsten (2009). These authors studied innovation in the biotech sector and the role that accounting played in the nonlinear innovation process. The scientific innovation under investigation was originally developed at Uppsala University in Sweden, but ended up at Stanford University, where it was eventually commercialised in the San Francisco Bay Area. Baraldi and Strömsten (2009) showed how the use of accounting information led to outcomes, which in turn started reactions by actors other than those that had been originally targeted, as in a chain of effects on a network level. For instance, an attempt to control the behaviour of a specific supplier induced reactions from the partners of this supplier. Many of these indirect effects were unintended, which meant that the focal actor basically ended up stimulating others to do rather different things than it had expected them to do in the first place.

Accounting for Prioritisations

As previously stated, according to the industrial-network approach, the business conducted in industrial markets consists of interaction in unique relationships with individually significant counterparts. This severely limits the extent to which a standardised approach is valid for accounting, when it comes to costing and revenue analysis. Analysis is likely to be less concerned with the costs and revenues of operating units, products, and geographical areas and more concerned with returns from specific inter-organisational relationships. No single type of inter-organisational relationship is "right" for a company in all circumstances, and the firm cannot just develop accounting systems that include a single design for all its relationships and expect it to be acceptable to all its partners. The central task for a company is to manage a diverse portfolio of relationships over time to maximise their long-term value (Tomkins 2001). The variety of the supplier and customer relationships implies that the company needs to prioritise, because it is unrealistic, if not downright impossible, for a company to adapt its operations to the satisfaction of all its customers and suppliers. Accounting has an important role to play in supplying the information required for the successive prioritisation of relationships with customers and suppliers (Håkansson and Lind 2007).

Dubois' (2003) empirical description of a purchaser's prioritisation of its maintenance and operations suppliers and the role of accounting in this process illustrates the arguments outlined earlier. The company under consideration selected five key suppliers with which it deepened its cooperation, with the primary aim of reducing indirect costs associated with purchasing, for example, the costs of warehousing, supplier handling costs, and administration. Representatives were selected from the company and its key suppliers to form 'commodity teams'. Involving just a few suppliers made it possible to tackle the indirect purchasing costs. Apart from the effects on supplier handling costs, the other indirect costs could only be reduced in collaboration with the suppliers. The role of accounting was to increase knowledge of the total costs of exchange as a whole, rather than to determine the costs of individual transactions. Both the supplier's costs and the buyer's costs were incorporated into the analysis conducted by the commodity teams. This meant using accounting to track indirect costs for the buying firm internally, and tracking the suppliers' costs. Both the buyer's costs and the supplier's costs were included in the total cost of the exchange. This meant another role for and use of accounting arising from the heterogeneity in the supplier base. The focus of accounting shifted the unit of analysis from the products to the relationships with prioritised suppliers, and thus, the content of the exchange with these suppliers became the subject of interaction, which made it possible to consider both the buyer's and the supplier's cost structures when deciding what products should be exchanged and how the transactions should be organised.

Lind and Strömsten's (2006) customer profitability framework provides another example of how accounting can support a firm when it needs to prioritise its customers. A few customers, namely, those with connective customer relationships, will be assigned such a high prioritisation that they do not need to pay for the resources the firm invests in them. This is, naturally, a position all customers want to be in; however, it is vital that these connective customer relationships contribute to the firm's other relationships (Lind and Strömsten 2006).

Most companies on industrial markets have a rather concentrated revenue base, meaning that just a small number of customers account for a large share of the revenue (Håkansson 1989). These customers, the integrative customer relationships, who often also have a dedicated unit in their counterpart working with them (i.e., a key account unit), might also be active in co-developing new products and/or processes (Lind and Strömsten 2006). These customers must certainly be prioritised, but they also need to be measured or considered differently from those customers that buy more standardised products. However, no company can or, indeed, should strive to have only close relationships, and, in fact, a company cannot adapt its products and production facilities for all its customers, nor can it form individual accounts for them all. Thus, they must prioritise the customers that buy standard products as well as modified ones, odd as it might sound. These so-called facilitative relationships should be measured in a more conventional way (i.e., annually and on a stand-alone basis). Hence, depending on what type of customer relationship exists, the focal firm should evaluate its customers and hence give them the appropriate prioritisation depending on the objectives of the focal firms for its entire portfolio of customers (Lind and Strömsten 2006).

A third study that discusses accounting for prioritisations is that of Håkansson and Lind (2004). In their study, the authors revealed how the Swedish cellular telecommunications company Ericsson and the Swedish telecommunication operator Telia used accounting to prioritise between their counterparts. Relationships were one key dimension when the two companies under investigation organised their operations. Each of the two companies dedicated individuals to work exclusively with a particular counterpart and specific relationships were an object in the accounting system. The prioritisation and differentiated focus on specific relationships was more strongly elaborated within Ericsson, which had a hierarchy of relationships units, than at Telia. Each of the relationship units was accountable for a specific customer relationship. These units acted as the customer's voice within Ericsson, competing with other internal units responsible for different customers with their own needs, each attempting to get the maximum amount of attention paid to their own customer's needs. However, the relationship units received different amounts of resources and had different possibilities to influence other units within Ericsson.

It can be concluded that Dubois (2003), Håkansson and Lind (2004) and Lind and Strömsten (2006) all presented empirical descriptions of accounting for prioritisations, albeit in different ways. Dubois (2003) and Lind and Strömsten (2006) both showed the role of accounting for decision making, that is, how accounting information is used when firms need to prioritise between the different inter-organisational relationships. Håkansson and Lind (2004), on the other hand, show the accountability aspect of accounting, that is, how accounting and control systems can be designed to make individuals act in accordance with predetermined company prioritisations.

Accounting for Networking

According to the industrial-network approach, dynamics play a vital role in industrial markets (Ford and Håkansson 2006). Business networks are always the result of an ongoing collective organising process. This incessant change, in combination with the strong interdependencies, creates a need for the firms to deal with constant network dilemmas (Håkansson and Ford 2002). The design and use of accounting in a business network is more about mobilising and influencing people within the focal company, and within its direct relationships and, onwards, to their counterparts' relationships to ensure that all work in a common direction, rather than the use of command strategies. Indeed, it can even be dangerous for a company to be too influential within its relationships and totally dominate the network of companies in which it is embedded because, if such a level of dominance were ever to be achieved, then the only source of wisdom and innovation in the network in which the company was imbedded would be the company itself (Håkansson and Ford 2002). Accounting has an important role to play in creating a dynamic structure that develops through co-evolution (Håkansson and Lind 2007). This means that the focus of the accounting and management control shifts from the optimisation and follow-up of preset goals to facilitation of the collective process of finding temporarily valid and mutually satisfactory "solutions". This is called accounting for networking. Accounting for networking implies that the primary role of accounting is not to find optimal governance forms (Van der Meer-Kooistra and Vosselman 2000; Dekker 2004) but rather to help create interaction between different companies which will lead to temporarily valid pragmatic compromises.

Håkansson and Lind's (2004) case study of the relationship between Ericsson and Telia illustrates this novel role of accounting. The authors found that Ericsson systematically used accounting to create units with partially overlapping accountabilities. Thus, Ericsson evaluated its individual units, that is, customer and technical units, on actions and measures that could not necessarily be controlled by the unit. For example, Ericsson's customer units were, to some extent, evaluated and rewarded through their customers' actions, that is, whether customers started to use a new software feature in its operations or not would be used as a measure of the performance of the unit. The overlapping accountabilities created a situation where each customer unit tried to influence Ericsson's development units to meet its customers' needs. This overlapping accountability created contradictions in Ericsson's network of relationships as people within the companies continuously needed to find new temporarily valid solutions. Accounting practices were used to handle the complexity produced by the interdependence and embeddedness of companies. Accounting helped to establish a structure that was not a solution to the coordination problems but rather a base facilitating a process that led to continuous adaptations of the 'solutions'. As Håkansson and Lind (2004, p. 67) put it: "This overlapping accountability provides the inducement to find new technical solutions as well as opportunities to develop them. The overlap forces the units to interact to find compromises that do not have to be fully satisfactory for either of the parties, because of their temporary nature."

In a similar vein, Carlsson-Wall et al. (2009) explored the role of target costing in inter-organisational product development. The empirical material was based on an in-depth case study of ABB Robotics, a large multinational company which manufactures, develops, and sells industrial robots, and some of its suppliers and customers. ABB Robotics and its suppliers and customers together reached viable pragmatic compromises. It was not possible, nor was it desirable, for just one company to direct all the development, as it was important to deal with numerous, and often conflicting, aspects and features in a holistic manner, to ensure that a viable compromise was reached. The development process also involved taking into consideration the needs and desires of a network of companies, some of which were part of the original development team, but including others that were mobilised temporarily to solve specific technological problems.

The characteristics of the development process had implications for the role of target costing. Target costing often failed to function as a hierarchical planning and evaluation technique following the "plan and execute" logic of development processes, as would have been assumed based on previous target costing literature (Ansari et al. 2007), and it was not used to find an optimal solution to a preset development problem. Rather, the target costing process was found to be more interactive and nonhierarchical. Frequently, unexpected events happened and situations arose during the product development projects, and target costing functioned as a means by which to frame pragmatic decisions that could be taken during collective problem solving. Target costing enabled a consensus to be obtained across firm boundaries about the priorities as it was used to coordinate product development projects, and formed the basis for rejecting technically viable solutions on the grounds of expense, when they failed to meet the target cost. Targets costing and the functional analysis took on a guiding role and gave focus to the problem solving. Thus, in the case study, target costing facilitated and directed knowledge integration between Robotics and its suppliers.

Like Håkansson and Lind (2004) and Carlsson-Wall et al. (2009), Baraldi and Strömsten (2009) found that the development process in a biotech case study was nonlinear. Many situations were concerned, predominantly, with collective problem solving and accepting temporarily valid compromises between companies with different objectives. The innovation process in Baraldi and Strömsten (2009) was described as a continuous combination of resources, where actors were trying to use accounting to control the behaviour of their counterparts, while at the same time being exposed to the control strategies of a different but possibly overlapping set of counterparts. For example, the innovators at Stanford University were aware of how the network that formed as a result of an innovation was comprised of customers, potential research partners, venture capitalists, and competitors, and they actively tried to determine the counterparts' agendas through their accounting and control systems. One way in which they were attempting to achieve this was by identifying the fact that a potential acquirer needed their products and know-how in order to meet their own future financial objectives. At the same time, their owners, three venture capitalist companies, demanded that they develop relationships with another customer, which also was a potential acquirer, so that the value of the company would not suffer.

The study by Baraldi and Strömsten did not focus on a focal actor, unlike the research presented in Håkansson and Lind (2004) and Carlsson-Wall et al. (2009). Baraldi and Strömsten (2009) showed how result, action, and personnel controls were used in different *combinations* by the various actors associated with an innovation within a network. Even if the joint controls existed, the study focused on how the actors developed their own controls, based on their own objectives, and how they tried to introduce innovation-specific benefits through the implementation of these controls. Patents, for example, worked as significant action controls because they hindered some actors in the network from pursuing research and commercialisation activity in certain areas associated with the innovation. However, at the same time, anything that was omitted from patents could be explored, and was taken advantage of by some actors. Further, personnel controls were used when selecting, informing, and linking actors to each other when this was considered to be desirable. Sometimes the selection of counterparts was made by third parties. Venture capitalists, for example, which were driven by explicit financial objectives, had a strong influence over the customers and research partners that inventors initiated relationships with. Result controls involved financial as well as nonfinancial information and worked as important signals to the actors in the network, showing historical success and clarifying future promises, and thereby also helping to recruit partners in the network and to scare unwanted interest off.

Håkansson and Lind (2004), Baraldi and Strömsten (2009) and Carlsson-Wall et al. (2009) all show that the dynamic nature of business networks implies that there is a need to continuously develop a network from the point of view of each individual company. The studies stress that accounting is used as one of the driving forces for creating a dynamic network structure with collective processes directed at finding temporarily valid "solutions". Accounting for networking often involves making prioritisations, as well as accounting for indirect effects. This was illustrated in Chapter 2, where in the process of turning around its business, Ducati had to change its important supplier relationships. One primary means of accomplishing this was to develop the economic analysis of the relationships. The company involved some prioritised suppliers in this joint development, and one of the results was a new way to account for costs and revenues across firms' boundaries, that is, accounting for indirect effects. Given the dynamic character of business networks, there is no reason to believe that this process will ever enter into a 'final' stage because there will always be the need to continue to adapt accounting and find new temporarily valid "solutions".

4 CONCLUSIONS AND TOPICS FOR FUTURE RESEARCH

In this chapter, we have addressed how the industrial-network approach challenges and influences the way we understand the design and use of accounting in networks. Building on the basic theoretical assumptions of resource heterogeneity (Penrose 1959; Alchian and Demsetz 1972) and interdependence (Richardson 1972), the industrial-network approach provides a particular view of business in industrial markets. The structure of business is conceptualised as a network of significant inter-organisational relationships between interdependent companies and organisations. The process of business is perceived to be a dynamic process of interaction between individually identifiable, interdependent companies and organisations. By applying the theoretical lens of the industrial-network approach, three implications for the study of accounting in networks were brought up: accounting for indirect effects, accounting for prioritisations, and accounting for networking. From the discussion of these, three general conclusions can be drawn.

First, accounting for indirect effects starts out from the need for any business organisation to take into account any important indirect effects arising from business activities directed toward other individual firms or organisations. The reviewed empirical studies (Dubois 2003; Lind and Strömsten 2006; Baraldi and Strömsten 2009) illustrated how firms can use accounting to make more informed decisions when calculations include indirect effects, but also demonstrate how accounting can be used to create indirect effects or to increase the awareness of indirect effects. In this way, accounting provides an important means by which to utilise and elaborate all kinds of indirect effects. In addition, it becomes vital to try to influence the counterparts' design for and use of accounting, as this will influence both the way in which the counterparts act and their ability to give vital information to the focal firm.

Second, accounting plays a key role in the prioritisation of customers and suppliers, albeit in ways that sometimes differ from those one might expect. Accounting is not only used for prioritising the supplier and customer that buys or sells most, but also for the evaluation of a combination of different inter-organisational relationships, for example, of integrative and facilitative relationships (Lind and Strömsten 2006). In the same way, the empirical illustrations showed that accounting is crucial for structuring the supply network for any manufacturer. Accounting information is used when selecting the key "system" suppliers and determining how these should function as hubs for a whole set of supplier relationships (Dubois 2003). Again, the indirect effects are often much larger than all of the direct ones.

Third, accounting for networking is concerned with how a firm manages in a dynamic network and the role that accounting may play in this process. One important ingredient in the development of accounting is that, in addition to developing inter-organisational accounting, firms need to develop their own intra-organisational accounting to incorporate different indirect effects and to "bring in" or to develop the interface with their counterparts' intra-organisational accounting systems. The overlapping accountabilities in the study by Håkansson and Lind (2004) are examples of such novel use of intra-organisational accounting. The dynamic character of business networks requires that the companies involved successively identify better ways to confront their own costs and revenues in conjunction with important counterparts. The firms also need to increase their combined abilities to calculate the internal costs and revenues in relation to changes in specific business relationships. In these ongoing efforts, each organisation can use accounting to try to "sell" its view of a network with the aim of mobilising others and creating collective action and mutually satisfactory solutions. These solutions are always temporarily valid in relation to what is coming next. Accounting for networking implies that the focus of accounting and management control is shifted from the optimisation and follow-up of pre-set goals to the facilitation of the collective process of finding temporarily valid "solutions". As shown in the studies by Håkansson and Lind (2004),

Baraldi and Strömsten (2009) and Carlsson-Wall et al. (2009), the primary role of accounting was to stimulate interaction between different companies with the aim of developing a continuously evolving series of pragmatic solutions through compromise, rather than to help to find a permanently valid solution to coordination problems.

So far, only a limited number of empirical studies have been conducted that apply the industrial-network approach. For the future, we envisage the interesting research opportunities currently available to scholars who are active in networks and accounting being taken up and elaborated upon, for example: There is a need for in-depth case studies where the various roles of accounting in the development of extensive business relationships are studied. How are intra- and inter-organisational accounting designed, and how are they used to take indirect (network) effects into consideration? As of now, a few studies have analysed these topics on an ad hoc basis (Dubois 2003; Lind and Strömsten 2006; Baraldi and Strömsten 2009), but no empirical studies have been conducted of how accounting for indirect effects is used on an ongoing basis.

In addition, there is little knowledge about how intra- and inter-organisational accounting is handled and used in relation to the development of firms, inter-organisational relationships, and networks. The studies by Håkansson and Lind (2004), Baraldi and Strömsten (2009) and Carlsson-Wall et al. (2009) indicate that, in many situations, accounting may put severe constraints on product development, but novel approaches to the design and use of accounting can also create new possibilities. More research is needed on how accounting can facilitate (instead of hindering) collective and nonlinear product development processes, where temporarily valid pragmatic compromises need to be made.

Finally, we perceive an opportunity to empirically and theoretically elaborate on how "assets" can or should be valued, given a firm's network context. In modern and contemporary accounting, the valuation of assets is closely related to the existence of a "market". Network resources have little or no external use outside the firm's network of embedded relationships and, therefore, are impossible to value in the same way. Informally, companies have begun to make such evaluations and it would be interesting to know more about how such valuation is done in practice. Related to this, we perceive a need for studies of the interface between organisational design and accounting in a network setting and a network's configuration. Accounting is an organisational device and, as such, must be related both to other internal organisational variables and to the inter-organisational network characteristics.

NOTES

1. www.impgroup.org.
2. The standard reference, when it comes to coordination of production activities, is that of Richardson (1972).

3. The two major references in relation to the resource concept are the seminal book by Penrose (1959) and the work of Alchian and Demsetz (1972).

BIBLIOGRAPHY

Alchian, A. A., and Demsetz, H. 1972. Production, information costs and economic organization. *American Economic Review* 62: 777–795.

Anderson, J. C., Håkansson, H., and Johanson, J. 1994. Dyadic business relationships within a business network context. *Journal of Marketing* 58: 1–15.

Ansari, S., Bell, J., and Okano, H. 2007. Target costing: Uncharted research territory. In *Handbook of management accounting research,* ed. Chapman, C. S., Hopwood, A. G., and Shields, M. D. Oxford: Elsevier.

Baiman, S., and Rajan, M. V. 2002. Incentive issues in interfirm relationships. *Accounting, Organizations and Society* 27: 213–238.

Baraldi E., and Strömsten, T. 2008. Configurations and control of resource interfaces in industrial networks. *Advances in Business Marketing and Purchasing* 14: 251–316.

Baraldi, E., and Strömsten T. 2009. Controlling and combining resources in networks. From Uppsala to Stanford, and back again. The case of a biotech innovation. *Industrial Marketing Management* (Forthcoming).

Carlsson-Wall, M., Kraus, K., and Lind, J. 2009. Accounting and distributed product development. *IMP-Journal* 3: 2–27.

Dekker, H. C. 2004. Control of inter-organizational relationships: Evidences on appropriation concerns and coordination requirements. *Accounting, Organizations and Society* 29: 27–49.

Dubois, A. 1998. *Organising industrial activities across firm boundaries.* London: Routledge.

Dubois, A. 2003. Strategic cost management across boundaries of firms. *Industrial Marketing Management* 32: 365–374.

Dubois, A., and Araujo, L. 2004. Research methods in industrial marketing studies. In *Rethinking marketing: Developing a new understanding of markets,* ed. Håkansson, H., Harrison, D., and Waluszewski, A. Chichester, UK: Wiley.

Dubois, A., and Gadde, L.-E. 2002. Systematic combining: An abductive approach to case research. *Journal of Business Research* 55: 553–560.

Easton, G. 2000. Case research as a method for industrial networks: A realist apologia. In *Realist perspectives on management and organisations,* ed. Ackroyed, S., and Fleetwood, S. 205–222. London: Routledge.

Ford, D., Gadde, L.-E., Håkansson, H., and Snehota, I., ed. 2003. *Managing Business Relationships,* 2nd ed. Chichester, UK: Wiley.

Ford, D., and Håkansson, H. 2006. The idea of interaction. *IMP Journal* 1: 4–27.

Frimanson, L. 2006. *Management accounting and business relationships from a supplier perspective.* Doctorial thesis, Department of Business Studies, University of Uppsala, Sweden.

Gadde, L.-E., and Håkansson, H., ed. 2001. *Supply network strategies.* Chichester, UK: Wiley.

Gadde, L.-E., and Håkansson, H. 2008. Business relationships and resource combining. *IMP Journal* 2: 31–45.

Hallén, L., Johnson, J., and Seyed-Mohamed, N. 1991. Interfirm adaptation in business relationships. *Journal of Marketing* 55: 29–37.

Håkansson, H., ed. 1982. *International marketing and purchasing of industrial goods. An interaction approach.* London: Wiley.

Håkansson, H., ed. 1987. *Industrial technological development. A network approach.* London: Croom Helm.

Håkansson, H., ed. 1989. *Corporate technological behaviour: Co-operation and networks.* London: Routledge.

Håkansson, H., 1993. Networks as a mechanism to develop resources. In *Networking in Dutch industries,* ed. Beije, P., Groenewegen, J., and Nuys, O. 207–223. Leuven-Appeldorn, Belgium: Garant.

Håkansson, H., and Ford, D. 2002. How should companies interact? *Journal of Business Research* 55: 133–139.

Håkansson, H., Ford, D., Gadde, L.-E., Snehota, I., and Waluszewski, A., ed. 2009. *Business in networks.* Chichester, UK: Wiley

Håkansson, H., Harrison, D., and Waluszewski, A., ed. 2004. *Rethinking marketing: Developing a new understanding of markets.* Chichester, UK: Wiley.

Håkansson, H., and Lind, J. 2004. Accounting and network coordination. *Accounting, Organizations and Society* 29: 51–72.

Håkansson, H., and Lind, J. 2007. Accounting in an interorganisational setting. In *Handbook of management accounting research,* ed. Chapman, C. S., Hopwood, A. G., and Shields, M. D. 885–902. Oxford: Elsevier.

Håkansson, H., and Snehota, I. 1989. No business is an island: The network concept of business strategy. *Scandinavian Journal of Management* 5: 187–200.

Håkansson, H., and Snehota, I., ed. 1995. *Developing relationships in business networks.* London: Routledge.

Håkansson, H., and Waluszewski, A., ed. 2002. *Managing technological development. IKEA, the environment and technology.* London: Routledge.

Håkansson, H., and Waluszewski, A., ed. 2007. *Knowledge and innovation in business and industry: The importance of using others.* London: Routledge.

Jahre, M., Gadde, L.-E., Håkansson, H., Harrison, D., and Persson, G., ed. 2006. *Resourcing in business logistics. The art of systematic combining.* Malmö and Copenhagen: Liber & Copenhagen Business School Press.

Johanson, J., and Mattsson, L.-G. 1992. Network positions and strategic actions—an analytical framework. In *Industrial networks—a new view of reality,* ed. Axelsson, B., and Easton, G. London: Routledge.

Kajüter, P., and Kulmala, H. I. 2005. Open-book accounting in networks. Potential achievements and reasons for failures. *Management Accounting Research* 16: 179–204.

Kraus, K., and Lind, J. 2007. Management control in inter-organisational relationships. In *Issues in management accounting,* ed. Hopper, T., Scapens, R. W., and Northcott, D. 269–296. Harlow, UK: Financial Times Prentice Hall.

Lind, J., and Strömsten, T. 2006. When do firms use different types of customer accounting? *Journal of Business Research* 59: 1257–1266.

Lind, J., and Thrane, S. 2005. Network accounting. In *Accounting in Scandinavia—the northern lights,* ed. Jönsson, S., and Mouritsen, J. 115–137. Malmö, Sweden: Liber & Copenhagen Business School Press.

Penrose, E. 1959. *The theory of the growth of the firm.* Oxford University Press.

Richardson, G. B. 1972. The organization of industry. *Economic Journal* 82: 883–896.

Tomkins, C. 2001. Interdependencies, trust and information in relationships, alliances and networks. *Accounting, Organizations and Society* 26: 161–191.

Turnbull, P. W., and Valla, J. P., ed. 1986. *Strategies for International Industrial Marketing.* London: Croom-Helm.

Van der Meer-Kooistra, J., and Vosselman, E. 2000. Management control of interfirm transactional relationships: The case of industrial renovation and maintenance *Accounting, Organizations and Society* 25: 51–77.

Wedin, T. 2001. *Networks and demand. The use of electricity in an industrial process.* Doctorial thesis, Department of Business Studies, University of Uppsala, Sweden.

12 Actor-Network Theory and the Study of Inter-Organisational Network-Relations

Jan Mouritsen, Habib Mahama, and Wai Fong Chua

1 A CONCERN WITH BOUNDARIES

For many decades, in Western management thought and practice, the concept of organisational boundaries seemed uncontroversial. Organisations were delimited and defined by their boundaries and the notion of 'the boundary' formed a firm basis on which organisational analysis could be conducted. This enabled the use of terms such as 'internal' versus 'external' events and entities, 'the organisation' versus its contextual 'environment', 'internalised costs' versus 'externalities', and so on. Such distinctions came to the fore in the 1960s, when general systems theory became associated with the metaphor of organisations as biological 'open systems' that interacted continuously with their environment (see Katz and Kahn 1966; Morgan and Sturdy 2000). And while the root metaphor of organisations (as machines, organisms, bundles of contracts, etc.) may vary, discussions of actual and possible organisational structure, culture, identity, the allocation of rights and obligations, and the development of mechanisms of coordination and delegation were made possible and indeed predicated on the sanctity of organisational space as identified by organisational boundaries.

Of course, organisational boundaries could not always be easily seen or touched, but they could be apprehended by eye when presented in diagrams and organisational charts. Such visualisation helped to consolidate the firm as an entity and placed everything else outside its organisational boundaries. In the diagrams, black lines cut up white space and separated those belonging to 'the' organisation from those outside it.

Recently, however, boundaries have become more controversial. The empirical observation is that firms spend more time and resources collaborating with others, for example, via complicated supply chains, networks, alliances, partnerships, joint ventures, and so on. As a result, identities have become more confusing. An 'external' party can be both a competitor in some market segments and a partner in others. Diagrams of organisations have also had to become far more complicated, encompassing many entities and requiring new writing technologies to enable their drawing. Instead of a few firm lines in space, there are now whorls of lines that pass through many nodes, some thicker than others, some longer, some of different colours, and some fuzzier—denoted by broken lines instead of firm ones. In addition, the temporal stability of boundaries has been called into question; boundaries have become more permeable and fragile—capable of being rearranged often and quickly. Research has begun to recognise that the organisational boundary is not a meta-explanation of organisational behaviour. Researchers have begun to invent new terms to describe firms that are neither the atomistic units theorised by economists, nor the social clans analysed by sociologists: network organisations, hybrids, public private partnerships, strategic alliances, action nets, and so on.

These different phenomena point to the diversity of perspectives that have been used to theorise the emergent controversy of boundaries. Our focus is actor-network theory (ANT)—a network perspective grounded in the writing of Bruno Latour, Michel Callon, and their associates. There is, however, some linguistic difficulty in studying empirical networks from a network perspective. The empirical network can be understood from many vantage points, such as transaction cost economics, contingency theory, structuration theory, and so on. Thus, empirical networks do not have to be studied from a network perspective. Within the network perspective, there are a few alternatives, including an alternative network perspective such as the industrial-network approach (see Håkansson and Lind 2004; see also Chapter 11). So, ANT is an approach among others from which the empirical network has to be studied with certain emphases, ambitions, and means of analysis which differ from those of the alternatives.

2 ACTOR-NETWORK THEORY AS A PERFORMATIVE APPROACH TO ENTITIES AND ASSOCIATIONS

ANT is not easy to summarise in just a few central points (see Latour 2005 for an introduction), but a central proposition is to advocate understanding social life through a *performative lens*. To understand what this means, it is useful to start from Latour's distinction between ostensive versus performative approaches to social life. The ostensive approach is how Latour frames the opposition to his favoured performative approach. Table 12.1 sets out the two contrasting types of research that Latour identifies. ANT is a performative approach, but a good understanding of what this implies can be gained by examining the meaning of the alternative, the ostensive approach.

The first principle concerns the *attributes of knowledge* of the world. The concern is to what extent researchers already know, before they start an investigation, the contours of a situation. The performative view maintains that the world can only be understood if the researcher knowingly disregards prior assumptions about the connections in it. This is to maximise surprise, as the world can be constituted very differently from situation to situation. Furthermore, this is not only a concern with local experiences, even if this is where analysis starts. A global perspective is interesting and relevant in the form that it enters the analysis. In most situations, many entities are not only local, but occupy positions from different time-space settings. Accounting systems such as target costing[1] procedures are rarely constructed in relation to the specifics of the local situation in which they are to be applied; in fact, they would have typically been designed in the past and therefore contain traces of the previous environments in which they had been designed and used. Likewise, target costing systems may tell a supplier that things have to be done, even if the system is remote, as it is mobilised by the focal firm. So, local issues are typically related to distant affairs and it is the task of the analysis to trace such relations.

The ostensive approach is different because many entities are ready-made. This means that they remain constant throughout the analysis. In ostensive models, the problem is neither the integrity of the entity (the variable) nor the type of causation envisaged; what is at stake is primarily whether the relation can be established or not. The question is rarely one of *how* the entity (the variable) may take many forms or *how relationships* can be interdependent. Therefore, in the ostensive approach, the researcher attempts to piece isolated fragmentary evidence together and establish verified propositions that hold across space and time. The ambition is to identify empirical generalisation about propositions that hold (in principle) always and everywhere.

This version of generalisability is alien to ANT. ANT assumes that generalisability is not universally interesting because it does not imply that researchers get more and more certain; generalisability stands in opposition to realism and therefore the more that researchers generalise, the less they describe the world. The more realistic the research, the more new entities have been found to account for observed interaction.

The second principle concerns the *attributes of actors*, including researchers. The performative approach suggests that all actors participate in forming the world. All actors, including researchers and nonhuman actors, interact and thus frame their specific segment of the world. All actors not only operate in the world; they also take part in framing it, translating it, making it accountable, and making it an accomplishment. Thus, they all take part in defining its boundaries and power. Additional propositions made by researchers are, if the research can gain enough support, part of the knowledge around which actors reorganise their world. This knowledge is fragile until it is embedded in the world. Thus, the production and consumption of knowledge happens at the same level.

This is contrasted by the ostensive approach, which, according to Latour, gives research a privileged position in the creation of knowledge. Here, Latour suggests, knowledge is produced by experts who generally know more than, rather than something different from, what is known by the lay actor. Lay actors are often (in the caricature) seen as being caused by culture, capitalism, contingency, or discourse, and therefore they act on the commands of others.

This emptying out of local knowledge is alien to ANT; if actors cannot act, there is no reason to include them in an explanation and, therefore, if external forces dominate the actor systematically, there is no reason to *include the actor in the analysis.*

The third principle proposed by Table 12.1 is that *actors are generally knowledgeable* about their situation. However, this does not mean that they necessarily have an understanding of all the entities that take part in constructing their network. Actors may be able to accomplish their interaction successfully, but typically there will be overflows or leakiness from all networks, and actors within the network may not be able to account for some effects produced in the network. The network is thus no source of stability. Actors construct their world, but do not seal it.

The ostensive contrast is that actors are notoriously bad informants who are assumed to know only part of 'their' world. The confusion thus facing actors is remedied by research which constructs larger contexts within which actors are located and serve functional needs. Actors deliver information, but their idea of causality is not taken into account. They become defined as carriers or as 'roles' necessary for totality outside the reach of the actor, to exist, develop, and thrive.

The process of letting the actor represent something else, such as unencountered environments, political struggles, or cultural predispositions, is alien to ANT. It insists that human and nonhuman actors have to be theorised in relation to their actual causality on the world rather than the causality defined by invisible macro-trends.

The radical consequence of this is the fourth principle, namely, that *no method guarantees* access to the entire world. Method is important not because it inherently produces a better description than the absence of method; method may be an important device with which to persuade certain actors. This persuasion may be genuine persuasion of others about the reasonableness of an account, and 'method' may be an actor in such an endeavour. But method will not produce a truth that is beyond doubt and dialogue. Researchers know some things; laypeople know other things. In practice, these diverse claims meet and are ranked vis-à-vis each other through a process where propositions about the world collide. It is not possible to know a priori when a scientific argument is stronger than a lay argument.

Against this, the ostensive approach maintains that truths have to be separated from untruths. The ability to do this is a methodical procedure by which false claims and double-talk are gradually evicted from our language. This ambition defines research as a process of becoming sure; it is a process of eliminating the wrong propositions.

Such an ambition may appear to be responsible; however, the performative position is that this will most likely kill the best ideas, which will not have been strong from their outset. So, rather than striving towards weeding out mistakes, ANT research is oriented towards finding the surprising relations that may provide new concepts and relations that allow actors another opportunity to speculate about matters of concern to them.

Summarising the message of Table 12.1, researchers encouraged by ostensive ambitions emphasise their preference to test verifiable propositions that are made prior to meeting the field. The key characteristics of the field are hypothesised a priori, and the key to success is the ability to design a comprehensive, ex ante model that is subsequently found to hold up through repeated testing. In important respects, an ostensive approach to the study of social life is an aspirational project founded on hope and belief in evidence-based expertise where it is possible to unlock the 'hidden' laws of social existence. The performative approach, on the other hand, suggests that researchers raise similar questions to those of other actors and find different practical ways of enforcing their definition of what society is about and how it functions. The focus, then, is not on what society 'really' is but on how society is practically constructed and understood. Given that the 'hows' of social fabrication are likely to be highly specific, the kinds of 'generalising' statements thought possible and made are far more subdued, but they are also more progressive because they identify new candidates to be taken into account, for example, in other situations where actors have to enact their world. In effect, performative accounts *add* vocabulary to actors and allow them to include more matters of concern in their repertoire of action.

Table 12.1   Ostensive and Performative Definitions of Reality (Latour 1986, pp. 272–273)

Ostensive Definition	*Performative Definition*
In principle, it is possible to discover the properties which are typical of life in society and could explain the social link and its evolution, though in practice they might be difficult to detect.	It is impossible in principle to define the list of properties that would be typical of life in a society, although in practice it is possible to do so.
Social actors, whatever their size, are in the society defined above; even if they are active, as their name indicates, their activity is restricted since they are only parts of a larger society.	Actors, whatever their size, define in practice what society is, what it is made of, and what is the whole and what is the parts—both for themselves and for others.
The actors in society are useful informants for those who seek the principles that hold society together, but since they are simply parts of society, actors are only informants and should not be relied upon too much because they never see the whole picture.	No assumption is necessary about whether or not any actor knows more or less than any other actor. The 'whole picture' is what is at stake in the practical definitions made by actors.
With the proper methodology, social scientists can sort out the actors' opinions, beliefs, illusions, and behaviour to discover the typical life in a society and piece together the whole picture.	Social scientists raise the same questions as any other actors and find different practical ways of enforcing their definition of what society is about.

3 RULES OF THUMB FOR AN ACTOR-NETWORK ANALYSIS

Actor-network theory thus provides a performative lens for the study of social relations including relations between accounting and inter-organisational relations or networks. It requires the researcher to be mindful of frailty, heterogeneity, multiplicity, and emergence. Our pragmatic rules of thumb for conducting such analyses are presented following:

> *Rule of thumb #1.* Treat all entities (variables, factors, elements, actors, systems, subsystems, etc.) as entities *in search for* boundary, power, and identity which are not given a priory. This means that, even if we can point out entities to be researched before the empirical analysis commences, we should be concerned about investigating whether they behave according to the initial expectations. Any entity may be drawn as a box that contains something, but in the analysis, the box always has to be dotted, because not only its boundaries but also its power and identity may be surprisingly different from our initial expectations. The boundaries can cause considerable surprise when elements that we thought would be part of the entity turn out not to be so. For example (see Mouritsen et al. 2001), it may be that we would expect target costing to convey to a subcontractor the unit cost to be striven after, but then when it turns out in the empirical setting that the target costing procedure only goes to the level of functional analysis, albeit justified as target costing, then we see that the entity can contain fewer elements than we had originally thought. Thus, the boundary is fragile. The power and identity of the entity can also be surprising when the entity works differently than we had anticipated. Using the same example as before, target costing may delegate innovation tasks to the supplier, but the target cost can also 'come back' and require the firm to change its competencies. When the target costing procedure is used to outsource innovation work, the innovative capabilities of the focal firm may change and investments in capabilities to coordinate various outsourced innovation activities may be increased. Here, the power of the target costing procedure is not only to influence suppliers' innovation activities; it also has a surprising influence on the capabilities of the focal firm.

> *Rule of thumb #2:* All entities are considered to be actors, whether they are human or not. Being an actor means being *able to bend the world around itself* and thus make the world speak its language in certain situations. Persons are obviously actors when they make changes to interactions with other people. A manager may persuade a subcontractor to invest more in innovation and then outsource the burden of investments in development work. It is more controversial that ANT also proposes nonhuman entities to be actors. The target costing system itself is an actor when it takes part in persuading the supplier to invest

more in innovation. This does not mean that the target costing system actually has purposes and intensions, but it does mean that it helps to persuade the supplier that it is a good idea to start innovating. The target costing system is an actor in the sense that, in the episode, in the situation, it makes a difference, so that what is proposed by the manager can be strengthened by the calculation provided by target costing. The knowledge and perspective provided by target costing persuades supplier B to engage with firm A.

Rule of thumb #3. An ANT analysis starts from observable practices rather than from an assumed context. The environment, including the culture, class struggle, discourses, and other external forces, are not accorded power before it can be shown how they will influence an interaction. Interaction may coalesce into a proposition about the environment, but the environment is then a summary of interacting entities rather than an external force. The target costing procedure may identify outsourcing of innovation to be important, but it is not possible to say a priori whether this is due to limited investment budgets or dynamic markets; we cannot know before the analysis how the 'wider concern' expresses itself. While it may be that even a limited investment budget can act as a higher market pressure for innovation, market pressures do not predict that the entity mediating this is the limited investment budget. In an ANT analysis, if context is important, it is identified by the analysis, rather than being assumed.

Rule of thumb #4. When analysing the power of entities, follow the actors in practice. Since entities do not have strong boundaries, and since their power and identity are not given a priori to understand their boundaries and power, the researcher has to *follow them in action.* This means that, to understand the power of target costing, the researcher follows over time how it gains identity and power. In the beginning, target costing was calculated as a unit cost; its functional analysis component became a qualitative proposition about the value and character of innovation. Over time, target costing changed both boundaries and identity. This development requires the incorporation of a temporal aspect in the analysis. To follow actors in action requires the researcher to track the changes to entities' boundaries, power, and identity over time. So, changes in C are related to changing relations between A and B. What comes first and how the emergence of change happens is an empirical question that has to be analysed over time. As a consequence, ANT has a preference for a *slow explanation* in the study of the transformation of entities.

Rule of thumb #5. All entities are coloured by their *relationships to other entities.* Entities exist in a network, with reciprocal relations between them. So, an entity is strong because it is involved in defining the boundary, power, and identity of other elements in the network. Generally, we can only understand the relationship between two entities, such as A and B, if we understand how another element, such as C, affects this relationship. In the example of target costing, two firms, A and B, engage in innovation-related activities and A outsources innovation to B. But how should we account for this interaction? By introducing C, the target costing principle, we observe how A and B come together and influence one another. When target costing is introduced, it is possible to observe how, gradually, B becomes increasingly innovation intensive, and A becomes increasingly able to coordinate insourcing of external technology and innovation. So, the relationship between A and B is coloured by the intervention of C. In ANT, any relation, even between two entities, has to be understood as containing at least three elements, because otherwise there will be no network.

These five rules of thumb are our quality criteria for an ANT analysis. They raise a number of interesting issues: Does the analysis consider the frailty of the entities? Does it consider how interactions between entities happen? Does it consider human as well as nonhuman actors? Does it consider the development of relations over time? How does it make up or identify the environment? These questions can guide the development of research questions, and of the approach and methodology adopted to answer them. But they are only rules of thumb, and much variation is to be expected.

4   ACTOR-NETWORK THEORY–BASED RESEARCH IN MANAGEMENT ACCOUNTING AND INTER-ORGANISATIONAL RELATIONS

Researchers using an ostensive approach to inter-organisational networks have been primarily interested in the emergence of the network as an empirical object. That is, they have been interested in the pervasive growth of linkages between autonomous firms in contemporary business. An empirical network is constituted of two elements: formal organisations in need of another's resources and differences in goals. There may be many ways in which firms are interdependent in this way. Supply chains suggest a linear interdependence where firm A receives something from firm B1 which it then transforms and ships off to firm B2. An interfirm network, then, is primarily a bundle of firms that interact in reciprocal ways so that patterns of communication and production can lead from and to any of the firms A, B1, and B2.

In this arrangement, accounting and other administrative technologies are introduced to make coordination possible. They (and other mechanisms of coordination) frame the relationship(s) and influence the mode of communication and interaction between the firms. This is a key feature of network operation because there are autonomous goals to be served. Therefore, as part of each firm, there are mechanisms that enable coordination. These mechanisms develop links. Yet these links are seen primarily from the perspective of A, B1, or B2 as the links lead away from the focal firm in each case, and reach out towards the other firms. The link is not a meta-mechanism that can be imposed by fiat; rather, it is proposed and accepted or rejected between the relevant parties, each of which can opt out of the relationship it they chooses.

In this way the empirical object 'network' has the following characteristics:

- Independent firms with autonomous goals
- A need for others' resources owing to the speed of transformation; the strategy of the firm changes faster than the firm, and therefore there is need for in- and outsourcing of resources.
- A set of coordinating mechanisms that link firms, and are proposed and accepted or rejected in the course of making the network, and
- There is no ultimate controller or manager of the network; however, there may be differences in power and influence between A, B1. and B2.

Thus, an ostensive approach emphasises the need to characterise networks and to test propositions about them. It requires a pre-specification of the key properties to be studied. For example, there might be interest in classifying networks by the type of ties between network entities (A, B, and C) achieved by considering certain principal questions: What do they buy and sell, how often do they trade, and how much do they spend with each other? Researchers might be interested in other questions, such as how many ties are there in total in the network, how often do they change, who has more or less bargaining power, and so on? It is desirable to test propositions about the relationships between characteristics. For example, researchers might be interested in testing the proposition that denser and fast-changing networks will require more coordination and less reliance on formal accounting controls. In an important sense, the central parameters of study are known (albeit hypothetically) before the analysis begins; that is, the key characteristics, the definitions, the relational forms, and so on are understood.

Such an approach is well illustrated in the following example of research on networks and the role of accounting. Van der Meer-Kooistra and Vosselman (2000) propose that networks might be organised into three main forms according to whether they are market-based, bureaucratic-based, or trust-based structures. The market-based structure is said to rely on vigorous supplier competition, regular measurement and evaluation, and the linking of rewards to realised output. In the bureaucratic-based pattern, frequent supervision of suppliers' employees, regular measurement and evaluation, and the link between reward and output are proposed. In contrast to the measurement focus of the market-based and bureaucratic-based patterns, the trust-based pattern is process oriented and culture based. It relies on the principle of procedural fairness and open commitment where rewards are but loosely linked to outputs. These three control structures are taken as given, and what Van der Meer-Kooistra and Vosselman (2000) focus on is explaining how certain transactional characteristics may lead to the cost-effective choice between these structures. For transactions characterised by low asset specificity, low risk, and low performance ambiguity, the market-based structure is proposed, and for those characterised by medium asset specificity, medium risk, and medium performance ambiguity, the bureaucratic-based pattern is suggested. In both the market-based and bureaucratic-based patterns, accounting is inserted to link rewards to output through the establishment of performance measurement systems. The trust-based pattern is reserved for transactions with high asset specificity, high risk, and high performance ambiguity. For this pattern, "open-book costing" arrangements are encouraged.

By contrast, the ANT approach to inter-organisational networks assumes that it is not possible to substitute or condense all the activities of a network with a set of priors. Instead, what is interesting is to identify as many entities that make up the priors as possible; these then become the posteriors of analysis.[2] So, the claim is that to study networks, we need to study how the network is practically accomplished, how the boundary is settled, how the firm is defined, how transactions are fabricated, and how the environment is stabilised. ANT is interested in *slowing down the explanation of the network*. This means that it wishes to look for 'surprising' candidates for explaining the network. It is interested in tracing the multiplicity of entities that take part in making the network what it is, for it is the interactions among these multiple entities that give effects to observed patterns in the network. In these interactive processes, the ANT approach prefers to see accounting as an *interdependent actor*.

The conceptualisation of accounting as an interdependent actor has two implications. First, accounting calculations are *network effects:* effects generated through the interaction of the multiple elements that make up the network. That is, the emergence, operations, and functionality of accounting numbers depend on the interactions between the constituent entities of the network. It is the interactions and the (re)distribution of relations among these constituents that determines whether a target costing system or some other type of accounting method should be adopted, and if so, how. Hence, in order to understand the functioning of accounting controls, researchers need to focus on the location of accounting within a larger set of connections among the constituents of the network.

Second, accounting numbers are not inert objects: when they 'circulate' in an inter-organisational network and become 'engaged' in various forms of negotiations and interactions, they produce effects. Accounting numbers may bring into existence particular stabilised spaces and times, either by acting as an intermediary or as a mediator. As intermediaries, accounting numbers transport meaning, strategies, routines, and power dynamics without transformation. When studied as intermediators, accounting numbers are understood to copy the properties of prospective network partners and represent the concerns facing the network and predict the future functioning of the arrangement. For example, costing reports are able to transport representations of prospective network partners and, through this, they predict the actions and effect of the network.

As mediators, accounting numbers not only transport, but transform, translate, distort, and modify networks and their constituent elements. They have performative effects when they allow other actors to engage in a discourse, to persuade each other, to act on other's interest, to colonise, to mobilise resources, and to speak for others. An accounting report, for instance, may not only represent but also change the meaning of actions, create new identities, redefine the boundaries of networks, and/or (dis)connect entities within networks of relations. In this regard, ANT researchers argue that accounting produces effects. Therefore, by conceptualising accounting as an interdependent actor, ANT researchers seek to focus analytical attention not only on accounting numbers per se, but on their connections and association within the network. It is these connections and associations that determine the performativity of accounting numbers.

When analysing accounting calculations, or more generally inscriptions formulated in financial or nonfinancial terms in reporting systems or in contracts, the ANT approach prefers to look at how these calculations and inscriptions gain power in the episodes and situations where they are materially present.[3] They are studied when they are in action and when they are seen to be influencing something. Accounting numbers gain their power/influence when they are able to embody the network of relations in durable forms and maintain their relational pattern across time and space. That is, the influence of accounting is not only based on the type of accounting that is done, but on what aspects of the relationships are and/or are not captured in the accounting numbers. For what is or is not captured in the accounting numbers may generate disorder, ambiguity, and asymmetry in the network of relationships. Following controversies, struggles, and resistances in the network will thus enable us to appreciate the influence and limits of accounting numbers

The general principles of the ANT research strategy previously outlined have been applied in various ways, hardly any in toto, in existing empirical accounting research. In order to illustrate how they enable new types of conclusions to be drawn, we use some of this material (unfortunately often our own, because the ANT approach is not much used in the study of accounting and inter-organisational control). This set of illustrations helps us to show the breadth of conclusions that the approach can develop. We suggest that many of the conclusions are counterintuitive, and thus have surprising implications about the role of accounting calculations in developing and mediating inter-organisational relations.

In the following sections we will show how accounting calculations can be actors in different types of inter-organisational and network settings and situations.

Understanding Accounting in Inter-Organisational Networks

Chua and Mahama (2007) apply the logic of ANT to the study of accounting in inter-organisational networks. They conceptualised accounting as an interdependent actor, which implied that they had to focus not only on accounting (in abstraction), but all the other constituent entities of the OzCom network they studied. Consequently, the authors identified and followed entities that were connected to the network, including Euro-Com, Atlantic, the Australian government, suppliers A and B, and many other multiple changing entities that were associated with the emergence and ongoing performance of the network. They show that the strength of accounting in the network depended on how it is involved in defining the boundaries, power, and identity of other entities in the network and how other entities in turn define accounting. For instance, in the formative year of the network, where *"time was the essence"*, Atlantic and EuroCom were influential in nominating the suppliers who were to be enrolled into the network, and this nomination was based on their prior interactions with the suppliers in another setting. In this process, accounting was less influential as business was made on a handshake. But as the network took shape, there was controversy over pricing, which led to controversy in the network. It was at this stage that the network engaged in experimentation with successive accounting measures, which eventually meant that the measures introduced altered the relationships within the network.

By focusing on relations within the entire network, Chua and Mahama (2007) have been able to examine how the emergence, operations, and functionality of accounting numbers were coloured by the network relations to which accounting was tied. They show that, in order to understand the performativity of accounting numbers in alliances, we need to understand the location of these numbers within a larger network of relational ties that extends beyond buyers and suppliers. But they also demonstrate that it will be difficult to understand the actions of OzCom and the suppliers without an appreciation of their relationships with the accounting systems that operated within and on the network.

The Agency and Performativity of Accounting Numbers in Inter-organisational Networks

Chua and Mahama (2007) demonstrate that human agency alone cannot be used to explain how networks come about and how they endure through time and space. They argue that networks are not wholly human, but also include a fragile and circuitous web of nonhuman entities. Within these networks, the nonhuman entities possess and do exercise agency that must be accounted for if we are to understand the emergence and situated functionality of networks. In the alliances they studied, accounting numbers, telecommunication network switches, and ready-made prices, among other entities, transformed things, left traces, stood for something, entered into account, and motivated others into action. That is, these entities acted; they organised and negotiated for something within networks of relationships. Chua and Mahama's (2007) study highlights a number of specific ways in which accounting acts.

First, the paper argues that accounting organises and brings about order, albeit temporally. This was demonstrated by the way a "fixed price schedule" allowed OzCom and its suppliers to bed down their supply contracts and how the "business process indicators (BPIs)" allowed the parties to establish provisional links between the efforts of the suppliers and the performance requirements of OzCom. The price schedules and the BPI then became the template for organising discussion between OzCom and its suppliers. Second, they show how accounting inscriptions retain the power to subvert the associations in a network. That is, while they have organising effects, accounting inscriptions also serve as conduits for generating ambiguity and disorder. The cost per subscriber number, the operation break-even analysis, and all other accounting inscriptions that were experimented with all created some form of controversy within the OzCom network. By inscribing and relating things, the BPI used in the OzCom alliance provided visibility over actions that had previously been invisible, and this led to the perception that OzCom was being "ripped off" by its suppliers. Consequently, the OzCom staff used labels such as "exploitative" to describe the character of the suppliers. This became a source of controversy and instability in the alliance. Third, the study also illustrates how accounting (when it interacts with other entities) can empower some actors and allow them to colonise others. The inability of OzCom to predict market growth led to the cost per subscriber measure empowering the suppliers, enabling them to appropriate the benefits of the network disproportionately. Finally, Chua and Mahama (2007) show how accounting inscriptions interact with other actors to recast networks in new ways. In the OzCom network case, it was the inability of accounting to hold together the complex web of technological and human actors that provide conditions of possibilities for not only altering the boundaries of the network, but also changing the power dynamics within the networks by enlisting more actors.

Mouritsen and Thrane (2006) analysed two roles of management technology, such as accounting systems and governance principles, in constituting the spread and boundaries of networks. They conceptualised management technologies as actors that mediate, shape, and construct inter-organisational relations through self-regulating and orchestration mechanisms. Self-regulating mechanisms allow interaction and exchange between partners in a network to occur unobtrusively, while orchestration mechanisms involve the structuring of these interactions. Both mechanisms are organised around various kinds of accounting calculations—such as transfer prices and intellectual capital statements—and around the construction of segmentation in the network that provides it with a topology of centres and peripheries.

Self-regulating mechanisms are oriented towards the exploitation of existing complementary relations and typically allow unobtrusive financial flows between partners. Through preset transfer prices and fees, self-regulating mechanisms help partners to rally around projects and customers without having to debate the distribution of proceeds from these engagements. This is important because much of the ideology of network participation is based on sharing and equality, which makes discussions about pricing and financial relations difficult as they are seen to concern the brutality of the market. Questions about the distribution of financial flows and concerns about ownership can disrupt caring and supporting relations. Self-regulation mechanisms allow the interactions and discussions between partners to be primarily about matters concerning what is offered to an external customer and therefore are more strongly associated with knowledge and competencies than financial relations.

Orchestration mechanisms are obtrusive. They are put in place to facilitate the structuring of network relations and they often represent the network as being more than its partner firms. Orchestration mechanisms distribute competencies across the network with a view to developing new network complementarities. In this way, orchestration mechanisms show how an individual partner firm is not only a part of the network, but also, to a certain degree, subordinate to the network. This can have dramatic effects; for example, in the extreme, it can force some partners to leave the network. Or the network can freeze ownership arrangements when some members of the network are more central to the flow of resources and knowledge than others. Orchestration mechanisms focus on decision making for the network entity, and partners may not benefit equally from the resulting decisions taken. While interaction is autonomous compared to network management when organised around self-regulating mechanisms, orchestration mechanisms typically require a decision at board meetings. Thus, orchestration mechanisms are mobilised narrowly in time and space, whereas self-regulating mechanisms flow more liberally, even if all self-regulating mechanisms have been approved at a board meeting at a certain time. This also means that they can be redone, and they are, but typically during board meetings.

Management control technologies are involved in constituting the boundaries of networks. Showing how network partners are related and by problematising how they should be related, management technology is integral to developing an inside and an outside in the network. This is what makes the network a network enterprise rather than just a network. Taking the form of an enterprise means that the network can reflect on itself with a view to transformation. Since transformation mobilises the network, rather than only individual firms, it is not strange that network partners find the operation of the network hopeful and frightening at the same time.

In addition, Mouritsen (1999) showed that, with the knowledge and information provided by a contribution accounting system, managers in BusinessPrint were prompted to consider how a larger proportion of the cost of the firm could be made variable. Because fixed costs in a contribution margin perspective are invisible, managers attempted to transform them into variable costs. How, though, was this to be brought about? *The answer was to turn* to outsourcing, which would transform fixed costs into variable ones. The contribution accounting system put pressure on managers to redesign their operations to fit the system's image of control.

Interestingly, however, the contribution accounting principle did not exist alone. Production managers proposed an alternative to the problems of invisible costs: namely, to develop an activity-based costing system. Drawing on this principle, managers would problematise visibility differently, as the fixed costs would no longer be a black box of costs, but a set of costs that could be traced via the relevant activities. This alternative calculation produced new types of effects because, in this situation, it was suddenly possible to envisage a much larger proportion of production as being directly controlled by the firm. Consequently, the surge was to insource production activities and to reduce the reliance on subcontractors.

The example shows that the very existence of knowledge presented by accounting calculations influences decision making. This is how accounting calculations are considered to be actors. They even set in motion a set of activities that remakes the boundaries of the firm. Using contribution accounting tended to extend the activities outsourced to suppliers, whereas using activity-based calculations tended to make production activities amenable to direct control within the boundaries of the firm.

A Roadmap and the Coordination of Inter-Organisational Space

In their analysis of mediating instruments, O'Leary and Miller (2007) identified the roadmap involved in coordinating the strategic investments between Intel and others who would use its technology to build new hardware and software. The road map stipulated the timing of the release of new and faster chip technology, its power and performance and its expected cost. This stipulation required Intel to do something, to make significant R&D investments. But Intel needed others to follow, and therefore it also needed a market where the technology could be useful. Faster chip technology would only be interesting if there were a market for it, and this, in turn, required users of the Intel technology to contemplate their product development, not only along the lines of the power of existing chip technology, but also along the proposed changes, to be introduced in the chip technology of tomorrow.

The road map made this coordination possible by describing the technology and making the progression of the power of technology possible. Hardware and software companies using the Intel chips should start developing their services and products in the knowledge that, in the future, the state-of-the-art technology would require very different software than was in operation at that time. The road map was able to make the future stable for the software firm as it made the stronger technology exist even if it still was a diagram rather than a fully fledged working chip. The road map made it real; it made it exist enough for other firms to organise themselves after it.

This is how the road map installed a collective concept of the power of technology. It delivered a simulation but it was not a mere prognosis of technological competence. It was much more a device for organising the future for many participating firms. It aroused their interest in investing, and suddenly the investments performed by the various parties were having an impact on one another. Further down the value chain from Intel, hardware and software firms would invest in such a way that Intel would increase its own investment. The reciprocity between these investments was substantial. Suddenly, through the intervention of the road map, investments were being committed. The road map persuaded participating firms to develop inter-organisational or network relations.

Transformations of the Focal Firm through Accounting for the Network

To learn how far the network goes, follow the actors you are interested in while they perform their activities. Look at the network while it is in action. This requires the researcher to look at things while they unfold. It is through action that things develop before they have been settled in a structure or a culture.

Mouritsen et al. (2001) show how the development of an integrated, lean supply chain occurred. LeanTech, a developer and producer of complex measurement systems for use in the TV industry, had long been interested in customising its products. This was a sensible strategy because the requirements of the various TV stations appeared to be highly variable. Therefore, quite sensibly, LeanTech developed a varied product line using a variety of different components. Customer orientation produced complexity in product development, in manufacturing, and in product variation. The supply chain was long because so many components were needed. This meant that LeanTech had to interact with many firms. Each interaction left a paper trail, and suddenly, by assembling the paper trails, the logistics manager was able to develop a sort of open-book system where he could calculate various economic effects of variability, complexity, and flexibility.

He was able to calculate inventory costs and cost of using a wide variety of components; he was also able to learn about suppliers' capacity utilisation; and he was able to learn about setup costs. In effect, he was able to open up the books of the suppliers and make calculations across the whole supply chain. This knowledge was used to problematise the customer orientation strategy. Rather than allowing the customer to propose any detail of a measurement system, the logistics manager suggested that, if the variation of components was reduced to about a third of its existing level at that time, by using more standard components, the economy of LeanTech could be radically improved. The open-book system inspired a thorough rethink of the firm's strategy. It was still to be close to customers, but a reduction in the hardware components was to be implemented to reduce the variety of components used. How, though, would it be possible to stay customer-oriented and to reduce the variation in component use? Gradually, managers found an answer: Rather than making hardware the entity of differentiation, the software could be a source of differentiation. If the hardware was to be standardised, it would be possible to manage production though a standardised, lean production process. Software could then be the source of customisation, and since it would be possible to develop software that was produced as a single package, it could be customised by barring the customer from certain facilities. Customers would get the entire software package, but not all its functionalities. In effect, the open book motivated the firm to adopt a strategy that involved differentiation outside the company, but which relied on a strategy of standardisation inside it. This changed the identity of LeanTech because it was no longer primarily a customer-oriented firm; it was more a firm managing production processes along a supply chain that spanned several firms.

This story shows how the accounting entity interrelates with other entities, such as innovation. Innovation gains identity by its problematisation in relation to the open-book calculations, and thus in relation to the call to make innovation a new and different issue.

Likewise, rather than assuming a priori that accounting numbers have an impact, and predicting the direction and magnitude of the effects, Chua and Mahama (2007) focused on observing the situated practice of accounting in order to understand what effect, if any, accounting has. They found that accounting has a stabilising effect (but only temporarily) and that the strength of these effects depended to a large extent on the elements that defied accounting calculations. For instance, rather than assume the effects of the cost per subscriber number, Chua and Mahama (2007) followed the practices that enabled or constrained its influence. They found that factors such as market demand and the subscriber base materially affected the performative effects of the cost-per-subscriber number. However, the failure of the cost-per-subscriber number to rein in costs led to experimentation with other accounting numbers. That is, by observing what occurred in practice, Chua and Mahama (2007) show the limits and also highlight the experimental nature of accounting practices. Had the authors assumed the effects of these inscriptions, they probably would not have discovered the rich insights into the performativity of these accounting inscriptions.

Following Accounting in Action

Chua and Mahama (2007) show that, to examine accounting in action, one needs to follow their chain of associations. The authors accomplished this by seeking to focus their analysis on the practical accomplishment of interacting (involving meanings, routines, strategic choices, and power dynamics) within networks and the observable effects of such interactions in time-space specific context. By following the associations in the alliance they were studying, they were able to show how suppliers A and B became enrolled in the network, and to appreciate the role accounting played in the enactment of the network, and the implication of this for the future of the alliance. Also, by following association, Chua and Mahama (2007) were able to study the multiple (and changing) ties and relays that connect both human actors and nonhuman entities and their influence on the choice and operation of accounting controls. In highlighting the importance of analysing networks in terms of associations, Chua and Mahama (2007) were able to bypass the human/nonhuman divide and to bring to the foreground how the two mutually constitute one another through the dynamic processes that bring networks into being and through the machinations that keep the elements of the networks in place, albeit temporally.

Knowledge about Accounting in Networks and Inter-Organisational Relations via Actor-Network Theory

What knowledge does ANT-based research deliver? This form of accounting research has probably resulted in the development of at least four types of management accounting proposition:

First, management accounting calculations or, more generally, inscriptions provide knowledge that often influences interactions. When knowledge is in the accounting format, it is difficult to argue against; it has to be incorporated in managers' responses. In this way, it can be difficult for the researcher to understand managerial action without knowing how the manager is equipped with management accounting knowledge of the situation. When target costing information or open-book accounting emerges, the managers change their priorities and engage in transforming the inter-organisational relationships.

Second, management accounting calculations can develop transformations in an inter-organisational arrangement that may be condoned in subsequent accountability situations. It can motivate the establishment of contracts and sharing rules between a focal firm and its suppliers, which influence not only the relation between the two entities, but also encourage the supplier to change its operations in response to insights obtained from its accounting system and then reapply the parameters stipulated in the focal firm's accounting calculation. For example, OzCom's development of a sharing rule changed the supplier's operations, which led to higher-than-expected costs. As a result of this, the contract and sharing rules had to be changed or abandoned. The inscription may have been adequate at the time of forming the rule, but it was insufficient to account for the strategies developed by the supplier. In consequence, the accounting had to be changed.

Third, inscriptions such as road maps influence investments among a set of firms, by predicting the pace of development in one firm. The road map acted by persuading other firms to develop complementary investments.

Fourth, management accounting calculation often develops the inter-organisational space when these calculations are in opposition within a focal firm. They help to frame and develop the boundary between the firm and its environment. When managers disagree about the proper course of action vis-à-vis suppliers or customers, they not only speak to each other; they also mobilise each other's management accounting calculation. The difference between a contribution accounting principle and activity-based costing is not only, or even primarily, a question about the true representation of the firm. On the contrary, in following the prescriptions of the two calculations through, managers start to make the calculations real by transforming the firm in their images. The contribution of accounting principles is to facilitate managers' strategies for outsourcing activities previously undertaken by the firm because then a larger proportion of the costs become variable and controllable. The contribution principle pushed the firm in a particular direction which is more prone to outsourcing. Activity-based costing can do the opposite: It can suggest ways of increasing the visibility of indirect, fixed costs and, suddenly, it can help to manage costs and develop processes. The more processes under the control of the firm, the more this development will be effective. Thus, activity-based costing can reduce the entities that are outsourced and generally justify a strategy involving insourcing.

5   CONCLUSION

The conclusions drawn earlier might be considered surprising, given the general evidence in the literature. The conclusions make accounting calculations, and inscriptions more generally, much more vivid and much more active than is usually suggested. This means that accounting calculations are not primarily to be thought of as tools that managers can use; instead, they have a more important role as they represent the knowledge that managers possess. Managers become powerless without the knowledge that they obtain from these calculations; furthermore, when this knowledge changes, the managers also change orientation and strategy. However, management accounting calculations are strong only within a situation where they are given power. This means that the contribution accounting system will probably only be strong if, generally, it is recognised that the firm may have a cash flow problem or other concerns that will make the contribution accounting problem relevant. Also, the road map will only be a relevant actor when hardware and software firms have to make huge investments towards a future that is conditioned by the R&D investments. The road map addresses the concern of multiple interconnected investments when decision makers are distributed over a network. So, the network built around the calculation gives it colour and relevance. This is required because, without relevance, the entity will no longer be an interdependent actor in the network.

This type of knowledge is formulated in propositions, but not in empirically generalised statements. Generalisation is often a valued property of research, and yet, it is not a universal good. Not all generalisations are interesting. Consider the following: Firms have accounting systems. Accounting systems use double entry bookkeeping principles. Both of these are (almost universally) true, but they are trivial, so generalisation of this type will not receive much attention. Generalisation has to be interesting to receive attention, and suddenly, generalisation is only an issue when particular interests can be assigned to it. This means that some actors implicitly or explicitly express a need for the generalisation. It is possible, then, to say that generalisation must be related to a matter of concern for it to be of interest to anyone.

What, however, should be the concern in management accounting research? Generalisation is not, as many would say, a mechanism with which to create knowledge about many entities because generalisation, the ANT approach claims, is a procedure of omitting elements from an explanation. Generalisation only focuses on elements that have similar status across cases, but, as ANT suggests, all elements contribute to the affairs that occur in a setting, and not only those that exist in some form in many settings. Therefore, generalisation, a process of reducing the number of facts, is a process of simplification. There is a trade-off where generalisation is concerned, since the more comprehensive the empirical generalisation, the less real the proposition.

It would be folly to deny a constructive role to empirical generalisation, but it would also be folly to assume that such generalisation will account for all entities in time and space. The ANT approach offers another account of the relevance of descriptions of the real, and this is based on the surprises it produces. By describing how an accounting system equips a manager with knowledge, and perhaps even with a motive in certain networks, ANT-based research provides surprises that identify new candidates with

312 *Jan Mouritsen, Habib Mahama, and Wai Fong Chua*

which to explain the development of an issue such as inter-organisational relations. ANT helps us to become surprised. This surprise is interesting and relevant not because it describes all cases, but because it offers new candidates to explain how management accounting becomes powerful. It is not difficult to generalise this, though, because the five rules of thumb described at the beginning of this chapter are large-scale generalisations. But the power is in the detail when new vocabularies are found, when new relations are found, when new contexts are found. These can be items of knowledge actors can use to meet their field anew. This can lead to reflection, which, in turn, will influence other settings and bring about change there. This knowledge is performative rather than ostensive. If properly equipped in a network, it performs and transforms new settings, rather than simply describing them.

NOTES

1. Target costing is a cost management process/technique that determines a market-based cost target at which products with specified functions and quality are to be produced to generate desired profits.
2. Priors are the entities assumed to be significant before an analysis begins and posteriors are second step analyses that focus on examining the associations through which entities gain form and significance.
3. Inscriptions are textual materials (e.g., reports, contracts, etc.) that are generated (or mobilised) and circulated within a network of relationships with the aim of influencing the thoughts and actions of members of the network.

BIBLIOGRAPHY

Chua, W. F., and Mahama, H. 2007. The effect of network ties on accounting controls in a supply alliance: Field study evidence. *Contemporary Accounting Research* 24: 47–86.
Håkansson, H., and Lind, J. 2004. Accounting and network coordination. *Accounting, Organizations and Society* 29: 51–72.
Katz, D., and Kahn, R. L. 1966. *The social psychology of organizations.* New York: Wiley.
Latour, B. 1986. The powers of association. In *Power, actions and belief—a new sociology of knowledge,* ed. Law, J. 264–280. London: Routledge and Kegan Paul.
Latour, B. 2005. *Reassembling the social: An introduction to actor-network-theory.* Oxford: Oxford University Press.
Morgan, G., and Sturdy, A. 2000. *Beyond organizational change.* Basingstoke, UK: Macmillan.
Mouritsen, J. 1999. The flexible firm: Strategies for a subcontractor's management control. *Accounting, Organizations and Society* 24: 31–35.
Mouritsen, J., Hansen, A., and Hansen, C. 2001. Inter-organizational controls and organizational competencies: Episodes around target cost management/

functional analysis and open book accounting. *Management Accounting Research* 2: 221–244.

Mouritsen, J., and Thrane, S. 2006. Accounting, network complementarities and the development of interorganisational relations. *Accounting, Organizations and Society* 31: 241–275.

O'Leary, T., and Miller, P. 2007. Mediating instruments and making markets: Capital budgeting, science and the economy. *Accounting, Organizations and Society* 32: 701–734.

Van der Meer-Kooistra, J., and Vosselman, E. G. J. 2000. Management control of interfirm transactional relationships: The case study of industrial renovation and maintenance. *Accounting, Organizations and Society* 25: 51–77.

13 Accounting in Inter-Organisational Relationships—The Institutional Theory Perspective

Robert W. Scapens and Evangelia Varoutsa

1 INTRODUCTION

In recent years, institutional theory has had a major impact on research in a wide variety of fields within the social sciences, including economics, sociology, political science, organisational theory, public administration, and also accounting. There is an extensive body of literature on institutional theory, which has been well summarised elsewhere (see, for instance, Nooteboom 1999; Brinton et al. 2001; Scott 2001). In the accounting literature, three particular types of institutional theory have had significant influences on accounting research, and especially on management accounting research. These are generally referred to as new institutional economics (NIE), old institutional economics (OIE), and new institutional sociology (NIS). However, with the exception of transaction cost economics (TCE), which is a particular branch of NIE, institutional theory has not been widely used to study accounting in inter-organisational relationships. Thus, the primary aim of this chapter is to explore how institutional theory could be used in such studies.

As there is no agreed definition of inter-organisational relationships, we will follow Oliver (1990), who defined inter-organisational relationships as "the relatively enduring transactions, flows, and linkages that occur among or between an organization and one or more organizations in its environment" (p. 241). However, in the literature, a wide variety of terms is used to refer to inter-organisational relationships, such as alliances, strategic alliances, inter-firm networks, collaborations, cooperative agreements, co-alignments, partnerships, business groups, joint ventures. From time to time in this chapter we will refer to writers who use such terms, and so, in referring to their work, we will use their own terms to refer to an inter-organisational relationship.

As the research using TCE to study accounting in inter-organisational relationships is reviewed in Chapter 10 of this book, we will not cover TCE (or NIE) in detail here. However, in order to distinguish the various forms of institutional theory in this chapter, we will contrast NIE with both OIE and NIS. We will also discuss the ways in which NIS, in particular, has been used in organisation theory to study collaborations and inter-organisational relationships more generally, and we will discuss the small number of studies which have used institutional theory to study inter-organisational accounting. Finally, we will point to the possibilities for future research using institutional theory to explore accounting in inter-organisational relationships.

In this chapter, we will first review the key features and differences amongst OIE, NIE, and NIS and indicate how research within these different strands of institutional theory is beginning to merge, and we will also indicate how structuration theory fits into this field of research. After briefly mentioning how institutional theory has been used to study accounting within organisations, we will describe some of the ways in which institutional theory (more specifically, OIE and NIS) have been used to study various types of inter-organisational relationships. This will enable us to indicate the potential of institutional theory for studying inter-organisational accounting, which will be explored in more detail in the subsequent section. Although there are only a relatively small number of studies that have adopted this perspective, we believe there is considerable potential for taking an institutional perspective in studying accounting in inter-organisational relationships.

2 INSTITUTIONAL THEORY

As we indicated earlier, there are different strands of institutional theory; however, they share a common recognition that organisations and decision making within organisations cannot be understood without considering the institutional context. In other words: institutions matter; but what are defined as institutions differ, and to a large extent, this distinguishes the different strands of institutional theory. Following we will briefly describe the nature and origins of the different strands of institutional theory which have had a particular influence on accounting research, and then, again briefly, outline how they have been used in management accounting research. This will provide an introduction to the use of institutional theory in studying inter-organisational relationships which will be discussed in the next section.

Old Institutional Economics (OIE)

The origins of OIE can be found in the work of the early American institutionalists[1]; in particular, Thorstein Veblen, Wesley Mitchell, John R. Commons, and Clarence Ayres (see Hodgson 1989; Langlois 1989). Although there were important differences in their views, they were all critical of the unrealistic assumptions of neoclassical economic models and the failure of conventional economists to study change. In particular, they rejected methodological individualism and its assumptions of rational economic behaviour. In more recent times there has been a renaissance of OIE, with contemporary writers seeking to build on the contributions of those early institutionalists (see, for instance, Hodgson 1989, 1993; Langlois 1989; Rutherford 1994). This more recent work is sometimes referred to as neo-OIE (Ribeiro and Scapens 2006), but for present purposes we will continue to label it as OIE.

As mentioned earlier, there are various definitions of institutions—even within OIE (and the other versions of institutional theory). But for the present purpose of outlining the OIE perspective, it will be sufficient to refer to an entry which appeared in 1932 in the *Encyclopaedia of the Social Sciences*.[2] This referred to an institution as "a way of thought or action of some prevalence and permanence, which is embodied in the habits of a group or the customs of a people" (Hamilton 1932, p. 84). This definition recognises the sociocultural character of an institution and emphasises the importance of habitual behaviour. Whereas habits are at the level of the individual, routines involve groups and, as such, are formalised or institutionalised habits (Hodgson 1993). Institutions impose form and social coherence upon human activity through the production and reproduction of habits of thought and action (see Scapens 1994).

One of the criticisms of the work of the early institutionalists was that it failed to produce a coherent body of theory. It is probably fair to say that even the more recent work in OIE has still not developed a body of theory. Instead, OIE can be characterised as a methodology, rather than a theory. Nevertheless, there is now a coherent and extensive research program that seeks to provide an alternative to traditional mainstream economics (Rutherford 2000). This research programme rejects the methodological individualism of neoclassical economic theory that portrays the individual actor as atomistic, passive, and rational.

New Institutional Economics (NIE)

NIE also recognises the importance of institutions. But in contrast to OIE, rather than rejecting the assumptions of neoclassical economics, NIE has sought to adapt them in order to bring institutions into mainstream economic analysis. However, within NIE, there are various strands of research, and work has been conducted in such areas as property rights and common law, public choice processes, as well as organisations; and a number of different theoretical approaches have been developed, including agency theory, game theory, and transaction cost economics (TCE). Although a detailed discussion of the various types of NIE is beyond the scope of this chapter, it is relevant to note that TCE has had a significant influence on accounting research, and more specifically on accounting research in an inter-organisational context (see Chapter 10).

As Hodgson (1999, p. 34)[3] noted: "it is a defining characteristic of the 'new' institutional economics that institutions act primarily as constraints upon the behaviour of given individuals". As such, a key difference between NIE and OIE is that, whereas OIE sees institutions as endogenous, NIE tends to treat them as exogenous variables. However, new institutionalists criticise OIE's focus on "behaviouristic" rather than rational choice models, and its failure to emphasise economising and improving economic efficiency (see North 1978; Coase 1983; Williamson 1987). On the other hand, OIE writers criticise NIE as too abstract and too theoretical, and they are critical of its more extreme and reductionist approach to individualism (Hodgson 1988). Nevertheless, despite these differences, NIE and OIE both recognise that institutions are important, and that they tend to be ignored in more orthodox economics (Rutherford 1989). But whereas OIE treats institutions as "taken-for-granted" assumptions which exist at the cognitive level, NIE regards institutions as the external rules or constraints that shape economic behaviour.

New Institutional Sociology (NIS)

As its name suggests, NIS emerged from the field of sociology rather than economics. Nevertheless, there are clear overlaps with OIE, since both emerged as a response to the "orthodox" or "rational" theoretical approaches in their respective fields. However, the early work in NIS differs from OIE because its focus was on the influence of the broader social, political, and economic institutions. In general, NIS asks how organisations are influenced by the institutions in their environments. Much of the research documents the impact of the state and professions on organisations, and traces the diffusion of new organisational forms and practices. For this purpose, institutions are defined as "those social patterns that, when chronically reproduced, owe their survival to relatively self-activating social processes" (Jepperson 1991, p. 145). The focus of much of this work in NIS is on how institutions shape the patterning of organisations and lead to homogeneity in organisational fields.

According to NIS, it is the search for legitimacy and resources that explains why specific organisational forms and procedures are diffused across organisations operating in similar settings, for example, similar environments (Scott 1992), societal sectors (Scott and Meyer 1992), or organisational fields (DiMaggio and Powell 1983). DiMaggio and Powell (1983) suggested that this process of diffusion can create pressures that lead organisations to become isomorphic with other organisations in their institutional field. Competitive isomorphism (Hannan and Freeman 1977), for instance through market forces, is not dismissed, but the emphasis is placed instead on three types of institutional isomorphism—coercive, normative and mimetic—that highlight the social and political dimensions of the environment in which organisations are located. The early NIS work tended to emphasise the structural nature of institutions. In other words, how organisations are moulded by institutional forces external to the organisation.

Rather less attention was given to the way in which institutions are created and how they change. The more recent work, however, is now beginning to explore such issues, as we will discuss following.

Although we have previously outlined what was initially three different strands of institutional theory, more recently the boundaries between them have started to dissolve. Next we will indicate some of the ways in which these different strands, and specifically OIE and NIS, are coming closer together.

Practice Variations

As we indicated earlier, a considerable amount of research has been conducted using NIS to explore how organisations respond to pressures from the institutional environment (for a summary, see Scott 2001). This research studied the convergent (isomorphic) processes through which organisations respond to institutional pressures and thereby secure legitimacy from the external stakeholders who provide their resources. The early work in NIS distinguished between the technical and institutional pressures, and focused extensively on the loose coupling of the systems designed to secure legitimacy (i.e., to respond to institutional pressures) and the systems used to protect the technical core of the organisation (and to respond to technical pressures). In much of this work, organisations were portrayed as passive entities seeking legitimacy by conforming to environmental pressures.

However, some writers have argued that organisations are not necessarily passive; they can act strategically in their response to institutional pressures (see Oliver 1991). As such, they may purposefully comply with external requirements by adopting specific formal structures and procedures, but in a manipulative fashion, in order to gain legitimacy and thereby secure the resources that are essential for their survival (Edelman 1992). However, the notion of decoupling these formal structures and procedures from their actual operations has been criticised in another stream of NIS research (see, e.g., Zucker 1977). It is argued that such decoupling conflicts with Berger and Luckmann's (1967) definition of an institution as "a reciprocal typification of habitualized action by types of actors" (p. 54), on which Meyer and Rowan (1977) drew in their seminal paper. Tolbert and Zucker (1996) claim there is "an inherent ambiguity in their underlying phenomenological argument, because the definition of 'institutionalised' itself contradicts the claim that institutional structures are apt to be decoupled from behaviour. *To be* institutional, structures must generate action. Consequently, institutional theory should focus on the institutions which shape the day-to-day activities and behaviours in organisations. As we point out following, such a focus is quite consistent with the way OIE has been used in management accounting research. But before doing that, we will note some of the more recent developments in NIS, which are bringing closer together the concerns of NIS and OIE (or, more specifically, the way OIE is used in management accounting research).

In more recent years, the early NIS research has been criticised for:

1. Treating institutional (or legitimacy) and technical (or economic) pressures as mutually exclusive, and failing to recognise that both types of pressures can be interdependent and confront organisations simultaneously (Dacin 1997; Scott 2001; for an accounting perspective, see Hopper and Major 2007). More specifically, economic and market pressures can be also institutionalised—that is, taken for granted. For example, in public sector organisations in many parts of the world, it seems to be increasingly accepted that business-like forms of management and increased competition can lead to more efficient public services.

2. Failing to recognise the processes through which institutions are created, adapted, transposed, and/or discarded (Scott 2001; Dacin et al. 2002; Seo and Creed 2002). In recent years a branch of NIS has become concerned with the idea of institutional entrepreneurship (Leca et al. 2006). This work has focused specifically on how institutions can be changed and on the role of individual actors (agents) in the processes of institutional change.

3. Failing to recognise power, agency, and interest at the organisational level (Scott 2001; Dillard et al. 2004; Lounsbury 2007). Recent research recognises that organisations comprise many different groups with different interests and power. So responses to institutional pressures are not automatic 'organisational responses', nor even necessarily a decision taken by the senior managers. They are more likely to be a complex process of social interaction between the various interest groups in the organisation (e.g.,, see Nor-Aziah and Scapens 2007).

Following such criticisms, NIS research has become concerned with the processes within organisations through which they respond to external institutional pressures. This has moved the focus of NIS away from processes of isomorphism and questions of why organisations appear homogenous, and towards the processes that shape practices within individual organisations (and organisational fields) and give rise to organisational heterogeneity. For example, Lounsbury (2007, 2008) calls for a greater focus on 'practice variations'. He argues that different logics can shape organisational responses to institutional pressures and, consequently, there can be variations in the way organisations respond. This does not mean that these responses are irrational; on the contrary, they are quite rational given the particular logic(s) within the organisation. Such research has notable similarities with the way in which OIE research has developed within the field of accounting research, and especially management accounting research, as we will see following.

Institutional Change

As we have just indicated, recent work in NIS has begun to explore the processes that shape practices within organisations. The studies of accounting change which draw on OIE also seek to understand processes of organisational change (and why organisations can be resistant to change). Although there are differences in the NIS and OIE studies, they can complement each other and, increasingly, they are focusing on similar issues. As we mentioned earlier, OIE developed in opposition to the assumptions of neoclassical economics, and it recognises that individuals operate in a specific social setting in which institutionalised rules and values, rather than some generalised principle of economic rationality, shape behaviour (Rutherford 1994; Scapens 1994). Burns and Scapens (2000) define an institution as "the shared taken-for-granted assumptions which identify categories of human actors and the appropriate activities and relationships" (p. 8). Such institutions can be located within as well as outside the organisation. In the majority of studies that use OIE to study management accounting change, the primary focus is on the institutions within the organisation (in the form of take-for-granted assumptions) rather than the institutions in the broader environment, which are the primary focus of studies that use NIS.

In studies of management accounting change, researchers have used OIE to explore the role of routines in shaping processes of organisational change. For example, Burns and Scapens (2000) developed a framework for studying management accounting change in which routines provide the conceptual linkage between actions and institutions. As well as drawing on such OIE writers as Hodgson (1988) and Tool (1993), their framework also drew on work from other areas, such as the evolutionary economics of Nelson and Winter (1982), Giddens's (1979, 1984) structuration theory, and certain strands of NIS (especially the work of Barley and Tolbert 1997; see also Barley 1986). More specifically, Burns and Scapens (2000) adapted the framework that had been developed in NIS by Barley and Tolbert (1997). Both sets of writers had been greatly influenced by the work of the social theorist Anthony Giddens, and especially his structuration theory. In view of the influence of structuration theory on some of the strands of NIS and the research which uses OIE to study management accounting change, it will be helpful to make some brief comments on Giddens's work.

In a paper in 2002 (to which we will return later), Greenwood et al. commented that NIS research has been primarily concerned to show how organisations respond in a similar fashion to institutional norms, while: "Much less attention has been given to understanding how the effects of isomorphism are brought about" (p. 58). This was despite a paper, written as long ago as 1980, in which two of the three authors of the 2002 paper contributed, and in which they examined "the problem of explaining how organisational structures change over time" (see Ranson et al. 1980, p. 1). In that earlier paper they referred to the work of, among others, Giddens (1976, 1977), arguing that *framework* and *interaction* (or in Giddens's terms, *structure* and *agency*) should not be seen as in opposition. Instead, they suggested that a more fruitful perspective would be to focus "upon the interpenetration of framework and interaction as expressing a relationship that is often mutually constituting and constitutive" (Ranson et al. 1980, p. 2). This draws on the ideas of the duality of structure, which Giddens subsequently consolidated in his seminal book, *The Constitution of Society* (1984), which set out in detail his structuration theory.

In their 1980 paper, Ranson et al. had talked about processes of organisational structuring, but in 2002 Greenwood et al. changed the terminology to "structuration", which they described as a "process of gradual maturity and specification of roles, behaviours and interactions of organisational communities" (p. 59). In other words, this is the process by which institutions emerge through repeated interactions within and between organisations. As we will see next, accounting researchers have drawn on both structuration theory and institution theory in management accounting research.

Institutional Theory in Management Accounting Research

Giddens's structuration theory has been used in accounting research since the mid-1980s, primarily to study management accounting change (see, e.g., Roberts and Scapens 1985; Macintosh and Scapens 1990, 1991; Scapens and Roberts 1993; Lawrence et al. 1997; Dillard et al. 2004; and Seal et al. 2004[4]). In this work, attention is given to Giddens's modalities of structuration—namely, signification (meaning), legitimation (morality), and domination (power). For Giddens, these modalities stand between agency and structure. As indicated earlier, agency and structure presuppose each other; structure constrains agency, as well as being produced and reproduced through it. However, according to Giddens, structure exists only in the form of memory traces, although it is manifest in social practices.

Drawing on the work of Barley and Tolbert (1997), Burns and Scapens (2000) replaced Giddens's notion of structure with institutions, and added a time dimension to provide a framework describing the process of institutionalisation. The main concern of their framework was to understand the processes through which management accounting rules and routines can come to be institutionalised within the organisation; in other words, how management accounting practices are shaped by the *"taken-for-granted* assumptions which inform and shape the actions of individual actors" (Burns and Scapens 2000, p. 8; emphasis in original).

In the Burns and Scapens framework, management accounting is perceived as a set of rules and routines that, together with other organisational rules and routines, allow for the production and reproduction of organisational life. As such, management accounting systems, for example the budgeting system, carry the values of rationality and financial orientation, which, if taken for granted, can become institutionalised. However, Burns and Scapens (2000) note that not all newly introduced accounting rules and routines will necessarily become institutionalised. In particular, if new management accounting systems and practices (or indeed any other new systems and practices) challenge the prevailing institutions in the organisation, they may not be reproduced and as a result may fail to become an institutionalised basis for actions and interactions. This framework has been used by various researchers to study management accounting change (see, e.g., Burns 2000; Busco et al. 2002; Soin et al. 2002; Burns and Baldvinsdottir 2005; Siti-Nabiha and Scapens 2005; Busco et al. 2006).

As indicated earlier, the Burns and Scapens framework can be located within OIE, but it also draws on, amongst other things, ideas from NIS. A number of other accounting researchers have drawn more directly on NIS to inform their studies of accounting change. In most instances, these researchers have focused on public sector organisations and, in particular, they have explored the introduction of the ideas of new public sector financial management into such areas as education, health care, local government, and, more recently, central government. Initially, such work focused on the processes of normative, mimetic, and coercive isomorphism, and adopted the ideas of decoupling.[5] Initially, it explored the separation of systems designed to secure external legitimacy and those used to manage the organisation, but subsequently it has sought to understand how the conflicting demands of multiple constituencies can be met and how external and internal contradictions can lead to conflict between different functional areas (examples include Johnsen 1999; Brignall and Modell 2000; Collier 2001; Modell 2001, 2003; Nor-Aziah and Scapens 2007). More recent work has begun to focus on practice variations, the way in which broader institutions can shape practices within organisations, and the role of agency (e.g., see Modell 2004; Modell et al. 2007; Modell and Wiesel 2008).

As we indicated earlier, a number of accounting researchers have used NIE, and in particular TCE, to study management accounting change and, more specifically, accounting in inter-organisational relationships. But as this is addressed in Chapter 10 of this book, it is not covered here. Later, we will discuss the few studies which have drawn on OIE and/or NIS to study accounting in inter-organisational relationships. First we will review studies that have drawn on NIS to explore inter-organisational relationships more generally.

3   INSTITUTIONAL THEORY IN STUDYING INTER-ORGANISATIONAL RELATIONSHIPS

In the previous section we reviewed the different strands of institutional theory and mentioned how they have been used in management accounting research. In this section we will explore how institutional theory, and more specifically NIS, has been used to study inter-organisational relationships. We will start by exploring how *collaborations* have been studied from an institutional perspective. The term 'collaborations' covers a broad range of inter-organisational relationships, and their study from an institutional perspective emphasises the diversity of influences that shape such relationships. As we mentioned earlier, NIS has highlighted the importance, for organisations operating in an institutional environment, of securing legitimacy by conforming to environmental pressures. Here, we will look at the importance of legitimacy in inter-organisational relationships and explore the role of trust and power. In so doing, we will seek to draw out the implications of this research for studies of inter-organisational accounting.

Collaborations

As indicated earlier, in studies informed by institutional theory, collaborations encompass a broad range of inter-organisational relationships. For example, Philips et al. (2000) defined a collaboration as "a co-operative relationship among organizations that relies on neither market nor hierarchical mechanisms of control" (p. 24). They argued that institutions supply the rules and resources upon which a collaboration is built, whereas the collaboration itself provides the context for the ongoing procedures of structuration that maintain the institutional (or organisational) field. Thus, to fully understand and explore the dynamics of collaborations (or inter-organisational relationships), it is crucial to examine the institutionalised patterns of rules and routines that are shaped by the institutional environment(s) of the partners. The early research, which adopted an institutional perspective to study collaborations, was inclined to emphasise the objective, external aspects of the institutional environment, and to view "institutional forces [as] another group of pressures that can either promote or impede collaboration" (Sharfman et al. 1991, p. 185). But, as we will see following, the later research has been more concerned with the way in which institutions can shape collaborations and their structuration.

Through their analysis of the formation of a new collaboration in the garment industry, Sharfman et al. (1991) observed that institutional forces can be more important than any explicit cost/benefit incentive. They concluded that the institutional field of a specific inter-organisational relationship comprises not only competitive pressures, but also institutional forces, either of which can promote or prevent the creation of new relationships. So, although TCE might explain the formation of inter-organisational relationships when they are due to competitive motives, it is unlikely to be sufficient for understanding the institutional forces that shape the nature of collaborations.

Philips et al. (2000) argued that "institutional rules and resources can be critical elements in the negotiations that constitute collaboration" (p. 30). Although their paper was analytical, and lacked empirical examples, it provided a structured theoretical framework that highlighted the importance of institutions in studying collaborations. Building on this framework, Lawrence et al. (2002) explored how the characteristics of a collaboration can transform existing institutional fields. Through a longitudinal case study of a small Palestinian nongovernmental organisation, they demonstrated that a collaboration can play a critical role in promoting change in the institutional field through the creation of "proto-institutions". Proto-institutions are the new practices and rules that stem from a specific collaboration, but can come to constitute new institutions which shape subsequent collaborations, provided they diffuse appropriately. Lawrence et al. (2002) emphasised that the interaction, structuration, and information flow of each collaboration can have significant effects on the degree to which a collaboration can initiate the creation of "proto-institutions" and thereby lead to the formation of new institutions. Similarly, Imperial (2005) argued that the shared policies, social norms, and rules that govern collaborations can become institutionalised and then reproduced in new collaborations. If the participants in every new collaboration had to determine new forms of governance, it would be a very complex and problematic matter, and so the institutionalised practices are likely to be reproduced.

In a study of international alliances, Parkhe (2003) adopted an institutional perspective to explore how relationships can be integrated even when the partners are drawn from widely dispersed institutional fields. In such relationships, he argued, the more diverse the institutional fields from which the partners are drawn, the greater the challenges that the inter-organisational relationship has to face. In his paper, Parkhe (2003) distinguished between social (meta), national (macro), corporate (meso), and operating level (micro) influences to categorise the exogenous and endogenous institutional influences that can shape inter-organisational relationships. This emphasises the complexity of the process of institutionalisation, and also the diversity of the institutional influences which need to be recognised when studying inter-organisational relationships.

This research demonstrates the importance of institutions in shaping the nature of collaborations. The institutionalised patterns of rules and routines provide the context in which collaboration becomes possible. However, this is not a one-way process. The practices and norms of existing collaborations can become institutionalised and thereby create the institutions which shape new collaborations. Thus, we should not see institutions simply as the objective external aspects of the institutional field, but instead recognise their structuration through the interactions taking place in ongoing collaborations. However, this can be a very complex process, with the interaction of meta-, macro-, meso-, and micro-level influences. As such, studies of inter-organisational relationships need to look beyond the economic context and explore the complexity and diversity of the institutions which shape, and are shaped by, those relationships. Lawrence et al. (2002) emphasised the importance of information flows in the shaping and structuration of the inter-organisational relationships. This suggests a need for studies of inter-organisational *accounting*—in its broadest sense. Such studies could look at the flows of information, as well as processes of accounting control. However, there have been relatively few such studies; we will discuss those that have been conducted in Section 4. However, in the institution theory literature rather more attention has been given to the *legitimacy* of the relationship. Although this probably reflects the legacy of the early research in NIS (described earlier), which tended to focus on the search for legitimacy in institutional environments, it also emphasises the importance of legitimacy for inter-organisation relationships.

Legitimacy

A substantial part of the institutional research into the various types of inter-organisational relationships is concerned with the issue of legitimacy. Such research recognises that the legitimacy of any such relationship is critical to its success and can be a source of competitive advantage. For example, Human and Provan (2000) explored how legitimacy is created through the evolution of inter-organisational relationships and argued that it is crucial to their success. They studied multilateral networks, which involve direct interactions among many member organisations that may have never interacted with one another before. These networks also often have an administrative entity that coordinates the interactions between the member organisations. Defining legitimacy as "a generalised perception that the actions, activities and structure of a network are desirable and appropriate" (p. 328), Human and Provan (2000) observed that different networks adopt different strategies to secure legitimacy in their institutional environments. By analysing two case studies of the formation and evolution of networks in the same industry, they found that networks can achieve legitimacy either through internal (inside-out) legitimacy building within the network (the more successful case) or through external (outside-in) legitimacy building in the institutional field (which in this instance was the less successful case). They argued that legitimacy building is critical to network success. Networks have to establish their legitimacy and, even though the inside-out strategy is likely to be the more successful, all networks have to address both internal and external factors, through the adoption of a dual legitimacy-building strategy that creates legitimacy both inside the network and within the wider institutional field.

Kumar and Andersen (2000) also argued that legitimacy is important for the success of inter-organisational relationships. They explored the connections between legitimacy and meanings. By meanings, they refer to the "interpretative significance" (p. 238) of the relationship to each partner. They identified three types of meanings and related each of these to three types of legitimacy (in each case, these are referred as pragmatic, moral, and cognitive, respectively). Pragmatic legitimacy refers to the recognition that the relationship is in the interests of the partners; moral legitimacy refers to the recognition that the relationship is the 'right' thing to do; and cognitive legitimacy refers to the recognition that the relationship is both natural and necessary. A subsequent paper by Kumar and Das (2007) developed these ideas further. Defining inter-partner legitimacy as "the mutual acknowledgement by the alliance partners that their actions are proper in the developmental processes of the alliance" (p. 1426), they argued that different types of inter-organisational relationships require different types of legitimacy and different levels of effort to attain legitimacy. Using the specificity of the investment, the extent of mutual dependence, and the chances of opportunistic behaviour (see Das and Teng 1998) to distinguish between different types of inter-organisational relationships, Kumar and Das (2007) argued that joint ventures require the highest level of effort to attain all three types of legitimacy, followed by minority equity alliances, and the least level of effort is required for nonequity alliances.

Dacin et al. (2007) also studied the importance of securing legitimacy in an inter-organisational relationship; but they identified five different types of legitimacy: market, relational, social, investment, and alliance. Market legitimacy relates to the rights and qualifications to conduct business in a particular market; relational legitimacy to the worthiness to be a partner; social legitimacy to conformity to social rules and expectations; investment legitimacy to the worthiness of the business activity; and alliance legitimacy to the validity or appropriateness of the relationship (see Table 1 in Dacin et al. 2007, p. 171). They argued that, without legitimacy in all these five respects, partners are likely to be denied access to crucial markets, and consequently the competitive advantage of the relationship is likely to be jeopardised.

These studies highlight (1) the importance of the legitimacy of the inter-organisational relationship for both the partners within the relationship and the other actors within the wider institutional field, and (2) the different types of legitimacy that are needed for a successful inter-organisational relationship. The interesting questions for accounting researchers are whether inter-organisational accounting can enhance legitimacy within and/or outside the network, and whether inter-organisational accounting can particularly enhance specific types of legitimacy. For example, is inter-organisational accounting more likely to enhance pragmatic legitimacy within the network, and/or its moral legitimacy outside the network (Kumar and Andersen 2000), or is it more likely to enhance market and investment legitimacy (Dacin et al. 2007)?

However, as Kumar and Das (2007) have pointed out, it is important to distinguish between legitimacy and trust. The fundamental distinction is that, while legitimacy implies a sharing of values and norms, trust implies the predictability of behaviour. Thus, "legitimacy, unlike trust, provides a more durable foundation for success, as a relationship founded on legitimacy is embedded in a shared view that the relationship is a proper one" (Kumar and Das 2007, p. 1432). Nevertheless, trust remains an important concept in the study of inter-organisational relationships, as we will see next.

Trust and Power

Social mechanisms, including trust, are generally regarded as important elements in business relationships (see, e.g., Zucker 1986; Sako 1992) because they determine the balance between cooperation and competition. Some writers link the concept of trust with power, as both can promote or limit the potential for cooperation (Lane and Bachmann 1997). However, the existing literature provides few theoretical analyses that combine trust and power, and even fewer that provide empirical evidence in the context of inter-organisational relationships. An exception is the work of Lane and Bachmann in 1997, which highlights the role of institutions and trade associations in the creation and shaping of inter-organisational relationships. Building on the work of Luhmann (1979), they considered *trust* to be a code of social interaction, and *power* the "functional equivalent" of trust. Drawing on data from the British and German kitchen furniture and mining machinery industries, they argued that in cases where 'strong' institutions exist (e.g., industrial associations and legal regulations), trust can become a social mechanism for coordination. In contrast, in environments where there are only 'weak' institutions, power may substitute for trust, because "system-power is a precondition for system-trust, rather than a different mode of regulation of interaction" (p. 250).

Marchington and Vincent (2004) went further and explored the role of trust and power at both the institutional and the interpersonal levels, and examined how trust and power influence inter-organisational relationships. Testing their framework through a case study of a manufacturing company, where they studied both its supply chain and its outsourcing activities, they argued that different factors encourage the inter-organisational relationship and its day-to-day management. They proposed a theoretical framework that comprises forces at three distinct, but interrelated, levels: institutional, organisational, and interpersonal. At the institutional level, which they argued is generally neglected in the literature on inter-organisational relationships, Marchington and Vincent (2004) drew on NIS to explore the influences that trade associations and government regulations have on such relationships. In addition, they recognised that inter-organisational relationships can be influenced by institutions at the industry level. However, they stressed that these (external) institutions may be modified *within* organisations (i.e., by organisational level forces). The final level, the interpersonal forces, stems from "backstage interpersonal dynamics", where "boundary-spanning agents" deal with day-to-day issues of management. This, again, emphasises the importance of recognising the influence of the diverse institutional forces (both internal and external) when studying inter-organisational relationships.

So, for accounting researchers, there are interesting questions concerning the roles of inter-organisational accounting (and information flows more generally) in shaping the nature and structuration of inter-organisational relationships. Specifically, there are questions related to the role of inter-organisational accounting in enhancing the legitimacy of relationships, both to the partners and to the other actors in the organisational field. There are also questions related to the trust and/or power needed to enable the relationship to emerge and to survive. In addressing such questions, it is important that the complexity and diversity of the institutional setting, which has been revealed in the studies outlined previously, is fully recognised. As we will see in the next section, these institutional influences have not been widely studied in the management accounting literature, although there are some studies of inter-organisational accounting which have adopted an institutional theory perspective. However, as we will point out in Section 5, there is much that remains to be done.

4   INSTITUTIONAL THEORY AND ACCOUNTING IN INTER-ORGANISATIONAL RELATIONSHIPS

As mentioned earlier, although various studies have used institutional theory to explore inter-organisational relationships, there are very few that focus on inter-organisational accounting. Following a general Google Scholar search, and a more targeted search of *Accounting, Organizations and Society*; *Management Accounting Research*; and *Accounting, Auditing and Accountability Journal* over the period 2000 to 2008, we identified only two papers which explicitly use institutional theory to explore inter-organisational accounting (and control). However, we also identified a further study which examines the way trust is constituted in inter-organisational relationships. As trust is an important issue in institutional theory, we will also review that paper in this section. We recognise that there have been far more studies that have used transaction cost economics to study inter-organisational accounting, but as these are discussed in Chapter 10 we will not review them here. The limited number of studies which we identified in the existing research literature leaves considerable scope for using the forms of institutional theory described in this chapter to study accounting in inter-organisational relationships (as we will discuss in the next and final section of this chapter).

The studies that we review next indicate the direction in which such research could progress. The first of these asks how inter-organisational cost management practices emerge, drawing on (and developing) some of the ideas of old institutional economics (OIE) previously described. This study explores the evolutionary processes within the focal organisation and both its suppliers and its customers, although it does recognise that organisational activity is embedded in the wider social cultural beliefs and values. The second study, however, looks at the wider institutions and reflects on the new institutionalised practices stemming from governmental initiatives on inter-organisational relationships. It shows that inter-organisational accounting can comprise a set of institutionalised practices, which are viewed as 'expert systems' by the participants in inter-organisational relationships.

In the first paper, Coad and Cullen (2006) adopted what they term "evolutionary thinking" to explore the emergence of inter-organisational cost management. Drawing on the works of Veblen (1898, 1909), Penrose (1959), and Nelson and Winter (1982), they identified three central concepts in evolutionary economics: institutionalisation, capabilities, and learning and change. Using these, they extended the Burns and Scapens (2000) framework to explore organisational capabilities to facilitate learning and change. In the context of inter-organisational relationships, these capabilities "might include rules and routines for inter-organisational budgeting and performance measurement systems, target costing, value chain analysis, activities-based costing and open-book accounting" (Coad and Cullen 2006, pp. 349–350). These rules and routines will be linked to the structural properties of institutions and can become the taken-for-granted assumptions which inform the actions of the actors who take part in inter-organisational relationships.

Based on a longitudinal case study of a small UK-based company that produces and markets customised school clothing, they examined how inter-organisational cost management (IOCM) practices emerge over time. They defined IOCM practices as the common efforts of buyers and suppliers aimed at reducing the cost and increasing the value of the product or activity of the supply chain. In their research they studied both sides of the supply chain: the suppliers and customers of their focal company.

This study highlights the institutions and capabilities that underpin the emergence of IOCM practices, the organisational routines promoting (or preventing) them, and the role of agents in the change process. Coad and Cullen showed how the introduction of a simple heuristic, based on value chain analysis, provided the basis for search routines which eventually led to 'unpredictable' modifications to activities, and to cost and organisational boundaries, that is, resulting in modifications that could not be foreseen at the start of the search process. The first stage relied on imitation. By drawing on process mapping and activities management practices previously employed in another company, the management successfully reduced their own costs and this encouraged them to explore their use of IOCM. The search routines developed the organisational capabilities and provided the basis for learning and change in cost management practices, practices that were subsequently replicated across the supply chain.

330 Robert W. Scapens and Evangelia Varoutsa

In contrast to the more traditional economic approaches, which focus on opportunity costs and marginal analyses of *known* alternatives, the heuristic approach illustrated in this study explains how *unknown* (i.e., unpredictable) outcomes can emerge. Coad and Cullen recognised the importance of path dependency, but argued that it lacks explanatory power and, hence, greater consideration should be given to *heuristics* in explaining evolutionary approaches (p. 363). Their paper also illustrates the blurring between intra- and inter-organisational phenomena. The company studied by Coad and Cullen first mimicked the practices of another company, and the routines which it had developed internally were subsequently replicated elsewhere in the supply chain.

Another significant point raised in their paper is related to the stability of inter-organisational relationships. In contrast to previous studies (such as those of Van der Meer-Kooistra and Vosselman 2000; and Dekker 2003), which attribute stability in inter-organisational relationships to the existence of trust and information sharing among the partners, Coad and Cullen argued that such stability is possible where potential conflicts and issues of power and politics are suppressed within the institutionalised routines as "institutional routines facilitate a truce in inter-organisational conflict" (p. 365; see also Scapens 1994). However, they also emphasised the need to recognise the relative power of the individual actors, which they derived from the wider institutional context. In addition, they acknowledged that they did not study the broader social, regulatory, and legislative influences in which organisational activity is embedded; they contrasted their work with that of Seal et al. (2004), which, amongst other things, reflected on the new institutionalised practices stemming from government initiatives on inter-organisational relationships. It is to their work that we now turn.

Seal et al. (2004, p. 73) "submit that a fruitful way of understanding inter-firm [inter-organisational] accounting is to see it as involved in the wider changes in the social relations of production that are characteristic of modernity". They proposed a theoretical framework that applies an institutional perspective to the study of strategic behaviour of key actors in inter-organisational relationships. In contrast to the existing literature, they shifted our attention to how inter-organisational accounting techniques can come to be embedded in a firm's institutionalised practices. Drawing on Giddens's structuration theory (see 1984), and his subsequent work on modernity (Giddens 1990, 1991), they analyse inter-organisational accounting as an expert system that mediates the interaction between actions (of supply chain actors) and wider social institutions over time.

Seal et al. (2004) argue that institutional arrangements are particularly important in supply chains because managerial action takes place outside and between conventional hierarchical organisational structures. Furthermore, as outsourcing often involves *disembedding* concepts of industrial organisation, strategic alliances and other forms of supply chain management can be interpreted as attempts to *reembed* the relations of production.

In this process, they argued, inter-organisational accounting can become an expert system that is produced and reproduced through the interactions between the supply chain actors and the wider institutional influences. For example, in their case study, we see the influence exerted by a governmental agency (the Department of Trade and Industry, DTI) through their encouragement of regional networks of firms, consultancies, training agencies, universities, and so on, which were aimed at equipping local firms to cope with the demands of increasingly global markets.

Through a case study of a company in the UK electronic industry, Seal et al. explored how techniques of inter-organisational accounting are shaped by and can become institutionalised practices. Their study followed the changes made in the company as severe market pressures led to attempts to improve its productive efficiency. In particular, it focuses on the creation of a cost management group (CMG), which was composed largely of accountants. This group was initially established to reduce costs by improving procurement activities though the establishment of closer relationships with suppliers, but its scope broadened over time as it took on production, commercial, organisational, and change management roles. Seal et al. argued that, in this process, the CMG came to represent an expert accounting system which operated across boundaries both within the company and outside it, as it was increasingly the repository of expert knowledge and the centre of a network of supply chain practices for the company and its suppliers.

The case study is divided into three phases, each representing the different relationships that the company had with its suppliers. Phase One, before the company was taken over by a Japanese conglomerate, the company was seen as an 'easy' customer by many of its suppliers, mainly because of the lack of a formal means of assessing of supplier performance. However, in Phase Two, after the takeover had occurred and several accompanying administrative changes had been brought about (including the appointment of a new procurement director), relationships with suppliers changed. New management practices and a supplier performance assessment system were introduced. During this phase, characterised by the introduction of management practices that encoded the new owner's philosophy and the actions of recently appointed managers, the focus was on reducing supply chain costs through the benchmarking of suppliers, value engineering, the identification of total costs of ownership, and the development of a sophisticated *supplier management programme*. However, during the third phase the emphasis shifted to attempt to improve the management and performance of the entire supply chain to the mutual benefit of all of its members. This was achieved through collaborations, which were encouraged and supported by the DTI initiative mentioned earlier.

By interpreting this case through structuration theory, the authors were able not only to identify mimetic influences from the company's institutional environment, but also to explore the impact of the strategic actions of key players in the supply chain. Although they did not find evidence of the types of techniques often advocated for inter-organisational accounting (such as open-book accounting; see Mouritsen et al. 2001), they argued that accounting could be seen as "a set of institutionalised practices that may be employed both within and between firms" (p. 89). They argued that the rhetoric of close relations in supply chains, which usually accompanies discussions of such techniques as target costing and open-book accounting, "has obscured the longstanding role of accounting in enabling transactions that are distanced through space and time" (p. 90). This recognises that accounting practices (even if not overtly inter-organisational accounting) are part of the institutional context that shapes the nature of inter-organisational relationships.

In drawing on structuration theory to study inter-organisational relationships, Seal et al. raised an important issue concerning the role of trust. Whereas some parts of the inter-organisational literature have debated the relationship between trust and control (see, e.g., Van der Meer-Kooistra and Vosselman 2000; Tomkins 2001; Dekker 2004), Seal et al. pointed out that structuration theory does not dichotomise trust and control, but instead sees trust as a generalised faith to abstract systems. This draws an important distinction between trust in abstract systems and trust in specific individuals, or even in a particular inter-organisational relationship. Such trust (in abstract systems) can contribute to the stability of inter-organisational relationships. This is somewhat similar to the point made by Coad and Cullen that "institutional routines facilitate a truce in inter-organisational conflict" (2006, p. 365; see preceding). Whereas the case studies of Coad and Cullen and Seal et al., seem to portray some form of trust in the inter-organisational relationship, even though trust *per se* was not the focus of their work nor an issue raised by the participants in the inter-organisational relationships, our third study in this section (Free 2008) illustrates that explicit attempts to build trust can have unanticipated consequences.

Although Free (2008) did not explicitly draw on institutional theory (as discussed in this chapter), he was concerned with "the organizationally embedded social context for trust and the complex relationship between trust and accounting practice" (p. 630). This is similar to the notion of institutions within organisations, as studied by the OIE-inspired work in management accounting, and he uses this notion to study the supply chains of large UK supermarket retailers. Furthermore, Free referred to the work of such institutional writers as Oliver and Zucker, and he described system trust as an institutional phenomenon. He also discussed trust in abstract systems (cf. Seal et al. 2004). In terms of the discussion of trust in the chapter, Free provides some important cautions.

In reviewing trust in the existing accounting literature, Free concluded that "there is a tendency to treat trust as a blanket concept . . . rather than one that is highly context specific" (p. 635). He drew on Giddens's structuration theory and notions of modernity to study a long-term relationship between a supermarket and one of its core suppliers. He referred to trust as a discursive resource and discussed how it can be manipulated. Even though the relationship under consideration dated back twenty years, it was jeopardised after the supermarket introduced the practice of 'category management'. Although there is no single definition of category management, it comprises an array of techniques designed to increase the competitive advantage of the supply chain and to allow the retailer to deal with fewer, but more sophisticated, suppliers. It is usually promoted as the catalyst for 'new' supplier-retailer relationships in which trust may be expected to play an important role.

However, the focus of the supermarket in this case seemed to be on improving financial measures through the implementation of category management, and this was not greatly appreciated by its supplier. As a result, the trust that had been established over the years was replaced by instability and tension. Free commented that, despite much 'trust talk', relations were shown to be inherently fragile as the new practices were absorbed by the supplier. Consequently, accounting practices, which (at least theoretically) promoted trust, actually damaged trust in buyer-supplier relationships. To use Giddens's notion of 'trust in expert systems', it could be concluded that, in Free's case study, the new accounting practices did not become embedded in the supplier-retailer relationships and, consequently, there was an absence of system trust. This contrasts with the study of Seal et al. (2004), where inter-organisational accounting was regarded as an expert system. Thus, more research is needed to explore why and how some systems of inter-organisational accounting can become embedded (or institutionalised) and provide a trusted basis for inter-organisational relationships, whereas, in other cases, such practices can damage trust.

In this section, we have reviewed the few studies that have adopted an institutional perspective to examine inter-organisational accounting. We believe there is considerable potential for adopting such a perspective for future research in this area, as we will describe in the following and final section of this chapter.

5 SUMMARY AND IMPLICATIONS FOR FUTURE RESEARCH

The research using institutional theory to study inter-organisational relationships, discussed in Section 3, emphasises the complexity of the institutional context of these relationships. For example, the work on collaborations illustrates the importance of understanding both the internal and external institutions of the partners in the relationship (see Philips et al. 2000). As we indicated earlier, from the perspectives of NIS and OIE, institutions are the recurring social patterns and taken-for-granted assumptions which give meaning to the actions and thoughts of the partners in an inter-organisational relationship. However, they should not be regarded simply as constraints shaping the nature of the relationship. The relationships themselves can shape the institutions and thereby influence the character of new relationships. Thus, it is important to be aware of the processes of structuration and institutional change when studying inter-organisational relationships.

As we saw earlier, the early NIS work distinguished between the institutional and the economic pressures on organisations. But more recent work has recognised that these pressures act simultaneously on organisations, and that economic pressures can themselves be institutionalised. Furthermore, these institutional pressures can be experienced at a number of different levels: meta (social), macro (national), meso (organisational) and micro (operating) (see Parkhe 2003). Thus, understanding the diverse institutional pressures, which can influence inter-organisational relationships, is a complicated, but very important issue. It is important because success of the relationship is likely to depend on whether it can gain legitimacy: that is, general acceptance that the relationship is desirable and appropriate both within the network (among the partners) and within the partners' own organisations. However, what is considered legitimate will be subject to institutional pressures at various levels. As we saw earlier, Dacin et al. 2007 referred to five types of legitimacy: market, relational, social, investment, and alliance. Thus, the nature and influence of institutions on inter-organisational relationships are complex and interrelated. Given this complexity in the institutional context of inter-organisational relationships, what are the roles of management control and accounting techniques? And how should institutional theory inform research into inter-organisational accounting and control?

Whereas NIE continues to adopt (albeit in an adapted form) the assumptions of neoclassical economics, an OIE (and/or an NIS) perspective would seek to understand the origins, nature, and implications of the taken-for-granted assumptions of the individual participants in the inter-organisational relationships. As such, NIE continues to rely on the behavioural assumptions of economics to analyse inter-organisational relationships, whereas the broader institutional perspective outlined in this chapter seeks to understand how the partners in inter-organisational relationships make sense of the nature of these relationships and their role, and the role of others agents, within them. For example, how do they handle the potential paradox involved in, for instance, cooperating with competitors and, in so doing, how do they come to redefine their own interests? What is the role of trust in such relationships?

As mentioned earlier, the recent TCE research has added the role of trust to the analysis of transaction costs. But as argued by Marchington and Vincent (2004), it is important to look at trust at three interrelated levels—institutional, organisational, and interpersonal. But whereas TCE explores trust at the organisational and interpersonal levels, little attention has been given to the institutional level. Furthermore, much of the TCE work on inter-organisational relationships tends to focus on the transaction costs of each specific relationship and, by treating each relationship as independent, TCE ignores the influence of the institutional environment, as well as any prior interactions between the partners. Such past interactions can affect the choice of partners and/or the governance of the relationship (Gulati 1998). In addition, TCE is concerned primarily with cost minimisation, whereas the purpose of many inter-organisational relationships is value maximisation (Gulati 1998). Moreover, TCE does not recognise all of the many benefits that the partners can gain through inter-organisational relationships, such as learning from partners, resource pooling, and reduction of environmental uncertainty (Faulkner and de Rond 2000).

However, in their study, which adopted an (evolutionary) institutional perspective to explore the emergence of inter-organisational cost management, Coad and Cullen (2006) argued that institutionalised routines can create stable relationships by facilitating a "truce in inter-organisational conflict" (p. 365). In other words, the routines of cost management could be acceptable to the various parties to the relationship, even though they have quite different interests and aims. This is likely to be the case where such routines are to be found in other—existing or previous—inter-organisational relationships in which the parties have been involved or of which they are aware—in other words, if the routines have become institutionalised. Thus, cost management routines and, potentially, other accounting techniques could become part of the broader institutional context which helps to give order to the complexity created by the diverse institutional pressures that influence the nature and character of inter-organisational relationships. More research is needed to explore the way in which accounting and cost management techniques can become embedded in the broader institutional context, and how such embedded techniques can shape the form and nature of future inter-organisational relationships.

Thus, drawing on both OIE and NIS, future research could explore why some accounting practices become institutionalised in inter-organisational relationships, while others do not. In contrast to the Coad and Cullen (2006) case, where inter-organisational cost management was replicated across the supply chain, in the case study reported by Free (2008), the attempts to introduce category management as a catalyst for new supplier-retailer relationships damaged the existing trust and the new accounting techniques did not become embedded in the relationships. To study how some accounting routines become institutionalised (whereas others do not), future research could usefully draw on the work of Greenwood et al. (2002) and Parkhe (2003), the Burns and Scapens's (2000) framework, as well as the evolutionary framework of Coad and Cullen (2006). Such research could explore the evolutionary processes through which management accounting and control practices develop, are maintained, and become embedded in inter-organisational relationships and examine how they can change over time.

In so doing, such research will need to be aware of the interaction between micro and meso institutions within the organisations and the broader macro and meta institutions of the institutional field in which the relationship is set. As we indicated earlier, the study by Seal et al. (2004) reflected on the influence of government initiatives on the development of inter-organisational relationships, and the way in which accounting, as a set of institutionalised practices, can come to be viewed as a trusted expert system, that is, as an institutionalised set of practices that can be drawn on by the participants in inter-organisational relationships. If accounting practices are viewed as an expert system, there is likely to be overlap between their use within individual organisations and their use within the inter-organisational relationships in which those organisations are involved. As Coad and Cullen (2006) observed, there can be a blurring of intra- and inter-organisational phenomena. However, as we know relatively little of the relationship between the accounting practices used within organisations which are participants in inter-organisational relationships, and their use of inter-organisational accounting, further research is needed in this area.

As just mentioned, Seal et al. (2004) recognised the importance of looking at the influences of broader institutions, but although they examined the impact of government initiatives, they did not explore in any depth the wider social cultural beliefs and values of the participants in the supply chain that they studied. However, as Parkhe (2003) pointed out (see Section 3), this can be particularly important when the partners in inter-organisational relationships are from dispersed institutional fields; for example, international alliances. Furthermore, it is important to recognise the meta and macro institutions when studying inter-organisational relationships in different countries. For example, emerging economies and economies with different socio-legal systems are likely to have quite different approaches to accounting for inter-organisational relationships—shaped in large part by their institutional environments. This institutional diversity is frequently ignored by TCE approaches to studying inter-organisational relationships.

Thus, much remains to be done and we believe that the institutional perspectives discussed in this chapter have an important role to play in studying accounting in inter-organisational relationships. Such research can explore the legitimacy of inter-organisational accounting in diverse institutional contexts, and explore how institutionalised (embedded) accounting practices can themselves facilitate the formation of inter-organisational relationships. However, it will be necessary to recognise the complexity and diversity of the institutional settings of the inter-organisational relationships. It is hoped that this chapter has helped to give some insights into the nature of this complexity and diversity, as well as pointing to opportunities for further research.

NOTES

1. Earlier, but less influential, work was undertaken by German and Austrian institutionalists in the last decades of the nineteenth century—see Scott (2001, p. 2).
2. The definition was cited approvingly by Hodgson (1993).
3. This conference paper of Hodgson was cited by Dequech (2002, p. 567).

4. The Seal et al. (2004) paper will be discussed in more detail later; see Section 4.
5. A number of these studies used Orton and Weick's (1990) distinction between loose coupling and decoupling.

BIBLIOGRAPHY

Barley, S. R. 1986. Technology as an occasion for structuring: Evidence from observations of CT scanners and the social order of radiology departments. *Administrative Science Quarterly* 31: 78–108.

Barley, S. R., and Tolbert, P. S. 1997. Institutionalization and structuration: Studying the links between action and institution. *Organizational Studies* 18: 93–117.

Berger, P. L., and Luckmann, T. 1967. *The social construction of reality*. New York: Doubleday.

Brignall, S., and Modell, S. 2000. An institutional perspective on performance measurement and management in the 'new public sector'. *Management Accounting Research* 11: 281–306.

Brinton, M. C., Nee, V., and Merton, R. K. 2001. *The new institutionalism in sociology*. Stanford, CA: Stanford University Press.

Burns, J. 2000. The dynamics of accounting change: Interplay between new practices, routines, institutions, power and politics. *Accounting, Auditing and Accountability Journal* 13: 566–596.

Burns, J., and Baldvinsdottir, G. 2005. An institutional perspective of accountants' new roles—the interplay of contradictions and praxis. *European Accounting Review* 14: 725–757.

Burns, J., and Scapens, R. W. 2000. Conceptualizing management accounting change: An institutional framework. *Management Accounting Research* 11: 3–25.

Busco, C., Riccaboni, A., and Scapens, R. W. 2002. When 'culture' matters: Management accounting change: Within processes of organizational learning and transformation. *Reflections: The Society for Organization Learning Journal* 4: 43–52.

Busco, C., Riccaboni, A., and Scapens, R. W. 2006. Trust for accounting and accounting for trust. *Management Accounting Research* 17: 11–41.

Coad, A. F., and Cullen, J. 2006. Inter-organisational cost management: Towards an evolutionary perspective. *Management Accounting Research* 17: 342–369.

Coase, R. H. 1983. The new institutional economics. *Journal of Institutional and Theoretical Economics* 140: 229–231.

Collier, P. M. 2001. The power of accounting: A field study of local financial management in a police force. *Management Accounting Research* 12: 465–486.

Dacin, T. M. 1997. Isomorphism in context: The power and prescription of institutional norms. *Academy of Management Journal* 40: 46–81.

Dacin, T. M., Goodstein J., and Scott, W. R. 2002. Institutional theory and institutional change: Introduction to the special research forum. *Academy of Management Journal* 45: 45–56.

Dacin, T. M., Oliver, C., and Roy, J.-P. 2007. The legitimacy of strategic alliances: An institutional perspective. *Strategic Management Journal* 28: 169–187.

Das, T. K., and Teng, B. S. 1998. Between trust and control: Developing confidence in partner cooperation in alliances. *Academy of Management Review* 23: 491–512.

Dekker, H. C. 2003. Value chain analysis in interfirm relationships: A field study. *Management Accounting Research* 14: 1–23.

Dekker, H. C. 2004. Control of inter-organizational relationships: Evidences on appropriation concerns and coordination requirements. *Accounting, Organizations and Society* 29: 27–49.

Dequech, D. 2002. The demarcation between the "old" and the "new" institutional economics: Recent complications. *Journal of Economic Issues* 36: 565–572.

Dillard, J. F., Rigsby, J. T. and Goodman, C. 2004. The making and remaking of organization context: Duality and the institutionalization process. *Accounting, Auditing and Accountability Journal* 17: 506–542.

DiMaggio, P. J., and Powell, W. W. 1983. The iron cage revisited: Institutional isomorphism and collective rationality in organizational fields. *American Sociological Review* 48: 147–160.

Edelman, L. B. 1992. Legal ambiguity and symbolic structures: Organizational mediation of civil rights law. *American Journal of Sociology* 97: 1531–1576.

Faulkner, D., and de Rond, M. 2000. Perspectives on cooperative strategy. In *Cooperative strategy: Economics, business and organizational issues*, ed. Faulkner, D., and de Rond, M. Oxford: Oxford University Press.

Free, C. 2008. Walking the talk? Supply chain accounting and trust among UK supermarkets and suppliers. *Accounting, Organizations and Society* 33: 629–662.

Giddens, A. 1976. *New rules of sociological method: A positive critique of interpretative sociology.* London: Hutchinson.

Giddens, A. 1977. *Studies in social and political theory.* New York: Basic Books.

Giddens, A. 1979. *Problems in social theory: Action structure and contradiction in social analysis.* London: Macmillan.

Giddens, A. 1984. *The constitution of society.* Cambridge: Polity Press.

Giddens, A. 1990. *The consequences of modernity.* Cambridge: Polity Press.

Giddens, A. 1991. *Modernity and self-identity.* Cambridge: Polity Press.

Greenwood, R., Suddaby, R., and Hinings, C. R. 2002. Theorizing change: The role of professional associations in the transformation of institutionalized fields. *Academy of Management Journal* 45: 58–80.

Gulati, R. 1998. Alliances and networks. *Strategic Management Journal* 19: 293–317.

Hamilton, W. H. 1932. Institutions. In *Encyclopaedia of the social science*, ed. Seligman, E. R. A., and Johnson, A. 84–89. New York: The Macmillan Company.

Hannan, M. T., and Freeman, J. 1977. The population ecology of organizations. *American Journal of Sociology* 82: 929.

Hodgson, G. M. 1988. *Economics and institutions: A manifesto for a modern institutional economics.* Cambridge: Polity Press.

Hodgson, G. M. 1989. Institutional economic theory: The old versus the new. *Review of Political Economy* 1: 249–269.

Hodgson, G. M. 1993. *Introduction to the economics of institutions: A manifesto for a modern institutional economics.* Cambridge: Polity Press.

Hodgson, G. M. 1999. *Structures and institutions: Reflections on institutionalism, structuration theory, and critical realism.* Paper presented at the *European Association for Evolutionary Political Economy Conference*, November 4–7, Prague, Czech Republic.

Hopper, T., and Major, M. 2007. Extending institutional analysis through theoretical triangulation: Regulation and activity-based costing in Portuguese telecommunications. *European Accounting Review* 16: 59–97.

Human, S. E., and Provan, K. G. 2000. Legitimacy building in the evolution of small firm multilateral networks: A comparative study of success and demise. *Administrative Science Quarterly* 45: 327–365.

Imperial, M. T. 2005. Using collaboration as a governance strategy: Lessons from six watershed management programs. *Administration and Society* 37: 281–320.

Jepperson, R. L. 1991. Institutions, institutional effects and institutionalization. In *The new institutionalism in organizational analysis*, ed. Powell, W. W., and DiMaggio, P. J. 143–163. Chicago: University of Chicago Press.

Johnsen, Å. 1999. Implementation mode and local government performance measurement: A Norwegian experience. *Financial Accountability and Management* 15: 41–66.

Kumar, R., and Andersen, P. H. 2000. Inter-firm diversity and the management of meaning in international strategic alliances. *International Business Review* 9: 237–252.

Kumar, R., and Das, T. K. 2007. Interpartner legitimacy in the alliance development process. *Journal of Management Studies* 44: 1425–1453.

Lane, C., and Bachmann, R. 1997. Co-operation in inter-firm relations in Britain and Germany: The role of social institutions. *The British Journal of Sociology* 48: 226–254.

Langlois, R. N. 1989. What was wrong with old institutional economics (and what is still wrong with the new)? *Review of Political Economy* 1: 270–298.

Lawrence, S., Alam, M., Northcott, D., and Lowe, T. 1997. Accounting systems and systems of accountability in the New Zealand health sector. *Accounting, Auditing and Accountability Journal* 10: 665–683.

Lawrence, T. B., Hardy, C., and Phillips, N. 2002. Institutional effects of inter-organizational collaboration: The emergence of proto-institutions. *Academy of Management Journal* 45: 281–290.

Leca, B., Battilana, J., and Boxenbaum, E. 2006. *Taking stock on institutional entrepreneurship: What do we know? Where do we go?* Paper presented at Academy of Management Meeting, August, Atlanta, USA.

Lounsbury, M. 2007. A tale of two cities: Competing logics and practice variation in the professionalizing of mutual funds. *The Academy of Management Journal* 50: 289–307.

Lounsbury, M. 2008. Institutional rationality and practice variation: New directions in the institutional analysis of practice. *Accounting, Organizations and Society* 33: 349–361.

Luhmann, N. 1979. *Trust and power.* Chichester, UK: Wiley.

Macintosh, N. B., and Scapens, R. W. 1990. Structuration theory in management accounting. *Accounting, Organizations and Society* 15: 455–477.

Macintosh, N. B., and Scapens, R. W. 1991. Management accounting and control systems: A structuration theory analysis. *Journal of Management Accounting Research* 3: 131–158.

Marchington, M., and Vincent, S. 2004. Analysing the influence of institutional, organizational and interpersonal forces in shaping inter-organizational relations. *Journal of Management Studies* 41: 1029–1056.

Meyer, J. W., and Rowan, B. 1977. Institutionalized organizations: Formal structure as myth and ceremony. *American Journal of Sociology* 83: 340–363.

Modell, S. 2001. Performance measurement and institutional processes: A study of managerial responses to public sector reform. *Management Accounting Research* 12: 437–464.

Modell, S. 2003. Goals versus institutions: The development of performance measurement in the Swedish university sector. *Management Accounting Research* 14: 333–359.

Modell, S. 2004. Performance measurement myths in the public sector: A research note. *Financial Accountability and Management* 20: 39–55.

Modell, S., Jacobs, K., and Wiesel, F. 2007. A Process (re)turn? Path dependencies, institutions and performance management in Swedish central government. *Management Accounting Research* 18: 453–475.

Modell, S., and Wiesel, F. 2008. Marketization and performance measurement in Swedish central government: A comparative institutionalist study. *Abacus* 44: 251–283.

Mouritsen, J., Hansen, A., and Hansen, C. Ø. 2001. Inter-organizational controls and organizational competencies: Episodes around target cost management/functional analysis and open book accounting. *Management Accounting Review* 12: 221–244.

Nelson, R. R., and Winter S. G. 1982. *An evolutionary theory of economic change.* Cambridge, MA: Harvard University Press.

Nooteboom, B. 1999. *Inter-firm alliances: Analysis and design.* London, UK: Routledge.

Nor-Aziah, A. K., and Scapens, R. W. 2007. Corporation and accounting change: The role of accounting and accountants in a Malaysian public utility. *Management Accounting Review* 18: 209–247.

North, D. C. 1978. Structure and performance: The task of economic history. *Journal of Economic Literature* XVI: 963–978.

Oliver, C. 1990. Determinants of interorganizational relationships: Integration and future directions. *Academy of Management Review* 15: 241–265.

Oliver, C. 1991. Strategic responses to institutional processes. *Academy of Management Review* 16: 145–179.

Orton, J. D., and Weick, K. E. 1990. Loosely coupled systems: A reconceptualization. *Academy of Management Review* 15: 203–223.

Parkhe, A. 2003. Institutional environments, institutional change and international alliances. *Journal of International Management* 9: 305–316.

Penrose, E. 1959. *The theory of the growth of the firm.* Oxford: Blackwell.

Phillips, N., Lawrence, T. B., and Hardy, C. 2000. Inter-organizational collaboration and the dynamics of institutional fields. *Journal of Management Studies* 37: 23–43.

Ranson, S., Hinings, C. R., and Greenwood, R. 1980. The structuring of organizational structures. *Administrative Science Quarterly* 43: 877–904.

Ribeiro, J. A., and Scapens, R. W. 2006. Institutional theories and management accounting change: Contributions, issues and paths for development. *Qualitative Research in Management and Accounting* 3: 94–111.

Roberts, J., and Scapens, R. W. 1985. Accounting systems and systems of accountability—understanding accounting practices in their organisational contexts. *Accounting, Organizations and Society* 10: 443–456.

Rutherford, M. 1989. What is wrong with the new institutional economics (and what is still wrong with the old)? *Review of Political Economy* 1: 299–318.

Rutherford, M. 1994. *Institutions in economics: The old and the new institutionalism.* Cambridge: Cambridge University Press.

Rutherford, M. 2000. Understanding institutional economics: 1918–1929. *Journal of History of Economics Thought* 22: 277–308.

Sako, M. 1992. *Prices, quality and trust, inter-firm relations in Britain and Japan.* Cambridge: Cambridge University Press.

Scapens, R. W. 1994. Never mind the gap: Towards an institutional perspective on management accounting practice. *Management Accounting Research* 5: 301–321.

Scapens, R. W., and Roberts, J. 1993. Accounting and control: A case study of resistance to accounting and change. *Management Accounting Research* 4: 1–32.

Scott, R. W. 1992. *Organizations: Rational, natural and open systems.* 3rd ed. Englewood Cliffs, NJ: Prentice Hall.

Scott, R. W. 2001. *Institutions and organizations.* 2nd ed. Thousand Oaks, CA: Sage Publications.

Scott, R. W., and Meyer, J. W. 1992. The organization of societal sectors. In *Organizational environments: Ritual and rationality*, ed. Meyer J. W., and Scott, R. W. 129–144. Updated edition. Beverly Hills, CA: Sage Publications.

Seal, W. B., Berry, A., and Cullen, J. 2004. Dissembling the supply chain: Institutionalized reflexivity and inter-firm accounting. *Accounting, Organizations and Society* 29: 73–92.

Seo, M. G., and Creed, D. W. E. 2002. Institutional contradictions, praxis, and institutional change: A dialectical perspective. *Academy of Management Review* 27: 222–247.

Sharfman, M. P., Gray, B., and Yan, A. 1991. The context of inter-organizational collaboration in the garment industry: An institutional perspective. *Journal of Applied Behavioral Science* 27: 181–208.

Siti-Nabiha, A. K., and Scapens, R. W. 2005. Stability and change: An institutionalist study of management accounting change. Accounting, Auditing and Accountability *Journal* 18: 44–73.

Soin, K., Seal, W., and Cullen, J. 2002. ABC and organizational change: An institutional perspective. *Management Accounting Research* 13: 249–271.

Tolbert, P., and Zucker, L. 1996. The institutionalization of institutional theory. In *Handbook of organization studies*, ed. Glegg, S., Hardy, G., and Nord, W. 175–190. Thousand Oaks, CA: Sage.

Tomkins, C. 2001. Interdependencies, trust and information in relationships, alliances and networks. *Accounting, Organizations and Society* 26: 161–191.

Tool, M. R. 1993. The theory of instrumental value: Extensions, clarifications. In *Institutional economics: Theory, method, policy*, ed. Tool, M. R. 119–159. Boston: Kluwer Academic Publishers.

Van der Meer-Kooistra, J., and Vosselman, E. 2000. Management control of inter-firm transactional relationships: The case of industrial renovation and maintenance. *Accounting, Organizations and Society* 25: 51–77.

Veblen, T. B. 1898. Why is economics not an evolutionary science? *Quarterly Journal of Economics* 12: 373–397.

Veblen, T. B. 1909. The limitations of marginal utility. *Journal of Political Economics* 17: 620–636.

Williamson, O. E. 1987. *The economic institutions of capitalism*. New York: The Free Press.

Zucker, L. G. 1977. The role of institutionalization in cultural persistence. *American Sociological Review* 42: 726–743.

Zucker, L. G. 1986. Production of trust: Institutional sources of economic structure 1840–1920. *Research in Organizational Behaviour* 8: 53–111.

14 Accounting in Networks—
The Next Step

*Håkan Håkansson, Kalle Kraus,
and Johnny Lind*

1 ACCOUNTING IN NETWORKS—THE NEXT STEP

An interesting picture has been painted of the state of the art of accounting in networks in this book. A number of theoretical approaches and accounting and managerial tools have been described, analysed, and discussed. It is evident that there are some similar conclusions running through all of the chapters, but there are also some noteworthy differences. By comparing and contrasting the conclusions here, we attempt to construct a platform for our interpretation of the research that needs to be prioritised on accounting in networks. In Chapter 2, Håkan Håkansson and David Ford made a distinction between theoretical and empirical changes explaining the contemporary interest for inter-organisational issues in accounting. The authors developed a 2×2 matrix with the degree of changes in the business landscape on one axis and the degree of changes in theoretical approaches to accounting on the other. The analysis of the four boxes in the matrix illustrated the dynamic interplay between the theoretical and empirical aspects of accounting in inter-organisational relationships and networks and explained and described the large variety of accounting issues and methods. One main conclusion was that both the business landscape and applied theories had changed and that these changes were, at least partly, independent of one another. This creates a complicated mixture of empirical and theoretical issues, of which only some are systematically related. The chapters that followed illustrated and augmented this conclusion.

Some of the authors have argued strongly that there seem to be some important changes in business practice that have been manifested in new roles and issues for accounting in different inter-organisational settings. John Cullen and Juliana Meira (Chapter 3) and Johnny Lind and Sof Thrane (Chapter 4) concluded that the obstacles imposed by contemporary accounting reinforcing the hierarchy have given rise to inter-organisational accounting practices, both in dyadic and network settings. Cullen and Meira analysed the maturity of the dyadic relationship and showed how it affected the design and use of inter-organisational accounting. Lind and Thrane, in contrast, distinguished between the way that an inter-organisational control system mitigated opportunistic behaviour, detailed cost information in the value chain, accounting that facilitates the simultaneous handling of heterogeneous customer and supplier relationships, and accounting information about direct and indirect effects of interaction with counterparts. In Chapter 5, Jeltje van der Meer-Kooistra and Pieter E. Kamminga discussed the issues of coordination, opportunistic behaviour, and relational atmosphere and the use of accounting to deal with these issues in a joint venture setting. Kalle Kraus and Cecilia Lindholm noted in Chapter 6 that the New Public Management trend, together with a trend towards cooperation within the public sector, have make it important to study the simultaneous operation of intra- and inter-organisational accounting in public sector organisations, as well as the connection between them.

Another argument that appeared in some of the chapters was that there seem to be some important changes in business practice that have been manifested in the development of new intra and inter-organisational accounting methods. One method, that of intra-organisational accounting, that is, customer accounting, in an inter-organisational setting was elaborated upon in Chapter 7 by Mikael Cäker and Torkel Strömsten. They identified challenges that needed to be acknowledged and which demanded response, and illustrated how customer accounting was applied in an inter-organisational context. In this book, a whole set of new inter-organisational accounting methods has been presented, such as open-book accounting, target costing, total cost of ownership, accounting for value chain analysis, and inter-organisational cost management. Some of these methods were analysed in detail by Martin Carlsson-Wall and Kalle Kraus in Chapter 8, where target costing was considered, and by Peter Kajüter and Harri I. Kulmala in Chapter 9, on open-book accounting. These two chapters demonstrated how these accounting methods transcend firm boundaries and encompass more than just the focal firm.

Shannon Anderson and Henri Dekker, Håkan Håkansson, Kalle Kraus, Johnny Lind and Torkel Strömsten, Jan Mouritsen, Habib Mahama and Wai Fong Chua, and Robert W. Scapens and Evangelia Varoutsa in turn argued strongly and convincingly that there is an interesting change taking place in the applied theories, too (Chapters 10–13). The application of the different theoretical approaches covered, namely, transaction cost economics, the industrial-network approach, actor-network theory, and institutional theory, raised a number of interesting issues with regard to accounting in networks, issues that were elaborated on in each respective chapter. Depending on which theory was applied, different issues were raised, although, interestingly enough, there was at least one common theme in these chapters, irrespective of the theoretical perspective applied; this concerned the *dynamics* of inter-organisational relationships and networks. Accounting in networks has a dynamic character, which was described in various ways by the authors and which we will summarise following.

Anderson and Dekker pointed to the importance of examining relationship dynamics, processes, and change and concluded that transaction cost economics may be successfully combined with other theories because it appears to be most useful for identifying when changes can be expected, and less useful for providing researchers with the tools required to study how and through which processes change takes place. Håkansson et al. stated that dynamics play a vital role in industrial markets in the industrial-network approach. They concluded that such dynamics imply that the primary role of accounting is not to devise optimal forms of governance but, rather, to help create interaction between different companies which will lead to temporarily valid pragmatic compromises. Mouritsen et al. concluded that, when applying actor-network theory to accounting in inter-organisational relationships, it is important to follow the actors in practice. This brings the dynamics to the fore, as following the actors in action requires the researcher to track and relate the changes over time to the boundaries, power, and identity of entities. Scapens and Varoutsa stressed the importance of dynamics when it comes to accounting practices and institutional contexts. They concluded that an important activity when using institutional theory to analyse accounting in inter-organisational relationships is to explore the (dynamic) process of how institutionalised accounting practices can themselves facilitate the formation of inter-organisational relationships and why some accounting practices become institutionalised in inter-organisational relationships, while others do not.

The existence of distinct and simultaneous changes in both practice and theory on accounting in networks is stimulating because there are so many different combinations of empirical and theoretical issues that can be identified. This is challenging for researchers and managers alike. There are so many possible research issues that can be formulated and, at the same time, there are so many possibilities for developing management practice. There is certainly a need for a substantial increase in knowledge that, hopefully, will lead both to the development of new theoretical models and concepts and to new managerial tools. We will try to provide an overview of some major future possibilities by identifying four dominant issues that are crucial for future development, two starting out from an empirical angle and two with a theoretical starting point.

There are two types of inter-organisational issues that are in obvious need of addressing from an empirical and managerial point of view. One has to do with an issue with its roots in the contemporary way of handling accounting: A key problem encountered by all managers is the effect of the very distinct boundary of the legal identity—the company. The second empirical issue that has arisen as a result of the new business landscape has to do with the handling of 'important others'. There is a need to develop and utilise interactive capabilities.

In a similar way, we can also identify two issues which are more theory-based. The first has to do with the existence of several theoretical approaches. These are both complementary and alternative. In both of these cases, it is important to identify their limitations and the assumptions underlying them. Given such knowledge, it becomes easier to discuss when their use is appropriate and/or how they should be adapted to specific circumstances. The second issue concerns how an entire set of theoretical models and concepts could be combined in a number of different ways to gradually craft a more general theory.

Important Issues Starting Out From Empirical Problems

The Boundary Issue

In principle, at present, all accounting starts out from the legal boundary of the firm, which leads to a number of difficulties when issues relating to the relationships between companies or organisations are to be embarked upon. One effect of this boundary is the development of special managerial tools for analysing inter-organisational issues, such as open-book accounting, but even with this accounting technique, the structure of the accounting is still based on the existence of the boundary. Open-book accounting helps in obtaining more information, but it does not help to get the information structured in a suitable way—the legal boundary is still embedded into the accounting structure. All companies wanting to develop more advanced inter-organisational accounting tools will have to deal with this problem. One noteworthy feature is that there is no obvious solution, such as simply eliminating the boundary, as all accounting builds on the existence of a boundary because it is this that gives the starting point for the identification of what should be taken into account. All accounting needs a dividing line specifying what should be included and what should be excluded. The question is, in other words, what alternative boundaries can be identified?

There are several alternatives to making the boundary the firm, such as defining the boundary to enclose two companies, thereby including the relationship between them. But a boundary may also be created around a chain of companies, or around a specified set of activities or resources. One important consequence of a network structure is that there is no optimal boundary that will be ideal for all issues in a network setting; instead, it is safe to assume that each company needs to use different definitions of its boundaries. Thus, there is a need to be able to use flexible boundaries in the accounting system, which may then be changed given the situation or type of issue under consideration. Furthermore, there will also be differences between different types of companies, which will substantiate the need for each company to work with a set of boundaries adapted to the context and to the issue of the moment. Furthermore, this means that determining the most suitable boundary will be an empirical issue, and therefore there is reason for all companies to experiment with their boundaries. This, in turn, will make it possible for boundaries to become a strategic issue and could bring accounting closer to the strategic development of each company. This type of development brings us to the second major empirical issue, the need for interactive capabilities.

The Need for Interactive Capabilities

The business landscape outlined in the empirical illustrations presented here gives reason to assume that interactive capabilities will become a key issue for many companies, as they are found to be for the company Ducati in Chapter 2. Such interactive capabilities are related to the choice of boundary as they may be seen as the ability of a company to manage its boundary, which, in this case, is seen as the interface between the company and related companies. This interface is not a dividing line, as is a classic "boundary", but instead it encourages systematic relating of the internal and external activities and resources. Interactive capabilities are capabilities to handle systemic interdependencies between what takes place inside and what is achieved outside the company. They are also about how to identify and follow up these interdependencies which may be technological and/or other resource-related interdependencies. Here, accounting is a key resource because it underlies the capability to understand how resources and activities interact across firms' boundaries, that is, how different combinations of resources across the boundary affect costs and revenues.

Two types of interactive capabilities may be distinguished. The first are one-sided interactive capabilities and have to do with the internal ability of a company to take advantage of the variation that exists among potential counterparts. Given that counterparts vary in their approach to interaction, the focal company has to have the ability to adapt to this variety and to deal with each of its counterparts. This includes utilising different accounting methods in different situations, amongst other things to assess and manage the effect of their willingness to cooperate and the extent to which they are prepared to adapt. The second type could be labelled two-sided interactive abilities because they refer to the capability of a firm to influence its counterparts when it wishes them to take part in a special type of interaction. Again, accounting is crucial, because it delivers the economic calculations that correspond to different solutions and, thereby, is vital for presenting many of the arguments that can be used when trying to convince a counterpart. The first type has a great deal to do with the ability to learn, adapt, and adjust to counterparts. The second has much more to do with teaching the counterparts and, therefore, with the ability to convince and to exert influence. In both of these cases, accounting has a principal role because it is the way costs and revenues are viewed and managed that is of greatest import. In other words, accounting methods are a central element in both types of capabilities.

Important Theoretical Issues

Identifying Theoretical Boundaries

For each theoretical approach, there are a number of developments that are needed, but most of these have already been covered in the earlier chapters. Here we want to take up two more general issues. The first has to do with limitations, or boundaries, in the existing theoretical approaches: In the empirical issues discussed earlier, we covered the problems associated with the existence of clear, well-defined boundaries, whereas here it is more or less the opposite that is under consideration. There is a deficiency of critical analysis of the different theoretical approaches suggested by the researchers who are applying them (although plenty of critical remarks are made about researchers applying other approaches!). There are two types of critical analyses that are needed especially. One has to do with the identification of the boundaries of the theoretical model in terms of the assumptions that are required in order for the model to work. It is important to identify such boundaries because they form the base for a discussion of how reasonable the approach is, given the empirical setting for the specific study. Such boundaries are also useful for all those who would like to compare or combine different theoretical approaches, or to find which is most relevant in a certain context.

The second limitation regards the interaction between the theoretical model and the way problems are formulated. There is always an important interaction between problems and theoretical approaches (known as the hammer-and-nail syndrome). Indeed, it is very often seen that a formulated problem is more a logical consequence of the model than of the empirical context. A critical analysis of the theory(ies) used can help researchers to avoid or at least be conscious of this. There is a need for more extensive analysis of the use of single constructs, as well as of entire theoretical models in relation to specific empirical inter-organisational phenomena. There are many descriptive and explorative studies—and they have certainly enhanced our general knowledge of the field—but now it is time to go beyond them. We need to get into deeper and more comprehensible applications Studies of this kind are especially needed to obtain a better understanding of the boundaries of the theoretical approaches, and theoretical approaches themselves become more useful when one can determine when they should not be used or for what purpose they should not be used.

Theory to Account for a Changed Business Landscape

A second general theoretical issue is very much a consequence of the earlier development. In Chapter 2, the possibility, or the need, to develop a new theory corresponding to the characteristics of a changed business landscape was highlighted. Given that the assumption that the business landscape has changed is a well-founded one, then studies trying to develop new theoretical constructs and models based on the features of the changed landscape will be required, and in great number. If some or all of the basic assumptions underlying contemporary economic theory can be questioned, there is certainly a need for researchers to consider to develop alternatives. There is a need for studies that start out from different assumptions, and which focus on different parameters. A whole set of different theoretical models and concepts is needed that, in turn, should be combined in a number of different ways to enable them to be crafted, gradually, into a more general theory. Whether this theory will eventually become a network theory or something else is an open issue.

The eventual form of the theory is far from only involving accounting. Take the developments during the present financial crisis, which started in 2007. The crisis has given a number of examples of how fragile network structures can be and how quickly they can turn against the companies involved. It has also made it very clear that we need much better theoretical models about this type of business landscape. This urgent need, combined with some special opportunities within the accounting field, described earlier as issues related to the boundary and interactive capabilities, opens up many opportunities within the field of accounting. Starting out from the issues prioritised by the companies, it might be possible to find and formulate interesting theoretical dimensions; accounting could be an area where innovations, in terms of new theoretical economic models, appears. The close interaction between practice and theory, which has made accounting somewhat difficult to research, might be turned to its advantage.

Contributors

Shannon Anderson is the associate professor of management at Rice University and a professorial fellow at the University of Melbourne's Department of Commerce and Economics. Her research focuses on the use of management accounting and control systems to facilitate the execution of operations strategy. In recent studies she has extended this line of questioning to the boundaries of the firm, studying how firms interact with suppliers, strategic alliance partners, and customers to enhance the performance of the value chain.

Martin Carlsson-Wall is a PhD student at the Stockholm School of Economics. His research relates to accounting in networks, particularly focusing on strategy, innovation, and project organising.

John Cullen is professor of management accounting at the University of Sheffield. His research is mainly focused on inter-organisational accounting, both in the private and public sector. He has also undertaken research studies on alternative governance structures, management control, and the use of empirically based case studies in teaching.

Mikael Cäker is assistant professor at the Department of Business Administration in the School of Business, Economics and Law at the University of Gothenburg. His research is mainly focused on the role of management accounting in lateral processes, with a specific interest in customer accountability, inter-organisational relationships, and lean-related initiatives. He also studies the potential inclusion of formal incentive systems in Swedish management style.

Henri Dekker is the professor of management control at the Department of Accounting at VU University in Amsterdam. His primary research interests relate to accounting and control in inter-firm relationships, business strategy and management control design, and performance measurement, target setting, and incentive compensation practices.

Wai Fong Chua is the senior associate dean of the Australian School of Business at the University of New South Wales. She has been a professor at UNSW since 1994 and was head of the School of Accounting from 2000 to 2006. She teaches and researches primarily in the area of management accounting. Her current research interests include the connections between accounting and strategising, the management of inter-organisational relationships, management accounting change, and the historical professionalisation of accounting. She is a current member of several editorial boards including the boards of Accounting, Organizations and Society and Contemporary Accounting Research.

David Ford is affiliate professor at Euromed Ecole de Management, Marseille. He is a founding member of the IMP Group of researchers and his research is into the structure and dynamics of business networks.

Håkan Håkansson is the NEMI professor of international management at the BI Norwegian School of Management in Oslo. He is one of the founding members of the international Industrial Marketing and Purchasing (IMP) Group. Publications mainly cover marketing, purchasing, and technological development in an international context. His present research interests, other than accounting issues, are related to networks and focus on innovations and knowledge development in the interface between science and industry. He is a member of a number of editorial boards and he is the editor of the *IMP Journal*.

Dr. Peter Kajüter is the professor of international accounting at the University of Münster. His research is concentrated on international financial reporting and management accounting. He is a visiting professor at ESMT, the European School of Management and Technology, and a member of the Working Group on Management Accounting of Schmalenbach-Gesellschaft für Betriebswirtschaft e.V.

Pieter E. Kamminga is assistant professor at the Faculty of Economics and Business at the University of Groningen. He conducts research in the field of management accounting. His research is predominantly on inter-firm transactional relationships, and in particular, on the management control of joint ventures. Professor Kamminga's current research deals with the dynamic aspects of joint venture relationships.

Kalle Kraus is assistant professor at the Department of Accounting at the Stockholm School of Economics. His research centres on the role of accounting in inter-organisational relationships and networks, both in the private and the public sector, but he also studies how the shareholder value trend and capital market pressure affect large companies listed on the stock exchange.

Dr. Harri I. Kulmala is docent at Lappeenranta University of Technology in Finland and works as CEO of FIMECC Ltd. He received his PhD in industrial engineering and management from the Tampere University of Technology. He has carried out scientific research and practical application development in the area of management accounting, especially in the networked business environment, for over ten years.

Johnny Lind is professor in management accounting and is centre director for the Accounting and Managerial Finance Unit at the Stockholm School of Economics. He is most active in the area of accounting in inter-organisational relationships and networks, covering both private and public sector organisations. His current research interests also include the interplay between capital markets and management control. He is a member of several editorial boards, including that of Management Accounting Research.

Cecilia Lindholm is assistant professor at the Department of Business Studies at Uppsala University. Her research is mainly focused on management accounting in the public sector, with a specialisation in inter-organisational cooperation between health care organisations. She also studies management audit and the association between legal and professional accountability in public sector organisations.

Habib Mahama is an associate professor at the School of Accounting and Business Information Systems at the Australian National University (ANU). He researches in the area of management accounting, with specific focus on management accounting controls in inter-firm relationships, management control of operational risk, and behavioural management accounting using both qualitative and quantitative design approaches.

Jeltje van der Meer-Kooistra is professor of financial management at the University of Groningen. Her research focuses on the governance and control of intra-firm and inter-firm transactions and relationships. She is particularly interested in the governance of (equity) joint venture relationships and the dynamic evolution of such relationships. She is a member of the editorial board of Management Accounting Research. She is director of the Management Accounting Research Programme of the Faculty of Economics and Business.

Juliana Meira is a lecturer at the Federal University of Pernambuco in Brazil and is a PhD student at the Management School of the University of Sheffield. The focus of her research thesis is the role of management accounting in inter-organisational relationships.

Professor **Jan Mouritsen**'s research is oriented towards understanding the role of management technologies and management control in various organisational and social contexts. He focuses on empirical research and attempts to develop new ways of understanding the role and effects of controls and financial information in organisations and society. His interests include intellectual capital and knowledge management, technology management, operations management, new accounting, and management control. He is currently an editorial board member for a series of academic journals in the various areas of management and business research, including accounting, operations management, IT, and knowledge management.

Robert W. Scapens is an emeritus professor at the Manchester Business School and the professor of management accounting at the University of Groningen in the Netherlands. He also holds visiting appointments at the University of Birmingham, UK; the University of Jyväskylä, Finland; the University of Siena, Italy; and is the Swedbank visiting professor at Lund University, Sweden. Together with Michael Bromwich, he was co-founder of Management Accounting Research, of which he is now the editor in chief. In his research, which is primarily in the area of management accounting, he uses both quantitative and qualitative methods; he has written extensively on research methodology and the methods of case research.

Torkel Strömsten is a researcher and lecturer at the Department of Accounting at the Stockholm School of Economics. His research interest is on the role that corporate governance and accounting play in industrial networks. Lately, he has conducted a major study that concerns the telecom company Ericsson and its relationship with the British telecom operator Vodafone. His primary interest was the role of governance and control in this relationship.

Sof Thrane is associate professor at the Department of Operations Management at Copenhagen Business School. He researches on the use of accounting in supply chains and inter-firm networks, with other research interests including innovation and cost management, and accounting in the public sector.

Evangelia Varoutsa is a PhD candidate at the Accounting Division of the Manchester Business School at the University of Manchester. Her research is mainly focused on changes in management accounting, the governance of inter-organisational relationships, and the role of the accounting information in such relationships.

Author Index

Subject Index

A

ABB Robotics, 192, 195–198, 202, 204–205, 208, 285
Abstract systems, 332
Accountability, 116, 121, 125, 131, 142–144; construction of, 115, 122, 123; inter-organisational, 9, 115, 140; managerial, 9, 115, 135, 136; overlapping, 73, 75; professional, 9, 115, 124, 132; processes of, 115; style of, 126; system of 123
Accounting for indirect effects, 280, 287–288
Accounting for networking, 284, 287–288
Accounting for prioritisations, 283, 287
Accounting in action, 11, 309
Activity-based costing, 65, 154, 157, 306, 310
Activity link, 170
Actor, non-human, 294, 295, 297, 299
Actor network analysis, rules for, 297
Actor-network theory (ANT), 8, 9, 14, 15, 22, 24, 292–312, 343, 344; and target costing, 191, 193, 204, 208
Agency, 229, 239, 303–304, 316, 319–322, 331; theory, 3, 10, 60, 64, 67, 76, 188, 193, 224, 227–228, 277
Agent, 227–228
Alliance decision, 11, 236, 262
Alliance evolution, 247
Ambiguity, 96, 301–302, 304
Appropriation concern, 12, 70, 108, 235, 239, 245
Architectural innovation, 195, 205

Asset, 17, 18, 19, 26; customers as, 177, 178; specificity, 62, 63, 64, 90, 98, 99, 117, 224, 235, 238, 239–241, 301
Assistant nurse, 128–129, 131–135, 138–140
Associations, 74, 302, 304, 309, 312, 327
Asymmetric information, 237

B

Balanced scorecard, 167
Bargaining power, 64, 86–87, 98, 300
Behaviour control, 7, 54, 56, 63, 247–248, 258, 262
Bidirectional relationship, 76
Bilateral governance, 23
BMW, 198–201, 205–206
Boeing, 187, 207
Boundary, 21, 27, 235, 237, 241–243, 249, 259, 345, 346; and actor-network theory, 292–293, 297–299, 301–306, 310, 318; and customer accounting, 171–174, 176; and the industrial-network approach, 270, 280, 286, 287; and institutional theory, 327, 329, 331, 343; legal, 6, 7; and open book accounting, 215, 216, 220, 224, 229; organisational, 1, 2, 5, 17, 31, 42, 49, 50, 53; and public sector organisations, 113, 115, 119, 120, 121, 126, 129, 133, 135–136, 141–143; and the resource-based view, 254–255; and target costing, 71, 185; theoretical, 347
Bounded rationality, 238–239
Budget, 5, 56, 63, 74, 88, 97, 298, 321; and public sector organisations,

For Product Safety Concerns and Information please contact our
EU representative GPSR@taylorandfrancis.com Taylor & Francis
Verlag GmbH, Kaufingerstraße 24, 80331 München, Germany